WANG AN SHIH
王安石
(VOL. I)

WANG AN SHIH

王 安 石

a Chinese Statesman and Educationalist
of the Sung Dynasty

(VOL. I)

BY

H. R. WILLIAMSON, M.A., D.Lit.

HYPERION PRESS, INC.
WESTPORT, CONNECTICUT

Library of Congress Cataloging in Publication Data

Williamson, Henry Raymond.
    Wang An Shih ... a Chinese statesman and
educationalist of the Sung Dynasty.

    Reprint of the 1935-37 ed. published by A. Probsthain,
which was issued as v. 21-22 of Probsthain's oriental
series.
    Bibliography: v. 2, p:
    1. Wang, An-shih, 1021-1086. 2. China--Politics
and government.
DS751.W35 1973   951'.02'0924 [B]   73-901
ISBN 0-88355-095-4

Published in 1935
by Arthur Probsthain, London, England

First Hyperion reprint edition 1973

Library of Congress Catalogue Number 73-901

ISBN 0-88355-096-2

Printed in the United States of America

TABLE OF CONTENTS
(VOL. I)

(i) Distribution of the Regular Forces.
(ii) Mounts for the Militia.
(iii) The Arsenal Board.

PREFACE

WANG AN SHIH (A.D. 1021–1086), of the Northern Sung Dynasty, was one of the most prominent statesmen of his time, and a prolific writer of both prose and poetry. In the latter capacity he attained to considerable fame. Of his work as a statesman, however, little has been heard until comparatively recent times.

His political theories and experiments were of a radical character, and were pushed with such tenacity against a powerful opposition that intense antagonism was aroused in influential circles. However, he gained the ear of the Emperor Shen Tsung, who elevated him to the highest administrative office in the Empire. For a period of eight years Wang An Shih was all powerful in his position as Prime Minister, and succeeded in putting his economic and militaristic ideas into concrete form in a number of measures which were styled the New Laws. After the death of Shen Tsung, his Royal friend and patron, Ssu Ma Kuang, his most powerful political opponent, was restored to power, and Wang An Shih lived just long enough to witness the complete reversal of his reform policy.

This drastic action initiated a period of forty years of political strife, during which the policy of Wang An Shih was made either the "butt" or the "banner" of rival factions. So engrossed were the statesmen of this latter period in their factious controversies that matters fundamental to the security and existence of the Empire were grievously neglected. The result of all this was seen in the national disaster of 1126, when the Golden Tartars, who had long been menacing the Empire from the north, launched the attack of which Wang An Shih had previously forewarned his countrymen, and to forestall which his reform policy had been mainly designed. The Tartars captured the Sung capital with the greatest ease, sent the chief members of the Royal family into exile, and compelled the rest to migrate south of the Yang Tzu river.

The party which had been antagonistic to Wang An Shih were particularly influential at the southern Court. A " scapegoat " had to be found upon whom the guilt for this national calamity could be laid. So they proceeded to launch a campaign of specious falsehood and defamation of the reformer in a frantic endeavour to convince those of their own and succeeding generations that Wang An Shih was solely responsible for the disaster which had befallen the nation. It is almost entirely due to the obloquies then heaped upon his name that the political work of Wang An Shih has until recent years remained unrecognized or has been grievously misrepresented or misunderstood. The accounts of his life and work which are found in the canonical histories of China are based on writings which emanated from this antagonistic school and betray their prejudices on almost every page.

One is therefore particularly grateful for the prominence which Liang Ch'i Ch'ao, one of the greatest of Chinese modern scholars, has given to the work of Ts'ai Shang Hsiang, who devoted many years of a long life to a careful investigation of the available evidence on the subject, and produced in 1804 a Critical Biography of Wang An Shih. The combined labours of these two scholars have succeeded in rescuing the political work of Wang An Shih from the oblivion in which it remained for so long. They have also contributed largely to the clearing of his name, with the result that considerable interest has been aroused amongst modern Chinese students of economics in his reform measures. By some of the more thoughtful of these he is now regarded as one of the most far-seeing, high-minded, courageous, and enterprising social reformers that their nation has produced. It seemed therefore desirable that there should be made available for the English reading public some account of the life and work of a man who is exciting such enthusiasm amongst his politically minded countrymen of to-day.

As far as the writer's knowledge goes, apart from two articles by Dr. J. G. Ferguson in the *Journal* of the North China Branch

of the Royal Asiatic Society, and an essay by Dr. C. W. Allan
in his *Makers of Cathay*, very little has been written on Wang
An Shih in the English language. In German Prof. Otto Franke
has issued an admirable treatise : Der Bericht Wang Ngan-
Schis von 1058 über Reform des Beamtentums. Ein Beitrag
zur Beurteilung des Reformators. Berlin, 1932.

The present work, therefore, is based almost entirely on
Chinese sources. In this connection it is to be regretted that
owing to the iconoclastic policy of his political opponents,
much of Wang An Shih's literary work has been wantonly
destroyed. He produced a dictionary and wrote extensively
on the interpretation of the Classical literature of China. But
unfortunately all that remains of this section of his labours
is the New Interpretation of the Government System of Chow,
styled the *Chow Kuan Hsin I*. In addition to this, there was
published in 1918 by the Sao Yeh Shan Co. what purports to
be a complete edition of the rest of the works which are extant.
This consists of eight volumes of poetry and sixteen of prose,
comprising his letters, inscriptions, essays, government
memorials, etc., and claims to be substantially the same as the
editions published during the Sung dynasty. A separate
edition of his poetry, consisting of fifty volumes with a commentary by Li Yen Hu (李 雁 湖) and claiming to be a reprint
of the Mongolian (元) edition as issued by the Ch'ing I Chai
(清 綺 齋) has been recently published by the Commercial
Press. These, together with the Chinese Histories and the
works of Ts'ai Shang Hsiang and Liang Ch'i Ch'ao referred to
above, form the main sources of the present work.

It has been found necessary to publish the work in three
volumes. The first gives a detailed account of the life and
political career of the reformer, indicates the nature and scope
of his reform measures, and contains translations of his chief
government memorials, and letters bearing on his character
and public life. The second outlines the history of the reform
policy after his death for a subsequent period of forty years
up to the downfall of the Northern Sung dynasty. It com-
prises studies of Wang An Shih's character and of the New

Laws, with critical material on his Times, the Sung Histories, etc. In this volume the traditional accounts of his life and work are fully translated, and Maps, Chronological Tables, and Indexes are included. The third volume is more particularly concerned with his literary work, and contains translations of all his important essays.

The work as now presented to the public was accepted by the University of London in 1931 as a thesis for the degree of D.Lit.

As the work is based principally upon Chinese sources, it has necessarily called for the co-operation of able and interested Chinese scholars. In this connection prime honour must be accorded to the Rev. Sun P'eng Hsiang who has rendered extremely valuable help. Thanks also are due to Professor Luan T'iao Fu, of the Shantung Christian University, who has contributed to the elucidation of many a difficult passage. I am indebted also to the Rev. J. P. Bruce, M.A., D.Lit., for guidance in the selection of the subject, and last, but not least, to my wife, who has laboured hard at the correction of the manuscript.

H. R. WILLIAMSON.

LONDON,
10th February, 1934.

CHAPTER I

ANCESTRY OF WANG AN SHIH

WANG AN SHIH (王 安 石) was born in A.D. 1021 at Ch'ing
Chiang Hsien (清 江 縣),[1] during the closing years of the reign
of Chen Tsung (眞 宗) of the Sung Dynasty. His family had
resided in Lin Ch'uan (臨 川), also styled Fu Chow (撫 州),
in the province of Chiang Hsi, for several generations prior to
An Shih's birth. But formerly the ancestral home had been
located at Tai Yuan Fu (太 原 府), Shansi province. The
removal to Lin Ch'uan probably took place in the time of his
great-grandfather, who was known as Wang Ming (王 明).
He held no official position, but his son, Yung Chih (用 之),
the grandfather of Wang An Shih, was an officer of the Imperial
Bodyguard.

An Shih's father is generally known as Wang I (王 益).[2]
As a youth of 17 he presented for criticism an essay to one Chang
Yung (張 詠), who was so impressed by the style and subject
matter of the treatise that he conferred a new literary designation
upon the writer. Henceforth he was to be known as Shun Liang
(舜 良), or "Noble Minister of the Emperor Shun".[3]

[1] Ch'ing Chiang Hsien is in Chiang Hsi province. Wang An Shih was born
during the term of his father's service there as Adjutant (P'an Kuan 判 官)
to the Prefect of Lin Chiang (臨 江). Taken from the Ancient Records
of Ch'ing Chiang Hsien (清 江 縣 古 跡 志), quoted by Ts'ai Shang
Hsiang (蔡 上 翔) in his Biography of Wang An Shih (王 荆 公
年 譜 考 略), vol. i, p. 1.

[2] Wang An Shih's father was born in 994, and gained his Chin Shih degree
in 1015. (Ts'ai Shang Hsiang, op. cit., vol. i, pp. 2 and 3.)

[3] The character I (益) in his father's name of Wang I (王 益) means
"Increase". But the idea signified by his original literary designation "Sun
Chih" (損 之) is that of "Decrease". Chang Yung thought the latter idea inconsistent with the hope of progress which the submitted essay justified. So he took
the character I (益), which was also the name of one of Shun's most famous
ministers, viz. Pai I (佰 益), and transferred the idea of that to the new
literary "style" which he now conferred, making it "Shun Liang" (舜 良),
translated as in the text.

1

We are fortunate in having from An Shih's pen an account of his father's life. As this affords some interesting resemblances to the character and career of An Shih himself, it will be worth while to reproduce the more important parts of this document here.[1]

"After gaining his Chin Shih degree [2] in 1015, my father was appointed to Chien An (建 安) as assistant to the magistrate. At first the people of the district were inclined to despise his youth, but after a time he so won their respect that even his superiors began to consult him on all important matters of administration. On one occasion when he was seriously ill the whole county joined in special prayer for his recovery.

"The people of this district had achieved notoriety through their habit of paying their taxes late, and during my father's term of office there the magistrate incurred the censure of the sub-prefectural official on this account. When my father heard of this he remarked that it was useless to blame the lower classes as long as the government employees continued to set them a bad example in this respect. So, accompanied by the local military officer, he arrested the clerks in the yamen, gave each man twenty strokes with the bamboo, and set them a time limit of three days in which to pay their dues. The strong action he took on this occasion so intimidated the people that they gave no further cause for complaint on that score. From this time my father's reputation as a courageous official began to spread abroad.

"Later he was transferred to Lin Chiang (臨 江), in the province of Chiang Hsi, as deputy-magistrate. His superior in this district was not of the highest character, and was frequently guilty of maladministration. On such occasions my father faithfully reprimanded him by quoting ancient precedents. A subordinate wrote a strong indictment of his colleagues, beginning at the top. But when he came to my father's name he held his pen.

---

[1] See his "Hsien Tai Fu Shu" (先 大 夫 述). Prose Works, vol. xvii.
[2] Chin Shih (進 仕), i.e. a graduate of the third degree in Literature.

" His next appointment was to Hsin Kan (新 淦), a neighbouring county. Although an interval of thirty years [1] has elapsed since he held that post, the officials and residents of the district still speak most highly of his administration of that district.

" Further transfers, accompanied by promotion of rank in each case, were made first to Lu Ling (廬 陵), modern Chi An Hsien (吉 安 縣), in Chiang Hsi, and then to Hsin Fan Hsien (新 繁 縣), in the vicinity of Ch'eng Tu (成 都), Ssuch'uan province. The latter place was overrun by bandits and outlaws. Shortly after taking up his new appointment my father seized several of the more desperate characters and made an example of them by banishment to a very forbidding neighbourhood. The rest were soon brought to order by generous and considerate treatment. In this way my father gained the confidence and respect of the whole district, so much so, in fact, that there was no necessity to inflict corporal punishment on any for a whole year.

" On the termination of his period of office there his rank was advanced to that of T'ai Ch'ang Po Shih (太 常 博 士) and he was promoted to the prefecture of Shao Chow (韶 州), in the province of Kuang Tung. This was a remote and somewhat wild district in which the I (夷) and Yueh (越) tribes resided. Amongst these my father was distressed to find that certain barbarous customs were prevalent, and noted in particular that distinctions between the sexes were not properly observed. He discovered that former intendants of his office had ignored this, thinking that as the people had become inured to their way of life it was impossible to institute any changes. My father observed that these tribes were, after all, members of the great human family, and so felt that it was incumbent upon him to instruct them in the important matter of relationships. He soon disposed of the idea that nothing could be done to remedy matters in this respect, and as a result of his efforts the men and women of the district were so influenced that they ceased to walk together in public places. One, Hu Yuan (胡 瑗), wrote a treatise

---

[1] According to Ts'ai Shang Hsiang, vol. iii, p. 8, the " Hsien Tai Fu Shu " was written on the occasion of his father's funeral in 1048.

which he styled 'Model Government' (政 範), which included
an account of my father's work at Shao Chow.

"Tigers abounded in the sub-district of Weng Yuan (翁 源),
which was under the jurisdiction of Shao Chow. My father
issued an order that steps were to be taken by the local officials
to eliminate this menace to the people's livelihood. Five tigers
having died (so the local official was led to believe), their heads
were sent on a barrow to my father at Shao Chow, together with
a scroll lauding his virtues and fame. My father refused to receive
the messengers, and returned the scroll to the official at Weng
Yuan to show his displeasure at such silly and obsequious conduct.

"A military guard of five hundred men from Ssu Ch'uan was
stationed at Shao Chow, who planned to revolt because their
reliefs had not come at the proper time. As Shao Chow was
an isolated spot a revolt of the soldiery would have caused great
embarrassment. The yamen officials were greatly alarmed. Not
so my father. He immediately apprehended five of the ringleaders
and sent them to the border of his district under escort. This
he did despite the urgent appeal of his subordinates that it would
be wiser to imprison them. Later, however, when it transpired
that the disgruntled troops had planned to rise in revolt that
very night if that was done, the wisdom of my father's action
was perceived and the people became more than ever submissive
to his administration.

"During his term of office at Shao Chow my father established
postal courier systems, erected market places, and built many new
roads. In everything he drew up the most detailed regulations,
with the result that the older residents remarked : 'Never since
Ling Hai [1] came under the sway of the Chinese Empire have we
had so fine an official as he.'

"After the mourning period for my grandfather [2] had been
duly observed, my father received the important appointment of
the Governorship of Chiang Ning (江 寧), i.e. the modern

[1] Ling Hai (嶺 海), the district of Kuang Tung, between the mountains
and the sea.

[2] According to Ts'ai Shang Hsiang, Wang An Shih's father returned from
Shao Chow in 1033, to keep the mourning period for his father. In 1036 Wang

Nanking. He gained the complete confidence of two successive Military Administrators there, who relied solely upon him in the administration of affairs. But, alas ! my father died while in this position, on the 23rd of the 2nd month of the year 1039, at the early age of 46.

"He scrupulously observed the Confucian code of ethics. With the single exception of his term of office in Ssu Ch'uan, where the distance made such action infeasible, he was always accompanied by his parents. While at Hsin Fan he refrained altogether from carousals and banquetings, and at the New Year festival the thought that he was separated from his mother and father was almost unbearable.[1] In his general manner of life he exercised the strictest economy, and was even parsimonious in the matter of his own food. But towards his parents he exercised the utmost generosity. In fact, he was frequently criticized as extravagant in his treatment of them. For he would occasionally have to borrow from others in order that they might not suffer from lack of good nourishing food.

"In the family circle he was never known to lose his temper or beat his children. At meal-times he would discourse freely and naturally upon the fundamentals of filial and loving conduct, dilate upon the causes for the rise and fall of states, and explain the reasons why good government is sometimes succeeded by a period of disorder. All this was done in an easy and delightful manner but showing that he himself possessed a feeling of responsibility for public affairs, which, in fact, accounts for the large amount of trust which others reposed in him.

"It was most unfortunate that his life was brought to a close before he had had full opportunity to make his contribution to the social order of his day."

Further information is gained from an introduction written by An Shih to a collection of poems made by his father, as follows :—

An Shih accompanied his father to the capital, probably to await further official appointment. This was granted in 1037, when he was appointed to Chien K'ang (建 康), another name for Chiang Ning. Ts'ai says the character " Ch'ang " (昌) is a mistake for " K'ang " (康). Op. cit., vol. i, pp. 2 and 3. (See p. 8, note 2).

[1] The Chinese try to get home to their parents if at all possible at New Year time.

"My father read very widely in his youth. But his chief ambition was to engage in public life and make a practical contribution to the welfare of the people. His busy life and early death prevented him from devoting much time to literary pursuits later on. However, one day as we were looking through his belongings we discovered over one hundred poems which had been either written or collected by himself. Although these are inadequate of themselves to give an idea of the real nature of his ambition, yet they do to a certain extent afford an insight into his character. They have, too, some ethical value in themselves. It was therefore felt by the family that they were worthy of preservation, and so I undertook to write this Introduction."[1]

Now, while recognizing that the maxim "De mortuis nihil nisi bonum" would hold particularly true of a son writing of a beloved parent, it is, nevertheless, possible to gain a fair insight into the character of Wang An Shih's father from the above memoirs. We find him a man of literary tastes, devoted to his family, and with a keen interest in the welfare of the people. He had a passion for justice, and was possessed of a determined will. He was fearless in administration, economical in his manner of life, and impatient with all manner of make-believe. In all these things he shows himself a worthy progenitor of one who later proved himself to be possessed of similar characteristics, only in greater and fuller measure.

The maiden name of Wang An Shih's grandmother was Hsieh (謝). By virtue of her son Wang I's rank and official record she received the honorary rank and title of Lady of Yung An (永 安 縣 君).

An Shih's father married twice,[2] first to a lady of the Hsü (徐) family. His second wife, who gave birth to Wang An Shih, was from the Wu (吳) family. Later she also had an honorary title conferred upon her, being styled the Lady of Ch'ang Shou (長 壽 縣 君).

---

[1] See his "Hsien Tai Fu Chi Hsu" (先 大 夫 集 序). Works, vol. xvii.
[2] See Commentary on Poem entitled "Reminiscences" (憶 昨 詩 示 諸 外 弟), Poems, vol. xx, p. 6.

CHAPTER II

HIS YOUTH (1021 1042)

WANG AN SHIH was the third of seven brothers,[1] two of whom,
An Kuo and An Li, are favoured with Biographical Notices in
the Dynastic Histories.[2] He had three sisters,[3] all younger than
himself, the eldest of whom was married at the age of 16 to
Chang K'uei.[4]

" In early years Wang An Shih was very fond of study, and
had an exceptional memory. In composing he wrote so fast that
the pen seemed to fly over the paper, and although he seemed to
be exercising no particular care, the work when completed was
remarkable for content and style." [5]

He accompanied his father to Shao Chow as a boy. They
returned from there to observe the mourning period for his
grandfather when Wang An Shih was 12.[6] In the year 1036,

[1] See Ts'ai Shang Hsiang, vol. ix, pp. 4 and 5. The names of the brothers
in order as there given are as follows : An Jen (安 仁), An Tao (安 道),
step-brothers of Wang An Shih, then An Shih himself (安 石), An Kuo
(安 國), An Shih (安 世), An Li (安 禮), and An Shang (安 上).

[2] i.e. (宋 史 本 傳) the Biographical Notices are translated in Vol. II
of this work.

[3] See Ts'ai Shang Hsiang, vol. ix, p. 5. The second daughter was married to
Chu Ming Chih (朱 明 之), the third to Shen Li Chang (沈 李 長)
of Yang Chow (揚 州).

[4] In the Obituary Notice written by Wang An Shih on the death of his eldest
sister, he describes himself as her elder brother (兄). The composition of the
text of this Notice was by the pen of Wang An Shih, but it was actually written
out by his youngest brother An Shang. See Works, vol. xxiv, p. 22.

[5] Biographical Section of the Sung Histories (宋 史 本 傳), Life
of Wang An Shih.

[6] Ts'ai Shang Hsiang, vol. i, p. 3. Also Works, vol. xvii, p. 29, where he says
that " in the year 1033 he accompanied his father from Shao Chow and met
Fang Chung Yung (方 仲 永) at the home of his uncle ". (The
expression " Ming Tao Chung " (明 道 中) must relate to either 1032 or
1033, as there were only two years with that designation. The probability is

7

when Wang An Shih was 15, he travelled with his father to the
capital, then located at K'ai Feng Fu, in Honan province.[1] In
the next year his father was appointed to the important post of
Governor of Chiang Ning, or modern Nanking, then termed
Chien K'ang (建 康).[2] Two years later, in 1039, when Wang
An Shih was 18, his father died.[3] The home of the Wang family
was maintained at Chiang Ning (江 寧) for some time after
this. Here, along with his two elder brothers, An Jen and An Tao
(who were children of his step-mother), Wang An Shih continued
his studies in preparation for the government examinations.[4]

In the year 1041 he proceeded to the capital for the preliminary
examination in connection with the Chin Shih degree.[5] While
engaged on this work he gained an intimate friend in the person
of one Li T'ung Shu (李 通 叔), a native of Fuchien. The latter

that it was in 1033. Lower down he talks of his return from Yang Chow seven
years later. That date is well confirmed as being in 1043. But Wang An Shih
was at home three years after his return from Shao Chow, so it might well be
that the interview referred to took place in 1036.)

[1] See Poem, entitled " Reminiscences ", below.

[2] The old name of Chiang Ning was Chien K'ang (建 康). Ts'ai Shang
Hsiang is of opinion that the Chien Ch'ang (建 昌) in the text of this poem
must be an error for Chien K'ang. There is such a place as Chien Ch'ang, which
is the modern Nan Ch'eng (南 城) in Chiang Hsi province, not far from
Lin Ch'uan (臨 川), Wang's ancestral home. But there is no record of his
father holding office there, whereas it is well known that he assumed the
governorship of Chiang Ning or Chien K'ang at this time. (See Ts'ai Shang
Hsiang, vol. i, p. 3.)

[3] See Ts'ai Shang Hsiang, vol. i, p. 1. Wang An Shih's father died at the age
of 46, having been born in 994. The Chinese way of reckoning ages one year
in advance of the Western custom accounts for the apparent discrepancy of one
year. In the case of Wang An Shih we have endeavoured to keep to the Western
way of reckoning. There is a note here that both Wang An Shih's father and
mother were buried at Chiang Ning.

[4] See Works, vol. xxi, p. 8. Memorial Essay on his friend, Li T'ung Shu.

[5] See Poem, " Reminiscences," below, where Wang An Shih refers to his
keeping of the three years' mourning period for his father. His father died in
the second month of 1039. But we need not posit a full three years for the
mourning period, as it was quite customary to allow twenty-seven months as
sufficient for this. It would probably be late in 1041 when Wang An Shih went
to the capital. The examination he was waiting to take is termed the Board of
Rites Examination by Ts'ai Shang Hsiang, vol. i, p. 1. It was probably another
section of the examination for the Chin Shih degree.

was unsuccessful in two attempts to gain his degree, and unfortunately was drowned, together with a friend, on his way home from the capital. He was then only 28 years of age. The news of his death did not reach Wang An Shih until nearly two years later, but evidently caused him great grief. His account of their friendship at the capital is worth reproducing. It reads as follows :—

"I have frequently been impressed with the way in which great men of the past attributed their progress in character to the stimulating and educative influences of friendship. I recognize my own inferiority to such in the matter of ability and character. In my early years I had no mind for study, and lacked those friends who might have stimulated and enlightened me in the struggle for character. It seemed as though I was doomed to live the life of an insignificant rustic. . . . But as soon as I met Li T'ung Shu at the capital I was attracted by his noble countenance. We held most helpful converse together, and unconsciously I was spurred on to imitation of him. His knowledge and literary ability were a constant inspiration to me and we began to exchange poems, through each of which breathed a spirit of frank and happy comradeship. Through my friendship with him I first became conscious of the possibility of becoming a worthy disciple of the ancient sages. While this may be attributed in part to the instruction I received from him I think it was chiefly due to his fine and gracious example.

"After he had tried twice unsuccessfully to gain his Chin Shih degree we bade each other an affectionate farewell, fervent in the hope that ere long we might meet again. But, alas ! during the next year after my appointment to Huai Nan, when I was making inquiries with a view to calling him to join me, the sad news of his death by drowning, together with his friend Ch'en An Shih, came to hand." [1]

An Shih was more successful than his friend in the degree examination, for he passed first class, being placed fourth on the Chin Shih list of 1042, the first name being that of Yang Chih

[1] Works, vol. xxi, p. 8.

(楊 寘).[1] The Dynastic Histories, which generally speaking
are greatly biased against Wang An Shih, suggest that this degree
was gained by the personal influence of " friends at Court ".
The extract from the History reads as follows :—

" Tseng Kung, a friend of Wang An Shih, showed some
essays of his to Ou Yang Hsiu (歐 陽 修). The latter noised
his name abroad, and as a result he was placed in the first class
at the Chin Shih examinations." [2]

The following is a translation of a letter which Tseng Kung
(曾 鞏) wrote to Ou Yang Hsiu :—

" My friend Wang An Shih writes in the manner of the
extreme ancients. His personal character is quite consistent
with his theories. He has already gained his Chin Shih degree,
but is known to very few people. As a matter of fact, he is
not anxious to get known. He is a sincere and self-respecting
person. To my own mind there have been few like him in
any age. There are thousands of mediocre folk whom we might
allow to go unrecognized and unemployed and it would be
no great loss to the State. But I feel that as things are at present
we should not permit Wang An Shih to be lost to the service
of the Empire." [3]

Now this is probably the letter to which the Dynastic History
refers.[4] It will be noted that Tseng Kung mentions that Wang

---

[1] Chan Ta Ho's Biographical Table of Wang An Shih, prefixed to Poetical
Works of Wang An Shih (詹 大 和 王 荆 文 公 年 譜).
Ts'ai Shang Hsiang notes that the names of Wang Kuei (王 珪) and Han
Chiang (韓 絳) were found together with Wang An Shih's name on this list.
All became members of the Grand Council later. Vol. ii, p. 1.

[2] Pen Chuan (本 傳).

[3] Liang Ch'i Ch'ao in Yin Ping Shih Ts'ung Chi (飲 氷 室 叢 集),
Life of Wang An Shih, chap. 5, p. 46.

[4] Tseng Kung (曾 鞏), also styled Tseng Tzu Ku (曾 子 固), a great
friend of Wang An Shih in his youth and throughout his life, wrote two letters
to Ou Yang Hsiu, one in 1041 and the other in 1042. Both of these may have
been written prior to Wang An Shih gaining his Chin Shih degree. However,
in neither of these is there any mention of Wang An Shih. Moreover, in a letter
written by Ou Yang Hsiu, evidently in reply to the second of these, sending
him an introduction for some Work, he makes no reference to Wang An Shih.
As there are no other evidences of correspondence passing between them at

An Shih had already gained his Chin Shih degree, so it could hardly be as a result of this recommendation that he was granted it. One cannot question the fact that in the times of the Sung Dynasty personal influence of those at Court was a large factor in determining the success of candidates at the official examinations. But even if Wang An Shih had such " friends at Court ", which in those days seems improbable, no one can question his eligibility from the literary standpoint for this degree. As will appear later on, he had most marked abilities in this direction. Later generations have either ignored or denounced his political theories and experiments, but he is universally lauded for his literary gifts.

The way in which he worked to gain this degree, and the fact that he actually took the examination in the regular manner, appears from a poem entitled " Reminiscences ", written by him on his return home from his first official appointment at Huai Nan in 1043 [1] :—

" These delectable haunts of my youth I recall,
This poor valley bedecked with the glory of Spring,
This homestead perched high with its short winding wall,
These beauteous glades sweetest memories bring.
The wild flowers and grasses all mingled in bloom,
The flashing of butterflies, bees on the hum,
My stout heart of youth, my desire for a name,
The feeling that Heaven had marked me for fame.

" The glories of Spring I have leisure to paint,
Others may mock but I feel no restraint,
High office awaits him who's skilled with the pen,
Mere descant of K'ung-Meng [2] makes beggars of men.

this time, we conclude that the statement in the Pen Chuan must have reference to this letter written either in 1044 or 1045. Ts'ai Shang Hsiang dates it in the fifth month of 1044, as Tseng Kung wrote a letter to Ts'ai Shen Hsin (蔡 深 信) at that time, in which he uses almost identical terminology to that used in the letter to Ou Yang Hsiu about Wang An Shih. Ts'ai traces the statement in the Pen Chuan to the Work of Ssu Ma Kuang, entitled Wen Kung So Yü (溫 公 瑣 語), and quotes it as an instance of deliberate falsification of the facts. (See Ts'ai Shang Hsiang, vol. ii, p. 2, and vol. iii, p. 1, also p. 3.)

[1] Poetical Works, vol. xx, p. 5.
[2] Confucius and Mencius.

At 15 I journeyed the long dusty road,
My father in the capital took up his abode.
The next year he took up a post in Chien Ch'ang [1]
In the 4th Moon our wee barque was moored in the Chiang.

" As I mused thus the thought flashed into my mind,
Time awaits not the pleasure of mere human kind,
If in youth we should fail to establish our name,
Old age would bring poverty along in its train.
So dead to the world I delve into my books,
The silence brings crickets from out of their nooks,
Ungifted and lowly I yet hope to share
The fame of such worthies as old Chi and Hsieh.[2]

" Then, alas ! dread misfortune o'ershadowed my fate
The death of my father left us all desolate.
What drooping of spirits, what sadness of mind,
What flowing of tears for one gentle and kind.
What mingling of grief of mother and child,
For three years we mourned in our home in the wild.
When lo ! rumour reached us the Court needed men,
Off to the capital to try fate with my pen.

" An essay embellished I proudly present
On humblest of services rejoice to be sent.
With gown of light blue and ivory ' hupan ' [3]
I take up a post for a year in Huai-Nan." [4]

The above facts, though meagre in themselves, give us a fair
insight into the character and experiences of Wang An Shih
prior to his taking up official appointment. Evidently he
accompanied his father to his various posts, devoting himself
to study with a view to following in his footsteps later on.

That he had high ambitions in those early years appears
also. He was determined, if at all possible, to equal in achieve-
ment the records of the most famous ministers of the Golden

---

[1] See p. 8, note 2.
[2] Chi (稷), Hsieh (契), famous worthies of the Yao-Shun regime.
[3] The hu-pan (笏 版) ivory tablet, part of the official insignia.
[4] Huai-Nan (淮 南), a political area of the Sung times covering modern
An Hui, Chiang Su, and part of Che Chiang.

Age of Yao and Shun. These ambitions excited the scorn of some of his associates, but that in no sense deterred him from persevering with his task. The life of the teacher was obviously not his object. He felt himself marked out for an official career and that in the highest circles.

But with all that in mind he also shows signs of a reticent and humble disposition, that he was not keen on pushing himself forward, but trusting that hard work and strict discipline would eventually win for him the recognition and opportunity which he deserved.

So far he had made very few friends. Possibly his wandering life would account for that. But we see how readily he responded to the friendly overtures of a man like Li T'ung Shu and how keen he was to imitate his virtues.

The characteristics which made Wang An Shih the man he was are already manifest. Powers of concentration on the job in hand, a masterful will, devotion to duty, high ambition combined with a love of his family and an unwavering loyalty to principle and friends are all present in due degree. Add to this his unusual literary gifts, and we see the man equipped for an official career, remarkable alike for its vigour and venturesomeness.

CHAPTER III

IN OFFICE AT YANG CHOW AND CHIN HSIEN
(1042–1050)

As has been indicated in the preceding chapter, Wang An Shih's first official appointment was made soon after his success at the Chin Shih examination. His degree was gained in the third month of 1042. He forthwith proceeded to Yang Chow (揚 州)[1] to take up the duties of under-secretary in the Military Headquarters of the Huai-Nan Circuit.

Han Ch'i (韓 琦), later better known as Han Wei Kung (韓 魏 公), was the Prefect of Yang Chow during Wang An Shih's term of office there, and apparently also held the concurrent post of Military Superintendent of the Circuit.[2] Evidently feelings of mutual respect were excited between superior and subordinate during this period, which later ripened into personal friendship. Political differences emerged during the period of Wang An Shih's greatest influence, which, however, in no way injured their personal relationships. After the death of Han Ch'i in 1075 Wang An Shih composed a poetical panegyric in his honour which includes the following lines :—

> " Withered and white-haired now,
> My novitiate I recall,
> I cannot, to my regret,
> Follow his funeral pall."

[1] Chan Ta Ho's Biographical Table. Yang Chow is situated in modern Chiang Su province, a few miles north of the Yang Tzu River, and on the west bank of the Grand Canal.

[2] See Ts'ai Shang Hsiang, vol. iii, p. 1, where it is stated that Han Ch'i left Yang Chow in the third month of 1045. Ts'ai also quotes the statement of the Wen Chien Lu (聞 見 錄) included in the text, and some others of kindred meaning which were written with intent to disparage the friendship of Wang An Shih with such a worthy man. However, the whole thing is very clumsily done, as witness the poem quoted in the text, and also the statement that Wang An Shih had really been working hard at his books, and not spending the night in carousing as the Wen Chien Lu would make out Han Ch'i to have suspected.

In the spring of the following year, i.e. 1043, he secured leave of absence, and after a long journey of some two months, during which he evidently visited his father's temporary grave at Chiang Ning, he arrived at his old home at Lin Ch'uan.[1] His natural longing for home is seen in the following poem :—

> " On the wide-spreading plain no hill greets the eyes,
> But temples and towers on the lowlands arise.
> From the highest of these I look out o'er the plain,
> And long for the old home in Chiang-Nan again
> The desire to return surged up in my breast,
> A longing so strong it could not be suppressed.
> As I sat at my desk my mind could but roam,
> So my kindly superior sent me back home.
> In the last month of Spring, on the turbulent tide,
> With strong oar and stout sail o'er the waters we glide,
> I rush to my home, my grandmother greet,
> What clasping of hands, what tears as we meet." [2]

During his stay at home he was grieved to find that a youthful acquaintance of the locality, named Fang Chung Yung (方 仲 永), who had given signs of considerable poetical genius in his boyhood, had failed to justify the promise of his earlier days.[3] Ts'ai Shang Hsiang deplores the practice of the local people in honouring this youth as the spirit of the mountain, at the foot of which he was born, on the ground that Wang An Shih's opinion would be that only as the man made progress and ultimately realized the possibilities of his natural endowment was he worthy of special honour.[4] Evidence of his close friendship with men like Tseng Tzu

---

[1] Works, vol. xviii, p. 28. Letter " Shang Hsu Ping Pu Shu " (上 徐 兵 部 書).

[2] See Poem, " Reminiscences," quoted in Chap. II.

[3] Works, vol. xvii, p. 29. " Shang Chung Yung " (傷 仲 永).

[4] Ts'ai Shang Hsiang, vol. ii, p. 4. Yun Lin T'u Chi Shu Hou (雲 林 圖 記 書 後).

Ku and Sun Cheng Chih (孫 正 之) is afforded by a letter
written as he took his leave of the former.[1]
He remained at home until the autumn of that year, as may be
gathered from the next stanza of the poem quoted above, viz. : —

"I mounted my horse and gave him the rein,
By old haunts and strange faces I ambled again,
Obsessed with the past, and without thought of the road,
On my sight bursts the view of this dear old abode.
I recalled how the children had played by my side,
Of their growth into manhood the signs I espied.

"Autumn has thrown her brown garb over all,
The bees hum no longer, the flowers all fall,
The heart of man droops with a myriad regrets,
The thought of our parting deep sadness begets.
Let us linger and feast, let us deep quaff the cup,
Let us drown all our grief, let us sing, let us sup."

His reluctance to leave home, which had led him to overstay
his leave, appears from a letter which he wrote to his Superior
Military Officer on the eve of his return to work. He apologizes
for not having started earlier, mentions the fact that he had
spent two months on the way home, and appeals to be excused
on the ground that it is natural to feel hesitancy about leaving
one's kith and kin.[2]
Indirect evidence as to Wang An Shih's tremendous energy
and devotion to his books is afforded by the Wen Chien Lu,
one of the main sources of those slanderous statements about
his character and relationships which have found their way into
the traditional histories. For we read there that, during his
novitiate in Yang Chow, Wang An Shih was accustomed to
read far on into the night and to get up so late and so hurriedly
that he had no time to wash before going to the office ! [3]

[1] Works, vol. xvii, p. 29. "T'ung Hsueh I Shou Pieh Tzu Ku" (同 學
一 首 別 子 固).
[2] Works, vol. xviii, p. 28.
[3] See p. 14, note 2. One wonders whether this is the source of the tradition
that Wang An Shih rarely washed his clothes or took a bath.

Wang An Shih completed his three years' apprenticeship at Yang Chow with little of further importance to record.

It should now be noted that according to the official regulations in vogue at the time, it was open to Wang An Shih at the conclusion of his three years' official apprenticeship to present a thesis to the supervisor of examinations at the capital with a view to seeking admission into the higher ranks of the official services.[1] As this was the one avenue to the ranks of the official hierarchy, naturally there was usually no diffidence on the part of novitiates to avail themselves of this privilege. Wang An Shih, however, proved to be an exception to the general rule, and refrained from presenting his thesis. The most probable explanation of this diffidence is that his family circumstances were such that he could not afford to take up residence in the capital and assume a position at one of the Bureaux at a merely nominal salary, both of which were necessary concomitants of success at this examination. It may be also that even thus early he wished to demonstrate his high-minded opposition to the conventions which demanded that a candidate for official position should be ready to state views which would be in accordance with those of the Supervisor of examinations if he wished to gain his approval and selection.[2]

However that may be, we find that in the year 1046 Wang An Shih was in the capital seeking another provincial appointment, which would better enable him to meet the financial needs of his family. There are two poems from his pen written in the capital during the fifth month of this year, from which we learn that a bitter north wind had sprung up and had brought hailstones as big as one's fist in its train. The commentator on these poems indicates that an earthquake was felt at the same time.[3]

During this visit to the capital Wang An Shih was accom-

---

[1] i.e. the " Kuan Chih " (館 職).

[2] See his essay on Promotion of Officials, " Chin Shuo " (進 說), translated in Vol. III of this work.

[3] Works, vol. ii, pp. 30 and 31 (丙 戌 五 月 京 師 作 二 首).

panied by a friend named Ma Han Ch'en (馬 漢 臣), who was his senior by four years and whom Wang An Shih regarded as an elder brother. As he was awaiting the result of his Chin Shih examination they were both taken ill, and unfortunately Ma Han Ch'en died in the sixth month.[1]

It was during this year that his friend, Tseng Tzu Ku, wrote to Ou Yang Hsiu the letter quoted in the preceding chapter, recommending Wang An Shih as a man of exceptional literary ability and as one of such rare qualifications that it would be a serious loss to the government if his services were not secured.[2]

In a letter which Tseng Tzu Ku wrote to Wang An Shih in the following year, i.e. 1047, he mentions that he had had an interview with Ou Yang Hsiu, to whom he had shown some of his compositions. He says, too, that these had greatly impressed him and had made him very desirous of making his personal acquaintance.[3]

Towards the end of 1046, or it may have been early in 1047, Wang An Shih received his first appointment as magistrate of a county district, being commissioned to Chin Hsien,[4] the modern Ning Po, in Chechiang province.

During his period of office there, which lasted until some time in 1050, the genius of Wang An Shih for reform and practical experiment asserted itself. The Dynastic History refers to his work there in the following terms :—

"During his magistracy at Chin Hsien he raised the dykes and mounds, drained the marshes and directed the streams, improving and extending the area of arable land. He loaned grain to the people on interest, thereby maintaining a constant supply of fresh grain in the Government granaries. The local people were gratified by this convenient and beneficial arrangement." [5]

[1] Works, vol. xxiv, p. 3.
[2] Ts'ai Shang Hsiang, vol. iii, p. 3.
[3] Ts'ai Shang Hsiang, vol. iii, pp. 4 and 5.
[4] i.e. (鄞 縣) Chan Ta Ho puts the appointment in 1046. But it must have been late in the year.
[5] Sung Shih Pen Chuan (宋 史 本 傳).

From a letter written to the Literary Councillor Tu Yen (杜 衍) we gather some idea of the conditions obtaining in this district during An Shih's tenure of office there. He writes :—

"This place is near the sea and there are numerous streams running from the adjacent valleys. The people ought never to suffer from either drought or flood. But for the last sixty or seventy years the officials have done nothing to conserve the water channels, or prevent silting of the ditches and streams. The people, too, have neglected the matter, so that the available water is all allowed to run off into the sea, and there are no facilities for ensuring a constant supply for the fields. Should there be no rain for ten days or so the streams and pools all dry up, and the people are in constant dread of drought. This I observe is due not to natural conditions so much as to lack of effort on the part of the local officials and people.

" Fortunately during my term of office here the weather has so far been favourable, and harvests have been good. So I am taking advantage of this to utilize the strength and time of the people to carry out extensive projects for deepening the channels and making reservoirs, so that all fear of drought may be eliminated for the future. Both young and old have gladly given themselves to this work. No doubt you will be pleased to hear of this scheme." [1]

From An Shih's writings we learn that he himself travelled through the district supervising and directing the work. He writes :—

" In the 11th month (1047) I set off from the city to get the work on the channels and watercourses started. In all I traversed fourteen different sections, resting at temples on the way. In each place I saw the people actually at work before leaving." [2]

Sorrow overtook him while at Chin Hsien in the loss of a baby daughter.[3] She was born in the 4th month of 1047 and died

---

[1] Works, vol. xviii, p. 22.
[2] Works, vol. xx, p. 7.
[3] Works, vol. xxiv, p. 26.

in the 6th month of the following year. An Shih wrote the tombstone inscription with his own hand. From this we learn that the child was of unusual intelligence and promise, and that her death caused her father great grief. He paid a special visit to the grave just before leaving Chin Hsien for the last time, and composed a short poem expressing the sorrow of his " farewell ".[1]

After he had been in Chin Hsien two years he wrote the following poem, which suggests that he was getting somewhat impatient with his lot, and more than ever desirous of making his way towards what he conceived to be the goal of his life, namely high official position at the capital. It suggests, too, that the poverty of his family was beginning to weigh him down and to be felt as a hindrance in the way of his advancement. The closing lines, however, suggest that he felt he was working for the future, and that prospects were not altogether hopeless. The poem is as follows :—

> " Closed seems the road to Fame,
> Poor is my home.
> Toil I must in this lowly place,
> 'Tis two years since I came.
> Bamboos and reeds the children plant,
> All awry.
> But breezes and mists in their midst will spring,
> Bye and bye." [1]

In a letter written to headquarters, the " Hsiang Fu " (相 府), in the eleventh month of 1047, he gives us further insight into his family circumstances about this time. He writes :—

" I lost my father while I was still a youth. My grandmother is of a great age, and it has long been necessary that adequate support should be provided for my family. But we are so numerous (lit. several tens) that, as we have neither lands nor property, their maintenance is a constant source of anxiety.

" It would, of course, be possible to provide them with the finest food and raiment if I were to abandon myself to corrupt

---

[1] Poetical Works, vol. xlviii, p. 9.

and dishonest practices. That, however, would be dis-
honouring to my father's memory and a violation of the
highest traditions of the Imperial service.

"It is essential that I should continue in some government
post, so I am appealing to the Court to enable me to provide
my father with a fitting burial." [1]

Further insight into his character may be gained from
a letter which he wrote to the Censor Sun (孫 司 諫) after
being two years at Chin Hsien. In this he protests vigorously
against an extra tax which the officials had imposed upon the
district to enable them to add extra police for the capture of
violators of the Salt regulations. He states that taxation was
getting so burdensome that people would have to sell their
land in order to meet their obligations.

He also speaks out courageously against the practice of those
conventional subordinates who were concerned merely with
the carrying out of their superior's orders, regardless of the
effect that such would have upon the livelihood of the people.
He notes, too, that usually subordinates were afraid of
protesting against any order from above, as such protest would
most likely be interpreted as disobedience." [2]

Towards the close of his period at Chin Hsien, sometime in
1049, he wrote the following two poems [3] :—

"Chrysanthemums I planted as I went on my way,
But their glory has faded as now I return.
Next year my term here will draw to a close,
I wonder who'll gaze on your colourful bloom.

"I uproot the bamboo from the foot of the hill.
By the meandering streamlet I plant it.
The new shoots already are thrusting their heads,
Through the soil that in Winter has nursed it.
As my term in this office will shortly expire,
I ramble oft hither to view it."

[1] Works, vol. xviii, p. 12. He returned home next year to bury his father.
[2] Works, vol. xviii, p. 30.
[3] Poetical Works, vol. xlvii, p. 13. Probably the absence was due to his father's
funeral.

An epidemic then broke out in the district which was sufficiently serious to bring from the emperor a specific prescription. Wang An Shih had this engraved in stone, and set up in the form of a tablet outside the gate of his yamen. He added the following by way of explanation :—

"We read in Mencius that the ancient rulers were compassionate and considerate in their government of the people. As I read this prescription from the emperor I mused : ' This is an instance of compassionate government. It is the duty of the throne to issue commands, and that of the official to make them known to the people. Both are mutually necessary if the people are to share in the blessings of orderly and progressive government. We have a gracious ruler on the throne. His solicitude and generosity penetrate to the uttermost bounds of his dominion. He has discovered a remedy for this disease which others have pronounced incurable. It is his gracious purpose to save the people from its ravages. If I in my humble sphere do not do my share and see that the people actually receive the benefits of his favour I shall be culpable in the eyes of all. So I have carved this prescription in stone and set it up in this public place that all may read it and make further inquiry unnecessary. Set up in the second year of Huang Yu (皇 祐), i.e. 1050, on the 28th day of the second month." [1]

The above quotations suffice to show that Wang An Shih carried out the duties of his office at Chin Hsien in a thorough-going and conscientious manner. He took a real and practical interest in the welfare of the people. So fine was his reputation for his good work there that even the Dynastic History cannot withhold its meed of commendation. For in the record of his life as there narrated, we read : "The local people were gratified by the measures he instituted for the improvement of their livelihood." [2]

The reputation of such a conscientious and public spirited official naturally enough soon reached the capital, where there

[1] Works, vol. xx, p. 7.
[2] Sung Shih Pen Chuan (宋 史 本 傳).

were not lacking those who were willing to recommend him for further promotion. In 1051 Ch'en Hsiang (陳 襄) recommended him together with Hu Yuan (胡 瑗), who afterwards became a very famous scholar. Of Wang An Shih he wrote :—

"He is a worthy and enlightened man, thoroughly versed in ancient lore, and already well known for his literary gifts and administrative ability " [1]

Evidently the " road to fame " was not to be closed against him for ever. His work at Chin Hsien was long remembered. Ch'en Chiu Ch'uan (陳 九 川) (1522–1526) writes :—

" During his term of office at Chin Hsien, Wang An Shih established a fine reputation. The people of the district erected many shrines to his memory, and even now regard him almost as a god. That he should thus be remembered after an interval of five hundred years is sufficient testimony to his character and ability for wise and beneficent government." [2]

---

[1] Liang Ch'i Ch'ao, op. cit., p. 46. Also Ts'ai Shang Hsiang, vol. iv, p. 5. The extract quoted here refers to Wang An Shih as already in office at Shu Chow.

[2] Liang Ch'i Ch'ao, op. cit., p. 53.

CHAPTER IV

IN OFFICE AT SHU-CHOW (1051–1054)

WANG AN SHIH was out of office for over one year [1] after the conclusion of his term at Chin Hsien. This interval is marked by the attempt of his friends at the capital to induce him to take the examination which would secure his admission to the higher ranks of the Government services. But this he steadily refused to do. Whereupon Wen Yen Po (文 彥 博), then Grand Councillor, recommended him to the throne along with Han Wei (韓 維). This was in the year 1051. The Dynastic History [2] has the following account of this :—

" Wen Yen Po, the Grand Councillor, recommended Wang An Shih for special promotion. He proposed that as he was of a modest and retiring disposition he should be exempted from observance of the customary procedure in regard to official promotion. He thought that this would serve as an example to the official classes in general, as it would tend to check their place-seeking rivalries."

Evidently the idea of Wen Yen Po in doing this was to secure for An Shih exemption from the examination, for his memorial of recommendation also contains the following [3] :—

" All scholars are desirous of taking this particular examination, but Wang An Shih is the rare exception. In his modesty he refrains from doing so. It would be difficult to find many of his disposition."

The result of this appeal to the throne was that a special mandate was issued ordering Wang An Shih to present himself

---

[1] See letter referred to under p. 25, note 2. There is confirmatory evidence that Wang An Shih returned from Chin Hsien in 1050 in his Inscription written for the San Ch'ing Tien (三 清 殿) at Fu Chow (撫 州). This is dated the 25th of the 5th month of 1050. Fu Chow was the prefecture in which his own home Lin Ch'uan was located. Works, vol. xx, p. 13.

[2] Sung Biography.

[3] Liang Ch'i Ch'ao, p. 46.

at the capital for this examination. The Dynastic History [1] continues : " A little later Wang An Shih was ordered to take the examination, but he refused." The emperor and high officials were doubtless full of curiosity to make the acquaintance of such an unusual man, but were not prepared to break with the traditional procedure regarding official promotion.

Fortunately there is included in his Prose Works a letter from Wang An Shih, which fully explains his reasons for refusing to proceed to the capital at this time to take the examination. This letter, or memorial, reads as follows [2] :—

" Owing to the great age of my grandmother, the fact that my father's corpse remained unburied : that my younger sister ought to be getting married and the numbers and poverty of my family, I have found it impossible hitherto to concur in your Majesty's request. . . . I am grateful that so far you have not compelled me to attend at the capital for the purposes of taking this examination and that, instead of blaming me as one who frames empty excuses for refusing to do so, you admire my modesty and reticence in refraining from taking this step.

" Possibly I might be deserving of the epithets ' Modest and retiring ' were I one who suffering from no embarrassment of family poverty should still seek to avoid the responsibilities of higher public office. But the facts are otherwise. I am bound to take into consideration the financial circumstances of my family and am compelled to choose what is for me the most advantageous course financially.

" Pardon me for mentioning the fact that I have been out of office for two years or so and that the aged and youthful members of my family are not yet adequately provided for. Just as I am on the point of resuming my official career (in the provinces) your order to attend at the capital arrives. To obey this would, I repeat, be inimical to my private interests. Therefore, I beseech your Majesty's gracious pardon, asking that you will give due consideration to my real motive for refusing,

[1] Sung Biography.
[2] Works, vol. ix, p. 12.

which is actuated solely by personal and family considerations. May I also appeal that you desist from further attempts to induce me to take this examination, and that you will give me your gracious permission to complete another term of official service in the provinces."

From this it is quite clear that financial considerations in the interests of his family determined Wang An Shih's attitude at this time, and that it was solely out of a sense of duty to them that he refused to proceed to the capital and take the first step towards advancement into the charmed circle of higher officialdom.

Thanks to the continued interest of Wen Yen Po, he was given promotion of rank to that of " Tien Chung Ch'eng ",[1] or 3rd Class Chamberlain of the Imperial Household, and given a new appointment [2] as Censor of Military Affairs at Shu Chow (舒 州), the modern Huai-Ning Hsien (懷 寧 縣) in the province of An Hui.

At this period the Emperor was desirous of keeping a close watch on the military officials in the various districts, with a view to curbing their power and preventing rebellion. So officials like Wang An Shih were deputed to act as representatives of the throne in the provinces to report on all military matters. He had the standing of co-Prefect in the district.

Details are lacking of his term of service at Shu Chow, with the exception of such information as can be gleaned from poems written there. But as in later life, after his retirement from the Grand Council, the title of Duke of Shu [3] was conferred upon him, it is reasonable to infer that his work in this district was characterized by some achievements worthy of public notice.

---

[1] (殿 中 丞.) An honorary title indicating rank or grade in the official service. There was a department at the capital styled the " Tien Chung Sheng " (殿 中 省), which was concerned with the affairs of the Imperial household, such as food, clothes, residence, medicine, equipment, and the like. Wang An Shih was given the rank of a third-class Chamberlain. This carried no actual responsibilities for affairs.

[2] Biographical Table of Chan Ta Ho.

[3] i.e. " Shu Kuo Kung " (舒 國 公), Biographical Table.

In one poem [1] written to his brother, An Kuo (P'ing Fu), recounting his arrival at his new post, he suggests that the place was off the beaten track, that visitors were few, and that he had no one with whom he could discuss the ancient lore. Another poem [1] was occasioned by the coming of rain on the 17th of the 7th month. When with this are related the facts outlined in his other poem,[2] entitled " Fa Lin ", or " Distribution of Grain " (發 廩), written towards the close of his period of service at Shu Chow, we may infer that the district was suffering from drought and famine.

The following is an attempted translation of this poem :—

" Free grants of grain were the regular rule
Of the kings of that ancient day.
But in recent times this has ceased to be
For the rich o'er the poor hold sway.
Not alone of the people does this hold true,
The State revenues come from like source,
The ruler defers to the rich and the strong,
Even Ministers buy their posts.
This is more than loyal hearts can stand
For the nine-plot system I long.[3]

" My purpose, alas ! I cannot fulfil,
So I serve in a humble sphere,
In this desolate place three years have passed,
Full of children their parents can't rear.
The order was given to disburse the rich grain
To save the helpless poor,
In this mountainous tract by vale and hill,

---

[1] Poetical Works, vol. xxxvi, p. 6.
[2] Poetical Works, vol. xvii, p. 5.
[3] Referring to the land system of the Yin or Shang Dynasty, under which the land was divided up into areas of fixed dimensions. These were subdivided into nine squares, the middle square being cultivated by the farmers of the other eight plots conjointly, the proceeds of the middle plot being regarded as Government revenue. The system was styled the " Ching T'ien Chih Fa " (井 田 之 法). The total area of the big plot was 630 acres or Mou (畝). The character " ching " illustrates the idea in its form (井). Cf. Legge, Works of Mencius, p. 240.

None keeps the wolf from the door.
When the wealthiest folk are in direst need,
What hope for the weak and poor?

" But once this place was wealthy and strong,
With rich meadows and keen sons of toil,
Conditions elsewhere one can easily gauge,
From their indolent work on the soil.
The poems of Pin by the famous Chow Kung,
Speak of vital affairs to the land,
I copy the text of the Seventh Moon ode,[1]
To enlighten the noble and grand."

Through this ode breathes that spirit of compassion for the
poor and opposition to the rich which characterized his attempts
at reform later on. His opening of the official granary and
distribution of the grain to the needy shows his readiness to
do all that was possible within the sphere of his own authority
to relieve the prevalent distress. It may be, though this is
nowhere expressly stated, that here as at Chin Hsien, Wang An
Shih made loans to the people on condition that when harvests
were good they should make repayment with interest. His
longing for the nine-plot system shows his desire to reinstate
the ancient order of communal ownership of the land, when the
people cultivated eight-ninths of a given area for themselves
and worked the other ninth for the Government. All this
reveals a mind already busy with the great problem of the
people's poverty.

From this poem, too, we learn that An Shih occupied this
position at Shu Chow for at least three years.

Though his sphere was somewhat remote, he was not forgotten by his friends in high place, for in 1053 Ou Yang Hsiu
submitted a memorial to the throne strongly recommending
Wang An Shih for promotion.[2] This reads as follows :—

" Everyone speaks most highly of Wang An Shih's character

---

[1] Odes, Legge's edition of the Chinese Classics, vol. xv, p. 226.
[2] I am following Chan Ta Ho here. Ts'ai Shang Hsiang, vol. iv, p. 11, and
Liang Ch'i Ch'ao, p. 46, both make this recommendation for the Censorate to
date 1056.

and learning. He is one who will hold on to his principles even though by so doing he should be involved in poverty. He is a man of very strong will, not easily swayed by extraneous influences. He has had a considerable variety of official experience, and has a real insight into the needs of the time. Though he has frequently been ordered to take the higher official examination, he has so far refused to do so. My appeal is that he be given a post in the Board of Censors."

This appeal evidently was not acceptable to An Shih. At any rate, he refused it on account of his grandmother's age.[1] But Ou Yang Hsiu continued to press An Shih's suit. At the conclusion of his term at Shu Chow he visited the capital to seek further appointment. In an interview with his friend, Ou Yang Hsiu, the latter evidently made the proposal that he should seek special favour from the emperor in An Shih's behalf, exempting him from the one-year period of unsalaried probation at the capital, if he would but take the prescribed examination. An Shih wrote him a letter [2] after the close of this interview which indicates his reaction to this suggestion. The letter reads as follows :—

" I am grateful for the opportunity you gave me at your home to-day, but I failed to express the whole of my mind to you. You understand that my reason for not taking this examination hitherto was due to the necessity of my providing the expenditure on weddings and funerals in my family, which prohibited my remaining for any length of time in the capital. My financial status has in no wise improved during recent years, rather has it got worse, for recently my two elder brothers [3] and a sister-in-law have all passed away.

" If perchance I should take the examination and be selected

---

[1] Wang An Shih's grandmother died this year, the tombstone inscription being composed by Tseng Tzu Ku. (Ts'ai Shang Hsiang, vol. vi, p. 11 ; also Biographical Table of Chan Ta Ho.)

[2] Works, vol. xviii, p. 15.

[3] i.e. An Jen (安 仁), who died in 1051 and was buried 1052 (Works, vol. xxiv, p. 1), and An Tao (安 道). See Works, vol. ix, p. 12, where he relates the death of his two elder brothers and his grandmother, also a sister-in-law.

for a post in one of the Bureaus at the capital, it would be necessary, according to the regulations, for me to remain there one year.   Should, however, the Court issue an order exempting me from this, and permit me to take up an outside appointment instead, a good deal of criticism would thereby be aroused, and that should be avoided.

" Should the Court again order me to take the examination I should feel bound to refuse on the ground of my family circumstances.   I know that you in your generosity would ensure the gratification of my wish in this matter.   But I am anxious to avoid the delay that would inevitably be caused by a repetition of these requests and refusals, as it would mean that I should not be able to proceed to a provincial appointment for some considerable time.   Already many months have elapsed since I ceased to draw my official stipend.   My family are dependent upon this, so the earlier I get this request of mine granted the happier they will be.   I feel that this is a matter which a generous minded man like yourself will feel in duty bound to help forward."

Ou Yang Hsiu still persisted in his attempt to introduce his protégé into higher circles, and was so far successful as to induce the Emperor to issue a special decree, not only exempting him from taking the higher official examination, but also excusing him from the one year's probation at the capital and offering him direct access into the higher ranks by appointing him to the " Chi Hsien Yuan " (集 賢 院) as assistant librarian [1] (Redactor) (集 賢 檢 理).   This appointment was offered him in an Imperial mandate dated the 22nd of the 3rd month 1054.[2]   The following is a summary of An Shih's first reply,[3] refusing the position :—

" I thank your Majesty for the despatch forwarded by messenger from the ' Chung Shu Sheng ' (中 書 省)[4]

---

[1] Works, vol. xviii, p. 15.
[2] Works, vol. ix, p. 13.
[3] Works, vol. ix, pp. 12 and 13.
[4] One of the three Government organs at the capital concerned with civil affairs.   These were styled respectively the Chung Shu Sheng (中 書 省),

offering me the appointment of assistant librarian. I am grateful for all past favours in not compelling me to take the examination on account of family circumstances. Recent losses in my family [1] and added responsibilities in connection therewith have only tended to increase my difficulties. That is the reason why I have now come to the capital to seek a further appointment in the provinces. . . .

" The court's favour in offering me this new appointment at the capital without demanding that I take the examination is altogether unexpected. If I refuse I shall be guilty of disobeying orders. On the other hand if I accept I shall feel that I have acted contrary to my principles. . . .

" I understand that your Majesty has extended to me the further privilege of exemption from the customary one year's probation and permitting me to spend that period in an outside appointment. But what pretext can I offer for thus forcing the court to break the long established precedent in this matter ?

" Again a new regulation has been recently issued that no official appointments are to be made on the recommendation of Court Ministers, unless such appointments should conform with established regulations and a formal order be issued to that effect. This appointment of mine has been offered on the recommendation of a Court Minister, and it is suggested that I should accept it on terms which do not conform with the regulations. This new regulation has been issued only ten days. I regret that I cannot be the first to break it.

" I hope then most earnestly that Your Majesty will, in the light of this, my honest intention, cancel this mandate, and appoint me to a post in the provinces consonant with my ability and deserts. In that way my superiors will be free of any charge of violation of the public regulations, and I shall

which would seem to have been the Chief Legislative organ, the Shang Shu Sheng (尚 書 省), which was the Executive organ, and the Men Hsia Sheng (門 下 省), which was the Chief Record Office, and exercised other functions such as the conduct of Ceremonial Affairs, etc.

[1] See p. 29, n. 3.

feel that my sense of duty has been loyally obeyed. I regret therefore that I must refuse this position, and appeal once more for a provincal appointment."

The higher powers refused to be satisfied with this explanation, and sent at least three other despatches urging him to accept the commission. Each time An Shih refused to consider it, stressing his sincerity in giving the reasons for refusal, denying that he had done anything or possessed any unusual qualifications such as might justify the consideration that was offered, and emphasizing the fact that he had been guided in his decision by considerations solely of what was right.

He stressed the fact that he was not unwilling to take the examination on any other ground than that of financial inability to conform to the regulations. He was convinced that no exceptions ought to be made to the regular procedure, and promised that when he should be free from financial embarrassment he would be willing to take the examination and accept such appointment as the Court saw fit to offer him.[1]

This incident has been elaborated at some length in order that the reader may be given further insight into the real character of Wang An Shih. His name has been defamed so excessively and for so long that it is incumbent upon one endeavouring to re-establish his reputation to produce adequate evidence. His critics are prone to assert that these repeated refusals to accept this appointment were but part of a clever device to enhance his reputation thinking that by arousing the desires of the Court to see such an unusual man in action he might be enabled to spring the more speedily into fame and high office.

Such criticism as this the above documents should serve to liquidate, for they show him to be a man of high principle, unwilling that special exceptions should be made to accommodate him, and determined at all costs to do justice to his family responsibilities. It is quite clear that it was An Shih's purpose to serve his country in some high and important

---

[1] Works, vol. ix, pp. 13 and 14.

capacity. There is also a sufficiency of evidence to show that he would not gain his object or further it in any way that would violate his stern sense of duty or involve him in any compromise with principle.

A letter (undated) [1] which he wrote to his friend, Li Tzu Shen (李 貲 探), will not be out of place here :—

" Men's circumstances change through a variety of reasons, and the motives underlying the acts and policies of great men differ greatly. But there is one thing common to them all. They held within themselves the ruling principle of action. They were, as it were, ' self-contained,' and ready for any emergency. They did not need to wait for a situation to present itself before deciding how to meet it. Just because they were of this type some of their actions may seem to others to be of a questionable character. But they themselves never had cause to regret any step they took. The slander of others left them entirely unconcerned. While I cannot hope ever to reach such a lofty standard, yet in my inmost heart I sincerely desire to do so."

Wang An Shih is known to posterity as " the Obstinate Minister ".[2] " Obstinate " he certainly was, but obstinacy of the kind which is born of a keen sense of right and duty may surely be forgiven.

---

[1] Works, vol. xviii, p. 7.
[2] Ssu Ma Kuang terms Wang An Shih "Hsien erh p'i" (賢 而 愎) acknowledging his worth and deploring his obstinacy at the same time. See the " Tzu Chih T'ung Chien Hsu Pien " (資 治 通 鑑 續 編), hereafter termed the " T'ung Chien ".

CHAPTER V

IN THE CAPITAL DISTRICT AND AT CH'ANG CHOW (1054-1057)

WE have seen in the preceding chapter that Wang An Shih's official friends were keen to secure for him some appointment at the capital. But the frankness with which he had communicated his financial difficulties to his patron, Ou Yang Hsiu, led the latter to realize that the post of assistant-librarian which had been offered him was not sufficiently lucrative. (It is important here to note that as An Shih's father and two elder brothers were dead, he was now the responsible head of the family.[1]) So he proceeded to secure for him a concurrent post as third grade Supervisor of the National Stud[2] (羣 牧 司 判 官). This appointment was referred to in Ou Yang Hsiu's recommendation to the throne as "an excellent financial post".[3]

As the expression "a concurrent post" is used, we infer that the position of assistant-librarian which An Shih had hitherto refused, was now also accepted by him. Details are lacking of his work in connection with these two appointments, which he held for about two years. His great friend, Wang Feng Yuan (王 逢 原), wrote him a poem at this time suggesting that though he was taking care of cows and sheep he had the qualifications for the chief position in the Empire.[4]

[1] After the death of a father the family responsibilities devolve on the eldest son.

[2] Biographical Table of Chan Ta Ho. The character used is "chien" (兼), indicating that the appointment was in addition to some other post held at the same time.

[3] Sung Biography.

[4] Biographical Table. Wang Feng Yuan likens Wang An Shih to the phœnix, one of the four great emblematical creatures of Chinese tradition. In this the phœnix is regarded as the most intelligent of the winged family, and was symbolic of the inauguration of a golden age. The implication is that Wang An Shih was regarded as a very exceptional man, and destined to do great things for his country. The other three emblematical creatures are the dragon, unicorn, and the tortoise.

34

At some time towards the close of his two years' service in these appointments he was given the position of magistrate of one of the counties in the capital district.[1]   But he held this for a very brief period, as we find him appealing for a country post again in 1056.   This appointment to one of the capital counties was probably gained through the friendly offices of Ou Yang Hsiu, for the following letter of recommendation [2] from his pen was written during 1056.   It reads as follows :—

"An Shih is already well-known for his learning and literary skill.   He is a man of the noblest self-respect and highest principle.   He is of well-informed mind, and possesses exceptional gifts of debate.   He is a man with just the right gifts for the time, one who could fill any office with credit."

For reasons which appear in the following letter of appeal for a change to a provincial post, An Shih found that residence in the capital precincts was inconvenient.   The following is a translation of the more important parts of this appeal [3] :—

"At a time when everything seems propitious, with a benevolent emperor on the throne, and when the people are looking to the high officers at court to institute good and beneficent measures of government, I find myself appointed to this position in the capital precincts.   I am aware that this post is one which all my friends and relations, and many of the high officials, have desired me to take up, and I quite appreciate the fact that normally it is a position in which at the present favourable time one should devote oneself wholeheartedly to the task in hand.

"But there are other considerations to be taken into account.

[1] See Works, vol. xv, p. 31, where, in the letter of thanks for his appointment to Ch'ang Chow (常 州), he mentions that he had been favoured with a district appointment in the Capital district, but that before there had been the chance to test his capacity in that post he had been transferred at his own request to a more convenient position (i.e. Ch'ang Chow, which was nearer his home).
[2] Ts'ai Shang Hsiang, vol. v, p. 8, where Ou Yang Hsiu recommends Wang An Shih with three others.
[3] Works, vol. xviii, p. 14.   "Shang Chih Cheng Shu" (上 執 政 書).

My object in entering upon official life was to provide the where-
withal to maintain my family.   But as the years have passed
I find that my circumstances have in no way improved in this
respect.   My mother is now getting advanced in years, and
the bodies of my two brothers and sister-in-law are still awaiting
burial.   I have, too, to think of my younger brothers who
will be wanting to get married.   These family perplexities
weigh on my mind to such an extent that I have no pleasure
in my present appointment.

" I am therefore beginning to realize that a position nearer
home, where it would be more convenient to attend to these
family duties, is absolutely necessary for me.   This is the
reason why I have sent in so many requests for a country
appointment during my two years' residence in the capital
precincts.

" There are other reasons in addition to that of my family
poverty and responsibilities for making this request.   I really
prefer to be in the provinces.   Moreover of late I have been
in very poor health, suffering from such bad headaches
that at times I get so dazed that I scarcely know what I
am doing.

" I realize that I ought to be devoting myself wholeheartedly
to the duties of this important position, as a mark of my
gratitude to the throne for giving me this favour.   But I fear
I have not the ability to transact the duties of such a responsible
post, so that even though my mind were at rest, I still fear
I could not carry them.   But when in addition to mental
perplexity I find myself suffering from serious physical disability, it is quite evident that I cannot carry on.

" So I have returned my official seal, and in accordance
with what I consider to be the correct official procedure now
await the punishment of the emperor for my delinquencies. . . .
I do not think it right to go on drawing my pay when I know
I am not doing the work, and realize my unfitness for the
position.

" I therefore appeal for a post somewhere in the south-east,
no matter how small and retired the place, in which I might

exercise my inferior gifts and limited knowledge and experience. . . ."

Response to this appeal was soon forthcoming, for in 1057 he was appointed as prefect of Ch'ang Chow in Chiang Su, the modern Wu Chin Hsien, not far from Nanking.[1]   His official rank was also advanced to that of " T'ai Ch'ang Po Shih " (太常博士).[2]   Shortly after his arrival at his new post, he wrote the following letter of thanks for the appointment :—

" I have already informed you that my aim in taking up official life was to improve my financial status.   But recently I have resigned an official appointment because of illness. I admit that such conduct as this would, with strict government prevailing, merit summary treatment.   I also remember with gratitude that Your Majesty transferred me from a position as assistant in the National Stud to that of magistrate of one of the capital counties, after I had made repeated appeals to be given a provincial post.   But before there had been time to see whether I had either the character or qualifications for that onerous post, illness overtook me, and in response to a frank and urgent statement of my circumstances, you eventually conferred upon me this new appointment, which is so conveniently situated for my purposes. . . . Now I would call your attention to the fact that these provincial districts suffer seriously from the constant changes that take place in the personnel of the officials administering them.   To my mind it is important that such officials should be allowed to remain for some considerable length of time in each post.   Take this district for example.   They have had bad harvests for several seasons, but the official has been changed no less than eight times during the last two years.   I fear that once the

---

[1] Biographical Table of Chan Ta Ho.

[2] Ts'ai Shang Hsiang, vol. v, p. 8. Letter of recommendation by Ou Yang Hsiu, in which Wang An Shih is referred to as " T'ai Ch'ang Po Shih " (太常博士) concurrently with his being in the Imperial Stud (羣牧判官).

residents have got over the troublesome business of my reception, my bodily weakness will, among other things, prevent me from making any real contribution to the needs of the place, unless I am permitted to stay on for some time. I hope you will bear this in mind, and if you can see your way to grant my request I shall be saved from a feeling of guiltiness, and the people will be duly encouraged." [1]

On his way to this new post at Ch'ang Chow he had visited his youngest brother, whom he had found ill at Ch'u Chow (楚 州), and had stayed with him and his fourth brother, An Kuo, for a period of forty days. He mentions that he actually took up his duties at Ch'ang Chow on the 4th day of the 7th month of this year, i.e. 1056. [2]

In a poem written to the Chief-Intendant of the Circuit, Shao by name, he refers to the disastrous losses which the district had sustained from floods. He expresses his determination to throw himself wholeheartedly into reconstruction work, and seeks the advice of his superior in connection with it. [3]

In two letters [4] which he wrote to headquarters from Ch'ang Chow he mentions that famine conditions were prevailing in the area : that the district hitherto had been very badly administered : that subordinates in the yamen had been doing pretty much as they pleased, and that serious defalcations had been discovered in the accounts. These defects he attributed in part to the fact that too many changes had been made in the personnel, and urging that it was essential for him to have a prolonged stay in the post if he was to make any constructive contribution and bring about any material improvement in the state of affairs.

He had not been in the position long, however, before the order came for him to take up the responsible position of

---

[1] Works, vol xv, p. 31.
[2] Works, vol. xviii, p. 16, Letter No. 3 to Ou Yang Hsiu.
[3] Poetical Works, vol. xxiv, p. 9.
[4] Works, vol. xix, pp. 6 and 7 (知 常 州 上 中 書 啟 and 知 常 州 上 監 司 啟).

Chief-Justice of the Chiang-Tung Circuit, in which Ch'ang Chow was situated.[1]   He raised objections to taking up this appointment, as it would involve him in considerable travel, and take him away from his family duties for too long at a time.[2]   However, it would seem that sometime in 1057, or early in 1058, his appointment was changed to that of Chief-Justice of Chiang-Tung.[3]

---

[1] There is some divergence of view between the authorities on the date of Wang An Shih's appointment to this post. In this I am following Ts'ai Shang Hsiang and Liang Ch'i Ch'ao. See Ts'ai Shang Hsiang, vol. v, p. 10, and also vol. v, p. 13.

[2] Ts'ai Shang Hsiang, vol. v, p. 12, " Shang Ts'eng Ts'an Cheng Shu " (上 曾 參 政 書).

[3] The commentator on Wang's Poetical Works, styled Li Chu (李 注) in Ts'ai Shang Hsiang's Work, indicates a definite date for this appointment as the 2nd month of 1058. See Ts'ai Shang Hsiang, vol. vi, p. 1.

CHAPTER VI

CHIEF-JUSTICE OF CHIANG-TUNG
(1058–1060)

ON the completion of a year's term at Ch'ang Chow (常 州) Wang An Shih received the appointment of Chief-Justice [1] of the Chiang-Tung circuit (提 點 刑 獄).[2] This geographically comprised portions of the modern provinces of An Hui, Chiang Su, and Che Chiang. The appointment carried with it the duties of oversight of the law-courts and prisons in the area, as well as investigation of legal decisions, and naturally involved him in a great deal of travelling.

Included in his Poetical Works are two poems written whilst on his journeyings through the circuit. The first of these [3] written to one Sun Shen Lao (孫 莘 老) suggests that he was travelling during the later winter and early spring. As this poem is interesting for the light it throws upon his feelings at this time, the following translation is attempted :—

"Bleak Winter is past, mild Spring has begun,
In this perilous pass I recall Wang Tsun (王 尊),

---

[1] i.e. " T'i Tien Hsing Yu " (提 點 刑 獄).

[2] Biographical Table.

[3] Poetical Works, vol. xxxi, p. 9. The Wang Tsun quoted in this poem was an official of the Han Dynasty. When travelling to a new appointment in Ssu Ch'uan they came to a very dangerous pass. The muleteer was inclined to turn back, but Wang Tsun urged him forward, saying that risks must be taken in the service of the State. A later appointee named Wang Yang turned back at this particular point in order to save his skin. An Shih dare not compare himself with Wang Tsun, for he realized that he himself was braving the dangers of the road in the first instance in the interests of his family, as that was the main reason for his entering upon official life. So this led him rather to think of Mao I (毛 義) of the Later Han times, who on receiving the news of his first official appointment, wept for joy, as it afforded him the means of keeping his family from poverty. Later, however, after his mother's death, he resolutely refused to take up any other appointment, as the necessity for earning such money as official life afforded no longer existed. See Commentary on this poem, also " Tz'u Yuan " in loco.

Who kept on his way, lest his critics should say,
He had turned from the path where his duty lay.
My own circumstances are of different degree,
Being much more akin to those of Mao I (pronounced -ee),
Who kept to the track,
Lest his parents should lack,
Still—this with my principles doesn't agree.
The breeze and the moon inspire me to song,
For quiet and study I fervently long.
But none understand me."

It has already been emphasized that Wang An Shih, during these early years of his official career, felt it incumbent upon him to continue in provincial appointments that he might have sufficient to maintain his family. But this necessity, while he accepts it dutifully, does not altogether satisfy his sense of the fitness of things. He evidently longed to be in a position where he could serve his country unfettered by such mundane considerations, and which would give him more time for scholarly pursuits.

The following extract from a letter to Chang Chi (張 幾) [1] makes this point very clear. He writes :—

" I know I have entered upon official life for the sake of a livelihood. This is of course contrary to my real principles.[2] But still one must have regard to the necessities of one's circumstances. Had I not taken up the government service, what other means of livelihood were open to me ? If I had adopted some other way of getting a living, I fear still greater violence would have been done to my sense of the fitness of things. So really I have no option in this matter."

In another letter to Wang Kai (王 該) [3] he writes :—

" My sole desire is to follow in the footsteps of Confucius. I look to him for correction when either in motive or in act I fail to do justice to the ideals I possess. It is certainly not

---

[1] Prose Works, vol. xviii, p. 36.
[2] i.e. he should not take office at a time when his own ideas could not be carried out.
[3] Prose Works, vol. xviii, p. 35.

my desire to remain in minor official posts, but I never forget those among the ancient worthies who through poverty were compelled to do so."

From the information at our disposal regarding Wang Ah Shih's conduct of so-called minor posts, we find little to which exception could be taken. He shows himself faithful to the duties of whatever office he took up, and his correspondence shows him keenly alive to the interests of the people. But all through there is a suggestion that minor posts did not satisfy him, and that he was but waiting his opportunity to serve the state in some higher and more influential sphere.

Two other letters written during these earlier days show him to be a true Confucian philosopher. The first,[1] written to his friend Sun Cheng Chih (孫 正 之), is as follows :—

"The real man has his time of straits, but he will never demean himself by weak conformity to conventional standards. Nor will he allow anything in his circumstances to override his principles. He will ever seek to improve his talents and cultivate his character. He will hold fast to his lofty ideals through every vicissitude of fortune, so that when his opportunity comes, and he stands in favour with the emperor, he may bring about such changes in his environment and so reform affairs as to make them conform to his ideals."

The second letter [2] written to Wang Feng Yuan (王 逢 原) reads thus :—

"The really great man trains himself for the service of the state, but his first concern is not to get power over the people but to get control over himself. I believe that Providence is operative not only in my own personal affairs, but also in the wider matters of empire. Confucius said, ' he who is not conscious that his course is decreed has not the making of a truly great man.' He also said, ' Whenever opportunity is afforded me for the application of my ideals

---

[1] Prose Works, vol. xx, p. 17.
[2] Prose Works, vol. xviii, p. 19.

to affairs of state, or my theories are rejected, I regard both alike as being ' providentially decreed '."

The career of Wang An Shih prior to his promotion to high office at the capital demonstrates that his desire to follow in the footsteps of Confucius was no vain or boastful ambition. He put his duty to his parents first, and was content to await the leadings of " Providence " [1] towards the wider and more influential sphere which he felt destined to occupy. Meanwhile he was training himself so as to be ready when the opportunity presented itself.

His plaint in the last line of the poem above, that " no one understands me ", must have reference to such matters as are raised here.   His critics were obsessed of the idea that his refusals to take appointments at the capital were all designed to give him that notoriety and arouse that curiosity which would eventually win for him abnormally speedy promotion.

But I think sufficient evidence is afforded by his letters and poems, as quoted above, to prove that he had no other motive in seeking country posts than that of making suitable provision for the financial needs of his family, and also with a view to enabling him to give such personal oversight as was necessary to his home affairs.

Another poem written in honour of Shen P'o Yang,[2] who evidently had held office in the Circuit prior to Wang An Shih, shows that he took a journey of several months duration through the district, and that he must have penetrated to some remote parts, for he complains that the language of the people is strange to him. He found that Shen P'o Yang was held in the highest esteem everywhere, and he is generous enough to acknowledge this in his ode.

In the " Life of Chow Lien Hsi " (周 廉 溪 年 譜) by Tu Cheng (度 正) it is recorded that the great philosopher, then 44 years of age, and Wang An Shih, who was then 39 and Chief-Justice of the Chiang-Tung Circuit, met together. " An

---

[1] i.e. " Ming " (命).

[2] Shen P'o Yang (沈 鄱 陽), Poetical Works, vol. xxxi, p. 10.

Shih was already famous as a Confucian scholar. The two conversed far into the night. This interview caused An Shih furiously to think, so much so that he could neither eat nor sleep."

This interview, if it occurred, which Liang Ch'i Ch'ao [1] is disposed to doubt, would have taken place in 1059.

The idea which the narrators of this supposed incident would convey is that Wang An Shih had found his master in Chow Lien Hsi, for he had disturbed his mental complacency to such an extent that sleep was impossible and food was neglected. Ts'ai Shang Hsiang disposes of this incident as a fabrication, together with one recorded of their earlier years, when it is stated that Wang An Shih was anxious to be regarded as a scholar, and sent in his visiting card three times to Chow Lien Hsi, who three times refused to see him.

It should be noted here that one of the features of this particular period is the rise of different schools of politico-philosophical thought, whose rivalries had serious effects upon the political situation. Chow Lien Hsi was one of the leaders of the Loyang School, whose later representatives were Ch'eng I and Ch'eng Hao, and later again Chu Hsi. The partisans of Wang An Shih came into serious conflict with this school later on, and in writings of a later date, it became common to insert slanderous statements regarding one another with a view to decrying the abilities and achievements of their rivals.

Ts'ai Shang Hsiang has made a careful examination of the biographies of Chow Lien Hsi and Wang An Shih and reaches

---

[1] Chow Lien Hsi is Chow Tun I (周 敦 頤), one of the five great philosophers of the Sung Dynasty. Liang Ch'i Ch'ao, after a close inspection of the biographies of Chow and Wang, concludes that they could not have met at all. He further adduces the fact that the particular quotation in Tu Cheng's work is from the writings of Hsing Shu (邢 恕), an adherent of the two Ch'engs, i.e. Ch'eng I (程 頤) and Ch'eng Hao (程 顥), who were of the same "School" as Chow, and who were eventually enrolled among the opponents of Wang An Shih's reform policy. He therefore disposes of the incident as a fabrication begotten of the prejudices of an opposing faction.

the conclusion that they could not possibly have met during Wang's tenure of office at Chiang Tung.[1]

However, it might be observed that even on the testimony of those who would revile his memory, Wang An Shih at this time " was already famous as a Confucian scholar ".

After he had been a year in his post as Chief-Justice of Chiang Tung, Wang An Shih returned to the capital to make a report on his work, and then presented his most famous memorial to the emperor Jen Tsung.[2] This memorial was styled the " Yen Shih Shu " (言 事 書), or Discussion of Current Affairs. Because of its inordinate length, amounting in all to 8,565 words, it has been called the " Wan Yen Shu ", or Memorial of a Myriad Words.

As Wang An Shih based his later reforms upon the ideas outlined in this memorial, a full translation is offered in the succeeding chapter. But in the interests of those readers who do not care to read through the whole of this lengthy and elaborate document, and also to show how the Traditional historians regarded it, a synopsis of the memorial as found in the Sung Histories may be referred to.[3]

This memorial is termed by Liang Ch'i Ch'ao " the greatest document on government since the times of Ch'in and Han ". This he does not merely on the grounds of its length, which in itself is remarkable, but because it exposes truly and adequately the weaknesses and defects of the current policy and administration.

There is some divergence of opinion as to the time of its presentation. But Ts'ai Shang Hsiang, followed by Liang Ch'i Ch'ao, dates it definitely in the year 1058, on the completion of one year at Chiang-Tung.[4] The history collated by Chu Hsi,[5] makes it antecedent to his taking up the appointment in the Board of Finance. It may be that the latter position

---

[1] Ts'ai Shang Hsiang, vol. viii, pp. 8-10.
[2] Liang Ch'i Ch'ao, p. 40.
[3] Sung Biography. See Vol. II of this work.
[4] Liang Ch'i Ch'ao, p. 40.
[5] i.e. The T'ung Chien Hsu Pien (通 鑑 續 編).

was offered him in consequence of the insight into current
affairs and the ideas for reform which this memorial showed
him to possess.

Included in his Works is a letter written to a friend, Wang
Shen Fu (王 深 父),[1] during his tenure of office in Chiang-
Tung, from which it is evident that he had met with some
criticism of his administration of the post.   He was charged
with being too lenient in his dealings with the officials of the
area, and because he had tackled only minor cases.

Wang An Shih admits that he had only incriminated five
officials so far, that in the majority of these cases he had imposed
fines only, and that in the most serious case he had punished
the recalcitrant official with dismissal.   He affirms too that he
had only taken this action because to do less would have given
him no " face " in making his report, but that he was no lover
of punishment of this sort.

However, he had his grounds for taking such a stand in
the fact that the government system was imperfect, and that
the government treatment of officials left much to be desired.
He therefore argued that to inflict severe penalties in such
circumstances was unjust.

He is grateful, however, for his friend's action in keeping
him informed of the criticism which is abroad concerning
him, and hopes that he will continue to admonish him in the
future.   He cannot admit, despite his friend's fears, that he
has acted wrongly in the matter, as he considers in the light
of all the circumstances obtaining, that he had given full regard
to the moral issues at stake.

One gathers from this letter the impression that Wang An
Shih denied that he had been too generous towards the
delinquencies of the officials under his jurisdiction, although
he admits that the great majority of them were not over
scrupulous, and concerned chiefly to keep in the good books
of their superiors.   The main point of his " apologia " is that

---

[1] Vol. xviii of Works, p. 6. This is one of seven letters written to Wang Shen
Fu, which are found in his Works. He died in 1065. (See Ts'ai Shang Hsiang,
vol. xii, p. 5.)

until reforms were introduced into the official system, and until there was an improvement in the conduct of government generally, it was both unjust and useless to mete out severe penalties.

Such criticism as was levelled at him in this connection he regarded as unenlightened and unavailing to change his purpose. This is prophetic of his later attitude, and accounts for a good deal of the misunderstanding and opposition which hindered him so greatly farther on.

His interest in the economical side of the people's life also is evident during his period in Chiang-Tung. He wrote about the Tea Regulations,[1] and affirmed that these were the severest and most burdensome feature of government policy in the south-east part of the country.[2]

A great friend of his, Wang Feng Yuan, with whom he had conducted regular correspondence, and whom he regarded as a kindred spirit, died in 1059, at the early age of 28, and was buried at Wu Chin Hsien in the prefecture of Ch'ang Chow.[3] This was a cause of great grief to Wang An Shih, as appears from the epitaph [3] which was composed by him, and also from a poem which he wrote in his memory.[4]

[1] Works, vol. xvii, p. 22.
[2] Works, vol. i, pp. 19 and 20.
[3] Works, vol. xxiv, p. 8.
[4] Ts'ai Shang Hsiang, vol. vii, p. 3. Also Works, vol. ii, p. 4.

CHAPTER VII

THE WAN YEN SHU (萬 言 書) 原 名 (上 仁 宗 皇 帝 言 事 書)

or

MEMORIAL OF A MYRIAD WORDS [1]

NOTE.—This Memorial was submitted to the Emperor Jen Tsung (仁 宗) in the year 1058, when Wang An Shih returned to the capital from the district of Chiang-Tung, where he had been acting as " T'i Tien Hsing Yu " (提 點 刑 獄), or Chief-Justice of the Circuit for one year.

" I, your Majesty's ignorant and incapable servant, have been honoured with your commission to take a part in the administration of one of the circuits. I feel it to be my duty, now that I am called to Court to report on conditions in my district, to bring to your attention certain matters affecting the Government. I presume to do this on the ground of the experience gained during my period of official service, and regardless of my own inability. I shall consider it most fortunate if my suggestions receive your careful attention, and if you can see your way to adopt such as seem in your opinion to be of a reasonable character.

" Your Majesty is well-known to be of a careful and economical disposition, endowed with great knowledge and wisdom, devoted and energetic in the discharge of your routine duties, and to be entirely averse to licentious and time-wasting pleasures. Your love for the people is cherished by all. Your method of selecting those whom people desire to be in the

---

[1] The title " Wan Yen Shu " is that given to this memorial in the Dynastc History of Sung, in the Biographical Notice of Wang An Shih. It means literally the memorial of 10,000 words. The actual number of words is 8,565. The title given to this memorial in Wang An Shih's own Works is that of " A discussion of (current) affairs ", translated as at the head of the Chapter.

highest offices of the State, in a public manner, and your appointment of them regardless of the opposition of slanderous and speciously clever folk, has never been surpassed, not even by the rulers of the Golden Age.[1]

" When one bears these things in mind, it might naturally be expected that poverty would be unknown in any homestead, and that the Empire as a whole would be gloriously prosperous.

" Such, however, is not the case. One cannot ignore the fact that the internal state of the country calls for most anxious thought, and that the pressure of hostile forces on the borders is a constant menace to our peace. The resources of the Empire are rapidly approaching exhaustion, and the public life is getting more and more decadent. Loyal and courageous hearts are becoming increasingly apprehensive as to the outcome of this unsatisfactory state of affairs.

" My own opinion is that all this is the result of the prevailing ignorance of a proper method of government. I realize that against this may be urged the fact that the Imperial laws are being strictly enforced, and that the regulations for the administration of affairs are quite adequate. My meaning, however, is not that we have no laws and regulations, but that the present system of administration is not in accordance with the principles and ideas of the ancient rulers.

" We read in Mencius,[2] ' When a ruler is sincerely loving, and generally known to be so, but the effects of his benevolent disposition are not realized by the people in any adequate way, it must be because the method of government is not moulded after the pattern of the ancient rulers.' We need look no

---

[1] i.e. the two emperors and three kings, by which are meant Yao, Shun, Yü, T'ang, and Wen-Wu, the last two being regarded as one, for Wen Wang never actually ruled as king. Credit, however, must be given to him for initiating the campaign against Chow, the notorious last emperor of the Shang Dynasty, so he is usually included together with his more martial confrère. Yao and Shun belong to the prehistorical period, but are usually dated as 2357–2205 B.C. Yü initiated the Hsia Dynasty in 2205 B.C., T'ang the Shang or Yin Dynasty in 1766 B.C., and Wu Wang founded the Chow Dynasty in 1122 B.C. As model rulers they represent the traditional Golden Age of Chinese history, though the Dynasties they founded in each case ended up ingloriously.

[2] Legge's Chinese Classics, vol. xi, book iv, pt. i, ch. i, v. 2.

further than this quotation to discover the reason for the defective character of the extant administration.

"I am not arguing that we should revive the ancient system of government in every detail. The most ignorant can see that a great interval of time separates us from those days, and our country has passed through so many vicissitudes since then that present conditions differ greatly. So a complete revival is practically impossible. I suggest that we should just follow the main ideas and general principles of these ancient rulers.

"Let us recall the fact that we are separated from the rule of these great men by over a thousand years of history: that they had their periods of progress and decline: that their difficulties and circumstances differed greatly. But although the measures they devised and adopted to meet their various circumstances varied in character they were at one in the motives which actuated them, and in their observance of the relative importance of affairs.

"Therefore I contend that we need only to follow their principles. I believe that if that could be done, the changes and reforms that would ensue would not unduly alarm the people, or excite undue opposition,[1] but would in the end bring the government of our day into line with that of the Golden Age.

"Though that is true, I am bound to admit that the present state of affairs is of such a character that even though your Majesty should desire to reform the administration it would be practically impossible to do so. It may be urged that as your Majesty is of such a careful and restrained disposition, your intelligence and wisdom, and your loving consideration for the people, are all that is necessary to success, provided that you devote yourself sincerely to the task. My reason for saying that the realization of your object is impossible is that there is an insufficient number of capable men to help you.

---

[1] Wang An Shih's hope in this connection was never realized, as his proposals excited the most vehement opposition.

Without these it is not feasible to reform the government so that it may conform to the pattern of that set up by the ancient rulers.

"My observation leads me to suggest that there never has been such a scarcity of capable men as exists to-day in the service of the State. Should it be urged that these men do exist, but that they are hidden away in the country districts, I would say that although I have prosecuted my search with diligence, I have found very few indeed.

"Does not this indicate that the method of producing such men is faulty? I may be permitted to quote my own experience of official life, for its adds weight to my impression that capable men are too scarce. In my travels through my Circuit,[1] extending over 300 miles, I have found extremely few officials who are able to carry out government orders in any satisfactory way, or who have the capacity to lead their people to fulfil their obligations to the State. On the contrary those who are incapable, negligent, avaricious and mean, are innumerable. In some prefectures there is absolutely no one who is capable of applying the ideas of the ancient rulers to current conditions, or of even explaining how such might be done. The result is that no matter how fine and complete the regulations and orders of the Court might be, the possible benefit of these is never realized by the people because of the incapacity of the local officials. Not only is that true, but the subordinates in the districts are able to take advantage of these orders to carry on corrupt practices and induce disturbances.

"Seeing that there is this scarcity of capable men in the provincial positions, even though you should have some amongst your Court Ministers who are capable of appreciating your intention to reform the administration, and even though they themselves be desirous to carry it out, it would still fail of realization. For when you take into account the immense size of the Empire, how can one or two such men ensure that all the people will derive the benefit of such ideas?

---

[1] i.e. through the Circuit of Chiang Tung (江 東).

" So this leads me to suggest that circumstances will prove too much for you. The statement of Mencius [1] is apropos, viz. ' The laws do not administer themselves automatically '.

" To my mind the greatest need of the time is the securing of capable officals. We should ensure that an increasing number of these should be made available for the services of the State, so that from this larger group we shall be able to select a sufficient number for our purpose, and secure the possibility of getting men into their right positions. Granted that, it should not be difficult, having due regard to time and circumstances, and acting always in accordance with the dictates of humanity and reason, to so reform the method of government administration that it will follow on the lines laid down by the ancient rulers.

" Although the modern Empire is the same as that ruled by the ancients, there is this scarcity of capable men in the government services, while in their day such men were numerous. How are we to account for that ? I believe it is due to our not having the right method of producing them.

" During the Shang dynasty the Empire was in the greatest confusion. Those in office were covetous and corrupt, the harbingers of decay and disaster, for they were not the right men for their posts. At the time Wen Wang came forth, capable men for the administration were all too few. But he trained the people in such a way that this defect was soon made good. He had no shortage of capable administrators, and he was able to use them in positions for which they were fitted. As we read in the ode,[2]

> ' Our joyous prince
> Can influence men.'

" His success is seen also from this :—

> ' Even the rabbit catchers
> Are lovers of virtue.' [3]

---

[1] Cf. Legge's Chinese Classics, vol. xi, bk. iv, pt. i, ch. i, v. 3.
[2] Cf. Legge's Chinese Classics, vol. iv, pt. ii, bk. i, pt. iii, ode v.
[3] An interpretation of Ode in Legge, vol. iv, pt. i, bk. i, ode viii.

" If the rabbit-catchers were of this character, we can be sure that those in government office were even more earnestly devoted to lofty ideals. It was because Wen Wang possessed this type of ability, that he induced submission of the foe whenever he organized military expeditions, and that the country was well governed in times of peace.

" We read in the Odes,[1]

> ' They bore their insignia with solemn gravity,
> As beseemed such eminent officers.'

" And again,

> ' The King of Chow marched on
> Followed by his Imperial army.' [1]

" These quotations illustrate the great fact that Wen Wang was able to ensure that civil and military officials all got positions suited to their individual capacity. This led to affairs being well organized and successfully administered.

" Later on, however, during the confused period of the Emperors I (夷) and Li (厲) capable men became scarce once more. When Hsuan Wang (宣 王) [2] came to the throne we find that only Chung Shan Fu (仲 山 甫) was sincerely devoting himself to national affairs. We read in the Odes [3] :—

> ' Virtue is light as a hair,
> Only Chung Shan Fu can lift it.
> I love him,
> But can do nothing to help him.'

" So the poet bewailed in piteous tones the scarcity of capable and loyal men who might have helped Chung Shan Fu with his noble purposes.

" However, Hsuan Wang was led to use Chung Shan Fu in such a way that men of his type were multiplied, and the scholars were so transformed as to become capable administrators, and in considerable numbers. Thus it became possible

---

[1] Cf. Legge vol. iv, pt. iii, bk. i, ode iv.
[2] 827–781 B.C.
[3] Legge, vol. iv, pt. iii, bk. iii, ode vi.

to reform the internal administration of the country, and to reduce to submission the rebellious tribes, and thus to recover the territory which Wen Wang had possessed. So we read in the Odes [1] :—

> ' They were gathering the millet,
> In those new fields,
> And in these new acres,
> Brought this last year under cultivation.'

" The reference here is to the ability of Hsuan Wang, who so influenced the people that they were led to cultivate useful gifts, in the same way as the farmer renews his land so that useful crops may be produced.

" We infer from this that the number of capable men available depends upon the ruler taking such a course as shall develop these gifts in the people, and on making it possible for such to bring their natural gifts to fruition. By this I mean that a proper method should be devised whereby such men can be trained, maintained, selected and appointed.

" Firstly, what is the proper method of instructing these ?

" The ancient rulers had a graded system of schools ranging from the National University (國) to the district and village schools [2] (鄉 黨). For the control and development of these, a considerable number of educational officers and teachers were appointed, who had been selected with the greatest care. The conduct of Court ceremonies, music, and Government administration were all part of the recognized Curriculum. So that the model held up before the student, and in which he gradually became well versed, was the example, precept, and fundamental principles of government observed by the ancient rulers. The students trained under this system were found to be of such ability and character as the Government required and could use. No student was received into the

---

[1] Cf. Legge, vol. iv, pt. ii, bk. iii, ode iv.

[2] The " hsiang " (鄉) was an area comprising 12,500 families, and the " tang " (黨) an area comprising 500 families.

schools who had not shown promise of developing such a capacity. But all who demonstrated that they possessed this potentiality were without exception received.

" This I consider to be the right method of training these men.

" Secondly, what is the proper method of maintaining them ?

" In a word, they should be given adequate financial provision ; they should be taught the restraints of propriety, and controlled by adequate laws and regulations.

" With regard to providing them with adequate financial resources, I would say that it is only natural for a man who is dissatisfied in this matter of financial provision, to proceed to all manner of loose and corrupt practices.

" The ancient rulers were fully cognizant of this fact, and drew up their regulations governing salaries, beginning with those who were allocated a share in the public services, although not on the recognized official roll, ensuring that they received sufficient to make up for what they had lost by being called upon for public work, necessitating absence from their agricultural or other pursuits. In increasing scale the salaries advanced, assuring each official of whatever grade sufficient to keep him honest, self-respecting, and free from corruption. They then made further provision for the sons and grandchildren of officials by their system of maintenance grants (世 祿). In these ways the ancient rulers ensured that the officials they employed had no undue anxieties during their own lifetime about the support of their families, or about exceptional expenditure such as was caused by weddings, funerals, and the entertainment of guests. They also so arranged matters that after their death their descendants should have no cause to grieve over an insufficiency of the means of life.

" Then as regards the necessity of inculcating in them the restraints of propriety, I would say that once you have satisfied a man's natural desire for sufficient financial resources, it is essential that he should be restrained by the ordinances of propriety, otherwise he will proceed to a reckless extravagance in everything.

" The ancient rulers were cognizant of this fact, and drew

up a series of regulations regarding weddings, funerals, sacrifices, support of the aged, banquets, presents, dress, food, utensils, etc., etc. Expenditure on these things was to be regulated according to the rank and grade of official. The aim was to adjust their financial outlay in an equitable manner, having due regard to their varying circumstances. A man might have a certain rank, which, if that alone was considered, would demand the expenditure of considerable sums on such things. But he might not possess the means to do the thing in the style which his rank required. The regulations provided for this contingency and he was not expected to conduct such matters in the lavish way that his rank alone would call for. But supposing a man had the means to meet all the requirements of high official rank on such occasions, but lacked the necessary rank which entitled him to make such a display, the regulations forbade him to do so, prohibiting the addition of the smallest fraction to the standard he was entitled to observe under them.

" Further as regards the measures to be devised for controlling the officials.

" The ancient rulers gave the officials moral instruction, as well as seeking to make them accomplished in the Arts. That having been done, those who failed to act up to the instruction they had received were banished to distant outposts, and were deprived of their official status for the whole of their life. They were also instructed in the restraints of Propriety. If they transgressed the rules in this sphere, the penalty exacted was banishment or even death.

" We read in the Wang Chih (王 制) section of the Li Chi (禮 記), [1] or Book of Rites, that if there was any delinquency committed in the matter of the proper clothing to be worn, that the prince of the State concerned should be banished.

" In the Book of History (書 經) in the section entitled ' Chiu Kao ' (酒 誥) [2] we read, ' Should information come to you that drinking is going on, you should without delay

---

[1] Book of Rites (禮 記), Chinese edition, vol. iii, bk. i.
[2] Cf. Legge, vol. iii, pt. v, bk. x, par. 14.

proceed to arrest the drinkers, and bring them to the capital for execution.'

" It may be urged that such matters as wearing the wrong clothes or getting drunk are very light crimes, and that banishment or execution for the miscreants were altogether out of proportion. The fact that the ancient rulers permitted such heavy penalties was with a view to unifying the customs of the country, and thus accomplishing the true aim of all government.

" By this imposition of the restraints of Propriety and the penalties of the Law, they sought to bring all alike into subservience and submission. But they not only relied upon the power of prohibition and inspection, they afforded in their own person an example of sincere and sympathetic conduct. In this way all those officials of high rank who had direct access to the presence of the ruler, were induced to carry out his wishes in a loyal manner. It was agreed that punishment should be inflicted upon the one who failed to do so. The ruler gave a sincere example of living out his precepts, and those of high rank learned to avoid doing the things of which he disapproved. The idea was that thus the majority of the people at large would need no penalties to keep them from unworthy practices.

" The above is the right method of maintaining the officials.

" Thirdly, what is the correct method of selecting officials ?

" The method adopted by the ancient rulers was to permit the country folk and students in the village or district schools to recommend those whom they thought had the requisite character and ability for appointment by the throne. Investigation was then made as to the real character and ability of such men, and each was then given a period of probation in some position suited to his capacity.

" It should be emphasized that in this investigation into the merits and ability of any candidate, personal observation or information from others were not the only factors on which the ruler depended. He never depended upon the judgment of any single individual either. A man's character was adjudicated by his conduct and his ability was tested by enquiry as to his views on current affairs. These having been ensured, he was actually tested out in some office for a time. As a matter of fact the meaning of the term 'investigation' was just this period of probation in actual employment. Yao's appointment of Shun was of this type. We can legitimately infer that this would be the procedure stringently followed in regard to other appointments.

"Now when we consider the vast extent of the Empire, and the enormous number of positions that have to be filled, one gets some idea of the large number of men that are required. We must acknowledge also that the Emperor cannot possibly investigate the character and ability of each and every one individually. Neither can he lay this responsibility on any individual, or expect him in a day or two to conduct such enquiry as would enable him to adjudicate the merit or demerit of any.

"So I propose that those whom you have already found by experience to be of good character and great ability, and to whom you have committed important responsibilities, should be entrusted with the task of selecting men of like qualifications. Also that these should be given an adequate period of probation in official life, after which they too should be allowed to make recommendations to the throne. When this has been done, and when the men recommended have been found to be worthy, rank, emoluments, and promotion should be conferred by way of reward.

"Fourthly, what is the right method to be adopted regarding the appointment of officials?

"The ancient rulers were cognizant of the fact that men differ in character, and their ability for actual work. They recognized that they were specially suited for certain definite tasks, and could not be reasonably expected to take up any and every kind of work indiscriminately.

"So they appointed those who had special qualifications for the work of Agriculture to the Ministry of Agriculture (like Hou Chi 后 稷). Those who were skilled in engineering they appointed to the Ministry of Works (like Kung Kung 共 工). The chief positions were reserved for those who had the finest character and greatest ability, those of lesser gifts and qualifications being appointed to subordinate posts.

" They further recognized the fact that it is only after a prolonged period in any one appointment, allowing one's superior sufficient time to learn of his real capacity and attainments, and for the people under him to become truly subservient and happy under his control, that the really worthy have the chance to display their worth, and on the other hand that the evil-minded may have their wickedness exposed.

" Hence they made provision for a prolonged period of probation, as the best method of testing the appointees. This being ensured, those of real character and ability realized that they would be afforded a full chance to carry their projects to a successful issue, and were not distressed by the prospect that possibly they could not carry out their ideas properly, or that they would be deprived of their just reward. On the other hand, idlers and negligent fellows, who have become inured to thinking that they might maintain their good name and position for a short time, would be stimulated to a more worthy view of their responsibilities, as they would be made aware of the certainty of degradation and disgrace which would ensue on a prolonged period of service, unless they reformed. Those who knew they possessed no ability for a certain post would refrain from assuming such on the same grounds.

" After a prolonged period of probation in any one appoint-ment, one's incapacity or unworthiness to occupy it, would certainly be manifest. This we have seen would deter unworthy or incapable men from embarking upon an official career. Still less would fawning and flattering folk find any inducement to compete for official position with this system functioning.

" So we see that due caution was paid to the selection of officials in those days, that they were given appointments for which they were deemed qualified, that they were kept in office for a sufficiently lengthy period, that they were regulated

and rewarded in a most careful manner, and were given freedom
and authority for the proper discharge of their duties.   They
were not hedged about by a minutiæ or regulations and
prohibitions, but were afforded a full opportunity for the
carrying out of their own ideas.

"The method adopted by Yao and Shun was of this order.
In the Book of History we read, ' There was an inspection of
the record of officials once every three years.   After three
inspections of this type, promotion and fame, or degradation
and disgrace were definitely decided upon.' [1]   This quotation
is apropos of my argument.   In the times of Yao and Shun
everyone knows whom they degraded, viz. the four villains
(四 凶),[2] while the men they promoted and maintained in
high office for the whole of life were the three worthy ones
(皐 陶, 稷, 契).[3] Promotion meant the conferring of higher
rank and the increase of their emoluments.

"That then is the correct method of appointing officials.

"The above represents what was the method in vogue in
those days concerning the instruction, maintenance, selection
and appointment of officials.   The ruler availed himself to the
full of the experience and advice of his great officers.   By their
joint help in seriously thinking of the best way of doing things,
they were enabled to put this method into effect.   As there was
no suspicion between ruler and minister, they were enabled
to carry out what they desired in the matter of government
administration."

[The following represents Wang An Shih's criticism of
current practices in regard to the main topics already raised
and his suggestions for reform.—Ed.]

"I.   *With regard to the method of instruction*

"It is true that nowadays each ' chow ' and ' hsien ' is
supposed to have schools.   In reality, however, these schools
are just so much ' bricks and mortar '.   For there are no

---

[1] Cf. Legge, vol. iii, pt. ii, bk. i, ch. vi, par. 27.

[2] The four infamous ministers (共 工, 驩 兜, 三 苗, 鯀) Kung
Kung, Huan Tou, San Miao, and Kun.

[3] i.e. Kao Yao (or Kao T'ao), Chi, and Hsieh.

teachers or real training carried on in them. It is true there are instructors in the National University ('T'ai Hsueh' 太 學), but these are not selected with any care. Court ceremonies, music and government administration have no place in the curriculum. I admit that the students have a vague idea that these things form part of the responsibility of those in public office, but they do not apprehend that these are the very things with which they ought to make themselves fully acquainted.

" In the main the instruction they receive consists of explanations of the texts of the Classics, analysed into sections and sentences. That, however, was not the ancient method.

" More recently a new method of instructing students to prepare for the official tests by writing essays has come into existence. This method, however, calls for the recitation and memorizing of an enormous amount of literature, and the candidate must devote himself strenuously to this task the whole day long if he is to achieve success. But even if success in this matter is gained, it does not qualify the best student for the ruler's position, or the less successful for the other public services. So that even if they should go on learning in these schools until their hair turned grey, and give themselves the whole day long to the attempt to conform to the requirements of their superiors, they would have only the vaguest notion of what to do when they were appointed to actual office.

" Not only does the present method of instruction fail to produce the type of man that is required, it actually spoils them so that they cannot become capable administrators. A man's capacity for government is best educed by specialization, and ruined by too great a variety of subjects to be studied. So we find that the ancient rulers in their search for capable men went to the factories for their artisans, to the farms for their agriculturists, to the markets for their commercial men, and to the schools for their officials. Each man thus had the opportunity of specializing in his own line, and was not compelled to study anything extraneous to the actual task of preparation for a particular job. It was felt that to do otherwise would be detrimental to the gaining of the specialized knowledge required.   The scholars were also prohibited from studying anything other than the methods and principles of the ancient rulers, the various heterodox ideas of the different schools being banned under strict penalty.

" The students of the present day ought to study methods of practical administration.   But either no instruction at all is given, or they have to exhaust themselves in strenuous cultivation of the art of essay writing.   The ancients gave their time and energy specifically to the study of practical administration, and yet not all developed equal ability for the same. But nowadays the time and energy of students is diverted into quite other channels, and they give themselves to useless studies. It is not to be wondered at that when such men are given government appointment very few find themselves capable of discharging their duties.

" I repeat that not only does the present system fail to produce the type of man required, it positively unfits them for the task of government administration.

" Further, in the times of the ancient rulers, the students were given instruction in both civil and military subjects.   It was also recognized that amongst the students there would be found some who had the capacity for high office, but that there would be others who would be suitable for only small posts.   There was recognition of the fact that men differed in capacity, and also in their suitability for different kinds of work.   In connection with the Military services, none who had not been specially trained in such matters were given positions, though those who had received such training were all given positions according to their ability.   The better qualified were appointed to the chief civil posts during peace, or to the chief military posts in a time of border trouble or war.   Those of lesser qualifications were appointed to the headship of the various civil groups,[1] or to the command of the different military

---

[1] i.e. the " pi " or unit of five families, the " lu " of twenty-five, the " tsu " of 100, and the " tang " of 500 families (比, 閭, 族, 黨).

units.[1] In this way the big Garrison posts, and the important Circuit positions were all filled by great men, who were at one and the same time both scholars and generals.

" Nowadays great emphasis is laid upon the distinction between civil and military matters by the students. The rule is that they confess to knowing nothing about military matters, being solely concerned with the civil services. So it comes about that important military positions are left to those who are termed ' military men '. These are often promoted from the hired levies, who in the main are the good-for-nothings of the country-side. For any who have the ability to maintain themselves alive in their own village are unwilling to offer themselves to the army. But these Garrison posts and other military commands are of the most vital importance to the country, and the selection of the right men for these positions ought to have the serious attention of the ruler.

" In ancient times archery and charioteering were studied by all official candidates, as being matters of the most urgent moment. In other respects they had regard to the individual capacity of the student, and no compulsion was exercised if it was seen that he was not adapted for that particular line. But it was expected that all able-bodied males would practise archery, only those who were physically incapacitated being excused that branch of learning.

" So in the district and village schools archery was a required subject. It was so because it was a necessary accomplishment for all who were to engage in official life. It was necessary for the entertainment of guests, it served to distinguish between the characters of men, and showed which men would make good colleagues. A place was always found for the practcie of archery on occasions of Musical Festivities, and in connection with the holding of great Ceremonies and Sacrifices. In the Book of Changes (易 經) we read :—

---

[1] i.e. the " wu " of five men, the " liang " of 25, the " tsu " of 100, the " lu " of 500, the " shih " of 2,500, and the " chun " of 10,000 men (伍, 兩, 卒, 旅, 師, 軍). From Chow Kuan Hsin I.

" ' Archery contributes to the protection of the State.' [1]

" From this it is clear that the ancients regarded archery not only as a ceremonial accomplishment but as one of the most powerful aids in time of war, as one means for ensuring the military prestige and protection of the State. It was used as an adjunct to the transaction of civil affairs, but it was also regarded as an asset to the conducting of military campaigns. On these grounds students devoted themselves diligently to the practice of archery, and those who became proficient in it were exceedingly numerous. So that when vacancies occurred in the chief military positions, the authorities had a large number of men from whom to choose.

" During student days candidates gained from their study of the principles and methods of the ancients, that character and deportment which earned for them the respect of their fellows in their own area. Later on they received appointments either at home or on the frontiers according to their special ability. This enabled the ancient rulers to devolve responsibility upon their military subordinates, and accounts for the fact that in those days there was no anxiety with regard to the military situation either at home or abroad.

" Nowadays, however, this most important responsibility, which should be carried by men selected with the greatest care, is thrust upon the shoulders of ' good-for-nothings ' who have been unable to maintain themselves in a bare livelihood in their own villages. That accounts for the fact that we have this constant anxiety about the situation on the borders, and explains why we are so concerned about the reliability of the regular army if the State should be endangered.

" The main contributing factor to this is the way in which present-day students regard the carrying of weapons as a disgrace, so amongst them we find none who are able to ride, shoot, or take part in any military manœuvres. This leaves us with no alternative but to depend upon the hired forces for the protection of the country.

---

[1] Book of Changes, Chinese edition, " Hsi Ts'e (繫 辭). Cf. vol. ii, p. 19.

"Further, the reason why the carrying of arms is regarded as a disgrace by the students, is because no proper instruction in military matters is given in the schools, and because no proper care is given to the selection of men for the military positions.

"This is an illustration of our not having the right method of instruction.

"II. *With regard to the maintenance of officials*

"The rate of salaries paid nowadays to officials is too low. With the exception of the very highly placed officials in the Court circle, all who have large families to support, engage either in agriculture or trade to eke out. Those in the lower positions like district officials (縣 官) are at the most in receipt of 8,000 or 9,000 'cash', while many only get as much as 4,000 or 5,000 a month. When the time during which they have to wait for appointments, and the intervals between appointments are taken into account, say over a period of six or seven years, we find that they only receive the equivalent of three years' allowances. So that they draw in actual cash an average of less than 4,000 or 5,000 'cash' a month. From this they have to provide the wages of a servant, and make provision for the support of their parents; and funeral and wedding expenses.

"It may be urged that a man of superior character will maintain his integrity and good name, even though he should be in very poor circumstances financially. It is also commonly said that a man of inferior moral character will remain mean even though he should become rich. But the mediocre man does not come within these general rules. In this case poverty induces moral degradation, and wealth helps him to maintain his good name. If we consider for a moment the whole of the educated class in the country, not more than 1 per cent may be classed as either superior or inferior men. Practically all are of the mediocre class, in whom, as I have just said, poverty induces moral degradation, and wealth helps to maintain their good name.

"The ancient rulers were cognizant of the fact that the great majority could not be compelled by force to adopt any line of action, and so adopted the mediocre man and not themselves as their standard. So they sought to lead men along the lines of their natural inclination, with the idea that by the adoption of a method which the ordinary man could observe and practice, they might be able to carry out their ideas for the empire, and ensure permanence for them.

" With the present scale of salaries, however, it is impossible for the ordinary man to be honest and self-respecting, and it is useless to expect that he should. So we find that the big officials both offer and receive bribes and presents, and carry on private business, thinking nothing of being regarded as ' corrupt '. The smaller fry of the official world practice all manner of device for making money, not only engaging in trade and barter, but even descending to begging. Once the officials have earned the reputation of being corrupt, they become negligent, caring for nothing but the holding of their positions. Real earnestness and devotion to the public cause become unknown. With official duties neglected in this fashion, it is of course impossible for government to make any sound progress. But when bribery is added, and intimidation with a view to ' mulcting ' the people, we see the implication of the statement that we are not providing our officials with sufficient financial help.

" Again, seeing that there are no regulations controlling expenditure on weddings, funerals, support of parents, clothes, food, and the appurtenances of life, everyone comes to regard extravagance as admirable, and economy as disgraceful. If a man has wealth he does everything in the most lavish style, merely following the line of his own fancy. As this is in no way prohibited by the authorities, the people begin to look upon it as the right thing to do. A man who is of straitened means, and who cannot live up to this conventional standard of doing things, constantly offends his relatives in such matters as weddings and funerals. So men are led to regard economy as something to be ashamed of. The wealthy seek for more wealth and become completely addicted to the lust for money, while the poor with their limited means exhaust their resources in the attempt to 'keep up' with them. It thus becomes doubly difficult for an official to be honest.

" This is an illustration of the statement that we are unable to restrain the officials by the rules of propriety.[1]

" It is of course well known to the officials of the intimate Court circle that your Majesty is strictly economical in your manner of life, and that you are hoping in this way to give an example to all your people. But these officials in their family life are recklessly extravagant, and do violence by their transgression of your prohibitions to the livelihood and morale of the people. Although this kind of conduct has already reached a serious stage, I have not heard of any of them having been either degraded or dismissed.

" The custom of the rulers in the Chow times was to inflict the death penalty on all who were found drinking in public, on the ground that if such practices were not rigorously repressed, it would involve great numbers in similar punishment. So they sought to deal with the evil at its source, and tried to ensure that comparatively few should suffer in this way.

" I know that the law in these days is particularly severe against avaricious practices by the officials. But on the one hand to issue such prohibitions, and at the same time to disregard extravagance and waste, is to lay the emphasis in the wrong place, regarding the non-essential as important, and disregarding that which is absolutely fundamental.

" One of the main criticisms of the present administration is that supernumerary officials are too many, especially considering the straitened condition of the exchequer.[2] It is true that the number of officials engaged is extremely large, but even when they were fewer and salaries small, the national Treasury was

---

[1] A note by Yao Nai (姚 鼐) of Ch'ien Lung's day, A.D. 1736–1796, says that this section beginning " It is, of course, well known . . ." to " absolutely fundamental" should be interchanged with the section below beginning " It may be urged . . . maintaining them ".

[2] " Hsien Kuan " (縣 官), the Court.

still short of funds. The matter of official salaries is a comparatively negligible factor anyhow.

" I have made no special study of the subject of finance, but I have made some enquiry into the methods of finance adopted by the ancient rulers. In a word, this consisted of using the resources of the people to produce wealth for the State, and to devote the wealth thus accumulated to meeting the requirements of the national expenditure. In those times we find they never experienced stringency in the national exchequer. But they did consider it calamitous not to make use of an efficient method of finance.

" At the present time we have no preparations for war on our hands ; the people are peacefully pursuing their various avocations, and are doing their utmost to produce wealth for the State. Yet we are constantly distressed by the prevailing financial stringency both in regard to the national Treasury and the people generally. The reason must lie in the fact that we have not secured the right method of administering the State finances, and that the authorities are unable to devise appropriate measures to meet the situation. Once the proper method is secured, and the necessary reforms made, I am sure, even though I may be considered stupid, that official salaries may be raised without causing the financial condition of the country to be adversely affected.[1]

" It may be urged that the laws and regulations for the inspection and control of the officials are both strict and adequate. But in the ethical instruction which we have given them, one would like to enquire whether they have been sufficiently enlightened concerning the punishments attendant upon their non-observance of the rules laid down. The same with regard to our efforts to restrain them by the rules of propriety, and in giving them their official charge. They should have been fully warned about the penalties for disobedience. Unless this preliminary work of admonition has been duly carried

---

[1] This and the following paragraph are the section proposed by Yao Nai to be interchanged with section denoted by n. 1, p. 67.

out, it would be wrong to inflict punishments in case of disobedience or transgression. The ancient rulers made these three features a matter of the greatest concern.

" Nowadays officials cannot be punished, because they have not had this preliminary tuition in admonition and warning. The procedure is of another kind. A multitude of trifling prohibitions hedge them about, and these are constantly being altered. They are so numerous and so detailed that the officials cannot even keep a record of them. So one need not point out that it is practically impossible not to offend in some cases. This is one of the great reasons why the laws and regulations of the Government are trifled with, and fail to be effective. For as things stand, it is quite possible that a veritable scoundrel might have the good luck to avoid incurring penalties, while the really loyal and good official might have the misfortune to get himself involved. This is what is involved in our inability to control the officials by the laws, and is one of the results of our failure to secure the right method of maintaining [1] them.

" III. *With regard to the method of selection of officials*

" The present method of selecting officials is as follows :— If a man has a colossal memory, can repeat extensive portions of the classics, and has some skill at composition, he is termed specially brilliant or worthy, and chosen for the highest grades of State ministers. Those who are not possessed of such retentive memories, or of such wide recitative powers, and yet have some skill in composition, showing their gifts of poesy and rhyming, are granted the ' Chin Shih ' degree, the highest of which are also eligible to be appointed to the high positions. It should need no discussion to show that the knowledge and skill which these men display in no sense of itself fits them for such places of authority and distinction. It is, however, the prevailing opinion, that this method which has been used so long has been proved capable of producing

[1] Yao Nai (姚 鼐) says the character " chih " (治) should be " yang " (養), maintain.

men suitable for these posts. It is then urged that it is quite unnecessary to alter the regulations, or to seek to follow the ancient practice in the matter. That I contend is faulty reasoning.

" Under the regime of the ancient rulers, although they most carefully observed the proper method of selecting their officials, they continued to be apprehensive lest the really worthy should in any way be hindered from gaining access to the highest positions in the land, and lest the unworthy should get mixed up with their betters. Nowadays when the ancient method is rejected, men of mere literary ability are regarded as worthy and efficient, as capable of fulfilling the reponsibilities of the highest office, and it is considered quite right that such men should be appointed thereto.

" It is of course reasonable to assume that some men of literary ability should prove themselves equal to carrying the responsibilities of high office, but mere literary skill [1] should not be the only factor to be taken into account, for on that score unworthy men might also be elected to these responsible positions. As a matter of fact nine out of every ten who are capable of administering the duties of these high positions have spent their lives in subordinate posts in the provinces, just because they did not possess the necessary literary ability, which as I have said, is of itself no real help to a man occupying an administrative position.

" The ancient rulers made a point of exercising the most scrupulous care in their selection of men for the official positions. For when the right men were secured, they could be entrusted with the responsibility of finding men of like spirit and qualities to fill other positions. In that way the whole of the government positions were filled by the men of the right type.

" But on our present system it is possible for an unworthy man to get into the most important positions, and if he were

---

[1] (雕 蟲 篆 刻) the "tadpole" style of writing, said to have been invented by the wife of one Ch'iu Hu (秋 胡) of Lu (魯). So these characters are used to denote inferior or minor literary gifts, especially when referring to oneself. " Tz'u Yuan."

to be allowed to follow the ancient practice, he would naturally introduce men of his own type into other Court positions, and eventually it would mean that the great majority of government posts were occupied by men unworthy of the honour, and incapable of discharging their responsibilities. Should an individual official of real worth and ability find his way to power, he would more often than not find himself embarrassed in having none who could assist him to carry out his ideas.

" If unworthy men were in the Court positions, they would alsò appoint men of their own kind to the provincial and district posts, and the pernicious influence of this would extend right through the official system. In which case, it would be useless to expect that the rule ' if a recommended man trangresses the law not only he, but also the one who recommended him should suffer like penalty ', should be of any help. It would simply afford another opportunity for the unworthy men to further their own evil purposes.

" One other basis of selection is a man's knowledge of the Nine classics, or the Five classics, or a special knowledge of One classic, or again on his knowledge of Law subjects. The Court has already realized that this knowledge is of no value for practical administrators, and has made certain modifications in the old system, requiring more a knowledge of the general ideas of the Classics. The men gained by this change are really no improvement on those gained by the old method. So a further modification was made later requiring men to understand the general classical ideas with a view to promoting those who were skilled in classical interpretation and practical applications. But these changes are of little value. For those who get selected by this method are still those of colossal memories and skill in composition. Those who really understand the ideas of the ancient rulers, and who are capable of applying them in a practical manner to government problems are not of necessity to be gained by this procedure.

" Still another type of official gets his appointment out of sheer favouritism. These are mainly the sons or brothers of those already in the government service. They have neither received any instruction in the schools, nor have they been examined by the authorities as to their ability. Many are those whom their own brothers or fathers cannot guarantee as to their morals. Yet they receive the commission of the Court and are granted both rank and office.

" Wu Wang (武 王) in recounting the crimes of Chow (紂) [1] included the following :—' He appointed men to office on the hereditary principle.' He meant to indicate by this that the appointment of officials on the hereditary principle, without regard to a man's ability or character, was the reason why Chow (紂) threw the country into confusion and eventually brought his dynasty to ruin. On that ground later rulers who achieved success in their administration refrained from adopting the method.

" There is still another set of officials to whom I should refer, namely the ' unclassed ' (流 品). The Court has already indicated by their designation that they are lacking in conscientious scruples, and limited their possibilities of promotion. That is as it should be so far. But these men are employed in subordinate posts in the districts, and this gives them a standing above that of the ordinary person. This can hardly be considered an observance of the dictum that ' the worthy should rule the unworthy '. From my own practical observation of officials over a large area, I find that there are many officials functioning who are of this ' unclassed ' type. But I know only two or three all told who are capable of assuming responsibility for affairs, and these without exception need to be closely watched lest they proceed to all manner of illegal practices.

" Under the ancient regime the sole basis of distinction was between the worthy and unworthy in moral character ; they observed no distinctions that could be described as ' social ' merely. Take the case of Confucius himself. Though he possessed the character of a sage, he served as a small official

---

[1] Book of History, pt. v, bk. i, pl. i, par. 5.

to the Chi (李 氏) clan. That, however, was no hindrance to his later becoming an important officer, as Minister of Crime (司 寇). Later, however, the idea arose that those who were of the lower or 'unclassed' type could hope for no high appointment under the government, the distinction being of a 'social' character. They came to regard themselves as belonging to the class devoid of self-respect.

" We know that there are instances of men who, according to current notions, had the ability and right to be selected and appointed to high office, and who have been rewarded with honours and dignities, being led astray in later life and falling into evil ways. If that is true, then what about those who are deprived of the prospect of gaining any high position, who are regarded by the Court as being ' outside the pale ', with strictly limited prospects of any kind ? Is it reasonable to expect that they should do other than demean themselves by malpractice of various kinds, and have also a reckless disregard for all restraints ?

" I have already referred to the faults in the current methods of selecting military officials. All that I said there and also above afford instances of the wrong method of selecting government servants.

" IV. *With regard to the appointment of officials*

" I have already indicated that the current method of selecting officials is wrong in principle. I have now to add that in the actual appointing of a man to office, no enquiry is made as to his real capability for the particular post to which he is allocated. All that is considered is his year of graduation, or his particular position in the examination lists. Or again instead of investigating his suitability for a certain position, regard is paid only to the number of years he has been engaged in the government service.

" On the basis of possessing literary ability a man may be appointed to a Financial post, then he may be transferred to a legal position, or again to an office connected with the Board of

Rites. One cannot expect anything else than that he finds it difficult to fill any office in any satisfactory manner, seeing that he is required to be ready to fill any position whatsoever. It is only natural in such circumstances to find very few who can fulfil their obligations in any one position. That had led in its turn to their falling into the habit of doing nothing at all. If a man receives an appointment to the Board of Rites, he is in nowise concerned about his utter ignorance of Rites, for the simple reason that he knows that those in the Rites department have never received any instruction in the business of their office. The same holds true with regard to those appointed to the legal positions.

" We find that gradually the people have become inured to the lack of instruction. They have consequently become absolutely bound by conventional notions and practices. I know it is true that there have been cases in which the Court has raised objections against the appointment of a man because he has not passed through the regular course of official procedure, but I know of no case of a man being rejected because he has not the ability for any particular post.

" Then I must refer to the current practice of frequent transfer of officials from one place to another. The fact that men are not allowed to remain in one office for any length of time prevents their superiors from getting to know them or their ability in any real sense. Again, those in inferior positions, because they have not had time to learn to respect superiors, are mostly unwilling to obey them. A worthy man has not sufficient time to bring his plans to fruition, and an unworthy man does not remain long enough in any one post for his evil disposition to manifest itself. There are other evils attendant upon this system, such as the burden which devolves upon the local population in the constant receptions of new officials, and the farewells to old occupants of the positions. There are too many defects in accounting and the keeping of records for which these constant changes are responsible. These are among the minor evils attendant upon this system.

" It ought to be a rule that appointments should be made for a protracted period, relatively longer periods being allowed to those who have control of greater areas, or particularly heavy responsibilities.   Only in that case can we expect a man to make some really valuable and constructive contribution to the state.   But the current practice is of a contrary type, many officials being transferred after only a few days in one post.

"There are then these defects in regard to the government system.   No care is exercised in the selection of officials, and they are appointed to positions regardless of their fitness or otherwise for them.   Officials are not allowed to remain in any one post long enough to make any effective contribution.

"Another defect I must now stress is that after they are appointed to office, they are not trusted to carry out their duties.   An official is hedged about by a multitude of minute prohibitions and hindrances, so that he simply cannot carry out any ideas he may chance to have.   This is one of the great reasons why those now in the government service are mainly unsuited for their positions.   Since you have the wrong men in office I realize that unless you should hedge them about in this way, they would proceed to all manner of lawlessness if given the slightest liberty.   That may be true.   But what I wish particularly now to emphasize is that history proves it to be impossible to secure proper government by merely relying on the power of the law to control officials when the latter are not the right men for their job.   It is equally futile to expect efficient government if, having the right men in their proper positions, you hedge them about by a multitude of minute and harassing prohibitions.

"Seeing that all the evils outlined above do exist, even though worthy and able men should find their way into the government service, it is just as if they were unworthy and incapable.

"Why is it that the Court refuses to suggest the promotion of a worthy and capable man, just because he has not passed through the recognized processes ?   Why do the big officers oppose such appointments ?   Why again, knowing that a man has neither the character nor ability for any position, does the Court fear to reject him simply because he has not been accused

of any crime by those in office? Why again do the great
officers refuse to agree to the rejection of such a man, though
they know he has not the capacity for the position they wish
him to occupy?

" The main reason for this confusion of ideas is a moral one,
no distinction being made between the worthy and unworthy,
the capable and the incapable.

" These things led me to say above that we fail in the matter
of appointing men to office, and that there are no proper
punishments for those who fail in their duty.

" If there is failure to secure the right method in regard to any
one of these matters, viz., the instruction, selection, maintenance,
and appointment of officials, it is sufficient to ruin the talented
men of the country. What state of things can we expect if all
four of these are present together? In that case it need occasion
us no surprise if the avaricious, negligent, and corrupt are
numerous, or that those who have real ability for government
administration are very few indeed.

" The Ode entitled ' Hsiao Min' (小 閔) says [1] :—

" ' Although the kingdom be unsettled,
There are some who are wise and some who are not,
Though the people may not be numerous,
Some have perspicacity and some have counsel,
Some have gravity and some have orderliness,
But we are going on like the stream flowing from a spring,
And shall sink together in a common ruin.'

" But the shortage of men of capacity in office, and the
impossibility of reviving the method of government adopted by
the ancient rulers, on that account, are not the only evils.

" The military situation, and the safety of the country are
involved. We cannot expect a continuation of past good
fortune in this respect such as might free your Majesty from
every cause for anxiety.

" We have before us the instance of Chang Chueh (張 角) of
the Han dynasty. With 360,000 men he rebelled, as it were

---

[1] Legge, Chinese Classics, vol. iv, pt. ii, bk. v, ode 1, v. 5.

in a single day. There was no one within his state able to
forestall him. We remember too the revolt of Huang Ch'ao
(黃 巢) of the T'ang dynasty, who brought about a general
uprising, and marched unopposed by either civil or military
official, right through the land. The ruin of Han and the downfall of T'ang can be traced to these two sources.

"After the downfall of T'ang, there was gradual deterioration
through the period of the Five Dynasties. Then the military
men were in power, and all the worthy men retired into private
life. It seemed as though they had completely disappeared in
fact. Those in power then ceased to pay any attention to the
rightful distinction between ruler and official, between superior
and subordinate. In those days it was as easy to change the
dynasty as it was to make a move in a game of chess. The
corpses of the people littered the field, and they considered it
most fortunate if they escaped with their lives. Disasters
of that type are brought about by the absence of capable men
in office.

" I am greatly concerned that at present, among your Majesty's
high ministers and officers, there are none who are exercising
any forethought on your behalf, or who are planning for the
permanence of the Dynasty.

" Let us recall the fact that Chin Wu Ti (晉 武 帝) lived
entirely in the present and made no plans for the welfare of his
descendants. Let us remember that during his time, those
who held office under him, were mere timeservers and
menpleasers : that the public life was utterly corrupt : that the
usual observances of propriety were spurned : the laws utterly
ignored, and that officials and people alike had no conscience
at all on these great matters. Anyone with the least intelligence
could foresee that it would result in disaster. This at length
came upon them ; there was utter confusion throughout the
land, and for over two hundred years China was in the grip
of barbarian tribes.

" I think with the gravest concern of your Majesty's
responsibilities in being entrusted with the care of this great
empire by the spirits of your ancestors. Their hope is that it

shall persist for endless generations, and that the millions of
your people will never know the pinch of poverty or the menace
of invasion. I implore your Majesty to note the reason for the
fall of Han and T'ang and the confusion and decadence of the
Five Dynasties, and to take warning from the calamity which
overtook Chin Wu Ti for his negligence and *laissez-faire*
policy.

" I trust too that you will make it quite clear to your ministers
that they should take steps to ensure the production of capable
men, and that they may make such plans for this object as may
be gradually carried into effect, seeking to adapt them to present
circumstances, without doing violence to the principles of the
ancient rulers. If such plans are made and rendered effective,
the capable men will be more numerous than can be employed ;
you will have no desire which cannot be fulfilled, and there
will be nothing that you cannot accomplish.

" When I first began to study Mencius,[1] and read that he said
' It is easy to carry out the government of the ancient rulers ',
I thought that that was really so. But later on when I came to
the place where Mencius was discussing with Shen Tzu (慎 子)
about the territory of Ch'i (齊) and Lu (魯), I realized that the
area governed by the ancient rulers was generally speaking
only about 100 li square.   Then I began to see that if a new
ruler were to arise he must induce the princes who were
controlling territory of 1,000 li or 500 li in extent to reduce their
area to some tens of li square. I began to doubt whether
Mencius, worthy and wise though he was, with wisdom and love
so great that he could unify the whole empire, could without
military force speedily reduce the territory of these princes by
80 or 90 per cent so that they should revert to the conditions
which obtained in the days of the ancient rulers.

" Later on again I began to take thought about the policy
of Chu Fu Yen [2] (主 父 偃) of which Han Wu Ti availed

---

[1] Cf. Legge, Mencius, bk. xi, pt. i, ch. i, par. 6 ; and also bk. vi, pt. xi, ch.
viii, pars. 6 and 7.

[2] (主 父 偃) of the time of Han Wu Ti, 140–86 B.C.

himself. His plan was to order the princes of states and rulers of territories to apportion as gifts of grace parts of their territory to their sons. At the same time the emperor fixed the titles and designations of these, bringing them all under the direct control of the ruler. In this way the territory got split up into smaller regions, the sons and brothers of the princes each getting their own share. But the plan ultimately resulted in the powerful and great princes being deprived of much of their influence, their large domains being split up into many smaller and weaker ones.

"Thus I came to see that by careful planning and estimating, and making the changes gradually, the large could be made small, and the strong weak, without revolts or rebellions, or the confusion and distress of war. The words of Mencius were seen after all not to be either extravagant or unreasonable. So to my mind it became clear that the difficulties in the way of one wishing to introduce such changes were not so formidable as might at first sight appear. So I repeat we should plan carefully for the changes that need to be made, estimate everything, and gradually introduce the changes. Then it will be comparatively easy to carry them out.

" But under the regime of the ancient rulers they were not so much concerned at what men left undone, as that they lacked the ability to do any particular thing. Again they were more concerned about their own inability to do things, or to get the people to do things, than they were about the people's inability to do them.

" What man naturally desires is to live well, earn a good reputation, gain honourable rank, and get good pay. The success which attended the efforts of the ancient rulers in training the people to become their officers, and in gaining the loyal obedience of their officials so that good government was made to prevail, was entirely due to their giving them what they desired. When an officer found himself incapable of discharging the duties of any post, he gave it up. But granted that he had the ability, he exerted himself to make himself still more capable, and naturally would not resign the chance of getting what he really desired. That is the implication of my first point above.[1]

" By the second [2] I mean that it was the practice of the ancient rulers to treat their officers handsomely, so that all who had any intelligence and ability at all, were enabled to make good progress. But it was considered vital that the emperor himself should give them an example of sincerity, and care, and devotion. This was with the idea that all might be stimulated to respond in a similar manner. So I say that their first concern was to rouse themselves to the task, rather than to be distressed at the inability of others.

" If your Majesty is sincerely desirous of securing a body of capable officials to help you, and I believe you possess this desire, all that is necessary is that you should devote yourself to the task.

" I have, however, observed that on former occasions whenever the Court has been desirous of introducing some reforms, that the pros and cons are most carefully considered at the beginning. But should some compromising and opportunist sort of fellow criticize the measure and evince some displeasure with it, the Court immediately desists and dare not go on with the matter.

" The laws are not set up for the advantage of any one special class. Under the regime of the ancient rulers, their laws were administered for the whole empire and its benefit. But we must bear in mind that their regime was instituted after a time of corruption and decay, when it was considered most fortunate that such laws could be instituted at all. If after setting up their laws, all the opportunists had been pleased to agree to their promulgation and there had been no opposition, then of course the laws of the ancient rulers would still have been extant.

" However, not only were the times most difficult for the setting up of the laws, but the opportunist officials were all unwilling to carry them out, so whenever the ancient rulers desired

---

[1] i.e. the concern of the ruler lest their people should be unable to perform certain duties.

[2] i.e. the ruler's concern at his own inability.

to carry anything of importance into effect, they had to have recourse to punishments. Only then could they carry out their original ideas.

" So we read in the Ode ' Huang I ' (皇 矣) [1]

'By punishments and extermination,
We eliminate opposition.'

" The reference here is to the way in which Wen Wang (文 王) carried out his ideas in the stabilizing of the empire. We find therefore that the ancient rulers, in their attempt to reform corrupt customs, and to create a body of capable officials, made their laws and regulations with firmness, and nerved themselves to the task even though they had to mete out strict punishments. They saw that there was no other way of carrying their plans through.

" Think for a moment of Confucius, who though a commoner by birth, travelled to all the states, giving advice to the princes, causing them to relinquish old practices; to oppose what they had once approved; and succeeded in rousing them to attempt tasks which they had formerly despised. Yet with all his energy and devotion, he was greatly hampered ultimately by their opposition. That, however, in no sense dissuaded him from his purpose, as he knew perseverence was the only way to ensure success. In his determination he may be classed with Wen Wang.

" Wen Wang is the greatest of all rulers, and Confucius the greatest of all sages. It is reasonable to suggest that all who are desirous of introducing reforms should act after their fashion. You exercise the power of regal sway, and occupy the throne of the ancient rulers. You have not the difficulty that they had in regard to this matter of punishment. There are some opportunists who show their displeasure by criticizing and opposing anything in the nature of reform, but they are nothing like so numerous as those who will be delighted with and approve of such a policy.

" You will therefore be at fault if you refrain from your

[1] Cf. Legge, vol. iv, pt. iii, bk. i, ode vii, v. 8.

purpose because of the displeasure or opposition of this conventional and opportunist body of opinion. If your Majesty is sincere in your desire to create a body of capable officials, I beseech you to tie yourself down to it absolutely. If in addition to having a policy of reform, you have the mind and will to carry out the same, gradually it may be, but nevertheless determinedly, you will be assured of success in your object, as far as I can see.

" Unfortunately, it has to be admitted that these matters which I present to your notice are not the subjects which these conventionalists discuss. Those who are regarded as critics of current events either regard them as impracticable, or so commonplace as to be beneath their notice. I know that there are amongst your great officers those who are exerting themselves to the limit of their power and intelligence to assist you. But in the main their ideas are confined to the detailed discussion of any proposal that is made, and it is this power of discussion which is held in esteem as a practical gift. The great officials regard such a gift as of the most estimable and rare variety, and so naturally enough, the Court is guided by such considerations in the selection of their officials.

" But they rarely or never touch upon those greater matters affecting human relationships, the laws of the land, the greater ceremonies and duties, the very things to which the ancient rulers devoted themselves so earnestly to understand and preserve. The moment anyone should raise discussion on any of these matters, the crowd begins to mock him as an unpractical idealist.

" Nowadays the Court goes into all the details and minutiæ of every proposal with the greatest deliberation and care. The officers of law and the laws themselves have been functioning for a prolonged period of time, but what of the visible results ? It is my earnest hope that your Majesty will give some consideration to these matters which are termed ' impracticable and commonplace '.

" In the early days of T'ang T'ai Tsung (唐 太 宗)[1] a great

---

[1] A.D. 627–650.

variety of idea and opinion prevailed amongst the advisors to
the throne.   There were such as Feng Te I (封 德 彝), who
thought that unless the methods adopted during the times of
Ch'in (秦) and Han (漢) were revived, the empire would
not only suffer, but cease to be worthy of the name.   There
was, however, only one man, Wei Wen Cheng (魏 文 正),
who was capable of really enlightening T'ai Tsung.   His
contribution to the administration, although it cannot be said
to have absolutely agreed in every detail with the ideas of the
ancient rulers, was nevertheless in general agreement with them.
So in a very few years, it was feasible to govern the empire
almost without the use of punishments.   Internally there was
concord, and on the borders peace, with willing submission of
the various tribes.   There has never been such a prosperous
age since the times of the three ancient kings (Yü, T'ang, and
Wen-Wu).

    " In the age of T'ang T'ai Tsung, the customs of the empire
were the same as now obtain, and the advice of Wei Wen Cheng
was considered impracticable or commonplace, but the fine
results of the adoption of his advice are patent to all.

    " The words of Chia I (賈 誼) are to the point.   He said,
' Many say to-day that moral instruction is not so effective
as the law and ordinances set up by the State.'   Why then do
they not compare the dynasties of Shang (商) and Chow (周)
with the dynasties of Ch'in (秦) and Han (漢).   (The former
emphasized moral instruction, the latter the law and ordinances.—
Ed.)   But it should be sufficient evidence to quote the instance
of T'ang T'ai Tsung.

    " Thus I have taken the opportunity of reporting on the
affairs of my office, to discuss with you matters vital to the
State.   I have been outspoken regardless of my own incapacity.
I have ventured to assert that there is a dearth of capable men
in the public service, and that there are none who are capable
of carrying out the ideas which your Majesty had in appointing
them.   I have also ventured to suggest, according to my own
observation and experience, that either the Court has not yet
secured the proper method of selecting and appointing officials,

or that the officials themselves are not permitted to make full and free use of their powers.

"These matters I regard as of first importance to your own enlightenment. If I were to hold my tongue on such things, and just present for your consideration one or two matters of trifling importance, asking you to estimate their relative benefit or injury, it would merely muddle your mind and be of no practical help to the government of the country. To act in that way would be foreign to my ideas of loyalty, so I trust your Majesty will give my proposals your careful attention, adopting such as you may think beneficial and appropriate. That I am convinced will make for the increasing well-being of your people."

CHAPTER VIII

RAPIDLY ADVANCING TO FAVOUR AT THE CAPITAL (1060–3). IN MOURNING (1063–7)

WANG AN SHIH was called to the capital from his post in Chiang-Tung to take up a position in the Bureau of Finance. Most of the authorities agree on the date at which this appointment was conferred, and the traditional Histories, which begin to favour him with a record of his commissions and doings from this date, state that the post was offered him in the 5th month of 1060.[1]

The Bureau of Finance was divided into three departments, one of which was concerned with the estimates of the National Budget, and the payment of official salaries, etc. It was to this department that Wang An Shih was appointed as one of three officials of the third rank.[2]

In his letter to the Minister Fu (富 相 公) acknowledging the receipt of the commission, he refers to the fact that he had hitherto felt compelled to refuse positions at the capital on the ground of financial stringency. He had to admit that as the position now offered him was a much more lucrative one he could not refuse it on that ground. But still he felt that as he had no special experience in financial matters, he was incapable of fulfilling the duties of such a post, and thought it would be much more in line with his training and ability if he were given a prefectural position.[3]

Evidently, however, his plea was ignored, and he was prevailed upon to proceed to the capital and assume his new duties.

One or two documents have been preserved which give us an insight into the working of his mind on financial matters at

[1] T'ung Chien, Chia Yu (嘉 祐), 5th year, 5th month, i.e. 1060.
[2] i.e. San Ssu To Chih P'an Kuan (三 司 度 支 判 官).
[3] Ts'ai Shang Hsiang, vol. viii, pp. 1 and 2. Also Works, vol. xviii, p. 13.

this time. The first is an inscription which he wrote upon the wall of the Vice-Minister of his department in honour of one Lü Chung Chih. From this we take the following extract [1] :—

" Finance is essential to every department of the national life. The administration of the nation's finances depends upon the existence of proper laws and regulations. But the observance of these depends again upon the officials. Should the right type of man not be forthcoming for official positions, then even though proper laws and regulations are extant they will not be observed. Should the laws and regulations be defective, even though there should be no scarcity of financial resources, they will not be efficiently administered. When the financial resources which are available are not efficiently administered, the public will take advantage of the situation to seize unlawfully the revenue that should go to the government, and competition will ensue between them and the ruler for the proceeds of the working of the financial regulations. Their rapacity is such that they will not be satisfied unless they are given rank, influence, and prestige. The result is that although possibly the emperor still retains his position, he is differentiated from the rest merely by a special designation. Even though he should be willing to exercise the strictest economy in food and clothing, endure physical hardship, and mental toil, with a view to ensuring a sufficiency of revenue and orderly government, I am convinced that he is bound to fail. If Yao and Shun needed to be greatly concerned about the promulgation of good laws and the securing of good officials for their administration, in order to ensure that the finances of the country should be properly controlled, how much more is it necessary that later generations should be anxious about such matters ?

" The officials of the Bureau of Finance hold a very responsible and honourable position. In case the extant regulations for the administration of finance should be unsatisfactory, it is incumbent upon them to take counsel with the emperor for their reform.

---

[1] Works, vol. xx, pp. 2 and 3.

" They should not be content merely with the observance of existing regulations, or with being careful about income and expenditure, or concerning themselves with the carrying out of the prescribed regulations as purely executive officers.

" Seeing that their duties are of so onerous a character, it is of the greatest importance to get capable men for the position, as on this depends the welfare of the whole nation. So the thing is to find men who demonstrate by their official record that they have the gifts for the times, and possess ideas which shall be of practical assistance to the emperor in the administration of the nation's finances. That was the idea of Lü Chung Chih (呂 沖 之)."

Further insight into his views on finance may be gained from a letter which he wrote to the Transport officer Ma at this time. We will translate the following extracts from this, viz.[1] :—

" The poverty of the national exchequer is due not only to extravagant expenditure. It is due chiefly to the failure of those responsible for the business to devise productive measures. It is necessary that an individual who is desirous of increasing his family resources, should be dependent for so doing upon the particular state in which he resides. It is necessary also that he who wishes to increase the financial resources of his state should depend upon the empire in order to achieve his object. It is equally true that he who would increase the wealth of the empire must look to its natural resources. . . . Otherwise the case would be very much like that of a father doing business with his own sons, and permitting nothing from outside to come in. . . . In which event, even though he should exhaust the resources of his sons, the family as a whole would still remain poor. . . . Many who make high-sounding proposals about the financial condition of the empire have nothing better to suggest than that the ruler should depend upon whatever revenue can be secured from the taxation of the people. But this is merely equivalent to the members of the family of the empire doing business with one another. . . . It is here that the great cause of the existing financial stringency lies."

<hr />

[1] Works, vol. xviii, p. 22.

In this same letter Wang An Shih proceeded to outline a scheme whereby economy might be secured, by stationing the regular troops in various districts centres, thus saving considerable expense on the transport charges in connection with transmission of military supplies to the capital.

One of the chief criticisms levelled against Wang An Shih by his contemporaries is that he laid too great an emphasis on financial matters. However, as will be seen later on, it is difficult to see how he could do otherwise in view of the conditions obtaining at the time.

The great fundamentals of financial administration which he outlines in the two preceding documents he sought to express and carry out in practical fashion during his term of greatest influence. His term in the Bureau of Finance, though very short,[1] evidently gave him an insight into the financial state of the country, which proved of the greatest value to him later on.

During his term of office in the Bureau of Finance, Wang An Shih was appointed a member of a commission of enquiry into the condition of affairs in the National Stud, of which Ou Yang Hsiu was then President.[2] It will be remembered that he had formerly acted as assistant in connection with that department. Probably as a result of his work on that Commission, he submitted a note of recommendation of Hsüeh Hsiang (薛 向), as superintendent of the department concerned with the procuring and breeding of horses for the government.[3] This he did on the grounds of his previous record in connection with the Transport service in Ho pei, and also in connection with the Salt Administration in Shensi. He thought that as the purchase of mounts was dependent upon the revenue from the salt lake at Chieh Chow, of which Hsüeh Hsiang was then in charge, that it would be a very convenient and beneficial arrangement to put him also in charge of the purchase of horses

---

[1] The Biographical Table of Chan Ta Ho says " hsun " (尋), i.e. short time.
[2] Ts'ai Shang Hsiang, vol. viii, pp. 4 and 5.
[3] Works, vol. x, p. 7 (相 度 牧 馬 所 舉 薛 向 劄 子). The actual recommendation was made later.

and their care in the Shensi area. There was plenty of spare pasturage land available in Shensi, on which the horses could be grazed, and they would still be near enough to their home environment to suffer no serious loss of condition. Further, as the land there was not under cultivation, there would be no loss of revenue such as was incurred by the present system of grazing the horses in Ho pei where the land was needed for cultivation. By transferring the main part of this business to virgin soil and freeing arable land for cultivation, not only would better and more horses be available for the government, but increased revenue would accrue also.

These extracts from his writings show that Wang An Shih was already thinking hard about financial matters, and that he had practical suggestions to make for the improvement of existing conditions.

His literary work was not neglected during this period. In addition to cultivating the friendship of Mei Sheng Yü (梅 聖 俞), a famous poet of his day, and a great friend of Ou Yang Hsiu,[1] he gave considerable time to reading through a collection of the T'ang poets which a colleague of his in the Bureau of Finance, Sung Tz'u Tao (宋 次 道), had brought from his home. This collection, according to Ts'ai Shang Hsiang, comprised the works of 104 of the lesser known poets of the T'ang dynasty.[2] Sung Tz'u Tao requested Wang An Shih to make an anthology of the finer pieces, which he proceeded at great cost of time and labour to do. Eventually this anthology was published under the title of " T'ang Pai Chia Shih Hsuan " (唐 百 家 詩 選), to which Wang An Shih wrote a preface. This work, which was the basis of much criticism later on, is still extant.

His residence at the capital, his work in the Bureau of Finance, and his writings, brought him into the public eye, and he was soon besieged with requests to take up fresh appointments. But before proceeding to give details of these, we will

---

[1] Works, vol. ii, 2, p. 12 (哭 梅 聖 俞), and Ts'ai Shang Hsiang, vol. viii, pp. 3 and 4.

[2] Ts'ai Shang Hsiang, vol. viii, pp. 12 and 13.

offer a translation of another of Wang An Shih's memorials on
State affairs, which was presented to the throne in 1060. This is
called the "Shih Cheng Shu" (時 政 疏), and reads as
follows :—

"In my study of history, I note that whenever an emperor
occupied the throne for a fairly long period, if he failed to be
fully conscientious and apprehensive about the discharge of his
duties, even though he may not have been cruel or oppressive,
confusion and distress resulted.

"Since the Ch'in dynasty, the three rulers who maintained
their thrones for lengthy periods were Wu Ti of Chin (晉 武
帝) Wu Ti of Liang (梁 武 帝), and Ming Huang of T'ang
(唐 明 皇). These three, although they may be termed wise,
far-seeing, and to a certain extent successful, after holding their
thrones for a long time, became negligent and careless. They
lost a real feeling of conscientious responsibility, they ceased to
think ahead and plan for the future, and began to presume that
no calamity could come upon them after such a protracted
period of peace and prosperity. But alas, when it was too late
for them to repent of such an attitude, calamity came upon
them, and although they themselves escaped with their lives,
their kingdoms fell into disgrace and ruin, their wives and
families suffered greatly, the blood of their people covered the
ground, and those who were not slaughtered were compelled
to suffer famine and slavery.

"It is inconceivable that a truly loving and filial ruler should
allow the kingdom of his ancestors to fall into decay or disgrace,
or that he who should be 'the parent of the people' should
endure the loss of their homes. And yet, such rulers as
the three mentioned above, through their complacency, and
presumption, were brought to such a pass, calamity coming
upon them swiftly and unexpectedly.

"The empire is a heavy responsibility. The best of laws and
regulations are necessary for its control, and an army of worthy
and capable officials are needed to preserve it. But unless the
ruler possesses this conscientious feeling of responsibility, these
officials will not be sought out, nor will these laws and

regulations be initiated.   If worthy officials are not employed, if the laws are not intelligently framed, and the precious months and years are allowed to pass vainly away, it will be fortunate indeed if no calamity occurs.   But I would emphasize the fact that when this time-wasting habit has been allowed to continue for a considerable time, it has invariably culminated in the greatest confusion.

" I humbly acknowledge that your Majesty is of an economical and restrained disposition, that you are of great intelligence and wisdom, and that your love for the people is sincere and strong.   But you have occupied the throne for a great number of years, and so it behoves you to be particularly solicitous and anxious, lest you should fall into the error of the three rulers mentioned above.

" According to my own observation, I regret that I cannot testify that government posts are filled with worthy and capable officials, nor can I say that the results of administrative work are such as should naturally follow from the laws and regulations that have been devised.

" In higher circles there is lack of sound policy, and much poverty is in evidence among the people.   Public life is gradually deteriorating and the national resources are steadily decreasing.   Your Majesty lives in a remote detachment from affairs, you neither seek for good officials nor demand that suitable laws and regulations for the times should be drawn up. It is this which has driven me to take thought for you, for I am compelled to admit that the situation gives grave cause for anxiety.

" It is possible that a conventional, *laissez-faire* policy, or even idleness and neglect, may bring no serious disaster upon the country for a certain period of time, but it should on no account be persisted in.   Because the three rulers I have mentioned above gave no heed to this vital matter, they brought upon themselves such terrible calamities, that even though they awoke to the necessity of providing good officials and efficient measures of government, they did so too late and it was impossible to save the situation.

"As I view things, there is still a chance to save the empire from the danger and disorder which looms over it, but if anything is to be done it must be done immediately. Otherwise the situation must be considered hopeless. I hope therefore that your Majesty will search for and multiply the worthy and capable in the government services, and that you will take steps at once to devise good and efficient laws and regulations.

"The History says, 'Unless the medicine disturbs, it will not be effective.' I would ask you to regard the state of the empire as an old disease that can only be cured by a temporary upheaval and some trouble, but I hope you will not shrink from this in order to find a sound and lasting remedy.

"I have been favoured with your appointment to the public service, and in my concern for the safety, progress and well-being of the empire, I involve myself in the guilt of being presumptuous by thus warning you. I would, however, implore your Majesty to give due consideration to my warnings, for I am confident that to do so will be for the great and permanent benefit of the empire."

The tone of this memorial, as Liang Ch'i Ch'ao points out, is more urgent than that of its predecessor, the Myriad Character memorial. Conditions were so desperate that Wang An Shih could not refrain from warning Jen Tsung at this time. But unfortunately he was too old and too thoroughly addicted to a *laissez-faire* policy to be able to change. He died two years after this memorial was presented.

But the moral courage and feeling of responsibility which this memorial displays on Wang An Shih's part is beyond all praise.

In 1061 he was appointed to the Chi Hsien Yuan as one of the responsible librarians.[1] The Historiographers' comment [2] on his acceptance of this post is as follows :—

"Prior to this Wang An Shih had repeatedly refused to accept appointments of this character, and this had led to much

[1] i.e. "Chih Chi Hsien Yuan" (直 集 賢 院).
[2] Sung Biography.

talk among the officials at court.   They had begun to think
that he could not be desirous of worldly advancement.   Such
gossip roused a good deal of curiosity, and created a great
desire in the court circle to make his acquaintance.   So that
whenever a good post was offered to him, the court was quite
concerned lest he should refuse it."

Such a position as he now took up would normally be
conditional upon his taking the examination [1] which so far he
had refused to do.   There is, however, no reference in the
Histories to this particular matter.   So we cannot say whether
he took it or not.   Possibly he exercised the privilege of not
taking it, as this had been extended to him several times by
special decree.

Promotion followed rapidly.   The History [2] notes that
when he notified his acceptance of the Librarianship everyone
at the capital was pleased.   He was soon offered the post of
Imperial Recorder, or Keeper of the Emperor's Diary.[3]   This
appointment he refused no less than seven times.   Eventually
a special messenger was sent from the court to offer the commission in person.   An Shih did his best to avoid the messenger,
who however followed him into the house imploring him to
accept.   An Shih withdrew into a private chamber, whereupon
the messenger laid the commission on his desk and returned.
An Shih sent the document after him.[4]

We gather from this batch of refusals [5] that his main reasons
for not accepting the post were that promotion of this character,
as it was not according to the regular procedure, would call forth
severe criticism, and that there were many officials on the
waiting list for such positions, who were senior to him.   For
him to accept would expose the high court officials to the
charge of having private preferences, and of showing the
" clique " spirit.

[1] i.e. the " Kuan Chih " (館 職).
[2] T'ung Chien under Chia Yu (嘉 祐), 5th year, 5th month.
[3] i.e. " T'ung Hsiu Ch'i Chü Chu " (同 修 起 居 注).
[4] Sung Biography.
[5] Works, vol. ix, pp. 14–16.

After a short interval the post was once more offered to him. This brought forth another batch of refusals, five letters [1] being written in all. From these letters we gather that family considerations were once more in the forefront of his thought; and that he had once again appealed for a provincial post, possibly to be near his mother, who was getting on in life, and was probably in ill-health at this time. She died the following year. He complains too of his own weakness through continual sickness.

However on this occasion he was not permitted to refuse the appointment.[2]

He was then promoted in rank to that of Secretary of the Board of Works,[3] and given executive responsibility in the Edicts Office.[4]   Concurrently he was made Supervisor of Justice in the capital, and chief officer of the Imperial Body-guard.[5]   All these appointments were made in the years 1061–2.

His independent spirit and indifference to popular opinion at this time are illustrated in the following incident which came under his notice as Supervisor of Justice.

" A certain youth had a fighting quail, which his friend asked of him as a gift.   When he refused, the friend, presuming on their intimacy, snatched the bird from him and ran away.   The owner gave chase, caught up to him, and in the scuffle which ensued injured his friend so seriously that he succumbed to his wounds.

" The Judge of K'aifengfu (the capital) passed sentence of death.   But when the decision came to An Shih for confirmation he refused to give it, contending that in the first instance this should be regarded as a case of robbery.   The owner of the

---

[1] Works, vol. ix, pp. 16–17.   Note the characters " tsai Tz'u " (再 辭), a second refusal.
[2] Biographical Table.
[3] i.e. the " Kung Pu Lang Chung " (工 部 郎 中), Biographical Table.
[4] i.e. Chih Chih Kao (知 制 誥).   The T'ung Chien refers this appointment to the 6th month of 1061.
[5] i.e. the " Kuan Kan San Pan Yuan " (管 幹 三 班 院).

stolen property in trying to apprehend the thief had inflicted mortal injury, but that should not be regarded as a crime at all. He therefore overruled the finding of the Judge, and impeached him for making an erroneous decision. The latter in his turn refused to abide by An Shih's ruling, and carried the case to the Chief Court of Justice. This Court upheld the decision of the Judge and demanded that An Shih should make a public apology. This he resolutely refused to do, whereupon the Censorate referred the matter to the emperor, who just ignored it." [1]

This was not the only instance in which Wang An Shih found himself in opposition to his fellow officials at this time, as the following incident, also taken from the Histories,[1] will show :—

" The Emperor issued a mandate that once an order had been issued from the throne, it was illegal to make any appeal for alteration and that it should be published forthwith. An Shih raised his voice against this, saying that if this mandate were allowed to stand, the She Jen (舍 人), officials appointed for the very purpose of censoring such mandates, might just as well be abolished. There were other considerations of a still more serious character to take into account. The matter proposed was dangerous constitutionally, as in effect it would render the officers in personal attendance upon the Emperor supreme in power. Even supposing that they should be above all private prejudices, there would be some so weak that they would not dare to consider the Emperor's interests only, while those who were of an arrogant disposition would take advantage of the measure to issue orders in their own name. The Censors would not dare to criticize or oppose such influential men and so very serious trouble might result."

These incidents reveal the presence of certain factors in the situation at the capital, and certain elements in the character of Wang An Shih, which together conspired in the end to bring about his downfall. On the one hand we perceive that

---

[1] Sung Biography.

he enjoyed the special patronage of men like Tseng Kung, Wen Yen Po, and Ou Yang Hsiu. The influence of such men with the Emperor had secured for him certain privileges and exemptions which naturally aroused the envy and jealousy of others who regarded themselves as his seniors in the service. While we may detect his own objection to such invidious treatment, his critics were unable to see in that anything more than a certain subtleness of mind which led to their regarding him as a cunning strategist.

He was also a man of very strong will, and held to his ideas of what was right with a stubbornness which the conventional official could not stand. His fight for the rights of the Censorate, an institution which the Chinese Government seems to find indispensable, shows that in the interests of what he considered to be the Constitutional practice he was ready to oppose the highest officials and even the Emperor himself.

The next year (1063) Jen Tsung (仁 宗), who had been on the throne for forty years, died,[1] and was succeeded by his nephew, Ying Tsung (英 宗). In the 8th month of this year Wang An Shih's mother passed away,[2] so in accordance with the Confucian canon of etiquette, he retired from official life, and returned to Chiang Ning (Nanking) where the home had been established since his father's death. There he remained for four years, keeping the prescribed period of mourning for his mother and devoting himself to the interests of his family and literary pursuits.

It must, however, be noted that in 1065 he was called by the new Emperor to take office. Included in his correspondence are three letters [3] refusing to accept whatever appointments were offered him. The first letter includes the phrase, quoted from the Court mandate inviting him to the capital, " Your mourning period is now ended." This letter is dated the 27th of the 7th month, 1065. That would be just two years

---

[1] " T'ung Chien."
[2] Biographical Table.
[3] Works, vol. ix, p. 18.

after his mother's death.[1]   He writes that he is ill and too weak to assume responsible office.   The second letter (according to Chan Ta Ho's Biographical Table) was written in the 11th month of 1066.   In this letter, while refusing the Court appointment he asks for a position in Chiang Ning, so that he need not leave his home.   In the third letter, which is of uncertain date, he mentions that he had been living idly for some time upon his official emoluments.   While realizing that he ought (out of gratitude for the past favours of Jen Tsung in giving him office despite his inability, and also in response to the grace of the present Emperor in not forgetting him) to obey his call to the capital, yet he found himself seriously embarrassed by family cares and his own ill-health.   So that he could do no other than ask for a post nearer home.   He promised that when his health improved and his family affairs were more settled he would be ready to proceed to the Court if required.

However, he did not enter the service of the Government in any active capacity during the reign of Ying Tsung.[2]   The latter died in the 1st month of 1067, and was succeeded by his son Shen Tsung (神 宗), under whom Wang An Shih was to attain to the highest office in the land, and to earn for himself that fame (or notoriety) which posterity has bestowed upon him.

---

[1] The prescribed period of mourning for a deceased mother was three years but for official purposes the period was shortened.

[2] Sung Biography.

CHAPTER IX

GOVERNOR OF CHIANG-NING FU, LITERARY COUNCILLOR

(1067–1068)

As soon as Shen Tsung came to the throne he endeavoured to get Wang An Shih back to the capital. The following is taken from the History,[1] viz. :—

" Throughout the reign of Ying Tsung, though called to Court several times, An Shih refused to go. Whereupon Han Wei and his brother Han Chiang, together with Lü Kung Chu and his brother, began to spread his fame abroad. Before Shen Tsung came to the throne Han [2] was acting as his secretary and tutor.[3] Whenever he made any suggestion which met with his master's approval, he would say, ' That is the idea of my friend Wang An Shih.' Later when Han Wei was offered the post of steward to the princes [4] he recommended Wang An Shih to take his place. From that time onwards Shen Tsung was most anxious to make his acquaintance, so that when he came to the throne he called An Shih to the capital. However, he refused to come. So the Emperor remarked to his ministers, ' During the reign of my predecessor Wang An Shih refused to come to court. This was disrespectful. And now that I have called him he still refuses to come. Do you think it is because he is really ill, or has he some other motive for not accepting ? '

" Tseng Kung Liang said that An Shih had the capacity for the highest office, and that it was impossible that he should be acting in either a deceitful or arrogant manner.

---

[1] " T'ung Chien " (通 鑑).
[2] i.e. Han Wei (韓 維).
[3] " Chi Shih " (記 室).
[4] " Shu Tzu " (太 子 庶 子).

98

" This, however, was not the only opinion, for Wu K'uei (吳 奎) went on to say, 'I worked with Wang An Shih when he was in the National Stud. I found him often advocating wrong courses of action, and he was very conceited in his opinions. His ideas were generally impracticable. If you must find him a post do so, but I fear he is sure to throw the Constitution into confusion.' "

The Dynastic History [1] supplements this with the statement that Wang An Shih deliberately cultivated the acquaintance of the Han and Lü families with a view to soliciting their good offices in securing promotion for him, and goes on to say that it was due to the influence and patronage of these men that An Shih rose to high office.

It was of course true that by this time An Shih had influential friends at Court. Men like Ou Yang Hsiu, Wen Yen Po, and Tseng Tzu Ku had all recommended him at various times, and pressed his suit with great persistence. But the idea that he cultivated the friendship of these and others with the one object of using them for his own purposes, seems foreign to his disposition as revealed in his own correspondence, and also in letters written about him by others. For instance, in a letter written to a friend, Sun Shao Shu [2] (孫 少 述), we read, " Heaven has given me a retiring disposition, and I have made very few friends. Such as I have are well-known to you." Tseng Tzu Ku (曾 子 固) in a letter of recommendation [3] stressed the fact that he was of a retiring disposition, and unwilling that his name should be blazoned abroad.

The traditional histories, being in the main the work of Scholars opposed to An Shih's reform policy, have sought by deliberate misinterpretation of the facts to present his portrait in the worst possible light. The whole question of the reliability of the Sung Histories, especially in their references to Wang An Shih and his reforms, is so important that we

---

[1] " Pen Chuan " (本 傳).
[2] Prose Works, vol. viii, p. 35.
[3] Liang Ch'i Ch'ao, p. 46.

have devoted a chapter to it.[1]   But as regards the passage now under discussion it will suffice to say that on the testimony of his opponents he was already of considerable fame as a scholar at this time,[2] and needed no extraordinary efforts on the part of his friends to bring him into the limelight.

The opinions of Tseng Kung Liang and Wu K'uei presage the great conflict of opinion about Wang An Shih's character and ability which was to be waged during the next few years.

In this incident we see too the beginnings of that relationship between the Emperor Shen Tsung and Wang An Shih, which was to be characterized by a rare intimacy and mutual confidence later on.   It is evident from the succeeding history, that in Wang An Shih the Emperor felt that he had secured the one man who could carry out his plans for the nation, and that Wang An Shih in his turn felt that Shen Tsung was an emperor who could and would utilize his methods and ideas for the welfare of the people.

It is to these factors, combined with changes in his family circumstances,[3] that we must look for the willingness which An Shih eventually showed to proceed to the capital and take important office under the new emperor.

Despite that, however, he was not so hasty in his acceptance of Shen Tsung's first offer as the Histories would have us believe.[4]   It was in the 3rd month (intercalary) of 1067 that he was called to take up the Governorship of Chiang Ning Fu,[5] where he was then residing with his family.   "It was the prevalent opinion that he would refuse it.   But when the mandate arrived he immediately assumed his duties."   So reads the History.[5]   But as a matter of fact Wang An Shih sent off a letter of refusal, as he felt too unwell to take up the duties of such a responsible post.   He asked that if it were impossible to give him a departmental post in the provinces,

---

[1] See Vol. II of this work.
[2] See Chapter VI above.
[3] His grandmother, mother, and father were all dead at this time.
[4] See below.
[5] "T'ung Chien" (通 鑑). See footnote at end of this chap., p. 108.

such as he had appealed for in Jen Tsung's day, he might be granted a sinecure.[1] This would enable him to devote himself to further study and literary work. But he would at the same time have opportunity to secure medical treatment and recruit his health. When that was regained he would not hesitate to proceed to the capital and take up any position which the Emperor should see fit to confer upon him.[2]

Further pressure was brought to bear upon him, but he did not actually take up his new duties until the winter of that year.[3]

From the letter of thanks which he wrote to the Emperor in connection with this appointment we gather that he had been allowed to retain the rank which his last appointment at the capital had given him, i.e. that of " Chih Chih Kao " (知 制 誥), Secretary of the Edicts Board. He had also been in receipt of certain emoluments from the court during his period of mourning and inactivity.[4]

It would seem that before he actually entered upon his duties at Chiang Ning Fu another offer was made by the Emperor that he should join the Literary Council at the capital. He was called to take up this important post in the 9th month of 1067.[5] This position would give him access to the inner Counsels of State, and make him eligible for promotion to Ministerial rank. The History [5] has the following details :—

" The Emperor was greatly displeased with Han Ch'i (韓 琦), who had occupied ministerial posts during the regime of three emperors, on account of the prevalent reports that he was assuming too much power. Tseng Kung Liang took advantage of this to strongly recommend Wang An Shih to the throne. When this came to the knowledge of Han Ch'i he was more determined than ever to resign, so he was

---

[1] " Kung Kuan " (宮 觀), residences conferred upon retired or sick officials who were of special merit. Each carried certain emoluments by way of pension.
[2] Prose Works, vol. ix, p. 18.
[3] Biographical Table. See p. 108, note 1.
[4] Prose Works, vol. xv, p. 5.
[5] " T'ung Chien " (通 鑑).

transferred to Hsiang Chow (相 州) with very high rank and emoluments.

"When he came to take his leave of the Emperor, the latter said with tears, ' Since you are determined to resign, I have felt bound to issue an order permitting you to do so.   But who is there who can take your place ? What do you think of Wang An Shih ? '

" Han Ch'i replied, ' He is more than capable for the office of Literary Councillor,[1] but he is not the man to occupy the position of Minister of State.' [2]

" To this the Emperor made no remark."

It has been said above that Wang An Shih was called to take up the office of Literary Councillor in the 9th month of 1067, but he allowed an interval of seven months to elapse before proceeding to the capital to assume his duties.   During the interim he must have been carrying on as Governor of Chiang Ning Fu.   The History notes that in the 4th month of 1068 he made his appearance in the capital, and that he was admitted by special favour to an Imperial audience.[3]

At this interview the Emperor enquired of him what he thought was the most pressing matter calling for attention in connection with the administration.   An Shih replied that the selection of the right method of government was of first consideration.   The Emperor then asked, " Would you say that the method adopted by the Emperor T'ai Tsung of the T'ang Dynasty (唐 太 宗)[4] was satisfactory ? "   An Shih

---

[1] " Han Lin Hsueh Shih " (翰 林 學 士).

[2] i.e. such as " Fu Pi " (富 弼).

[3] " T'ung Chien " (通 鑑), also " Pen Chuan " (本 傳).

[4] Emperor, A.D. 627–649. " One of the greatest rulers that China ever had. His reign of twenty-two years formed the ' Golden Age ' of the T'ang Dynasty. He gathered about him the best ability of the day, both among statesmen and soldiers.   Under the guidance of Wei Cheng (魏 徵) among others, he established a government which was the model for subsequent ages. . . . Learning was encouraged and schools were founded.   Government methods were reformed. At the same time he did not neglect the military branch of the service. Many of the border tribes that had been making trouble upon the frontier of China with immunity were now taught that a stronger hand had assumed the direction of affairs." (Outlines of Chinese History by Li Ung Ping.)

replied, " But why talk about T'ang T'ai Tsung ? You should take Yao (堯) and Shun (舜) as your models.[1] Their method of government was simple and direct, comprising all that was essential without undue complications, and so not difficult to carry out. Later students of their method, however, in their inability to apprehend the real nature of their system, have come to regard it as beyond the capacity of others to imitate."

The Emperor replied, " But that is setting me a very difficult task."

An Shih was given a concurrent post as Expositor,[2] which gave him further opportunities of presenting his theories of government to the Emperor. On one occasion he detained him at the close of a general audience for a private interview.[3] In the course of their conversation the Emperor remarked that it was only after T'ang T'ai Tsung had secured the help of Wei Cheng,[4] and Han Chao Lieh[5] (漢 昭 烈) the assistance of Chu Ko Liang (諸 葛 亮),[6] that they were able to carry out their great achievements. He also expressed the opinion that these two ministers must have been very great men, and such as are not found in every generation.

To this An Shih replied, " If your Majesty really feels ready to attempt to imitate Yao and Shun, you will certainly need the help of such ministers as Kao (皋), K'uei (夔), Chi (稷), and Hsieh (契).[7] If you would become a ruler like Kao Tsung

---

[1] 2357-2205 B.C.   The model rulers of Chinese traditional History.

[2] " Shih Chiang " (侍 講), " Pen Chuan " (本 傳).

[3] " T'ung Chien " (通 鑑), also " Pen Chuan " (本 傳).

[4] See p. 102, note 4.

[5] Better known as Liu Pei (劉 備), founder of the Kingdom of Shu (蜀) in the time of the Three Kingdoms, A.D. 221-263.   Liu Pei died A.D. 222.

[6] Chu Ko Liang was his loyal adviser and minister.   It was to his assistance that Liu Pei owed his gaining of the Kingdom of Shu, and had he continued to listen to his counsel he would not have suffered his crushing defeat at the hands of Wu (吳), which led to his downfall and death of grief.

[7] Kao (皋) is (皋 陶) Minister of Justice under Yao, also under Shun, K'uei (夔) was Minister of Music.   Hsieh (契) was Minister of Education under Shun, and Chi (稷) was Minister of Agriculture.

(高 宗)[1] you must have a minister such as Fu Yueh (傅 說).[2] But as a matter of fact, Wei Cheng and Chu Ko Liang are scarcely worth mentioning, as they are not regarded with any great esteem by those who understand the best methods of government.

" But when one takes into account the vast extent of the empire, and that there is constant distress through the lack of able men to assist you to govern it, and when I consider again the fact that you are not yet sure as to the right method of government to adopt and that you have not yet sincerely made up your mind to trust your ministers to put it into operation, I fear that even though you should find a minister who had the character and ability of a Kao, or a K'uei, a Chi, a Hsieh, or a Fu Yueh, he would be swamped by a horde of smaller men, and would depart with his proposals in his pocket. . . . "

" But," rejoined the Emperor, " every generation has its ' mean men '. Even the halcyon age of Yao and Shun was not free from them, for were there not the four notorious ministers ? " [3]

" That is true," replied Wang An Shih, " but it was by virtue of their ability to recognize these men as villains, and by punishing them according to their deserts that Yao and Shun became so famous. If they had allowed them a free course to execute their pernicious ideas, do you imagine that men of such calibre as Kao, K'uei, Chi, and Hsieh would have been content to serve such a sovereign for the whole of their lives ? "

---

[1] i.e. Wu Ting (武 丁), 1324–1265 B.C. Famous for two things, the way in which he obtained the services of an able minister, Fu Yueh, and the expedition he led against the Tartars. In his search for a successor to Kan P'an, his prime minister, he is said to have appealed to God, and to have had revealed to him the features of the man who could take his place. He thereupon made a picture of the man of his dream, and ordered a search to be made for him. A mason was at length found who answered to the description given, and was made prime minister. This was Fu Yueh (傅 說), who proved to be the right man for the place, for under his guidance the country prospered within and was respected without. (Li Ung Bing, Outlines of Chinese History.)

[2] See last note.

[3] i.e. Huan Tou (讙 兜), Kung Kung (共 工), K'un (鯀), and San Miao (三 苗), all of the Emperor Shun's day, and all punished by him.

The year 1068 was characterized by severe drought and famine, north of the Yellow River, so a proposal was made by the Grand Council that on the ground of financial stringency the customary gifts to the officials should this year be withheld at the time of the winter solstice celebrations.   This matter was referred by Imperial mandate to the Literary Council.[1]   During the discussion on this important matter, Ssu Ma Kuang and Wang An Shih conducted a first-class debate on the subject of the national finances.

Ssu Ma Kuang advocated that the Court and officials should set an example of economy to the people, and that this was the best way of relieving the prevailing financial distress.   To this Wang An Shih replied, " In the times of the T'ang dynasty, Ch'ang Kun[2] surrendered his special food allowance (as a contribution towards the relief of the famine victims).   But the general opinion was that as he realized his inability to cope with the situation in any adequate way, that not only should he have surrendered his food allowance and other emoluments, but should have resigned from office altogether."

He followed up this by saying that the financial straits in which the National Treasury found itself was due to the fact that those in control lacked the requisite knowledge and ability in financial affairs.

To this Ssu Ma Kuang rejoined, " But skill in finance consists merely in the ability to scoop up the shekels by increasing the poll-tax."

" Not so," retorted Wang An Shih, " a skilled financier secures a sufficiency of revenue without increasing the taxes at all."

" Nonsense," scornfully replied Ssu Ma Kuang, " the possible total revenue from the country is of a fixed and definite amount. If the people get less, then the government receives proportionately more, and vice versa.   But if you take from the people (after the fashion that you propose) it will be still more

---

[1] The Hsueh Shih (學 士), " T'ung Chien " (通 鑑).
[2] (常 袞).

detrimental to their livelihood than an increase in taxation involves." [1]

He followed this up by asserting that Wang An Shih's proposals were akin to those of Sang Hung Yang (桑 宏 羊) [2] who led Han Wu Ti (漢 武 帝) grievously astray thereby.

It is quite possible that Wang An Shih had some adequate reply to make to this insinuation, but it is not recorded in the Histories. The account goes on to say that the Emperor, seeing little hope of the debate reaching any satisfactory conclusion, terminated it by saying that " although he agreed with the idea of Ssu Ma Kuang, it was not expedient to carry it out ".

The History then goes on to relate the fact that Wang An Shih had taken advantage of his being in charge of the drawing up of Imperial mandates at this time to introduce the incident of Ch'ang Kun,[3] which was really a threat to the legislative and military officials. So they refrained from further mention of the subject.

The incidents related in this chapter show amongst other things that both Shen Tsung and Wang An Shih were possessed of the loftiest ideals for the future of their country. An Shih

---

[1] " T'ung Chien " (通 鑑). Evidently Ssu Ma Kuang's idea was that the capacity of the country for revenue was of a fixed amount, and that it was impossible for any increase to be made in that without detriment to the people's livelihood.

[2] Sang Hung Yang (桑 宏 羊), Minister of Finance under Han Wu Ti, 140–86 B.C. Instituted the Equalization Regulations (平 準 法), which were devised with a view to saving transport charges on grains for the State revenues, and also for levelling up prices by establishing government Bureaus for purchasing grain when cheap and plentiful at a price slightly higher than current rates and selling again when scarce and dear at prices lower than current rates. In this way profits which usually went to the Grain Combines were received by the Government. It is said by some authorities that the people were not taxed above the normal, but the government had sufficient for financial needs. Another tradition is that represented by an augurer that Sang Hung Yang should be boiled alive, and then the rain would come. This was evidently spoken in a time of drought, when it was customary to examine into the conduct of government to find the cause for heaven's displeasure thus revealed. (From the " Yu P'i T'ung Chien Chi Lan " (御 批 通 鑑 輯 覽). But see fuller note under Chapter on Equitable Transport Measure, pp. xvii–xix.)

[3] See p. 105.

was ambitious enough to imagine that a revival of the " Golden Age of Yao and Shun " was possible under Shen Tsung. The latter, while somewhat diffident of his own capacity, was beginning to feel that under the tutorship of a man like Wang An Shih, great and splendid reforms were possible. But the influence of Ssu Ma Kuang was very considerable, and as his views failed to coincide with those of Wang An Shih, the Emperor found himself in a very difficult position, for to incline towards the one was to lose the support of the other. So while it is obvious that at heart the Emperor was disposed to give his confidence to Wang An Shih he had in a measure to defer to contrary opinions at this point as a measure of expediency.

We see, too, in this chapter the setting of the field between the two great and outstanding characters of the period, viz., Ssu Ma Kuang and Wang An Shih. The latter was the " Radical ", the former the " Conservative " leader of the times. In the debate which has been outlined above, we see their two points of view emerging. Wang An Shih was out for some great constructive measure which would increase the revenue of the State without imposing further burdens upon the people. Ssu Ma Kuang could not see as far as that, and was content to advocate measures of economy in the public expenditure.

It will be noted also that Wang An Shih was fearless in his denunciation of those whom he would dub " The Conventional Inefficients ",[1] i.e. those who were afraid of instituting changes because of the trouble that was involved, or those who would hold on to their jobs and emoluments despite their obvious incapacity.

His opponents, however, were prevented from taking any drastic action against him at this time because he was manifestly in favour with the Emperor, so although we find him already faced with formidable opposition it was more or less suppressed.

We see, too, that the Canonical Histories betray their prejudices on every page. Ssu Ma Kuang is the " hero "

[1] (因 循 流 俗).

and Wang An Shih the "villain" of the piece. His appeal to Shen Tsung to become another Yao or Shun is interpreted as a piece of adroit flattery to win the Emperor's favour. His reference to the great ministers of the ancient regime, and the necessity of securing such to help the ruler to attain his object, is regarded as a piece of unmitigated arrogance. The eclipses, earthquakes, floods, and drought which characterized this year or two were all regarded as being connected with An Shih's villainous plots and schemes, and should have been a sufficient warning to the Emperor not to use such a man in the public service.[1]

But more of that anon. What has been said above will suffice to show the reader that Wang An Shih was facing a task of superhuman difficulty in taking up office at this juncture, and that, due to the prejudices of the Historians of the period, any attempt to portray the character of such a statesman is beset by peculiar difficulty.

---

[1] There is divergence of views between the various authorities as to the date on which Wang An Shih actually took up this appointment. Chan Ta Ho says clearly that he took it up in the winter of 1067 (冬 方 就 職). In Wang An Shih's letter of thanks for the appointment carrying his acceptance of the post, he uses the expression (經 涉 歲 時), which seems to imply that he had delayed for about a year before obeying the order to take up the post. This order was issued in the third intercalary month of that year. We need not take the expression in Wang An Shih's letter of thanks as equivalent to twelve months. It might be a general term for eight or nine months, which would bring the date to some time in the winter, as Chan Ta Ho suggests. However, Ts'ai Shang Hsiang and Liang Ch'i Ch'ao regard his acceptance of the post as having taken place soon after the commission reached him.

This question also affects the time at which he took up his duties as Literary Councillor. The Histories date this in the 9th month of 1067. See p. 102. Liang and Ts'ai both accept this as correct. However, in the "T'ung Chien" under that month the commentator states that he waited seven months before actually proceeding to the capital to take up the appointment, which would bring the date to the 4th month of 1068, when we read of Wang An Shih's being called to the Imperial presence by special privilege. Chan Ta Ho puts the appointment of Literary Councillor in 1068 without indicating the month. However, when we come to Wang An Shih's own Works, we find that he wrote the Imperial permission to Han Ch'i to retire to Hsiang Chow in the 9th month of 1067, which, if the History is correct in the date of the latter event, implies that Wang An Shih must have been acting as Literary Councillor then. The document permitting Han Ch'i to retire to Hsiang Chow is found in vol. xii, p. 3, of his Works.

CHAPTER X

APPOINTED VICE-GRAND COUNCILLOR
(1069)

WANG AN SHIH, in his capacity as Expositor of the Literary Council, continued to disturb the placid atmosphere of the court with his unconventional theories and bold statements.

Owing to the long drought and prolonged famine, the Emperor, in accordance with the customary procedure on such occasions, was keeping to his private rooms, fasting, and denying himself the pleasure of musical diversion and entertainment. This led An Shih to remark that calamities such as drought and famine were part of the natural order of things, and had no essential connection with the way in which public affairs of state were conducted, or the way in which this or that person behaved.

Fu Pi (富 弼), who had just been appointed Grand Councillor, heard of this statement, and said with concern, "The Emperor should stand in awe of Heaven. If he fails in that respect, he might proceed to any lawlessness."

So he memorialized the throne in a document of several thousand words, vigorously discussing the whole subject. In the interview which the Emperor granted him after the receipt of this memorial, he said, "The appointment of men to the Administration is the most important matter with which your Majesty has to deal, and you should make it your first consideration to enquire into the character of those you wish to employ. You should not allow your personal preferences to rule in such a matter as this. If you do, and continue to follow your tendency to set people prying into matters extraneous to their office, you will give to evil-minded and specious fellows just the opportunity for which they seek.

"I have noticed, too, that gradually certain changes have been introduced both at the capital and in the provinces, which must be the result of mean men bringing their theories and proposals before you. This type of person delights in activity and change, so that suggestions of an unusual character are bound to be made. If only the Court will maintain its usual placidity and calm, affairs will be conducted according to the regular and long-established procedure, and these mean folk will cease to think they can get in.

"I beseech you to look carefully into this question so that you may be saved from vain regrets." [1]

Evidently all this was directed against Wang An Shih, whose growing influence with the Emperor was a menace to the prospects of the conventional type of official. To these he must have appeared as a mischievous busybody, worming his way into the Emperor's confidence by his high-sounding proposals for reform. If his policy should gain the approval of the Emperor, they could see their own prestige and influence gradually but surely diminishing, so they roused themselves to poison the mind of the Emperor against him by every possible device.

Fu Pi's attempt seems to have failed to influence Shen Tsung to any appreciable extent, however, for at the close of the above account, so the History goes on to say, the Emperor was still desirous of availing himself of Wang An Shih's advice and assistance.

This brought T'ang Chieh into the field. He was vice-Grand Councillor at this time, and felt it incumbent upon him to warn the Emperor against giving An Shih scope for the trial of his theories.

So he said that Wang An Shih would find it very difficult to fulfil the duties of high office satisfactorily.

" Do you mean," enquired the Emperor, " that he lacks the requisite literary skill and classical knowledge, or that he has not the administrative or executive ability for such a post ? "

T'ang Chieh (唐 介) replied, "He is a keen scholar, but bigoted in regard to the ancient lore. So his proposals are quite impracticable. If he should be employed in some high administrative capacity, he will necessarily suggest numerous changes."

[1] " T'ung Chien " (通 鑑).

Feeling, however, that his little effort had failed to produce an appreciable effect on the Emperor, T'ang Chieh sought out Tseng Kung Liang (曾 公 亮) and expressed his fear that Wang An Shih would soon be promoted and given full opportunity to try his theories, that such an experiment would inevitably bring distress and confusion in its train, and that the nobles ought to give the matter their attention.

The Emperor then sought the advice of his private reader, Sun Ku (孫 固), as to whether he thought Wang An Shih might be appointed to the Grand Council.

Sun Ku replied, " He has great literary abilities, and to employ him in some merely advisory appointment would be excellent. But for the office of State Minister greater capacity than he possesses is required. For that he is too petty and small. If you are wanting really well-qualified men for such a post, then I would mention Lü Kung Chu (呂 公 著), Ssu Ma Kuang (司 馬 光), and Han Wei (韓 維)."

" But," dolefully continues the record,[1] " the emperor persisted in his idea of giving An Shih further promotion and in the 2nd month of 1069 issued the decree appointing him vice-Grand Councillor, with the concurrent post and rank of ' Yu Chien I Tai Fu ' (右 諫 議 大 夫), or Advisor to the ' Chung Shu Sheng ', the Chief Legislative Organ of the Government."

The vice-Grand Councillors to whose number An Shih was thus appointed were usually three in number,[2] and were generally present at meetings of the Grand Council, of which they acted as executive officers. They were entitled " Ts'an Chih Cheng Shih " (參 知 政 事).

In the course of a conversation[3] with him at this time the emperor remarked, " People have but a superficial knowledge

---

[1] " T'ung Chien " (通 鑑).

[2] In addition to the three regularly appointed vice-Grand Councillors there were two others who were regarded as of equivalent rank and took their place at their conferences, viz. the President and Vice-President of the Board of War (樞 密 院 使 and 樞 密 院 副 使).

[3] " T'ung Chien " (通 鑑), also " Pen Chuan " (本 傳).

of you, they imagine that you are only conversant with literary theories and that you have no knowledge of practical matters."

To this An Shih replied, " But a knowledge of classical theories is exactly what is requisite for the conduct of affairs."

" Then," said the emperor, " what is to be your first contribution ? "

" The greatest need of the times," replied the new vice-Councillor, " is to transform current thought and practice and to set up (new) laws and regulations."

This reply delighted the emperor.

Wang An Shih was now 47 years of age, in the prime of life, with unique equipment of mind and spirit. He stood high in the favour of the emperor, who was determined to give him an opportunity to put his theories for the improvement of the country's condition to the test. He realized the serious need for initiating radical and far-reaching reforms, and had the highest ideals and strongest hopes for the future. But the horizon was already dark with foreboding. The jealousy and hatred of many of his contemporaries would shortly bring about him a storm of calumny and opposition which would make his task peculiarly difficult. In this sense the words of his critic T'ang Chieh were all too true, " he would find it very difficult to fulfil the duties of high office."

There were, however, other difficulties in the situation besides those which were more personal. If these are to be understood, and the nature of Wang An Shih's task rightly estimated, it is necessary that the reader should have some general idea of the conditions obtaining during his lifetime. For only in so far as one appreciates the state of the Chinese Empire under the northern Sungs generally, and particularly in the times of Jen Tsung, Ying Tsung, and Shen Tsung, can the contribution which Wang An Shih sought to make be properly evaluated.

With this object in view the reader is referred to Vol. II of this work, in which the attempt has been made to give some account of the nature of the times.

Chapter XI

PREPARATIONS FOR FINANCIAL REFORM; BEGINNING OF OPPOSITION

(1069)

THE problem of the national finances was the first to which Wang An Shih gave his attention after his promotion to the office of vice-Grand Councillor. Liang Ch'i Ch'ao says that "the financial state of the Sung Dynasty reached its nadir in the later years of Jen Tsung's reign" (1023–1063).[1] (This matter is discussed in some detail in the second volume of this work.)

We read that prior to this Jen Tsung had instructed Ssu Ma Kuang to investigate the financial situation and had requested him to devise measures for the reduction of government expenditure. We read further that a special Bureau had been established for this purpose. But apparently all that was done was to make a comparison between the figures for 1042 and the budget for the current year, and to send in a report on the differences that existed between them.

In the second report, presented a little later, pointing out that the annual income was inadequate to meet expenditure, Ssu Ma Kuang indicated that the reason for this deficiency was extravagance. Gifts to officials and others were too lavish. There were too many supernumeraries. The personnel of the Royal Household was too great. The Standing Army was too large, the emphasis being on numbers to the detriment of their efficiency. It was therefore essential that the emperor should take counsel with his officers, both civil and military, and also with the officials of the Revenue Office in order that the necessary adjustments should be made to save what was unquestionably a critical situation.

[1] Liang Ch'i Ch'ao, p. 114.

It was possible, he thought, to effect some reduction in the expenditure, but it would have to be done very gradually. It was certainly impossible to make any considerable reduction immediately.[1]

Wang An Shih has an essay on Current Extravagance,[2] written possibly during the reign of Jen Tsung, which it will be well to include at this point. It reads as follows :—

" The people are the special object of Heaven's love and nurturing care, but the ruler is the one on whom they set their hope (for the maintenance of the means of life). The Sages, in accordance with Heaven's ideas, established rulers for the people, with the main object of securing peace and ensuring prosperity for them. These things depend upon the proper regulation of public life and the maintenance of correct customs. Any change that takes place in such matters is of vital consequence to the life of the people, and in proportion as their spirit is affected so the prosperity or decadence of the State is at stake. It is, therefore, a question to which the most careful attention should be given.

" The good ruler maintains an economical standard in public life, extravagance being recognized as a great evil. If extravagance is not controlled it soon reaches an irremediable stage, when the people, in order to satisfy their lust for power and prestige, are ready to exhaust all their resources.

" It should be remembered that the productive activity of Heaven is limited by the seasons, and that the power of men to avail themselves of such is limited also. But the state expenditure is incessant and knows no bounds. Unless some method of control is devised, then the wealth gathered at these fixed seasons and by this limited means, will lead to the poverty of the people on the one hand and the reckless extravagance (of certain classes) on the other.

" Since the inauguration of the Sung Dynasty, thanks to a

---

[1] Liang Ch'i Ch'ao, p. 114, quoted from Shih Huo Chih (食 貨 志).
[2] Prose Works, essay entitled " Feng Su " (風 俗), vol. xvii, p. 18.

succession of four sage-like rulers,[1] the empire has gradually been reduced to order, and the laws and constitution have been definitely promulgated. Taxation has not been of an over-burdensome character, and public services have been equitably apportioned. The present has never been surpassed for its tranquillity.

" In view of these considerations, it should follow as a matter of course that every family should have enough for its needs, and every man sufficient for his maintenance.

" Yet the facts are otherwise. The poorer classes cannot clothe their children properly, even in the coarsest of cloth. The serving and labouring classes persist in their cunning and deceitful practices. The reason for this is that we have not eliminated corrupt and pernicious customs.

" The influence of the Sage proceeds from that which is near to what is more remote, from within to without. The capital city is the place where the fashions are set, the centre towards which the faces of the people are turned, and the standards of which they are inclined to imitate.

" It is difficult to get the official clan, with their wealth and abundance of possessions, to adopt an economical way of life. They readily fall into extravagance. On occasions of ceremony their raiment and equipages are marvellous. They make constant changes in their utensils, and other appurtenances. The influence of all this rapidly spreads throughout the land.

" The consequence is that the artisan class devote themselves to the production of useless articles, and the commercial world concentrates on the securing of rare goods which by their very nature are difficult to obtain. The desire for strange and wonderful things grows from year to year, and ability to make frequent changes becomes estimable. So we find that a thing

---

[1] These four must have been T'ai Tsu (太 祖), 960–975 ; T'ai Tsung (太 宗), 976–997 ; Chen Tsung (眞 宗), 998–1022 ; and Jen Tsung (仁 宗), 1023–1063. The essay would probably be written in Ying Tsung's reign, although it is possible that it was composed in the later years of Jen Tsung.

is cast aside before it is damaged at all, and that those who still follow the old fashions are made a laughing stock.

"The rich strive to outstrip their fellows, and the poor are ashamed of their poverty. The latter say, 'I too am a man. I suffer lack while he (the rich) gets honours and possessions in such abundance.' So they turn to ways of envy and emulation, devoting their whole energies to the attempt to outstrip their fellows. The result is that among the lower strata of society there are those who exhaust the resources of a lifetime in one mad moment of extravagance. But there is no forest so big that it cannot be consumed by a prairie fire, and no sea or river so large that it can ever fill a leaking vessel.

"When modest and simple customs are cast aside, covetous and corrupt practices become the norm. This in its turn leads to the exhaustion of the resources of both high and low. The people generally become depraved and the officials lose their reputation for honesty. Cruelty and oppression come to be regarded as the proper course while those who are of a dutiful and self-respecting character are considered base and uncultured.

"The economically minded and upright become few, while the money-grabbers get numerous. The wealth of the rich parades itself in every corner of the city, while the corpses of the poor fill the ditches in the wild.

"It is but natural for a man to take pleasure in life when his mind and body are free from anxiety and distress, and that when his mind is troubled by physical suffering he begins to lose his desire to live.

"In such a case as this the laws are powerless to prevent trouble. In fact this is the very reason why the penal code is not respected, or effectively administered.

"A great flood may be caused by a small hole in the river bank and a tiny sprout may grow up into an enormous tree. It is easier to prohibit certain things at the beginning than to save the situation later on.

"So we ought to take steps akin to the practice of the ancient rulers, and demand that all wares be handed in for inspection before being put on the market. All who are producing articles of a useless, extravagant or immoral character, or anything which is inclined to deprave the people, should be punished. Such articles and utensils as are permitted to be used by various grades of society should be classified with a view to limiting the expenditure on such things.

" Artisans and merchants who are promoting the production and sale of luxuries should be heavily taxed to make their trade difficult and shameful. When the people perceive that it is useless to go on producing articles of luxury, and that punishment and shame await those who carrry on the trade, they will be forced into the fields, and as more land is brought under cultivation, there will be no lack of food.

" If this is made clear to all, the control that is exercised in the capital will naturally lead to the whole country being brought into line."

In one respect Wang An Shih shows himself in sympathy with the idea of Ssu Ma Kuang, namely, that an example of economy and simple living needed to be set by the official and wealthy classes, particularly those resident at the court and in the capital. But he goes further than Ssu Ma Kuang in his endeavour to deal radically with the problem. He would bring the law to bear upon the producer of articles of luxury. By inflicting severe penalties upon producer and distributor he hoped to put a check upon the extravagances of the rich, which he feared would sap the vitals of the nation's economic life. Agriculture would be fostered, as the labour which had been engaged upon the production of useless articles would be diverted to the more profitable work of farming.

This essay was written before Wang An Shih entered upon his own career as a financial reformer. It demonstrates not only his keenness to deal with the economic problems of his time but shows also that he had a clear perception of the causes of the prevailing poverty, and that he had practical remedies to suggest for current ills.

So one is not surprised to find that immediately after entering upon his new duties as vice-Grand Councillor, it became his first concern to make certain radical proposals for the financial betterment of the State.

To begin with, he felt it necessary to get control of the Bureau of Finance.[1] This seems to have been a separate unit of the Administration, functioning independently of the other organs of Government. To gain his object he felt it necessary to establish a new Bureau which would make the old one of a subordinate and dependent character.

His appeal for the establishment of this new Bureau is included in the Histories, as follows [2] :—

" In the times of the Chow Dynasty there existed a Bureau called the ' Ch'uan Fu.' [3] This was set up with a view to controlling the Monopolists or Combines,[4] for the adoption of such measures as would distribute the wealth of the nation more equitably, and conduce to the relief of the poor. In succeeding generations the proposals of men like Sang Hung Yang and Liu Yen (劉 晏) [5] may be said to conform generally to this older idea.

[1] i.e. The San Ssu (三 司).

[2] T'ung Chien.

[3] (泉 府) Finance Bureau which controlled supplies, distribution, and prices, aiming at sufficiency of revenue for the State without inflicting any undue hardship upon the people.

[4] " Chien Ping " (兼 并), really " Plutocrats ", wealthy merchants, and officials who controlled finance and trade.

[5] Liu Yen (劉 晏), i.e. Liu Shih An (劉 世 安) of the T'ang Dynasty. In the reign of Tai Tsung (代 宗), during the years A.D. 763–5, was Grand Councillor, and later Minister of Transport, Taxation, etc. He paid first attention to the livelihood of the people, one of his favourite quips being that if the numbers of the people were increased, the revenues would increase in proportion. Evidently he was a skilled financier, the revenues from Salt being increased tenfold during his regime. The revenues from Salt alone were sufficient to provide for all military and transport services. He balanced up supplies throughout the country, and provided a courier system with fixed sections, over which they transmitted the prices of commodities from place to place. He so managed affairs that the regulation of food prices were all in his own hands. Prospects of good harvests or bad were all known by him beforehand, and preparations to meet emergencies of surplus or dearth duly completed. In the first year of Te Tsung (德 宗), i.e. 780, he was put to death by order of the emperor. This was resented by the whole empire. (From the T'ung Chien Kang Mu (通 鑑 綱 目).) But see further notes in Vol. II of this work.

" The scholars of those days, however, failed to comprehend the idea of the ancient rulers in adopting such measures, and thought it equivalent to the government engaging in trade competition with the people. They therefore opposed the idea on the ground that it was inconsistent with the dignity of the ruling class.

" Despite that, however, I now wish to suggest to your Majesty that with a view to reforming the financial state of the country, we should adopt the ' Ch'uan Fu ' idea, in order that the authority over all monetary matters might revert to the throne." (i.e. the government would get the advantages which the plutocrats had received hitherto.)

The emperor having shown his approval of this suggestion, An Shih went on to discourse upon the difficulty of finding the right men for the carrying out of his new scheme, and urging that particular care be given to the selection of each individual appointed for the work, lest through the unsuitability of one or two the activities and plans of the many should be brought to nought. He illustrated his point by referring to the case of the great emperor Yao, who though he only employed one man to regulate the great floods of his time (i.e. Kun), failed to secure the right man for the task. In this new financial reform movement they would have to employ considerable numbers of men, so the chances of failure were proportionately increased.

" This," says the historian, " was said because Wang An Shih was still not quite convinced that the emperor was going to give him his full confidence."

However true or false that may be, the emperor agreed that one unsuitable man could prevent any large measure of success, and he forthwith issued a mandate for the establishment of a Bureau, which was to be under the direct control of the emperor. It was styled " The Bureau for the promulgation of measures of financial reform ",[1] which we will call for short " The Financial Reorganization Bureau ".

This was in the 2nd month of 1069, the same month as

---

[1] " Chih Chih San Ssu T'iao Li Ssu " (制 置 三 司 條 例 司).

that in which Wang An Shih was appointed vice-Grand Councillor.

The Imperial decree, authorizing the establishment of this new Bureau, is as follows [1]:—

"I realize that it is necessary to enrich the empire before it can be brought to proper order. But at the present time the revenues of the Court are insufficient, while the financial condition of my people remains grievously straitened. I have therefore commanded my ministers to set up a special Bureau under the personal supervision of the crown, with a view to rectifying this deplorable state of affairs.

"The specialist in administration is born of experience, for it is experience which makes him intelligent as to the causes for success and failure. So now I am looking to my ministers for help in the more equitable administration of finance. For as they are men who are thoroughly versed in the subject they will ensure its unadulterated success, and their advice be such as can be carried into effect.

"I realize that the true way to improve the financial condition of the country is to increase its resources. But at the same time we must ensure that everyone has a sufficiency of the means of life.

"So I thoroughly disapprove of proposals which involve burdensome taxation, for they not only deprive the people of their means of subsistence, but arouse resentment against the ruler.

"Wherefore I command all officers of the Board of Finance and all officials who exercise supervisory functions in the provinces, as well as all officials both at the capital and elsewhere, that within a period of two months from the date of receiving this mandate, they shall report on the working of the existing financial regulations."

Although this was an Imperial Mandate, it is quite easy to detect the hand of Wang An Shih in it. Certainly the main points of the edict about the engagement of financial specialists and increasing the resources of the empire, while at the same

[1] Liang Ch'i Ch'ao, p. 111.

time assuring the people of a sufficiency of the means of life, are all fundamental tenets of An Shih's policy. After the new Bureau was set up, Ch'en Sheng Shih (陳 升 之), President of the Board of War,[1] and Wang An Shih were appointed as Directors of the whole business. It was quite natural that the emperor should enlist the co-operation of the one who had made the original proposition for the establishment of the Bureau.

The reference to burdensome proposals of taxation was a hit at the conventional financier, and the whole scheme of getting control of the financial administration and its proceeds into the power of the Crown, was directed against the activities of the wealthy Usurers and Trade Monopolists, who, instead of using their wealth for the initiation of industrial enterprises which might have benefited the poor, were evidently content to live lives of luxurious idleness upon their ill-gotten gains. These gains came from the exorbitant rates of interest which they charged on loans made to the poor, whose insignificant resources were eaten up in annual or monthly payments to their rich creditors.

If this state of things were allowed to continue, the rich persisting in their work of grinding the faces of the poor, and at the same time squandering their gains on their luxuries and pleasures, the capital resources of the country must gradually get exhausted and the livelihood of the common people become more and more difficult.

It was therefore part of Wang An Shih's policy to secure for the Government some of the profits which had been accumulating in the hands of these usurers and monopolists. This necessitated full control by the Government of all financial matters, and led Wang An Shih later to devise various schemes for making state loans to the people at lower rates of interest than those demanded by the wealthy moneylenders.[2] As this

---

[1] " T'ung Chien."

[2] The rates of interest exacted under Wang An Shih's regulations were usually 2 per cent per mensem, i.e. 24 per cent per annum. But the rates demanded by the moneylenders were more than that, ranging between 30 per cent to as much as 50 per cent. Two per cent per mensem is considered quite normal in China to-day.

would deprive this rich class of their chief source of income, it
is easy to see that they would form one of the chief obstacles
in the way of so drastic a financial reformer.

Wang An Shih had been thinking on these problems for
a long time, as the following attempted translation of one of his
poems [1] written in his earlier years will show. It bears the title
of " The Monopolists " (兼 幷) and reads :—

> " In the Golden Age solicitude
> Marked the way of the ruling clan.
> Wealth was gained in a rational way,
> Whether for State or for man.
> The emperor wielded unquestioned sway,
> As the Dipper [2] rules in Heaven.
>
> " The public income and outlay
> Every item he could scan.
> Monopolies then were considered a crime,
> And heavy the punishments ran,
> Neither power nor influence could such men gain,
> So severe was the legal ban.
>
> " But later conditions were quite reversed,
> The people were hard to rule.
> Ch'in Wang erected a wonderful shrine
> To widow Ch'ing's memory.[3]
> Duty and Right lost their true might,
> The great books were allowed to decay.
> Though the ancient way was not forgot,
> Its mention brought mockings and play.
>
> " Who most money brought,
> Was most able thought.
> The rulers knew no other way.

---

[1] Poetical Works, vol. vi, p. 6.

[2] i.e. the " Great Bear " (北 斗), regarded as the fixed centre of the stellar
system, round which all other constellations revolve and so applied to the
emperor.

[3] This widow amassed enormous wealth from a monopoly in cinnabar.
She was so powerful that none dare offend her. Even the emperor thought it
well to keep in her good graces, hence the memorial, although it must also be
said that she was of good repute.

Monopolists ruled, whom Confucianists schooled
In Conservatism failed to gainsay.
In a hundred ways the lust for gain
Was able to win the day.
Selfish men the mart controlled,
Even officials joined the fray,
But the people, ah ! the people,
Most pitiable they."

The poem indicates clearly some of the pernicious tendencies of Wang An Shih's time. The wealthy money-lenders and trade-monopolists not only made things very hard for the poor, but they were proportionately influential in matters of state, even the ruler having to show them considerable deference. The Confucianists of the time also come in for their meed of scorn, as they failed to raise their voices against the tyranny and corruption which such a state of things involved. Nor are the official class allowed to go scot free. In many cases, perhaps the majority, the high officials were of the money-lending class themselves.

The last two lines of the poem show how the plight of the common people under this regime of wealthy oppression weighed on the mind and heart of Wang An Shih.

All that has been said above will serve to show his motive in appealing that this Financial Reorganization Bureau should be set up, and also accounts for whatever keenness he himself showed that he should have a prominent share in its activities.

Lü Hui Ch'ing (呂 惠 卿) was appointed to help in this Bureau, also Su Che (蘇 轍) and Chang Ch'un. The former gained this post on the recommendation of Wang An Shih, who regarded him as the one man of the time who could apply the ancient classical lore in a practical manner to current affairs. It was generally thought that most of the documents, regulations, etc., which were drawn up and promulgated by this Bureau were from the pen of Lü Hui Ch'ing, but it was also well understood that the ideas behind them all were those of Wang An Shih.

The Histories [1] state that Tseng Pu (曾 布), for whom Wang An Shih secured a post in the Chung Shu Sheng (中 書 省), where he had full opportunity of knowing what memorials were being sent in to the throne, was of great assistance to the officers of the new Bureau by stiffening the mind of the emperor against any attempt to hinder the activities of the reformers.

An effort on the part of Wang An Shih to induce his friend Liu Shu to join the staff of the new Bureau is reported to have elicited the following reply :—" The Emperor has now begun to look to you for advice in matters of public import. What you ought to do is to devote your attention to the exposition of the principles of Yao and Shun, and not give first place to financial policy."

The History states that Liu Shu refused the invitation, whereupon Wang An Shih broke off friendly relations with him.

It is evident from this that the Emperor was lending Wang An Shih special support at this time. This apparently gave rise to considerable trepidation in Court circles. In the Histories we find the writers and commentators on events interpreting an eclipse of the sun which occurred soon after his appointment as vice-Grand Councillor as a sign that he was about to get the whip hand of the Emperor.

One also gets the impression that scholars in attendance upon the Emperor were supposed to regard such mundane matters as financial questions as beneath their notice, and that they should confine themselves to instruction of the Emperor in general moral principles, hoping thereby to bring about by the force of his personal example the necessary reform of public life.

This incident also suggests that Wang An Shih was giving his prime attention to the economical side of things.

We see in it, too, the fact that Wang An Shih's determination to embark upon a practical experiment of his political theories was leading to the severance of some old friendships. If that was the case, it was only to be expected that malice and bitter

[1] T'ung Chien.

opposition should be aroused amongst those at Court who were already envious of his influence, and of different schools of political thought.

So at this juncture we note that the historiographers give free play to their superstitious fancies. They attribute the breaking of the Yellow River banks, the incidence of floods, earthquakes and the like, as evidence of Heaven's displeasure with the Emperor for placing too much confidence in his new minister.

Even the death of a fellow vice-Grand Councillor, T'ang Chieh, which occurred in the fourth month of this year, is laid at the door of Wang An Shih. The History relates that he was a man of bold speech, and that he frequently engaged in hot and sharp debate with the new Councillor. Wang An Shih was also obdurate in maintaining his own point of view. After one of these debates, in which the Emperor sided with Wang An Shih, T'ang Chieh got so angry that as a result a carbuncle appeared on his back from which he died.[1]

But to return to the Financial Reorganization Bureau. One of the next things done under its auspices was to conduct an investigation into the State accounts. All the books connected with the national revenue services were called in for inspection and audit. Some of the books sent in were found to have unbroken seals, many of them being twenty or even thirty years old. This was accounted for by the system of official bribery prevalent at the time, the auditors guaranteeing the " correctness " of all accounts on which the proper amount of " hush money " had been received. Corresponding difficulties were made for those who refused to pay up. This gives us some idea of the corrupt state of the revenue service.

The new Bureau next investigated the annual budget. Every item of expenditure was closely scrutinized, and definite amounts re-estimated for the ensuing year, both for the general

---

[1] An Shih's own son, Fang (雱), also died in this way, so the Historian relates, as the result of temper following his being rebuked by his father. He, too, is said to have " grown a carbuncle on his back ". " T'ung Chien " under 1076, 7th month.

expenditure and the Great Sacrifice. In this way a saving of about
40 per cent was effected. This substantial reduction was made
almost entirely on Court expenses, which reflects very
favourably on the character of the Emperor Shen Tsung,
showing his willingness to give practical help in this necessary
measure of economy.

It was, of course, too much to expect that Wang An Shih
would devise measures that would *increase* the national revenue
all at once, but in the matter of *reduction* of expenditure, he
succeeded where Ssu Ma Kuang had failed.

In addition to reducing expenditure, the new Bureau made
substantial increases in the salaries of officials. For the capital
district a total increase of 410,000 " strings " was made, and for
the provinces an extra amount of 689,000 " strings " was
allocated for the pay-roll.[1]

The Bureau then proceeded to appoint a special Commission [2]
of eight, who were to travel through the country and make
investigation into agricultural, irrigation, and river problems.
They were also to report on the current methods of taxation
and the regulations for public services. Ch'eng Hao (程 顥),
afterwards to become so famous as a writer and philosopher,
was one member of this Commission. The historian is at a loss
to account for such a fine man consenting to serve under Wang
An Shih, but presumes he must have had good reasons for
doing so.

This Commission was appointed in the fourth month of
1069. A note in the Histories under the sixth month informs us
that the court officials, generally speaking, thought that in
Wang An Shih they had secured a very capable and energetic
man. It is therefore reasonable to suppose that even Ch'eng Hao
held a similar opinion of him at this time.

---

[1] Liang Ch'i Ch'ao, pp. 114 and 115.

[2] These eight men were Liu I (劉 彝), Hsieh Ch'ing Ts'ai (謝 卿 材),
Hou Shu Hsien (侯 叔 獻), Ch'eng Hao (程 顥), Lu Ping (盧 秉),
Wang Ju I (王 汝 翼), Tseng Hang (曾 伉), and Wang Kuang Lien
(王 廣 廉).

There was, however, one notable exception in the person of Lü Hui (呂 誨) of the Censorate. He was the only one who dared to speak out against Wang An Shih on personal grounds, although thus early opposition to his proposals and criticism of his procedure had resulted in the transfer of four men of note to provincial appointments. These were T'eng Fu,[1] the governor of the capital, who had enjoyed the intimate friendship of the emperor, and of whose influence An Shih is said to have been afraid ; the Literary Councillor Cheng Hsieh,[2] who was to raise a great storm later : and two other important officials, one the Royal Chamberlain, Wang Kung Ch'en (王 拱 辰), and Ch'ien Kung Fu (錢 公 輔), clerk to the Edicts Board.

The account of Lü Hui's attack is given in detail in the Histories, from which the following extracts are taken :—

" He met Ssu Ma Kuang on his way to court, and being asked what particular business he had to introduce, replied : ' The document I have up my sleeve, which relates to the new vice-Grand Councillor.'

" ' But,' asked Ssu Ma Kuang, ' what is the use of criticizing one with whom all are so pleased ? '

" ' True,' rejoined Lü Hui, ' Wang An Shih is very popular just now, but he is not only obstinate, prejudiced, and a lover of flattery, he is also deceitful and untrustworthy. In speech and appearance he gives the impression of being an honourable and loyal man, but at heart he is crafty and treacherous. His appointment to high office will spell disaster for the nation.' "

He then sent in a memorial to the throne, impeaching Wang An Shih in the most virulent terms, terming him a hypocrite, eloquent but dangerous, insolent and overbearing, and a secret enemy of the State. He then enumerated ten points on which his charges were based, synopsized as follows :—

1. His refusal to make apology in connection with the fighting quail case showed him to be proud and insolent

---

[1] (滕 甫) T'eng Fu.
[2] (鄭 俠) Cheng Hsieh.

to his superiors. His refusals to take office under the Emperor Ying Tsung without any reason other than his personal convenience is added proof of this.[1]

2. While refusing minor appointments, he had accepted without hesitation more important positions like that of the Governorship of Chiang Ning Fu and to the Literary Council. So that he is shown to be actuated solely by motives of personal advantage.

3. His appeal that he might be allowed to sit in the Imperial presence in his capacity as tutor shows his ignorance or contempt of the distinctions which should exist between the Emperor and his ministers.

4. Since he has assumed the office of vice-Grand Councillor he has repeatedly made excuses for remaining behind for private conference with the Emperor, after the other ministers have left, and has used this opportunity for persuading the Emperor to affix his seal to certain important documents. In this way he has shown his disloyalty to his colleagues in the Council. Moreover, his craftiness is seen in this, as if the affair under discussion went well he could assume the credit himself, but if things went awry he could lay the blame at the door of the Emperor.

5. His decision on the Tengchowfu case [2] showed him to be actuated by personal considerations and motives of private vengeance.

6. He is partial to his own relations, as in the case of his brother, An Kuo (安 國), for he pressed his eligibility for promotion despite the opinion of the examiners, who placed him low down in the list. He is also so arrogant and

---

[1] See Vol. II where the whole matter is discussed in detail.

[2] This was the case of a woman who had attempted to kill her husband because of his ill-treatment. She had confessed to the crime. The local official proposed that she should not be called upon to suffer the extreme penalty of the law, because of her confession. Wang An Shih supported this proposal, but was strenuously opposed by Ssu Ma Kuang. The case was held in abeyance for over a year, when Wang An Shih's point of view was accepted, and a new law framed that in such crimes as this if confession of guilt should be made the penalty should be that of two grades lighter than for murder.

presumptuous that none dare oppose him. But his door is besieged with office-seekers who rely upon his personal favour for promotion. This faction-forming policy is a menace to the constitution.

7. He has exceeded his lawful authority by making appointments without reference to the Grand Council, and shown himself an innovator of dangerous precedents in this connection.

8. He is so self-willed that he can brook no opposition from his colleagues. He was responsible for the death of T'ang Chieh,[1] and so now no one dare resist his will.

9. He allied himself with the treacherous Chang P'i Kuang (張 弼 光), who proposed that your Majesty's brother, Ch'i Wang (頎 王), should be removed from the court. This shows him to be a promoter of schemes for separating the royal family.

10. He is plotting to gain supreme control of the government through the influence of his partisans in the financial and military departments. This is shown particularly in his recent suggestions for the Financial Reorganization of the State.

He has already appointed three of his own party to high office, and sent eight of them into the country on the pretext of devising measures of economy. This will only throw the whole country into turmoil, and prove injurious rather than beneficial. This is already apparent.

Lü Hui then wound up his indictment with a further warning against Wang An Shih's specious persuasiveness. He prophesied that if the Emperor continued to place his trust in such a traitorous scoundrel that all the honest and loyal officials would feel compelled to desert the court, and great confusion would result. He said he had proofs that Wang An Shih possessed no real forethought, but was simply out to introduce changes, and to do things differently from others. In con-

---

[1] (唐 介) T'ang Chieh.

clusion he affirmed that the eloquence and blandness of Wang
An Shih were mere devices to cloak his evil intention.[1]

This indictment, with its ten points, is taken up again in
the chapter on Wang An Shih's character.[2] But it will be well
to indicate at this point the opinion of Liang Ch'i Ch'ao, on
the reason for this outburst. This he finds in the Dynastic
Histories, in the biographical sketch of Lü Hui, as follows :—

" Chang P'i Kuang submitted a memorial to the throne
appealing that the emperor's brother should be transferred from
the court to a principality. This enraged the Emperor's mother,
and caused the Emperor to demand the punishment of the
memorialist, as he had attempted to create divisions within the
royal family. Wang An Shih protested that Chang P'i Kuang
had committed no crime, and in the end he was not punished.
Lü Hui, vexed beyond measure at this failure of his attempt to
incriminate the memorialist, and in hatred of Wang An Shih
for the attitude he had taken up on the question, submitted this
indictment."

On the evidence of the Dynastic Histories, it would appear
quite clear that Lü Hui was actuated by personal motives in
this attack. Liang Ch'i Ch'ao goes into his charges with considerable detail, and makes them appear to be of very trifling
significance.

Evidently the Emperor thought so too, for he ignored the
memorial, which later was returned to Lü Hui. The latter
thereupon resigned his office as Censor, and was transferred to
Teng Chow as prefect.

[1] " T'ung Chien."
[2] See Vol. II of this work.

CHAPTER XII

ECONOMICAL TRANSPORT AND DISTRIBUTION MEASURE PROMULGATED

OPPOSITION GROWING (1069—7TH AND 8TH MONTHS)

THE Financial Reorganization Bureau having been duly established, Wang An Shih was now ready for his first experiment in practical economics. This took the form of a measure designed to save expenses on the transport of grain from the provinces to the capital, and at the same time to ensure that supplies would be more equitably distributed throughout the country. Grain was the common substitute for tax-moneys in those days, and great expense was involved in conveying it from local centres to the capital, where great quantities were required for the military. Other commodities, too, such as silk or cotton, were accepted in lieu of cash for taxation purposes, and the measure applied equally to these.

The measure had other features, the particulars of which will appear as the history and objects of the measure are unfolded below.

The memorial which initiated discussion of the idea was submitted by the Financial Reorganization Bureau,[1] and was drawn up by Wang An Shih himself. It reads as follows:—

"Among the tax regulations of the ancient rulers[2] due regard was paid to the relative distance over which the grains and other tax-goods had to be transported. So that within the area of the royal domain the weight and type of grain

---

[1] Prose Works, vol. 17, pp. 22 and 23.

[2] " Five hundred li constituted the Imperial Domain. From the first hundred li, they brought, as revenue, the whole plant of the grain ; from the second they brought the ears ; from the third they brought only the straw ; but had to perform other services ; from the fourth they gave the grain in the husk ; and from the fifth the grain cleaned." From the Shu Ching, section iii, bk. 1, pt. ii, ch. iv, 18. Legge's translation. This is supposed to relate to the times of the Emperor Yü, i.e. in the twenty-third century B.C.

131

demanded by the officials varied in proportion to every hundred li of radius from the capital.

" From the states external to the royal domain, local products were accepted by way of tribute.

" In addition to this other regulations were extant, which by a system of exchange and transfer of goods from one place to another, aimed at a more equitable and efficient distribution of the country's resources.

" By this method of control and organization of the produce and wealth of the country, dearth of supplies in any one district was obviated and articles injurious to the morale or livelihood of the people were eliminated. Surplus stocks which would have had to be stored unprofitably by the people were bought up by the government officials, to await offers by out-of-season purchasers.

" These various measures were not designed solely with the idea of making profit for the government.

" Financial resources are essential to every organized State, but justice and equity are equally essential to financial administration. That being admitted, it is only right that the relative ease or difficulty of transport should be taken into account in assessing the taxes : that the quantities required should be subject to adjustment in accordance with circumstances : due regard should be paid to the question as to whether the goods called for are found in a particular district or not, and whether they are available at the time, and that authority for fixing quantities, weights, and methods of collection and distribution should be properly determined.

" At present there is constant anxiety about the state of the National Finances. Those who administer them are bigoted in their adherence to the old faulty methods. There is utter lack of co-operation between the capital and the provinces, and no means whereby surplus in one district and dearth in another might be mutually adjusted.

" The amount demanded from the various circuits remains a fixed annual figure. It is impossible under existing regulations to arrange that larger quantities of grain should be procured from a district that reports bumping harvests and convenient transport facilities, or that less than the stipulated amount should be demanded from a district where famine conditions and high prices obtain.

" The expense involved in transporting the grain from distant places amounts to twice or five times as much as the original price, and then when it gets to the capital it has to be sold for half the cost. The officials of the Finance Bureau and the Transport Officers of the different circuits are solely concerned with securing the amount stipulated by the specified date, and every possibility of adjustment according to circumstances is ruled out.

" When war arises, or some great ceremony like the Border Sacrifice is held, involving the country in extraordinary expenditure,[1] officials are sent out to make special levies. This happens, however, almost every year. So that those who are responsible for the collection of the national revenues have to resort to all manner of subterfuge in order to be ready for every emergency. In addition to that, in their anxiety lest they should be unable to meet the requirements of the annual budget, they frequently manipulate matters [2] in such a way that the people are called on to pay double the amount of the regular taxes.

" Then, again, the Court often asks for goods which are not procurable in a particular district, or that are out of season. This gives the wealthy traders and big merchants their opportunity. Taking advantage of the government's demands

---

[1] There were two great State Sacrifices each year, the " Chiao " (郊), or sacrifice to Heaven, which took place at the time of the winter solstice, and the sacrifice to Earth (社), " She," which took place at the Summer Solstice. Great expenditure was involved on these occasions, not only on the necessary preparations, but also on special gifts to the officials.

[2] " Chih i che pien " (支 移 折 變), transfers of taxes collected under one head to another purpose, and other accommodations, which in the end resulted in the people having to pay double, as taxes once diverted could never be recovered, and extra levies had to be imposed to meet the deficiency under the original head.

and the people's extremity, they are able to get the control of the market and prices.

"In view of all these considerations we, your ministers, suggest, as the Transport Officer of the six circuits [1] supervises the land tax, and also the trade taxes from the monopolies in tea, salt, and alum, and as the greater proportion of military and civil expenditure is derived from these sources, that he should be granted a sum as working capital, partly in cash and partly in goods, which will enable him to meet every exigency of supply and demand for the government services. This fund will enable him, as he is conversant with local conditions, to adapt his demands to them, and to exercise his discretion in purchasing and selling according to circumstances.

"He will be able to buy the goods that are required by the government in the cheapest market and as near to the capital or other distributing centre as possible.

"He should therefore be authorized to sell any goods that may be in stock in the granaries or warehouses so as to have in hand a sum that will meet the regular demands of the Court for the current year.

"In this way the control of prices and the collection and distribution of the nation's resources will come more into the hands of the government.[2] Dearth and surplus will be mutually adjusted. Transport will be more economically managed, and much expense and trouble will be saved. This will tend to eliminate burdensome methods of taxation, and the farming class will be proportionately relieved. In these ways it is conceivable that both the government revenue will be adequately

---

[1] These I make out to be Huai-Nan (淮 南), Liang Che (兩 浙), each regarded as one, Chiang-Nan-Tung (江 南 東), or S.E. Chiang, Chiang-Nan-Hsi (江 南 西), or S.W. Chiang, Ching-Hu-Pei (荆 湖 北), and Ching-Hu-Nan (荆 湖 南). These were the great grain-producing areas.

[2] The big merchants had been getting rich out of the difficulties of the people in meeting the court demands, as they had been manipulating the purchase and sale of stocks themselves. This had given them considerable influence and control of the market and prices as well. Wang An Shih now proposed that this control should be transferred, at least in part, to the Government.

provided for and the resources and livelihood of the people suffer no serious injury."

This proposal was accepted by the Emperor, and in the 7th month of 1069 issued in the form of an Imperial mandate.[1] Hsieh Hsiang (薛 向) was appointed to supervise the carrying out of the measure, in his capacity as Chief Transport Officer of the six circuits, which were known as the Chiang (江), Che (浙), Ching (荆), Huai (淮) area. Hsieh Hsiang's appointment to that area in the 4th month of this year had caused considerable commotion at Court.[2]   Charges of corruption in connection with his previous post in the Salt Administration had been brought against him, but Wang An Shih had supported the appointment against spirited opposition on the part of Fan Ch'un Jen (范 純 仁), Ch'ien Kung Fu (錢 公 輔), and the current holder of the position, Chang Ching (張 靖).

Hsieh Hsiang was granted a loan of 5,000,000 " strings " [3] from the Imperial Treasury with which to initiate the scheme, which was styled the " Equitable Transport and Distribution Measure ".[4] In return for this loan he was to guarantee delivery to the Court of 3,000,000 bushels of grain annually.

The mandate also authorized him to nominate his own assistants for the work, which he proceeded to do in the persons of Liu Ch'en (劉 忱), Wei Ch'i (衛 琪), Sun Kuei (孫 珪), Chang Mu Chih (張 穆 之), and Ch'en Chien (陳 倩).[5]

Critical memorials poured into the Court during the next month. Some directed their criticisms against the personal

---

[1] " T'ung Chien," where the heading in large type reads " Hsing Chun Shu Fa " (行 均 輸 法), indicating that it must have been carried into effect. The later statement in the Dynastic History (然 均 輸 後 迄 不 能 成) that it was not carried out must be interpreted to mean that it was withdrawn after some period of experiment. But see below.

[2] See " T'ung Chien " under 4th month of 1069.

[3] A " string " is 1,000 copper or other metal coins. These coins were connected by a string passed through a hole in the centre. One thousand of these was the common unit of currency.

[4] " Chun Shu P'ing Chun Fa " (均 輸 平 準).

[5] Dynastic Histories, Sung Shih, Shih Huo Chih (食 貨 志).

character of Hsieh Hsiang, but all were levelled at the new measure in particular and Wang An Shih's policy in proposing it in general. These memorialists included such influential names as Liu Ch'i (劉 琦), Ch'ien K'ai (錢 顗), Li Ch'ang (李 常), Fan Ch'un Jen (范 純 仁), and Su Che (蘇 轍).

Su Che submitted two memorials,[1] the gist of which is given below, viz. :—

" In the times of Han Wu Ti (140–87 B.C.) frontier wars were incessantly waged, and very great expenditure was incurred upon the building of the palaces. In consequence of this the State finances got into a seriously straitened condition. The merchant Sang Hung Yang then submitted a proposal that the Government should take over the purchase and sale of grain in order to relieve the financial stringency. His idea was that grain should be bought up in large quantities when cheap and plentiful, and sold out again when scarcity occurred and high prices ruled. This proposal was adopted and styled the ' Equitable Price Measure ' (平 準 法).

" Although it is usually thought that this involved no increase of taxation, and that at the same time the State revenue was adequate for all purposes, nevertheless, it cannot be considered to have been a good thing. . . .

" The officials who administered the measure were corrupt : exactions increased as time went on, and in the end serious injury was done to the livelihood of the people. So that when Han Chao Ti (漢 昭 帝) succeeded to the throne (86–73 B.C.), the scholars roused themselves to oppose the measure and succeeded in getting it rescinded. Only then were the people pacified.

---

[1] Dynastic Histories, Sung Shih, Shih Huo Chih (食 貨 志). There seems some uncertainty as to whether both these memorials were by Su Che (蘇 轍) or not. There is general agreement about the first section ending with the words " a good thing " as in the text. With regard to what follows there are some records, viz. the Dynastic Histories and the " T'ung Chien Chi Lan " (通 鑑 輯 覽), which say it was by Su Shih (蘇 軾). The " T'ung Chien " says it was by Su Che.

" Now, however, the same idea has been revived. The great majority are against it, the general opinion being that the new measure will be still more detrimental to the people than that of the Han times. For one thing it is said that the officials who have been selected for the business are not the equals of Sang Hung Yang for ability and knowledge, and that their method of operation is inferior to his.

" Yet the Court has broken through the well-established tradition, and given them a free hand to prosecute their profit-seeking policy. Serious injury is bound to result. . . .

" Great initial and regular expenditure will be involved in the employment of this horde of officials with their account books, etc. In the purchase of the grain the usual malpractices will be in evidence, haggling over the quality, and demanding bribes, so that in the end the prices paid by the government will be in excess of those current amongst the people. And in the matter of sales the same defects will be in evidence. The money which the government has put into the business will never be recovered. Even should some profit accrue from the operation of the measure, it will mean less revenue for the State than would be gained by taxing the merchants in the usual way."

Fan Ch'un Jen, who held important office in the Censorate, also vigorously denounced the measure and attacked the character of Hsieh Hsiang. He then proceeded to warn the Emperor against Wang An Shih's schemes for enriching the State and strengthening the military arm. He asserted that in his love of fame he had forgotten his principles. He had dubbed the old and loyal servants of the throne " Conventionalists " and " Time-servers ". Any who differed from his point of view he characterized as " Useless ", while those who took his side he termed " Worthy gentlemen ". Already he had gained great influence over large numbers at Court, and even the Emperor himself was giving him encouragement. If this was allowed to continue there was no knowing to what lengths he would go.

He then appealed that those officials who had been dismissed or transferred for opposition to Wang An Shih's policy should be recalled and reinstated, and as a final thrust demanded the resignation of Wang An Shih himself.[1]

His appeal went unheeded, so he resigned. The Emperor refused to accept this resignation, and offered him the Principalship of the National University, which he again refused. After consultation with the Emperor, Wang An Shih suggested that Fan Ch'un Jen might be appointed to the Edicts Office. This he indignantly refused, saying : " This is an attempt to seduce me by an offer of personal advantage. Unless the Emperor avails himself of my advice even the highest paid post in the government service would make no appeal to me." [1]

Whereupon he sent in the memorial a second time. This annoyed Wang An Shih so much that he demanded severe punishment for Fan Ch'un Jen. However, the Emperor suggested more considerate treatment, and so he was appointed to Ch'eng Tu (成 都) as Transport Officer. After arrival at his new post his opposition to the measure in no way decreased. He even went so far as to forbid the local officials in his circuit to carry it out.

Such conduct naturally aroused the wrath of Wang An Shih, who got Fan transferred to a less important post.[1]

Other opposition even more serious was aroused at this time on account of Wang An Shih's attitude to the Teng Chow Fu case, noted above.[2]

Liu Su (劉 述), of the Board of Punishments, and the Censors Liu Ch'i and Ch'ien K'ai, charged him with malicious interference with the course of justice and of trespassing on the authority of the properly constituted Financial officials. They urged further that he had lightly altered the long-established laws on his own initiative, and appealed that he should forthwith be dismissed from office to placate the people.

In addition they called for the dismissal of Tseng Kung Liang (曾 公 亮) and Chao Pien (趙 抃), who were An Shih's servile adherents.

---

[1] " T'ung Chien " under 8th month, 1069.
[2] See Chapter XI.

The upshot of all this was that the three memorialists were transferred to provincial appointments. The Historian relates that Wang An Shih demanded that Liu Su be imprisoned, but that in the end more generous counsels prevailed.[1]

Three other officials suffered degradation in rank and transfer of position on account of their opposition to Wang An Shih at this time. These were Ting Feng (丁 諷) of the Board of Punishments, Wang Shih Yuan (王 師 元) of the Courts of Justice, and Sun Ch'ang Ling (孫 昌 齡) of the Censorate.

What was still more important was the defection of Su Che, who hitherto had associated himself with the Reform Party and had held actual appointment as Secretary of the Financial Reorganization Bureau. Having sent in the memorials noted above, and evidently finding himself out of sympathy with his colleagues, especially Lü Hui Ch'ing, he publicly attacked Wang An Shih's policy as impracticable.

The History [1] notes that An Shih demanded that he be severely dealt with, but that owing to the intervention of Ch'en Sheng Chih he was transferred to Honanfu (河 南 府) as Judge.

The above extracts from the Histories will convey to the reader some idea of the nature and extent of the opposition to Wang An Shih and his policy at this time.

The final word of the Historian on the " Economical Transport Measure " is that in the end it was not actually put into effect.[2] No reasons are given. It may be that the opposition was so strong that after a time it was withdrawn. But the more probable explanation is that it was supplanted by a later proposal, styled " Trade and Barter Measure ",[3] which incorporated all the essential features of its forerunner.

Three things should be noted in winding up this chapter. The first is that the idea of this first attempt at practical

---

[1] " T'ung Chien " under 8th month, 1069.

[2] Dynastic Histories, where we have the words 然 均 輸 後 迄 不 能 成.

[3] i.e. the " Shih I Fa " (市 易 法), see later chapter.

economics was in itself very good. The difficulties of transport in those days were, of course, enormous. The expenses of transporting the tax-grain from distant places to the capital were one of the most serious questions connected with the budget. The making of the Grand Canal [1] was with a view to facilitating the transport of this tax-grain and other goods. If a large proportion of these transport charges could be saved by giving the transport officials liberty to sell grain in distant places and buy it from a place much nearer the capital with the proceeds, if, again, they had liberty to purchase when cheap and sell out when dear, and had freedom to arrange exchanges of goods at their discretion, the measure must have been profitable to the Government.

The people, too, should have benefited by it. The work of transport would be lightened, and their own contribution to the public services correspondingly decreased. The balancing up of supplies at which the measure aimed would also work beneficially for them, and the provision for times of dearth which the regulations included must have been welcome.

The second thing to note is the emphasis which opponents of the scheme lay upon the character of the officials operating it. Here rather than in the character of the measure itself must we look for the difficulty of carrying it into beneficial effect.

---

[1] The Grand Canal now joins Hangchow (杭 州) with Tientsin (天 津). The work was commenced in the time of Fu Ch'ai (夫 差), King of Wu (吳), 494–472 B.C., who carried it from Hang Chow into Chiang Su. It was extended during the times of the Sui (隋), T'ang (唐), and Northern Sung (宋) dynasties. The most memorable contribution was made by Sui Yang Ti (隋 煬 帝), 605–617 A.D., who during his reign completed 5,000 miles of canals. The Grand Canal was extended to Lo Yang (洛 陽), which was his capital, or, at least, connected with the Yellow River so that direct transport was possible between the Yang Tzu River (揚 子 江) and Lo Yang. In the Mongol Dynasty the capital was located at Peking, and so the Canal was connected with the Pei River (北 河) to T'ung Chow (通 州), a few miles out of Peking. In the Northern Sung Dynasty the capital was K'ai Feng Fu, which is situated on the Yellow River, and so would be in direct connection via the Grand Canal with the great grain-producing areas. (See Boulger, " A Short History of China," p. 26.)

Su Che laid his finger upon the right spot when he said that the usual malpractices and defects of administration would be in evidence in the operation of this as of previous measures of its kind. The character of Hsieh Hsiang was evidently under suspicion,[1] as a good deal of the criticism connected with this particular measure was levelled at him. But that was not the only difficulty. The matter would be in the hands of local officials chiefly, and with these the traditional practice of " squeeze " and " bribery " would account for a full share of the spoils. In this as in all the other measures which Wang An Shih instituted, this difficulty was practically insurmountable, and accounts in large degree for the lack of success attending them. But of that more anon.

The third point to note is that this measure was not in itself an innovation, but was a revival of the more ancient measures. The " Ch'uan Fu " of the Chow Dynasty, and the " P'ing Chun Fa " of Sang Hung Yang in the Han Dynasty, also the different measures of Liu Yen in the T'ang Dynasty, were all its true antecedents.[2] It was one of Wang An Shih's favourite sayings that he was a follower of the ancient precedents, not in detail, but in idea. In this sense he is to be considered a true disciple of his master, Confucius, who said of himself : " I am a transmitter and not an originator." [3]

---

[1] Liang Ch'i Ch'ao, pp. 299, 300, asserts that Hsieh Hsiang was an honest and very able official. He had been recommended by Wang An Shih as long ago as 1060 for a post in connection with the procuration and breeding of horses for the Government services, and now he recommended him for the onerous post of Transport Officer for the chief grain-producing area of the empire. Later on he was again recommended as Minister of Finance, and in this, as in his other appointments, accomplished many reforms. He was the equivalent of Liu Yen, according to Liang Ch'i Ch'ao, and is given great praise by the Sung historians. But what occasions him great surprise is the fact that Wang An Shih's patronage and employment of such a worthy and capable official is not mentioned in these Histories.

[2] See Chapter XI and notes in Vol. II of this work.

[3] Confucian Analects, book vii, ch. i. " Shu erh pu tso " (述 而 不 作), translated by Legge " A transmitter and not a maker ".

Chapter XIII

PROMULGATION OF THE AGRICULTURAL LOANS MEASURE

Opposition Grows in Strength : Many Important Personages Resign : Wang An Shih Supreme (9th Month, 1069—12th Month, 1070)

At least 80 per cent of the Chinese are engaged in agriculture, and are dependent upon good harvests for their livelihood. Granted the prevalence of normal conditions, the farmers have sufficient for their regular needs, and after a succession of good years usually have a surplus, which enables them to meet extraordinary expenditure such as is entailed by weddings, funerals, and other occasions of a ceremonial character.

Very frequently, however, it is the " abnormal " which confronts them. Drought, flood, locusts, and other field pests, the exigencies of the political or military situation, all these either singly or in combination reduce the farming class to financial extremity, and they are reduced to the necessity of borrowing.

Borrowing is one of the greatest evils of the Chinese social life. One is amazed at the high rates of interest which are charged by the ordinary moneylender, 25 per cent per annum being considered quite normal. Students borrow for their education, parents borrow for the wedding expenses of their children, children borrow for the funeral expenses of their parents, and all these loans are contracted at such high rates of interest that frequently they spend the rest of their lives trying to get free of debt. It often happens that people pay half their annual earnings in interest to the moneylender.

In the times of the Sung Dynasty the farming class were dependent upon the moneylenders and powerful families for these necessary loans, and it was with the main object of relieving the agriculturists of the intolerable burden of the usury which they exacted that the Agricultural Loans Measure was framed.

Briefly put, the scheme comprised the conversion of the stores of grain in the Government granaries into a capital fund, which was to be available for distribution to the people at the rate of 2 per cent per mensem, or 24 per cent per annum. These loans were to be distributed in the spring and repaid in the summer or autumn. The rate of interest charged, as we have already suggested, seems enormous to the Westerner, but it was a very much lower rate than was being charged by the plutocrats, against whose pernicious activities the measure was also directed.

In setting up this particular measure Wang An Shih and his colleagues in the Financial Reorganization Bureau professed to be following ancient practices. In essence the scheme dates back to the times of the Chow dynasty, if the Chow Li (周 禮), the book on which Wang An Shih based most of his reforms, is to be attributed to that time. Anyway, it would seem that it is not later than the times of the Usurper, Wang Mang, 46 B.C.–A.D. 23.[1] The impression that was current in those days would seem to be that it really represented the system that was in vogue in the times of the great Duke of Chow, and for the purposes of this study we will let that assumption remain.

Su Che (蘇 轍) makes this clear in the following memorial [2] submitted to the throne, viz. :—

" Loans are essential to the farmer and the merchant. To prohibit the contracting of loans by these classes would be to drive the people to starvation. If moneylending is to remain a monopoly of the wealthy classes, inhumane practices will inevitably arise. They will exact more than 50 per cent of the loan in interest. Property and even clothing will have to be sacrificed to make the repayments. Great distress is thereby inflicted upon the people, and no advantage accrues to the government.

[1] See vol. lix, *Journal of North China Branch of R.A.S.* Article by Hu Shih on Wang Mang. Also Appendices, pp. xix–xxi.
[2] Liang Ch'i Ch'ao, p. 199.

" In the times of the Chow Dynasty [1] it was possible for the people to negotiate a loan from the officials on terms that were considerate for both parties.   In my opinion every district should be permitted to institute a government loan system, but the privilege of contracting loans should be confined to residents of repute."

Historical instances of the carrying out of similar measures occur in the case of Duke Ching of the Ch'i State (齊景公), 546–488 B.C., the minister Tzu P'i of the Cheng State (鄭子庋), and also by a city official, Tzu Han, of the Sung State (宋司城子罕).[2]   Although definite dates are lacking for the last two, their measures must have been operative prior to 222 B.C., when the empire was united under the first emperor of Ch'in (秦始皇帝).   Under the regime of Wang Mang loans for purposes of funerals, burials, or sacrificial purposes could be contracted without interest, but repayment was demanded after very short intervals, extending at the most to three months.   Other loans required for working capital were also provided for at what was termed a " moderate rate of interest ".   There is some uncertainty as to what these rates were.   According to one book of the " Han Shu ", the rate was 3 per cent per month, but according to another it was " not to exceed an annual interest of 10 per cent per annum ".[3]

In Wang An Shih's day the Transport Officer of the Shensi Circuit (陝西), Li Ts'an (李參) by name, had made a practical and profitable experiment with a measure of this kind.   He devised it primarily with the object of gaining a sufficiency of grain for the military located in his area.   He issued an order to the people that they should make an estimate of the amount of grain they would need for their own use in the current year, and to report on the quantity which might be reckoned as " surplus ".   With a view to ensuring that this " surplus " grain should be at the disposal of the officials, he

---

[1] Referring probably to the " Ch'uan Fu Chih Kuan " (泉府之官). See Chap. X, p. 118.

[2] Liang Ch'i Ch'ao, p. 188.

[3] See article on Wang Mang as above, p. 228.   Also notes in Vol. II of this work.

would advance to the farmers an amount of money which would be equivalent to the value of the grain. When the grain was reaped the farmer would repay the loan (in grain) with a certain percentage extra by way of interest. This loan system was called " Ch'ing Miao money " (青 苗 錢), or " Green Sprout money ", because the loans were disbursed in the spring when the wheat was just sprouting. After several years of experiment with this system, the government granaries had a surplus stock of grain for future emergencies.

As the measure which Wang An Shih devised was based on this, and more ancient precedents, he adopted the name of the Shensi measure and called it the " Green Sprout Measure ", which we have translated " Agricultural Loans Measure ", as that gives a better idea of its real character.

A capital fund was essential to the inauguration of the scheme. We have already discoursed on the depleted state of the National Exchequer in those days, so it was useless to expect help from that quarter. There were, however, in all the districts, considerable stocks of grain stored away in the government granaries. Of these there were two kinds, one known as the " Ch'ang P'ing Ts'ang " (常 平 倉) or " Emergency Granary ",[1] and the other as " Kuang Hui Ts'ang " (廣 惠 倉), or " Charity Granary ". In the former, surplus stocks of grain were kept by the government in readiness to be sold out to the people in times of dearth, at fixed government prices. In the latter was stored the grain that was reaped from ownerless land which had been appropriated by the government, and which was distributed in famine times for relief purposes.

Wang An Shih proposed that the stocks in the emergency granary should be used to form the capital fund wherewith to start the new system. Ssu Ma Kuang opposed the conversion of these stocks for this purpose. It would appear, however, from the document in which the Financial Reorganization Bureau appealed for the promulgation of this measure that these granaries were not serving the purpose for which they were

---

[1] T'ung Chien, Hsi Ning, 2nd year, 9th month.

originally intended, and that the people were getting little or no benefit from them.

This document was as follows [1] :—

"The stocks in the Government Granaries in all the districts amount to the value of 15,000,000 'strings'. The Granary Laws hitherto obtaining are being very badly administered, so that the possible advantages of the old system are not being realized. We propose that the present standards of measure be retained, that suitable arrangements be made for selling the grain when the market is high at slightly cheaper prices than those ruling outside, and that when grain is plentiful and cheap it should be purchased at a price slightly in excess of the market rate. We also suggest that the transport officers should be given liberty to demand either money or grain for the land tax according to the convenience of the people, and to exchange or dispose of stocks at will, but in all cases the grain should be valued at current rates.

"Further, that after the fashion of the 'Ch'ing Miao Regulations' as operating in Shensi, the people shall be permitted to contract loans either of money or grain, to be repaid at stipulated times, in summer and autumn, with interest at the rate of 2 per cent per mensem. The borrower should be free to repay either in money or grain. In cases where distress has been encountered through floods or drought, the repayment of the loan might be deferred to the next harvest. In this way not only would ample provision be made against drought, but the plutocrats would be prevented from exacting double the normal rates of interest in the intervals between the exhaustion of old stocks and the new harvest.

"Under the existing Granary Regulations it has been the practice to keep in stock the grain collected at harvest season until a time of shortage and high prices comes round, when the grain would be sold out. But those who could take advantage of this were very few, being practically confined to the leisured folk of the city and environs.

[1] T'ung Chien, Hsi Ning, 2nd year, 9th month.

" The aim of the present proposal is to ensure that an adequate stock be kept in all districts, to sell when grain is dear and to buy when it is cheap. By regulating the market prices (by our own) we hope to make it possible for the farmer to get on with his work at the proper season. The plutocrats will no longer be able to take advantage of the people's extremity. This is a measure in the interests of the people, the government deriving no financial advantage therefrom. It is also in line with the ideas of the ancient rulers, who did their utmost to introduce advantageous arrangements for agriculturists.

" We appeal that a number of officials be sent out to supervise the working of this measure in accordance with the needs of each particular district, and that each sub-prefecture appoint an assistant-inspector. These should be responsible for the collection, transport, and distribution services.

" We propose that a beginning be made in the Circuits of Ho Pei (河 北), Ching Tung (京 東), and Huai Nan (淮 南), and that later on, when the measure shall have assumed workable shape, it should be extended to all districts.

" Finally we suggest that the grain in the ' Charity Granary ' (廣 惠 倉), after the needs of the aged and poor have been met, should be administered on the same lines as the stocks of the ' Emergency Granary '."

Such was the scheme, but before it became law considerable discussion took place and serious opposition was aroused. As soon as Wang An Shih and Lü Hui Ch'ing had definitely decided to introduce the measure they made known the details to Su Che and others, asking for their unreserved criticisms.

In the course of the discussion Su Che said ; " Your idea of making loans to the people with a view to their relief is quite right, and the proposition as such is a good one. But the difficulty lies in the character of the officials who are to supervise the disbursement and collection of the loans. They are sure to act arbitrarily and nothing which you can devise in the way of preventive measures will be effective. Even the respectable folk will take advantage of the system, the rich delaying repayment as long as ever they can. Extra punishments will have

to be devised and inflicted and the work of the local officials
will be increased.   Liu Yen (劉 晏) did not use this method
of making loans, so why not just revive his ideas ? " [1]   (i.e.
use the Emergency Granary Laws without any loan system
attached.)

Wang An Shih replied : " That is quite a reasonable view
of the thing. I will think more about it."

" So," says the Dynastic History,[2] " for over a month Wang
An Shih made no reference to the Agricultural Loans Measure."

But the Transport Officer of the Ching Tung Circuit, Wang
Kuang Yuan (王 廣 淵), reported that the poor farmers in
his Circuit were unable to begin their farming work that spring
and that the moneylenders were taking advantage of their
extremity to exploit the people.   He therefore appealed that
a grant of grain to the value of 500,000 " strings ", or the cash
equivalent, should be allocated to his Circuit, that he might
make loans to those in distress.   He thought that if this were
granted he could raise interest to the amount of 250,000
" strings " (50 per cent per annum).   This idea appealed to the
Emperor, and as the proposal was in line with Wang An Shih's
new measure, he began once more to give his attention to it,
and to regard it as a practicable proposition.   Wang Kuang
Yuan was called to the capital for a special interview on the
subject, and it was eventually decided to promulgate the measure
by Imperial decree.   A sum of a million " strings " was released
from the Imperial Treasury to purchase grain for the Ho Pei
Circuit.

This was in the ninth month of 1069, and in accordance
with Wang An Shih's original suggestion a beginning was made
with the three circuits of Ho Pei, Ching Tung, and Huai Nan.[2]

For the next two months the Court resounded with noisome
controversy, the lead of the opposition being taken by Ssu
Ma Kuang.

---

[1] Evidently a loan system had been connected with the operation of the
Granary Laws, though possibly only in the form of grain. This appears from
Wang An Shih's letter to Tseng Kung Li (below).
[2] T'ung Chien, Hsi Ning, 2nd year, 9th month.

He first of all directed his shafts against Lü Hui Ch'ing, who was Wang An Shih's most active associate at this time. The question of his appointment as tutor to the heir apparent and as " Imperial Expositor " having been mooted by Wang An Shih, Ssu Ma Kuang took the opportunity of asserting that Lü Hui Ch'ing was a very clever man, but a thoroughly deceitful and evil-minded person.   He averred that Wang An Shih, who was himself of good character, albeit self-opiniated and obstinate, and unacquainted with practical matters, was suffering in reputation through his association with a man of this type. He contended that Lü Hui Ch'ing was the mind behind the new measures, and that Wang An Shih was merely helping to carry out Lü Hui Ch'ing's ideas.

He also felt it incumbent upon him to warn the Emperor that very great dissatisfaction was being expressed by the great officers at the way in which so many had been promoted recently without regard to the usual procedure, and that this discontent was spreading amongst the people generally.

The Emperor took up the cudgels in Lü Hui Ch'ing's behalf, saying that he had been quite struck with his intelligence in the Imperial Council, and that he had been impressed with his many other excellent qualities.

Ssu Ma Kuang demurred to this, saying that although he possessed outstanding literary and oratorical abilities, he was of a perverse disposition.   There had been very able ministers of former dynasties, such as Chiang Ts'ung (江 充) of Han (漢) and Li Shun (李 訓) of T'ang (唐), but their influence had been exercised to the detriment of the ruler's reputation and the distress of the people.

" To this the Emperor kept silent." [1]

Ssu Ma Kuang continued the fight with Lü Hui Ch'ing himself in the presence of the Emperor, both waxing hot over the question of the reform of the laws and regulations, the latter maintaining that changes should be introduced only when absolutely no alternative was possible, the former contending

[1] T'ung Chien, Hsi Ning, 2nd year, 9th month.

that under the old regime regular periods were observed for reconsideration of the laws and the opportunity afforded for making the desired changes. The implication of Ssu Ma Kuang's remarks was that Lü Hui Ch'ing and his associates were altogether too radical, and that the changes they were suggesting and making were quite uncalled for.

Ssu Ma Kuang further complained that in the setting up of the Financial Reorganization Bureau they had infringed upon the legitimate authority of the Board of Finance, and asserted that it was the duty of high ministers of state to guide the Emperor in moral principles, and not by financial proposals such as the new bureau was making.

This incited Lü Hui Ch'ing to make a vehement reply, and a very serious situation was averted only by the personal intervention of the Emperor, who earnestly exhorted the two contestants to confine themselves to the discussion of principles and leave personalities alone.[1]

Then Ssu Ma Kuang turned his attention to the Agricultural Loans Measure. He admitted that the poorer people might be ready enough to borrow the money, but ventured to raise the question as to their readiness to repay.

He quoted an instance from the times of T'ai Tsung (太 宗), when in the Ho Tung Circuit the practice of government-purchase and sale of grain was instituted to pacify the distressed people. The prices offered by the officials were very favourable at the outset, and so the people were happy enough to do business with them. But later on, when market prices rose the official prices remained the same, and as the people were compelled to sell to the officials at the old rates the measure became a constant source of trouble in the area. He was afraid that in the case of the Agricultural Loans Measure something of the sort would be in evidence.

He reminded his opponent that not only did the government refrain from exercising compulsion in this matter, even the wealthy moneylenders likewise refrained from so doing.

---

[1] T'ung Chien, Hsi Ning, 2nd year, 9th month.

By way of reply the Emperor called his attention to the fact that this type of measure had been operative in Shensi for quite a long time, and that there had been no complaints from the people about it. To this Ssu Ma Kuang retorted : " I am a Shensi man, and all I have heard and seen of this particular measure is decidedly bad. Although this measure was inaugurated at first without the government approval, the local officials could operate it in a manner definitely deleterious to the people's livelihood, how much worse would conditions be once the measure gets government backing ? "

When the Emperor reminded Ssu Ma Kuang that the clamour and opposition of the people arose from their custom of resisting every measure of the government, he said that the whole matter ought to be looked into, and that after all the affairs of the Financial Reorganization Bureau were the concern of three men only, Wang An Shih, Han Chiang, and Lü Hui Ch'ing. He was astonished that the Emperor should imagine that he could conduct the affairs of the country in sole consultation with these.[1]

In the tenth month the Grand Councillor, Fu Pi (富 弼), resigned on the ground that he could not stand the way in which Wang An Shih was carrying on. He had sought to resign on several occasions, ostensibly on the pretext of illness, but really because he had been unable to hold his own with that persistent and mischievous agitator.

The Emperor expressed his concern at the prospect of losing the services of so old a servant of the dynasty, and sought his opinion as to who might take his place. On Fu Pi's suggesting that Wen Yen Po would do very well, the Emperor made no remark for a while, and then asked if Wang An Shih would be suitable. Fu Pi expressed no opinion either one way or the other.

His resignation was eventually accepted and he was transferred to Po Chow (博 州).[2]

Ch'en Sheng Chih (陳 升 之), who thus far had been

---

[1] T'ung Chien, Hsi Ning, 2nd year, 9th month.
[2] T'ung Chien, Hsi Ning, 2nd year, 10th month.

associated with Wang An Shih in the affairs of the Financial
Reorganization Bureau, was promoted to the Grand Council
in Fu Pi's place. After the appointment had been made, the
Emperor, being somewhat apprehensive as to the impression
it might have made upon the Court, sought Ssu Ma Kuang's
opinion on the question. The latter replied :—

"Men from Min (閩) are crafty and dangerous, while men of
Ch'u (楚) are too casual and lack a sense of responsibility.
The present Grand Councillors (Tseng Kung Liang (曾 公 亮)
and Ch'en Sheng Chih) are from Min, and the two vice-Grand
Councillors (Wang An Shih and Han Chiang) are from Ch'u.
They are bound to fill the Court with their fellow provincials
and those of their own faction, in which case how can you expect
public life to be characterized by purity and nobility ? "

"But," replied the Emperor, "Ch'en Sheng Chih appears
to me to be a man of outstanding ability and intellect, and well
versed in government administration."

"He lacks strength of character," retorted Ssu Ma Kuang,
"and would be quite useless in a great emergency. Every man,
no matter how able and intelligent he may be, needs the help
of loyal and straightforward associates. Only then will he be
kept on the right lines. A wise ruler should see to this in the
selection of his high officials."

"Then," continued the Emperor, "what would you say
to Wang An Shih (for his associate) ? " [1]

"Some people say he is a schemer and an evil-minded man,"
replied Ssu Ma Kuang, "but in my opinion that is going much
too far. But I must repeat that he is not practically minded,
and that he is altogether too self-willed."

After Ch'en Sheng Chih had been promoted to the Grand
Council, he began to play for his own hand to the detriment
of his old colleague, although the history notes that Wang An
Shih had pressed for his promotion in order to get still further
help for his projects. Gradually, however, Ch'en Sheng Chih
conveyed the impression that he had not been of one mind with

---

[1] T'ung Chien, Hsi Ning, 2nd year, 10th month.

Wang An Shih for some time. In particular he urged upon the Emperor the undesirability of a Grand Councillor being in special charge of a Bureau like that established for financial reorganization, and suggested that the present was a convenient opportunity to dissolve it.[1]

Wang An Shih, quoting the ancient precedent of ministers of State having particular charge of a department like education, war, works, justice, etc., urged that it was not unreasonable for a Grand Councillor to have charge of the Financial Reorganization Bureau.

Ch'en Sheng Chih was, however, obdurate, saying that if a Grand Councillor was put in charge of a Bureau for reorganizing everything in connection with the government, the idea was reasonable enough, but for an official of such high standing to be in charge of a special Bureau of that type was out of the question.[1]

Wang An Shih held on with his usual pertinacity, arguing that every item of expenditure above a hundred " cash " which the Chief Legislative Assembly wished to approve, or any instance of promotion to the Board of Finance which they wished to recommend, had to be submitted to the Grand Council in the form of a memorial before anything could actually be done. (This, in effect, provided Ch'en Sheng Chih would hold on, would make the Financial Reorganization Bureau the supreme and final authority in all matters of finance.) So it would be in no sense derogatory to the dignity of a Grand Councillor to continue as Head of the same.

Ch'en Sheng Chih remained unconvinced and resigned his co-directorship of the Bureau. He was succeeded by Han Chiang (韓 絳), whom the History notes as one who supported each and every proposal of Wang An Shih which came to the Emperor for approval. This appointment was made in the eleventh month of 1069.[1]

Further progress in connection with the prosecution of the Agricultural Loans measure was now reported. The experiment

[1] T'ung Chien, Hsi Ning, 2nd year, 11th month.

in the three Circuits was reported by the Financial Reorganization Bureau to have been successful, and that it had met with the approval of the people, of whom large numbers had expressed themselves as desirous of taking up the loans. They therefore appealed that the Transport Officers of all Circuits should be ordered to inaugurate the measure, and that three special officials should be appointed in each Circuit to supervise the working of it, in addition to being responsible for any other schemes which the Bureau had under consideration.

So in the eleventh month of 1069 the mandate was promulgated, appointing forty-one officials for this purpose.

This brought Ssu Ma Kuang once more into the field. He wrote a long letter [1] of 3,300 words to the Financial Reorganization Bureau, quoting many classical allusions, and criticizing in severest terms the defective and dangerous character of the Agricultural Loans Measure. This was answered by Wang An Shih himself in the following fashion [2] :—

"I acknowledge receipt of your favour. It is obvious that although we have been able to maintain friendly relations over a considerable period, we cannot reach a common mind on matters of public import, due doubtless to our different ways of viewing such things.

"It would be preferable to give you a lengthy and detailed reply, but I fear that such might not receive your proper attention. Although I am conscious that this brief reply may seem to you to be lacking in courtesy, yet as it deals with the main points raised in your letter sufficiently well, in my opinion, I hope the apparent brusqueness may be overlooked.

"One of the great aims of the Confucian scholar is to ensure that whatever statement he makes shall be representative of the actual facts. If that can be attained, then nothing else matters.

"I gather that you think I have trespassed upon the authority of other officials, that I am out to make trouble, that my sole

---

[1] Ts'ai Shang Hsiang, vol. xvi, p. 6, questions whether this document is entirely from the pen of Ssu Ma Kuang, suggesting that possibly additions by other hands have been incorporated.
[2] Works, vol. xviii, p. 8.

concern is to make revenue for the government, that I resent criticism, and that I have incurred the resentment of the whole empire in consequence.

"On the contrary I think I have done nothing but what the Emperor has commanded me to do, that all of my proposals for the revision of the existing regulations have been discussed in the open forum of the Court before being proceeded with, and that the actual execution of such measures of a new character as have been approved has been delegated to the proper authorities. That cannot surely be interpreted as an infringement upon the authority of others.

"I also consider that I have adopted the government method of the ancient rulers with the one object of relieving the people of their economic distresses and the eradication of certain great public evils. Such surely cannot be interpreted as the act of a trouble maker.

"My proposals for financial reform are in the interests of the empire as a whole (not only in the interests of the government but also of the people). That surely cannot be termed the policy of a 'tax-gatherer' actuated by considerations of financial gain alone.

"I regard myself as an exposer of fallacious arguments and the foe of specious talkers. But that is not being 'resentful of criticism'.

"And as regards the fact that critics and slanderers are numerous, I knew long ago that this was bound to come.

"The governing class has been addicted to a policy of *laissez-faire* too long. The great scholars and officials for the most part do not give much thought to matters of state, regarding the *status quo* and the good opinion of the majority as the *summum bonum*. But the Emperor is desirous of altering all this, and as for myself I am determined to render him any assistance in my power regardless of the number of my enemies.

"The case being such, noisome opposition and disturbances are only to be expected. When P'an Keng (盤 庚) decided to remove the capital,[1] not only the officials, but the general

---

[1] Shu Ching, Legge's edition, part iv, book vii, pt. i, 1.

populace as well, resisted the idea. But P'an Keng did not on that account desist from his purpose. He felt that his decision had been made after full consideration of all the circumstances, and that there was no reason for altering it.

"I will admit that if you mean that during my term of office I have been unable to carry through any project of great benefit to the people that your criticism is just. But I cannot admit the cogency of your contention that a policy of quiescence and conservatism is what the country needs to-day.

"With my regrets that I cannot see you personally, and assuring you of my sincere regard, I remain. . ."

This letter speaks for itself, and the main points of Ssu Ma Kuang's criticism stand out from the reply.

Several months elapsed before the measure was put into force, and then only in three Circuits. It was only after the experiment had been pronounced successful in this limited sphere that it was applied to the whole country. Full opportunity for discussion had been afforded at Court, and Su Che had been given special opportunity to express his views upon it.

There is strong reason for suspecting the prejudiced character of the canonical histories, but they cannot wholly be discounted, so we will now give extracts of the more important incidents and criticisms concerned with the progress of this measure as given by them.[1]

"After the forty-one officials had been appointed to supervise the carrying out of the measure throughout the country, they made it their first object to get the people to take as much money as possible in the way of loans, so that they might please Wang An Shih and get 'kudos' for their zeal. The poor were quite keen to take the loans, but the richer classes were quite unwilling to do so. So the officials compelled all classes to take the loans proportionately to their tax classification, and with a view to making this effective they caused local committees of ten to be formed from the rich and poor alike.[1]

"Wang Kuang Yuan, Transport Officer for the Ching Tung

---

[1] T'ung Chien, Hsi Ning, 2nd year, 11th month, etc.

Circuit, compelled first-class residents [1] to take fifteen ' strings ', and proportionately in descending order, the fifth class taking one ' string '. This roused a good deal of opposition amongst the people, who complained of the injurious character of the measure. But in spite of that Wang Kuang Yuan reported that all the people gratefully welcomed the measure.

" This brought forth public criticism from the censor Li Ch'ang and also from Ch'eng Hao (程 顥), who affirmed that Wang Kuang Yuan was exploiting the people in his desire to gain bigger profit for the government, and that he was administering the measure in such a way that it was certain to increase the distress of the people.

" Liu Hsiang (劉 庠),[2] Transport Officer of the Ho Pei Circuit, refused to distribute the loan money. After his decision had been made known at Court, Wang An Shih said : ' Wang Kuang Yuan carries out the measure to the utmost of his ability, and meets with public criticism, whereas Liu Hsiang who does his best to hinder it is in no way opposed. If that is allowed to continue, what hope is there of getting general approval of the measure ? '

" So," says the History, " the criticisms of Li Ch'ang and Ch'eng Hao were ignored." [3]

The year 1069 closed with the resignation of Chang Tsai (張 載), the famous philosopher, from the post of redactor to the Ts'ung Wen Yuan (崇 文 院). In giving a sketch of his character and views the Historian recounts an interview which he had held with Wang An Shih on some occasion or other, at which the following conversation is said to have taken place :—

" What is your opinion of the New Laws ? " asked Wang An Shih. " If you will but co-operate with others in their good

---

[1] This appears from a memorial submitted by Han Ch'i. See Ts'ai Shang Hsiang, vol. xvi, p. 1. In this the fifth class were not allowed to take more than a " string " and a half, the fourth class three " strings ", the third class six " strings ", the second class ten " strings ", and the first class fifteen " strings ".

[2] Later to cause Wang An Shih considerable annoyance as governor of K'ai Feng Fu.

[3] T'ung Chien, Hsi Ning, 2nd year, 11th month.

efforts, you will get due credit for it. But if you try to teach others about matters in which they have superior knowledge to yourself,[1] they will rightly refuse to carry out your orders," was the deep reply.[2]

The next year, 1070, opens with the account of the transfer of Chang Fang P'ing (張 方 平), who had held high office in the chief administrative assembly, to a provincial appointment. He had been one of the opponents of Wang An Shih's promotion to the hierarchy, and was a determined critic of the reform policy. At Wang An Shih's instigation, he had been degraded once before. "On this occasion," continues the record, "in spite of the emperor's wish to give Chang another appointment at the capital, Wang An Shih succeeded in getting him transferred to Ying T'ien Fu (應 天 府).

In the 2nd month of 1070 Han Ch'i (韓 琦) submitted the following memorial [3] :—

"I note that in accordance with the Imperial decree recently promulgated in connection with the Agricultural Loans, that great stress is laid upon the benefits which this measure will bring to the common people. It also emphasizes the fact that it will prevent the rich from taking advantage of the extremity of the poor to exact heavy rates of interest. It also claims that the government will not benefit financially from it.

"But according to the regulations now in force, farmers and

---

[1] The actual expression used is "like teaching a jade-cutter to cut jade" (如 敦 玉 人 琢 玉).

[2] There is a note in the Histories about a large increase in the number of sinecures which occurred about this time, and suggests that Wang An Shih was responsible for this, as so many of the Court officials had been compelled to leave the Court through opposition to his policy and that it was found necessary to make provision for them in this way. This, however, is controverted by Liang Ch'i Ch'ao (pp. 204-5), who asserts not only that the system of pensioning off prominent officials in this way had obtained long before Wang An Shih took up office at the capital, but that he was actually prepared to consider the abolition of these sinecures on the ground of their costliness. He traces the source of the slander to the "Ch'ih Pei Ou T'an" (池 北 偶 談) of Wang Yu Yang (王 漁 洋), which in turn quotes the Shih Shih Cheng Kang (世 史 正 綱) of Ch'iu Wen Chuang (邱 文 莊) as authority.

[3] T'ung Chien, Hsi Ning, 3rd year, 1st month.

merchants alike are ordered to borrow 1,000 ' cash ' and repay 1,300.[1] This is surely a case of the officials lending out money on interest, and therefore the original purpose of the measure is being contravened. I know that according to the provisions of the measure compulsion of any sort is supposed to be prohibited, but the fact remains that unless compulsion is exercised none but the poorer classes will take the loans, and they will find it very difficult to repay. As time goes on it will be found necessary for the general community to assume responsibility for the repayment.

" All that is necessary to ease the financial situation is that your Majesty should exercise strict economy, for then the people will follow your example. There is absolutely no need to send out these revenue-seeking officials into the whole country, for they only disturb the people. I implore you to recall those who have been specially appointed to supervise this new measure, and to instruct the Circuit superintendents of justice (提 點 刑 獄) to put the old Granary-laws once more into effect."

The Emperor showed this memorial to Wang An Shih, with the remark, " Han Ch'i is a straightforward and loyal official. Although he is serving in a provincial appointment he does not forget his duty to the Court. It seems that what we at first thought would be of benefit to the people is turning out to be injurious. How can we expect traders and merchants to take these loans ? Yet it appears that the officials are compelling them to do so."

Wang An Shih changed countenance as he said : " If the wishes of the people are consulted there is no harm at all in the merchants also borrowing."

He then replied to the memorial of Han Ch'i in the following terms : " If we were acting like Sang Hung Yang (桑 宏 羊), whose sole object was to fill the private purse of the emperor, we might justly be termed ' profiteering officials '. But the fact is that in reviving this measure as handed down from the Duke of Chow (周 公) we are solely concerned with the relief of the

---

[1] The promoters never intended to loan out money without interest. This was an essential part of the scheme to ensure its continuity and success.

poor and the repression of the rich. The enrichment of the national coffers has not entered into our calculations, so it is quite unreasonable to brand this as a profiteering measure."

It was obvious, however, that the Emperor was not quite convinced by this statement, and was not a little hesitant as to the advisability of pushing the measure. So Wang An Shih, on the pretext of being unwell, kept to his rooms. The Emperor, in fact, wished to issue a mandate authorizing his ministers to recall the measure, but Chao Pien (趙 抃) requested him to wait until Wang An Shih should have recovered from his illness before doing so.

Wang An Shih then asked to be relieved of his post. Ssu Ma Kuang was deputed to write the Emperor's reply. This he did, and incorporated the following sentence : "The officials are in a ferment and the people greatly distressed." This incited Wang An Shih, and he took up the matter vigorously, contesting every point. The Emperor told Lü Hui Ch'ing to intimate his regret to Wang An Shih. Han Chiang then appealed to the throne that Wang An Shih should be retained. Having been called for an interview with the Emperor, Han Chiang said : "The real cause of all the trouble in the country lies in the fact that the influential officials are forming factions, and are determined to hinder your Majesty's purpose to carry out the laws of the ancient rulers."

This statement won the approval of the Emperor, who raised Wang An Shih once more to his old office, and he proceeded to press his advocacy of reform with greater vigour than ever.

He instructed Tseng Pu (曾 布) to write out a reply to Han Ch'i's memorial. When this was ready he ordered it to be carved in stone, and sent out copies to every district in the empire. This led Han Ch'i to argue the case with greater intensity. He affirmed that Wang An Shih was deliberately warping the meaning of the Chow Li (周 禮) [1] with a view to

---

[1] i.e. the Chow Kuan (周 官), on which Wang An Shih professed to base most of his reform measures. He wrote a new interpretation of this classic, styled the "Chow Kuan Hsin I" (周 官 新 義). For details see the Literary Section in Vol. III of this work.

misleading the Emperor. This statement was, however, ignored.

The Emperor at this time was greatly concerned about the relationships of Wang An Shih and Ssu Ma Kuang. He was anxious to use both, but the feeling between the two at this time was such that the one or the other had to go. Wang An Shih was consulted by the Emperor as to the advisability of giving Ssu Ma Kuang a post of greater authority. Wang An Shih replied : " He is working against the government. So are all his associates. If you give him higher office and a share in the inner counsels of state, the result will be that all who think differently from me will attach themselves to him as their leader."

Ssu Ma Kuang had been offered the post of vice-President of the Board of War [1] during Wang An Shih's temporary absence from Court (noted above). This he had refused, saying : " Your Majesty should find out whether a man is loyal or not, and what contribution he has to make to the government before appointing him. If you give him position and emoluments simply out of personal favour, and make no use of his advice, that is simply abusing the government system. From the standpoint of the official concerned, to take position and emoluments in such circumstances is simply robbing the government treasury, for it means that one will be given no real opportunity to save the people from their distresses. I should be grateful if your Majesty would abolish the Financial Reorganization Bureau, recall the officials who have been specially appointed to supervise the new measures, and revoke the Agricultural Loans measure. If that is done I care not whether you use me in office or not.

" In distributing the loans in connection with this measure, the officials, in their fear lest the money should never be repaid, compel the poor to seek guarantors amongst the rich. When the poor find themselves unable to repay they disappear, while the rich, who cannot abscond, are called upon to pay for them. If this is allowed to continue, after the lapse of ten years or so

[1] T'ung Chien, Hsi Ning, 3rd year, 2nd month.

the resources of the poor will be exhausted and the rich will have become poor. The ordinary methods of grain distribution will have become non-operative. There are the dire possibilities of war to be faced, with consequent famine. The result will be that the fields will be full of the corpses of the poor, and the more sturdy elements will overrun the country as bandits. Such, as I see it, will be the outcome of this measure."

Ssu Ma Kuang submitted nine memorials of this type, but as they synchronized with Wang An Shih's restoration to favour, Ssu Ma Kuang was allowed to refuse this new appointment, the edict which had been issued conferring it upon him being recalled. Fan Chen (范 鎮), who was friendly with Ssu Ma Kuang, and who was in control of the department which dealt with the transmission of edicts, twice sent back this mandate of " recall " to the Emperor, who in the end was compelled to hand it to Ssu Ma Kuang direct. Fan Chen then sent in his resignation, on the ground that he could not accept responsibility for compelling the Emperor to act unconstitutionally. His resignation was accepted.

Han Ch'i also resigned his superintendency of the Ho Pei Circuit and, at the instigation of Wang An Shih, the Emperor accepted his resignation.

These were resignations of very important personages, and all were the outcome of the promulgation of the Agricultural Loans Measure. It will be well, therefore, at this juncture to interpose a letter of Wang An Shih, written in reply to one from Tseng Kung Li (曾 公 立), as this explains more clearly the objects of the promoters, and the reasons for administering it in the way which had called forth such an outburst of hostile criticism. The letter reads as follows [1] :—

" You have written me about the Agricultural Loans Measure. I would begin by making the general remark that it is not in the interests of the wicked to see good government prevailing. So the moment they see that something opposed to good government is mooted, they support it blindly. Their interest is not in the law.

[1] Works, vol. xviii, p. 9.

" The hatred of Mencius of those who discussed ' profit '
was directed against those who planned to get revenue for the
government, either without any consideration for the people
or for their own personal gain.

" My critics' particular type of ' government ' waits until
conditions have become so serious that animals are fed with
food which the people need, or deaths have occurred from
famine, before taking any steps to relieve the situation.

" True ' government ' is concerned, and concerned most
intimately, with matters of finance, and it is one's bounden
duty to engage in work of this kind. More than half of the
' Chou Li ' (周 禮) is connected with finance, but Chow
Kung was surely not a ' profiteer ' ?

" Evil-minded folk compose their plausible arguments to
confuse the issue, deceiving both small and great. But what
can they do against the clearly expressed willingness of the
people for the promulgation of this measure ? It was said at
first that the people would not ask for the loans. But we cannot
cope with the demand. Then it was said they would not repay.
But so far there has been no difficulty on that score either. The
reason is to be found in the fact that the people naturally find
the measure to their interest.

" Of course, I quite see that it would be better if we could
reduce the interest to 1 per cent per mensem, or even lend the
money without interest at all. It would be better still perhaps
to give the people the grain outright, and not regard it as
a loan. Why, then, is 2 per cent necessary and regarded as the
only alternative to free relief ? Simply because the work is
to be continued in the future, for failure to make such a good
work permanent would show faulty thinking somewhere. If
we failed there, we should hardly get the credit of ' being
benevolent without waste '. It is therefore necessary to have
a loan system of some kind.

" There are the salaries of the officials concerned to be paid ;
transport charges must be met ; we must prepare for some
losses through people leaving their homes in times of drought
or flood ; there will be losses from rats and birds. We must

also plan for the exigencies of famine years, when free relief will have to be administered. The question is whether this can be done on anything less than the 2 per cent basis.

" This basis of 2 per cent per mensem was considered all right in connection with the Granary Laws (常 平 倉 法), so that there should be no objection to our adopting this basis in connection with the new measure.[1]

" If you will take the opportunity to discuss again this matter with those who are thoroughly conversant with the principles on which it has been framed, you will find that all I have said above is in strict accordance with regular law, and that the conventional critics are not worth the time you would have to spend on them in eliciting their point of view."

So Wang An Shih, despite the formidable character of the opposition, backed by the approval of the Emperor, and the loyalty and energy of his associates, Han Chiang and Lü Hui Ch'ing, kept steadily on his way. He was convinced that the measure was in the interests of the poorer people : he was therefore prepared to ignore a great deal of the opposition arising from official quarters, because he knew the measure was detrimental to their interests, and therefore their enmity was to be expected. It was, for instance, not in the interest of the official class that Wang An Shih should reduce public expenditure by 40 per cent, the major portion of which would have gone to the officials in food and robing allowances. The measure was openly directed against the profiteering proclivities of the wealthy moneylenders, many of whom were of the official clan, so it was quite natural that they should raise their voices against it.

The depleted state of the national exchequer and the administrative expenses connected with the measure made it necessary that some interest should be charged on the loans. It was better that the poor should pay 24 per cent per annum to the government than that they should pay 40 per cent or even 50 per cent to the wealthy moneylenders.

---

[1] This is additional proof that under the " Granary Laws " loans were possible.

Tseng Kung Liang, having reported that in the capital district much trouble had been caused through the officials having to chase down people who were compelled to receive the loans but were unwilling to take them, Sun Chueh (孫 覺) was sent to investigate the facts of the case. He reported that the people were unwilling to do business with the officials. "For this," says the History, "he was degraded and transferred to Kuang Te Chün (廣 德 軍)."[1]

In the 4th month of 1070 Lü Kung Chu (呂 公 著) submitted a memorial which contained the following[2]:—"No ruler has ever thought he could govern the empire without the confidence of the people. The ancient rulers used neither compulsory methods nor measures of intimidation, nor did they bring overbearing arguments to bear." Lü Kung Chu also refused to appoint Lü Hui Ch'ing to the Censorate, an act which led to his degradation and transfer to Ying Chow (潁 州).

Chao Pien summed up the current situation pretty well in the following memorial[2]:—

"Wang An Shih is overbearing and self-opinionated, accusing the generality of critics of being mere conventionalists. He pushes his own ideas against the opinions of the great majority. He is misleading the people, embellishing his faults. We have seen the remonstrances of the censors go unheeded and how they have lost their posts through their stand. Ssu Ma Kuang has felt compelled to refuse the appointment of vice-President of the Board-of-War.

"Public affairs should be considered and dealt with in the light of their relative importance. Financial profit is of minor concern; it is far more important that we should carry the people with us. The few officials who are particularly interested in the promulgation of the new laws are also of minor concern; it is of far greater consequence that the retention or dismissal of the great officials near the throne should be thoroughly considered. To ignore what is of greater importance in favour of what is of lesser consequence, and to retain a minor

[1] T'ung Chien, Hsi Ning, 3rd year, 3rd month.
[2] T'ung Chien, Hsi Ning, 3rd year, 4th month.

advantage at the expense of a major one, cannot be of any benefit either to the empire or to the dynasty."

This memorial was accompanied by his request for resignation, which was accepted, and he was transferred to Hang Chow (杭 州).

The following incident is also significant of the trend of events at this time [1] :—

Li Ting (李 定), who in his youth had been a pupil of Wang An Shih, had gained his doctor's degree, and had been appointed to Hsiu Chow (秀 州) in the south. On his return to the capital he was met by Li Ch'ang (李 常), who said to him : " You have just come from the south, what are the people there saying about the Agricultural Loans Measure ? "

Li Ting replied : " There are none who are not pleased with it."

" But," said Li Ch'ang, " the whole Court is wrangling over this business. You had better not talk like that in public."

" I only know how to speak the truth, but evidently I do not know the capital," was the reply.

This remark naturally was very gratifying to Wang An Shih, who immediately recommended Li Ting for higher appointment. In an interview which he had later with the Emperor, the latter inquired about this measure, whereupon Li Ting confirmed his former remark by saying that the people all thought it very beneficial.

From this time the Emperor turned a deaf ear to all criticisms of the new measures, and ordered that Li Ting be appointed to the Board of Censors, without observing the usual procedure. This met with severe criticism as being too arbitrary, so Li Ting was transferred to the Board of Examinations. This met with further opposition on the part of three officials in the Edicts Office, viz. Sung Min Ch'iu (宋 敏 求), Su Sung (蘇 頌), and Li Ta Lin (李 大 臨), who objected to anyone being given an appointment of this character without passing through the prescribed grades of promotion. They therefore returned the

---

[1] T'ung Chien, Hsi Ning, 3rd year, 4th month.

Emperor's order. Back and forth it went four times with the same result. In the end all three were deprived of their posts for obstructing the Imperial commands, but the people praised them for their courage.

As further trouble arose over Li Ting, the censor Ch'en Chien (陳 薦), losing his position for indicting him of not keeping the regulation mourning period for his mother, Li Ting was again transferred, this time to the University as a teacher. Three others, viz. Lin Tan (林 旦), Hsieh Ch'ang Ch'ao (薛 昌 朝), and Fan Yü (范 育), lost their posts for criticism of this new appointment. Li Ting himself got quite concerned at the trouble he had stirred up, so he asked to be relieved of this last appointment. Eventually he was given a position in the Edicts Office.[1]

Ch'eng Hao (程 顥) next advanced to the attack with the following memorial :—

" It is impossible to carry into effect a measure which almost everyone regards as impracticable. How can we expect the recent policy to succeed, involving as it does the loss of good and loyal officials, and the obstruction or rejection of the opinion of the vast majority ? How can this insult of the great and noble by the small and mean lead to anything good ? What can be the advantage of treating the loyal and orthodox as specious and traitorous ? All it can lead to is that unworthy men will make some small name for themselves, and profiteering officials will get rapid promotion. The public morale is rapidly deteriorating, which is positively a national calamity."

This matter was referred by the Emperor to the Legislative Assembly (中 書 省) for public discussion. Wang An Shih got angry with all who spoke and fiercely remonstrated with them. Ch'eng Hao mildly reproved him, saying : " The affairs

---

[1] Ts'ai Shang Hsiang controverts the accusation against Li Ting's character, affirming that Li Ting was truly a good man, loyal to his parents, in support of which no better evidence can be adduced than that he resigned his office to attend to the needs of his father. He concludes that Li Ting was unaware that he had committed any unfilial act in not observing the mourning period for his (supposed) mother. For he did not know she was his mother ! See Ts'ai Shang Hsiang, vol. i, of the Tsa Lu, p. 10.

of the empire are not the concern of one man, nor are we going to follow the opinions of one. I beseech you to control your temper and listen to what I have to say."

"After this," says the History, "Wang An Shih became a little more reasonable."

Further criticism followed from Chang Chien (張 戩), Wang Tzu Shao (王 子 韶), two censors, also from Li Ch'ang (李 常), who affirmed that the people were being compelled to pay interest on money that had not been distributed. On the demand for names being made of him, he refused to disclose them on the ground that he was not a censor. All three asked to be relieved of their posts, and all were transferred. Ch'eng Hao, for whom Wang An Shih had the greatest respect and with whom he had hitherto been quite friendly, was offered appointment as Chief-Justice for the Western Circuit. This, however, he refused.[1]

All this opposition and this succession of resignations caused the Emperor and Wang An Shih some anxiety, and it became a moot point as to whether it would not be advisable to place the Financial Reorganization Bureau under the Chief Legislative Assembly (中 書 省). Hitherto it had been organized separately and independently of all other political organs, having been established by special decree of the Emperor. It was felt possibly that the maintenance of this specially privileged institution might have accounted for a lot of the opposition, and the mind of the Emperor at least seemed to be working in the direction of the affiliation of this special Bureau with some other political organ.

From all that has been recounted above it will have become clear to the reader that very soon it was going to be a case of "Wang An Shih contra mundum". All the regular officials of the censorate had resigned and it had become necessary for him to get one of his own particular friends, Hsieh Ching Wen (謝 景 溫), appointed to that office, so that a semblance at least of maintaining the duties of that important department of government administration should be retained.

[1] T'ung Chien, Hsi Ning, 3rd year, 4th month.

Wang An Shih then began to think seriously about the proposal to affiliate the Financial Reorganization Bureau with the " Chung Shu Sheng ". At first he demurred to the idea on the ground that his proposals and regulations were not yet completed. However, by transferring Han Chiang, his colleague in the Bureau, to the Chief Legislative Assembly, the affiliation was made. It was still possible, however, for the affairs of the Bureau to be managed much as the reform party pleased, for under the affiliation scheme it was made a department of the Board of Revenue, the head of which was Lü Hui Ch'ing.[1]

Another step towards centralization was made directly after this, the department of the Chief Legislative Assembly (中 書 省), which had controlled civil appointments, being divided into two branches, one for civil and the other for military appointments. In this way the Board of War, which had hitherto been responsible for military appointments, became less influential and the President of the Board, Wen Yen Po (文 彦 博), was deprived of much of his authority.[1]

In the 7th month of 1070 Feng Ching (馮 京)[2] supplanted Lü Kung Pi (呂 公 弼) in the vice-Presidency of the Board of War. The latter had frequently exhorted Wang An Shih not to be so radical in his reform policy, and to be a little less keen on pressing his own ideas. A draft of a memorial criticizing the new laws was found in his despatch case, and this led to his transfer to T'ai Yuan Fu (太 原 府).

Su Shih (蘇 軾), who was director of the Imperial Historical Bureau, was requested by the Emperor to give his opinion on current affairs.

In his reply [2] he expressed the opinion that the Emperor was not lacking in intelligence and that he did not suffer from lack of energy or determination, but that he was too anxious for speedy results. He thought also that he was too ready to hear advice from too many quarters (i.e. from other than the old

---

[1] T'ung Chien, Hsi Ning, 3rd year, 5th month.
[2] T'ung Chien, Hsi Ning, 3rd year, 7th month.

guard), and that he promoted men to high office too hastily. A little less activity would be wise, and it was foolish to meet trouble half-way.

The Emperor said he would give these points his serious consideration, and expressed the hope that all his ministers would be equally frank in their criticism.

News of this interview soon leaked out, and caused Wang An Shih considerable displeasure. So with the idea of getting Su Shih into trouble he secured for him the very difficult post of Chief-Justice of K'ai Feng Fu. However, this resulted in Su Shih enhancing his already high reputation by dint of much hard work and pertinacity.

Taking advantage of his popularity, he submitted several memorials, criticizing the reform policy. He contended that the only method of successful government was to get the good-will of the people. He pointed out that the Financial Reorganization Bureau had in effect supplanted the Board of Finance. He called attention to the fact that those in charge of this Bureau were but youths, and that the forty-one officials who had been sent out into the provinces under their auspices had seriously damaged the prestige and majesty of the empire by their emphasis on mere profit.

For nearly a year now the Emperor's high ministers had busied themselves with financial matters. And yet the much vaunted talk about the prosperity that was bound to come was so much balderdash. One only heard about the expenditure of enormous sums of money and the employment of great numbers of men.

After criticizing a scheme which had been propounded for clearing the waters of the Pien River and making the adjacent land suitable for rice-growing, which he affirmed was impracticable, and a word about the rumoured innovation of a Public Services Tax, Su Shih continued :—

" Agricultural loans have been prohibited from very ancient times, and yet your Majesty has now made them part of the regular laws of the country. Although you say that compulsion in the matter is forbidden, can you guarantee that some tyrant of a ruler or some wicked official will not in the future introduce oppressive practices in connection with it?

"Han Wu Ti (漢 武 帝) adopted the proposal of Sang Hung Yang to remedy the prevailing financial distress, a proposal which reduced to its simplest terms means 'Buy cheap and sell dear'. But it was termed 'Chün Shu' (均 輸). In those days commercial firms were practically out of commission (because the government was doing all the business) and robbers were abundant (because there was no prospect of getting a living any other way), and the State was wellnigh ruined. You may infer that this is what is involved when the loyalty of the people is lost.

"The reason for the rise and fall of states is to be found not in their military strength or weakness, but in the depth or shallowness of the public morale. The persistence of nations in history depends upon the quality of their national life and not upon their economic status. . . .

"Jen Tsung's regime was most benevolent. He had a properly regulated procedure for the selection of men. He did not concern himself with the exposure of the faults of his predecessors, and did nothing whatever to alter the old laws. Those who examine his achievements might say that he failed to reach the ideal, that in military matters he failed nine times out of ten, and that in financial matters he only just managed to meet his bills. But on his death the opinion of the whole empire was that his had been a benevolent reign. Why? Because he thought solely of how to treat his people with kindness and justice, and sought to make peace and righteousness the main characteristics of the public life.

"Now, however, critics observing that the officials of his later years were mostly of the conventional type, and that little of moment was done, seek to improve on the administration of those days by introducing a policy of oppression and supervision. They talk of saving the present generation by wisdom and ability. So a crowd of new people have been called in who, it is affirmed, by their courage and zeal are going to produce speedy results. But one not only fails to see any benefit accruing from this policy, but perceives many evidences of oppressive and money-making schemes. No improvement in the morale of the people can possibly result from such a policy.

" Then with regard to the Censorate. In olden days the censors were at liberty to discuss anybody or anything without let or hindrance. Even the Emperor himself, and the highest ministers of state, stood in awe of them. I do not say that every Censor is of necessity a man of the highest character, or that all their criticisms should be regarded as just. But it is essential that they should be encouraged to speak out boldly on all public questions, and that their office should be respected, so that assistance may be rendered towards the suppression of evils the moment they arise.

" I remember hearing my elders remark that the opinion of the censors was always in line with the opinion of the country, and that it was usually just. But nowadays these opinions are angrily expressed, resentments and incriminations of a slanderous character intermingle, so that it is easy to see to what a low state public opinion has been reduced.

" My fear is that gradually all power will pass into the hands of a few individuals, and that the Emperor will be left desolate. When constitutional practices are ignored, then anything might happen. My prayer is that your Majesty will do all that can be done to preserve the old system of government."

The Historian goes on to say that Wang An Shih was doing his utmost at this juncture to get the Emperor to assume supreme authority and to entrust him with sole responsibility for affairs. So Su Shih took advantage of his opportunity to set the questions for the Doctor's Degree examination, to propound the following :—

" Duke Wu of Chin (晉 武 公), by acting on his own initiative, reduced Wu (吳) to submission, but Fu Chien (苻 堅), in his attack on Chin (晉), was completely defeated by assuming all authority himself. Huan Kung of Ch'i (齊 桓 公) obtained the leadership of the princes by entrusting all authority to Kuan Chung (管 仲), whereas Duke K'uai of Yen (燕 噲 公) suffered defeat by trusting implicitly to the counsel of Tzu Chih (子 之). Explain why in these cases the adoption of the same policy produced entirely contradictory results."

This greatly annoyed Wang An Shih, who ordered the censor Hsich Ching Wen to produce an indictment against him. He failed, however, to find just cause for so doing. But this led Su Shih to seek a provincial appointment, and he was soon transferred to Hang Chow (杭 州) as Governor.

Under the 8th month of this year the History [1] records an invasion of the Hsia tribes in the north-west and the appointment of Han Chiang as Pacification Commissioner for Shensi and Ho Pei. Wang An Shih would have undertaken this work himself, but matters at the capital were developing in such a way that this was impossible.

For one thing Lü Hui Ch'ing had resigned to fulfil his mourning obligations. This gave Wang An Shih an opportunity to get another of his party, Tseng Pu (曾 布), installed as expositor in the Ts'ung Cheng Tien (崇 政 殿),[2] where he would be able to keep track of all the memorials that were presented. The History notes that he was of very poor qualifications and generally ignored. After a while he had to be transferred, Wang An Shih succeeding in getting him into the Land Revenue department as Head.[3]

In the 9th month Liu Hsiang (劉 庠)[4] was appointed governor of K'ai Feng Fu, and began to prove himself a thorn in the side of Wang An Shih. As he gave many signs of unwillingness to adapt himself to the ideas of the reform party, Wang An Shih sent for him to talk matters over. However, Liu Hsiang refused to go, saying : " Since Wang An Shih was appointed vice-Grand Councillor, he has done nothing that is in accordance with the dictates of humanity. What use is there in going to see a man like that ? "

---

[1] T'ung Chien, Hsi Ning, 3rd year, 8th month.

[2] Evidently the Imperial Council Chamber where memorials were presented.

[3] The Financial Reorganization Bureau had been incorporated with the Board of Land Revenue (司 農 寺). It was therefore a most important position strategically for the Reform party.

[4] See p. 157, note 2.

Later on he submitted a memorial criticizing the reform policy. He was called by the Emperor for an interview, and was asked why he refused to co-operate with the powers-that-be and to assist those who were doing their best to improve political conditions. He replied : " I recognize the Emperor as my sole master. I refuse to submit to the authority of Wang An Shih."

Tseng Kung Liang (曾 公 亮) resigned at this time on account of advanced age. The History says that he had given Wang An Shih half-hearted help, but even that was given simply out of envy of Han Ch'i. Su Shih had once criticized him for failing to control Wang An Shih. Tseng had replied : " The Emperor and Wang An Shih are as one man ; in fact, they are like Heaven itself (not to be resisted)." The History insinuates that he was allowed to resign because he did not flatter Wang An Shih sufficiently.[1]

Feng Ching (馮 京), an ardent supporter of the reform movement, was now appointed vice-Grand Councillor, and Wu Ts'ung (吳 充), another prominent supporter, was appointed vice-President of the Board of War. This latter post was the equivalent of a vice-Grand Councillor and carried with it the same privileges.

At this juncture all the important positions in the government were held by members of Wang An Shih's party, and so criticism of their policy could but prove futile, i.e. if the ordinary channels were to be used. There was, however, another channel open to them in the existing examination system, so in the essay which had to be presented on these occasions his opponents found a fine field for voicing their views. It was customary for the Emperor to look over those essays which had been awarded special merit.

In the 9th month of 1070 a particularly pungent one was presented by Lü T'ao (呂 陶), of T'ai Yuan Fu, as follows [1] :—

" Your Majesty has just recently assumed the throne. I trust you will not be deceived by this new theory of finance and neglect your old and trustworthy officials. I hope that you

---

[1] T'ung Chien, Hsi Ning, 3rd year, 9th month.

will not engage in war, or presume that you are another Yao and Shun. Your own mind may be favourably disposed towards the reform policy, but the whole empire is of contrary views. Will you not examine yourself, and consider what may be the consequences of your present attitude ? "

The Emperor asked Wang An Shih to read this essay, but before he had got half-way through he was spluttering with rage and was quite unable to finish it. So it was handed to Feng Ching who, after reading it, remarked, " There is some ground for the opinions expressed."

'Another essay of over 9,000 words by K'ung Wen Chung (孔 文 仲) was accorded special merit by the supervisor of examinations. This was solely concerned with criticism of the new laws.

In the same month Ssu Ma Kuang asked to be relieved of his post of the Han Lin Academy [1] (翰 林 院). The Emperor received him in a special audience, and said : " Wang An Shih and you used to be good friends in the past, what has made you doubt him ? "

Ssu Ma Kuang replied : " All who oppose him, such as Su Shih, for instance, ruin the prospects of their official career, being regarded as enemies of the Constitution. As for myself, though ready to suffer cashiering or degradation of rank, I wish to fulfil my bounden duty. And as for being friendly with Wang An Shih, who was a greater friend of his than Lü Kung Chu ? But in the end he was ruined by him."

Ssu Ma Kuang's resignation was accepted, and he was transferred to Yung Hsing Chün (永 興 軍).

Further resignations followed. In the 10th month Ch'en Sheng Chih (陳 升 之), formerly close associate with Wang An Shih, feigned illness for a hundred days, and then resigned on the death of his mother. The History [2] says that he and Wang An Shih had been at cross purposes for some time, and

---

[1] T'ung Chien, Hsi Ning, 3rd year, 9th month. This was the final break between Ssu Ma Kuang and Wang An Shih in matters of policy.
[2] T'ung Chien, Hsi Ning, 3rd year, 10th month.

that the main reason was that Wang An Shih was constantly trespassing on his authority.

Fan Chen (范 鎭), Literary Councillor,[1] also sent in his resignation. The grounds which he gave were that his criticism of the new laws had been ignored, and that two of his nominees for office, Su Shih and K'ung Wen Chung, had not been given appointment. He also cited Wang An Shih's support of unworthy men like Li Ting and Wang Shao (王 韶). He also quoted the dismissal of worthy men like Sung Ming Ch'iu, Su Sung, Li Ta Fang, and others, all for insufficient reasons. He declaimed further on the injurious character of the new measures, on Wang An Shih's misinterpretation of honest criticism, and his diversion of the Emperor's generous purpose to unjust ends.

Wang An Shih's hand shook with rage as he grasped this memorial, and he wrote out a vehement reply. This led to Fan Chen's resignation and the loss of all favours to which he was entitled. In his farewell interview with the Emperor he said : " Your Majesty should take counsel with all your officials, and learn the real facts of the case. This hindering and perversive group ought to be eliminated, and the old guard of loyal officials restored. By their sincere counsel they will bring back peace and prosperity to the nation."

The History [1] relates that the people lauded him for his strength of character.

Despite this formidable array of resignations, Wang An Shih continued to persevere with his policy, as succeeding chapters will show. All that has been quoted above of the discussions of the reform policy is taken from the traditional Histories, and no criticism has been made of the feasibility or otherwise of the statements made. Opportunity will be taken in other parts of this work to criticize the reliability of the traditional Histories in general, and some of the references to Wang An Shih in particular.

---

[1] T'ung Chien, Hsi Ning, 3rd year, 10th month.

CHAPTER XIV

THE MILITIA ACT PROMULGATED

(12TH MONTH, 1070)

THE account of the promulgation of this measure, which is styled the Pao Chia Fa (保 甲 法) or Militia Act, appears in the History [1] under the date of the 12th month, 1070, just prior to the announcement of Wang An Shih's promotion to the office of Grand Councillor, the highest administrative post in the State.

Only a brief sketch of the character and course of the measure is given by the History at this point. It will be our purpose in this chapter to give a fuller account of its rise, nature, and progress.

The Militia Act in its essence and objective partook of the nature of a Conscription Measure, and was designed to meet the pressing need of the country for radical and extensive military reform.

Both the Emperor Shen Tsung and his minister, Wang An Shih, were aware of the perilous condition of the Empire from the military standpoint. The aggressive tactics of powerful neighbours in the north and north-west [2] represented an ever-increasing menace to the peace and stability of the dynasty. Serious losses of territory had been incurred under former rulers [3] in those areas, the disgrace of which both ruler and

---

[1] " T'ung Chien."

[2] i.e. the " Liao " (遼) or " Iron " Tartars, the " Chin " (金) or " Golden " Tartars, and the Hsi Hsia (西 夏) or Tanguts to the north-west. The two former are generally spoken of as the Ch'i Tans (契 丹), sometimes spelt Khitans.

[3] Sixteen districts had been ceded to the Ch'itans by Shih Ching T'ang (石 敬 塘) of the Posterior Chin Dynasty (後 晉 紀), A.D. 936–943. Two additional districts, viz. Cho (涿) and I (易), were lost to them in 988–9 by T'ai Tsung. The Hsi Hsia rose to considerable power during the reign of Jen Tsung (仁 宗), 1023–1063, occupied large stretches of territory in the north and north-west of modern Shensi, and exacted considerable tribute from the Sungs by the peace of 1043. " Outlines of Chinese History," pp. 170, 180.

minister were determined to wipe out. The standing army, though large,[1] was poorly equipped and generally inefficient; such people's corps as existed were incohesive and lacking in the martial spirit, and the attitude of the officials and people generally was characterized either by indifference, wilful or ignorant, or by a stoical pessimism.

The financial condition of the country was also in a parlous state, and gave but poor promise of any great increase in numbers or improved equipment of the regular forces.

There seemed to be only one solution to the problem, and that was to introduce some form of conscription and, following on the lines of ancient precedents, initiate some policy that would make soldiers of the people.

The practice of maintaining a standing army on the payroll of the country seems to have originated with the first emperor of the T'ang dynasty.[2] Prior to that the people were liable to be called upon for military service at any time. There were, of course, ancient regulations extant which conditioned and controlled this system, and it was to these that Wang An Shih, following his usual procedure in such matters, looked for justification and principles in devising his own particular measures.

The ancient precedent for his Militia Act was found in the " Ch'iu Chia Fa " (丘 甲 法) of the Chow Dynasty.[3] The requirements of his measure were based on a unit (丘) of 128 families, from which normally 128 men would be called upon

---

[1] At the opening of Shen Tsung's reign, 1068, the Standing Army numbered 1,162,000 men.

[2] Boulger, " A Short History of China," pp. 27, 28.

[3] The land under the Chow Dynasty was divided up into plots of 900 acres, subdivided into nine smaller plots of 100 acres each. Each of these smaller plots was leased to one family on condition that they shared the work of cultivating one of the nine in the interests of the Government, the proceeds reckoning as their contribution to taxes. This division of the territory was known as " Ching " (井). Four " Ching " formed a larger division known as " I " (邑), which was held by thirty-two families. Four " I " formed a still larger territorial division known as " Ch'iu " (丘), leased to 128 families. It was on this that the " Ch'iu Chia Fa " was based. The acre represented 6,000 square feet, the foot being roughly equivalent to the linear " foot " of to-day.

for war or other government service of an urgent character. But as animals, carts, and other equipment were necessary for such purposes as well as men, the specific regulations called for one cart, four war horses, twelve oxen, three officers in armour, and seventy-two troopers from the unit.[1] No doubt this was still regarded as the equivalent of one soldier from each family.

That would seem to have been the older regulation, for in the "Chow Kuan" (周官), or Official Regulations of the Chow Dynasty, the civil classification of five families to the unit (比) was coterminous with the military classification of five soldiers to the unit (伍), the civil unit of twenty-five families (閭) being coterminous with the military unit of twenty-five soldiers (兩).

Wang An Shih sought further support for his ideas in the fact that similar measures had been adopted by famous rulers and law-makers of the later Chow times (the Ch'un Ch'iu or Feudal period), such as Kuan Chung of Ch'i (齊之管仲), Tzu Ch'an of Cheng (鄭之子產), and Shang Yang of Ch'in (秦之商鞅). In the Han Dynasty Chung Ch'ang T'ung (漢之仲長統) had also revived the method.[2]

One other factor of a preliminary character needs to be considered before we proceed to give a detailed account of the Militia Act as such.

During the reign of Jen Tsung (仁宗), A.D. 1023–1063, this ancient system had been reinstituted in a modified form under the designation of the "I Yung" (義勇), or Volunteers. These were one type of "Hsiang Chun" (鄉軍), or Local Levies, who were enrolled as reserves to the regular army on the basis of property qualification. Most of these were from the better class of residents. Those of the first and second classes provided their own crossbows in addition to making a small monetary contribution, while those of the third class were provided with weapons by the Government. Twice a year they were given some training in military drill and

---

[1] "Tz'u Yuan."
[2] Prose Works, vol. x, p. 2.

tactics in the sub-prefecture, being provided with food and expenses during the training period.

The Volunteers were liable to be called upon for local duty in rotation, or for guard duty in nearer or more distant places. During the period 1041–8, when the I Yung were first organized, the system seems to have been confined to three circuits, Hopei (河 北), in which there were 180,031 men on the register, Hotung (河 東), which reported 77,079, both for the period mentioned, and Shensi. But for this circuit the only figures available are for the years 1064–8, when 156,873 men were enrolled.

During the reign of Ying Tsung (英 宗), 1064–7, every family was required to provide one Volunteer for every three males. The age limit was fixed at between twenty and thirty years. They had their own officers. Rewards of rank were made to those who showed special skill in archery or cross-bowmanship, or to those who showed particular zeal in raising their own corps or undertook the erection of forts and the provision of garrisons. Although this is stated to apply specifically to the Shensi Circuit, it seems to have been more or less the general rule throughout the three Circuits (above).

There was also another type of People's Corps organized under the name of " Kung Chien Shou " (弓 箭 手) or Bow-men. These were confined mainly to the border districts, where in return for leases of land they held themselves in readiness for police or border duty.[1]

It was therefore Wang An Shih's purpose to extend and make more efficient this system of People's Corps. This would ultimately place at the disposal of the Government a much bigger and more efficient fighting force than then existed. It would also bring about a reduction in the numbers of paid troops. In this way not only would expenditure on the regular army be considerably minimized, but provision would also be made for weeding out the incapables and inefficients. The farmers were a stolid and self-respecting class of men. Could

---

[1] Synopsized from the Dynastic Histories, " Sung Ping Chih " or Military Organization of the Sung Dynasty, vol. 187, section 140, subsection 1.

these but be converted into a potential fighting force, and given military training at such times as would not interfere with their agricultural work, the nation would reap the benefit both in prestige and stability. The problem of the paid soldier's return to civil life would thereby be partly solved, and the efficiency and economy of the military arm be secured at one and the same time.

The details of the measure changed from time to time, but the following were the regulations as at first promulgated, viz.[1] :

1. Ten families to form a platoon or "Pao" (保).

2. Fifty families to form a company or "Ta Pao" (大 保).

3. Ten companies to form a regiment, or "Tu Pao" (都 保).

4. Units of less than ten families to be attached to a neighbouring platoon.

5. Each platoon and company to be officered by a resident property owner with the requisite ability. Each regiment to have a commander and vice-commander who had the respect of the men. All officers were to be elected locally.

6. Each family in which there were two or more able-bodied males must provide one for the platoon. If there were more than two males in the family, other members who had the strength and spirit for the work might also enrol. In the wealthier families, if only one male were available he should also be enrolled, provided he was physically fit and had the right spirit.

7. Bows and crossbows would be provided by the Government when the Militia were in attendance at the drill grounds. But it was permitted to practise at other times with any weapons not probibited by the law. It was planned to give military instruction to all who enrolled.

8. Each company was required to provide five men who would act as night watchmen in relays. Captures of thieves and seizures of stolen goods, when reported, would be suitably rewarded.

[1] " T'ung Chien " under 12th month, 1070.

9. If within the bounds of any Militia unit cases of robbery, murder, incendiarism, adultery, kidnapping, teaching or practising forbidden rites, manufacture of poisonous drugs, etc., occurred, and the matter was not reported by the nearest unit, penalties would be inflicted. Nothing which did not come under the purview of the law was to be reported.

10. If more than three robbers should have taken shelter within the bounds of any Militia unit for a period of more than three days, and the matter was not reported by a neighbouring unit, even though they could prove they were ignorant of the matter, the neighbouring unit would be penalized for such slackness.

11. This new measure was first to be carried out in the capital circuit (京 畿), then extended in order to the five circuits of Yung Hsing (永 興), Ch'in Feng (秦 鳳), Hopei (河 北), Ching Tung (京 東), and Ching Hsi (京 西), and later again gradually extended to the whole empire.

From the above outline it appears that the object immediately before the promoters of the scheme was to raise a local police force. It was, however, a force which could readily be transformed into a potential fighting unit, which was Wang An Shih's ultimate purpose.

The Emperor at first raised some objections to the scheme, preferring that something on the lines of the " Tsu Yung T'iao Fa " [1] (租 庸 調 法), or system of conscripted labour

---

[1] The system of taxation and conscripted labour extant during the T'ang Dynasty, 618–905 A.D. The Government granted to one family a piece of land one " ch'ing " (100 Chinese acres, equal to 15·13 English acres) in extent. From this 10 bushels of grain were to be contributed to the Government annually. This was termed " Tsu " (租). The holder was also required to contribute two rolls of silk, and 3 oz. of fibrous silk. If cloth was offered in lieu of silk, then the length was to be increased by one-fifth ; 3 lb. of hemp was also demanded. If money was offered in lieu of these goods 14 oz. of silver was demanded. This was termed " T'iao " (調). Apart from these contributions of money or goods, twenty days' labour was to be given to the Government annually. In years which contained an intercalary month twenty-two days' labour were exacted. Goods

and service of the T'ang dynasty, might be revived.   To this Wang An Shih demurred, on the grounds that although it was quite practicable, and had certain advantageous features such as limiting the area of land which the wealthier classes might hold, and encouraging the labouring classes to work for themselves, it could only be introduced gradually and the benefits which might accrue would be realized too slowly altogether for the purpose they had in view.   He thought further that as the existing regulations regarding the Volunteers and other local levies allowed for their support while on public duty, it was unnecessary to make the provision for the poorer classes which the " Tsu Yung T'iao Fa " guaranteed.

He would suggest that a beginning might be made with the bigger scheme they had in mind by encouraging the existing Volunteer Corps.   There were some defects which might be remedied.   As the volunteers were mostly of the respectable residential families, it would be wise to treat them as befitted their class.   It was, for instance, wrong to seal them on their wrists or backs, involve them in great expense for reviews and drill, and use them for the transport services.   " These things are resented already, and if we add the liability of being called upon for actual warfare we must expect them to be still more resentful and unwilling."

Feng Ching (馮 京) interposed a remark that the volunteers who entered for tests in archery had been suitably rewarded by the Emperor.

Wang An Shih rejoined that it was unfair to make tests in archery the sole avenue to preferment.   There were many who had not the strength or skill for that who needed some other inducement.   And it was wise that some special advantages should be offered to induce many more men to volunteer for this Corps, and that those who refrained from joining should

could be offered in lieu of labour, 3 ft. of silk being regarded as the equivalent of one day's labour. On the other hand, if an extra twenty-five days' labour was offered, all the items under the " T'iao " heading were cancelled, and if additional labour of thirty days was volunteered, all other taxes were remitted. This labour was termed " Yung " (庸) (taken from the " Tz'u Yuan ").

suffer corresponding disabilities. In some way or other they must transform the spirit of the people, and arouse their martial spirit.

He suggested, therefore, that much better prospects of promotion should be offered to selected stalwarts from the countryside. That from the first they should be given some recognized official rank, and that they should have the same prospects of promotion as those enrolled in the regular forces, amongst whom it was possible for a man to rise to the rank of a " Tz'u Shih " (刺 史), i.e. the equivalent of a sub-prefectural official.

As these men would serve in a voluntary and honorary capacity, some saving in official salaries would thereby be gained, and a much greater spirit of willing co-operation would be developed amongst them.

He had the further idea that some of the higher officials might be induced to officer these Volunteers, thereby enhancing their prestige.

" These suggestions," records the Historian,[1] " received the approval of the Emperor."

It is evident from the above that Wang An Shih intended to keep the Volunteers [2] functioning at the same time as he was initiating the new Militia Act. They were already possessed of some sort of organization and had received some training. The new scheme would take time to develop. It would therefore be unwise to abolish the Volunteers before the Militia were

---

[1] Most of the material in this section is taken from the Dynastic Histories, vol. 192, section 145, Military subsection vi, District Corps iii (宋 史 兵 志), also from vol. 191, section 144, Military subsection v, District Corps ii.

[2] In the period 1041–1048 there were 180,031 Volunteers (I Yung) enrolled in the Hopei circuit and 77,079 in Hotung. In Shensi for the period 1064–8 the numbers were 156,873. While it was Wang An Shih's ultimate purpose to bring the Volunteers under the Militia Act, it was very difficult to carry into effect. The two schemes were operating together for some time. It was not until 1082 that they were finally amalgamated. In the period 1075–6 the total figures of the Volunteers in the five circuits of Hopei, Hotung, Hopeihsi, Yung Hsing, and Ch'in Feng amounted to 247,537. (Dynastic History, vol. 191, section 144, v, ii.)

ready. So as one step towards the goal he suggested their retention temporarily with such reforms and advantages introduced as would induce them to serve in larger numbers and with a better spirit.

The next step was to make some suggestions about the regular army Wang An Shih urged that the most pressing need from the standpoint of the national finances was to make considerable reductions in their numbers. It should be noted that the Standing Army at the opening of Shen Tsung's reign (1068) numbered 1,162,000 men.[1]

To this suggestion the Emperor demurred, contending that the numbers had already been considerably reduced compared with the figures in Jen Tsung's day, and that the troops in the Hopei and Shensi areas had already been reduced below the safety line.[2]

Wang An Shih agreed that there was an element of danger in reducing the numbers of men available for military service. But if the present numbers of hired troops were to be maintained on the pay-roll the finances of the country must continue to be in a parlous state.

So he felt that two things were essential. The people in the northern Circuits must be induced to go in for some form of military training, which would gradually make them an efficient fighting force, and the regular army should be combed out and made more effective. But the chief need was for the revival of something akin to the ancient system of making soldiers of the people. Apart from that there was no hope of making the country strong and stable.

He then suggested that the number of regulars stationed in the capital and precincts was altogether too large, that these might be distributed in different parts of the country to serve the interests of both economy and efficiency, and that the Emperor's anxiety for the safety of the capital might be allayed by transferring relays of the Volunteers there.

To these suggestions there was considerable opposition.

[1] Dynastic Histories, p. 184, note 1.
[2] Liang Ch'i Ch'ao, 155-6.

The Emperor feared that removal of the paid forces from the capital was dangerous policy, as once the regulars got scattered he might lose a certain measure of control, and rebellion on the part of military leaders was a thing he was most anxious to guard against. Others, like Wen Yen Po, argued that to introduce the local levies into the capital might bring in the riffraff from the countryside, and that they would be a constant menace to good order. As a compromise Ch'en Sheng Chih suggested that the Volunteers or other local levies might be gradually introduced into the prefectures adjacent to the capital. But he thought it unreasonable to expect that such corps could be utilized for distant garrison duty or actual warfare.

This brought from Wang An Shih the following rejoinder :—

" Prior to the times of T'ang (唐) there were no regular hired forces at all. The ordinary people were used both for garrison and war duty. Everything depends upon the quality of the officers that are secured. If we can devise suitable treatment and encouragement for them, there need be no anxiety about the value and efficiency of the People's Army."

The Emperor having been prevailed upon to admit that the most far-sighted policy was to have both regular forces and militia available for the defence of the empire, Wang An Shih proceeded to press for the reform of the regulations governing the regular army.

In an attempt to justify Wang An Shih's persistence in this advocacy of reduction of the hired troops, and of introducing his Militia Act, it will be well at this juncture to give the considered opinions of other prominent contemporaries on the subject. We have already seen that the standing army at the opening of Shen Tsung's reign numbered over a million. This force, according to Liang Ch'i Ch'ao, absorbed more than two-thirds of the total revenue.

The following memorials, submitted during the reign of Jen Tsung (1023–1063), indicate the necessity for some policy of reform in this connection :—

Ou Yang Hsiu wrote, about 1040 :—

" For thirty-three years there has been peace. All the soldiers who have had any experience of war are either dead or decrepit. Those who have been recruited later know nothing of actual warfare. During this period of peace they have been provided with all the necessaries of life, and have become both haughty and indolent. When they move guard they must have coolies to carry their bedding, while those on duty at the capital hire men to transport their grain. How can we expect such men as these to endure the hardships and perils of actual warfare?

" The weakness of our forces has been exposed recently by the defeat sustained on the western frontier by our troops under Ch'i Tsung Chü (齊 宗 舉). If only the troops were hardy and efficient it might be considered justifiable to expend the resources of the farming class upon their maintenance. But what reason have we for maintaining the mere pretence of an army, composed as it is of such proud, lazy, and useless men?

" The ancient practice was to give the strong and robust fellows of the farming class military drill and instruction in the intervals between the agricultural seasons, keeping them free for their farming work at other times. But this practice no longer obtains. The recruiting officers go out in times of dearth, measuring the height of the men, testing their strength, and enrolling them in the standing army. Those of better physique are drafted into the Imperial Army (禁 兵), while those of inferior standard are allocated to the Provincial Corps (廂 兵). The recruiting officers are rewarded according to the number of recruits they enrol. In times of dearth and poverty it is only natural that there should be competition to enter the army. So it has come about that after every period of famine, the strong and robust have been found in the army, while the older and feebler folk have been left on the fields.

" I am not unaware of the criticism that if such men were not received into the army at such times they might turn to banditry for a living. But the pity is that while such critics are conscious of the danger that these men might become robbers for a short period, they seem completely to overlook the fact that once they are enrolled in the regular army they become robbers for practically the whole of their lives (i.e. they consume the revenue provided for their maintenance by the farming classes, but give nothing in return).

"In ancient times the old and feeble were allowed to take their ease while the young and strong undertook the work of farming. But now the opposite is the case. The young men idle around while the older folk are left to get on with the arduous labours of the fields. If all were to engage in agriculture, they would, of course, have to eat the coarsest food, but the moment they join the army they are assured of abundance of good food and a comfortable job for the rest of their lives. No wonder the number of those engaged in agriculture is decreasing all the time.

"My contention is that the present army system is an abuse of the people's loyalty and a grievous imposition."

Take again the following extracts from a second memorial, also from the pen of Ou Yang Hsiu (歐 陽 修) :—

"Nowadays the officials are afraid of calling upon the army for any service. They use them only when there is absolutely no other alternative. In such cases they are almost cringingly courteous, using such expressions as 'May we borrow or hire your services for a short time'. Even in official despatches the term 'hiring' is used, so the soldiers say laughingly to one another, 'The official is hiring us.'

"It is, of course, quite right that rewards should be given for meritorious service. But now the system obtains of rewarding all without discrimination, disbursements amounting to 800,000 or 900,000 'strings' being made once in three years, at the time of the Great Ceremony (大 禮). The officers simply dare not withhold these gifts when the time comes round. But on receiving them, not only do the soldiers feel no shame at receiving rewards which they in no wise deserve, but begin to quibble over the amount given, and create a disturbance if they think they have been granted too little. They assemble together with their sticks and staves, and threaten to attack the Imperial Commissioner.

"Such arrogance as this is due to mismanagement, and the absence of regulations for their proper discipline and control . . .

"So long as our army fails to win the respect of our foes on the one hand, and acts so arrogantly at home on the other, the permanency of our dynasty, which has existed now for over eighty years, cannot be guaranteed. Confusion and disorder are bound to increase. Everything is dealt with in such a casual and negligent manner that conditions are approaching those of the preceding five dynasties, which is surely most pitiable."

The following memorial, presented by the chief censor, Fan Chen (范 鎮), in the period 1056–1064, throws further light on the conditions obtaining, viz. :—

"Though taxation is heavy the revenue remains insufficient. The chief cause for this is to be found in the size of our standing army. It is said that this is essential to our frontier policy, as we must be prepared for the Ch'itans (契 丹). But, as a matter of fact, the Ch'itans have made no incursion southwards for over fifty years. Why? Because it is much more to their advantage to go on receiving our handsome tribute gifts of money and silk, and to maintain the peace. But supposing they were to decide to launch an attack. In that case I venture to predict that the only defenders of our cities north of the Yellow River would be found to be composed of women and girls. For the soldiery who are stationed in the districts, and who engage in no farming or other productive work, would be found quite useless.

"And yet we continue to maintain them at the expense of the people. The policy of creating and maintaining a standing army leads to a great decrease in the numbers of those engaged in agriculture. This, of course, means that great areas of arable land lie fallow. This in its turn involves the people in heavier taxation and an increase of the burden of public services. So the loyalty of the people gets strained, and cannot be relied upon.

"On the contrary, the policy of raising Militia or People's Corps, making soldiers of them while they continue their work of farming, tends to eliminate these evils. The number engaged in farming operations is not decreased, more land gets tilled, taxation is lighter, and the loyalty of the people remains staunch and true.

"It is surely preferable to prepare to meet the Ch'itans by a policy which ensures the loyalty of the people than by pressing a policy which tends to deprive the State of such an asset. I am convinced that if we pursue our present policy our resources both in money and men will be exhausted before the enemy appears. Whereas our revenue will be sufficient and our military strength more than adequate, if we adopt a policy of making soldier-farmers of our people . . ."

Su Shih (蘇 軾) also sent in a memorial on this subject, from which the following extracts are taken, viz. :—

"It is very bad policy to assemble the troops in one place unless they are given work to do. Take an illustration. Here is a piece of land 100 'ch'ing' in extent. The pasturage upon it is sufficient for 4,000 horses. It is surely common sense to assemble the animals on this land rather than transport the fodder from the land to some distant place to feed the horses there. Our soldiers are assembled at the capital, but the food for them has to be transported from the distant places of the empire, from Huai-Nan (淮 南), Hupei (湖 北), and Hunan (湖 南).

"The soldiers ought to be engaged in farming so as to provide their own keep.

"There is the further matter of periodical transfers of the regulars from the capital to the borders for garrison duty. Once every three years this takes place, and involves the Government in great expense. This calls for heavier taxation of the farming class, and puts great burdens on those who are responsible for the transport services. And all this in a time of peace.

"My suggestion is that the local levies be given better training. In order to raise the expenses for this work the regular forces should be reduced. If you offer the local levies better facilities and conditions they will soon respond with energy and loyalty, so that after a while they will be equal to the regulars.

"If this is done, any great concentration of troops at the capital will be unnecessary. You will only need to keep enough there for the Imperial bodyguard. The enormous expense of transport of supplies from great distances to the capital will also be saved, and this constant transfer of forces will be rendered unnecessary. I calculate that more than half the present expenditure will be saved in this way."

A second memorial, also from Su Shih, adds fresh information. It reads as follows :—

"A man may be considered an efficient soldier between the ages of 20 and 40 years. But according to the present regulations he lives on the State for another twenty years (the disbandment age was 61). Obviously he cannot render good and effective service for the whole of that period. We ought to disband half our existing regular forces on this ground alone, and save half the expense of their maintenance. But we have more troops than ever on the pay roll. They are mostly old and decrepit, not half as efficient as troops of the former days. Recruits are drawn for the most part from the good-for-nothing class, whose youth has been dissipated by wine and chess. They soon find themselves unfitted for the rigours of military service, and regret that they joined up. But as it is impossible for them to earn a living if they return to civil life, they hold on in the army.

"My proposal is that no new recruits should be accepted who are over thirty years of age, and that the age limit for retiring be fixed at fifty. If it be possible I would suggest that for new recruits a contract be made whereby they agree to serve for ten years only. This would enable them to maintain their self-respect during their soldiering days, and obviate any feelings of resentment when they are called upon to retire.

"It is one of the greatest defects of our national life to-day that the people as a whole are not versed in arms. The ordinary civilian fears the soldiers and the latter tyrannize over the common people. As the people generally are not given military training they are under the additional disability of not being able to resist robbers or deal with other marauders in any effective way.

"I would therefore further propose that all able-bodied

males have a turn at soldiering for a certain definite period, and that afterwards they should return to civil life. In that way the nation as a whole would become a potential fighting force, and both bandits and invaders would be intimidated into quiescence."

All these proposals have much in common with the policy later initiated and carried through by Wang An Shih. During the reign of Jen Tsung, when these proposals were made, it was impossible to carry through such a drastic scheme of military reform as these proposals involved, largely because of the vacillating character of the Emperor himself. Shen Tsung was a man of stouter heart and greater determination. So that when Wang An Shih made his proposals, together they were able to carry into effect much of what Ou Yang Hsiu, Fan Chen, and Su Shih had only been able to suggest.

However, even in Shen Tsung's time, with such a determined character as Wang An Shih for protagonist, the new policy was not initiated easily. There was much opposition from the great officials and considerable hesitancy on the part of the Emperor himself.

For one thing he was afraid of the trouble which disband-ment in large numbers might cause, and quoted the opinion of the officials in charge of the Board of War that mutiny similar to that which occurred in the reign of T'ang Te Tsung (唐 德 宗) [1] might arise. To this Wang An Shih replied :—

" Let your Majesty but do what is right and carry out con-scientiously what you feel to be the obligations of sound government. Let perfect frankness obtain between ruler and people in this matter, and your fears will prove to have been utterly without foundation. The mutiny to which you have

---

[1] In A.D. 780 T'ien Yüeh (田 悦) was in charge of Liao Ch'eng Hsien in Shantung. He had 70,000 armed men under his command, and he was generally regarded as a loyal officer. But Hung Ching Lung (洪 經 綸), Chief Administrator of the Hopei circuit, ordered him to disband 40,000 of these. T'ien Yüeh made a show of disbandment by ordering his men to return to their farms. However, after a short interval he brought the men back to their old military stations. The following year these troops rebelled, and T'ien Yüeh arrogated the title of King (王) to himself (Tz'u Yuan).

referred arose through the Emperor giving his confidence to
the wrong man, and in so doing he was led to do serious injustice
to a loyal servant of the throne. I pray that you will act with
determination in this business, issue orders that reduction of the
hired forces be undertaken gradually and in accordance with
carefully considered regulations."

It is evident that orders for further reductions in the regular
army must have been issued after this, as the following memorial
from Ssu Ma Kuang [1] testifies :—

"Already large numbers have been disbanded,[2] and these
are naturally resentful and despondent. But as they comprise
weak and timid men for the most part, they have not so far
attempted any serious rebellion against the Government.

" But no one can guarantee that there will be no such revolt
if this policy of disbandment is persisted in. Great alarm and
disturbance has been manifest in every district where your
edict has been published, especially in those parts which are
more intimately concerned in it.

" I admit that if you were now to recall the mandate the
State would suffer serious loss of prestige, and it might lead to
disobedience on the part of the haughty troops in future cases,
but at the same time I feel that if the order is not withdrawn
it will be practically impossible to prevent the people's

---

[1] Quoted Liang Ch'i Ch'ao, p. 164.

[2] During the years 1068–9 considerable reductions had already been effected.
In 1068 a mandate was issued that troops in the sub-prefectural districts which
were not up to regulation standard should be disbanded. These troops were of
the 2nd grade (廂 軍). The same order decreed that all troopers of the
1st grade army who failed to meet the regulation requirements should be transferred to the 2nd grade forces. All who failed to come up to the standards of
the 2nd grade force should return to civil life. A later mandate permitted (*sic*)
all over 50 years of age to return to civil life. (According to the old regulations,
61 was the retiring age for soldiers.) The same order permitted the enlistment of
able-bodied and efficient 2nd grade men under 45 years of age on full pay. This
applied to those who hitherto had been in receipt of half-pay only. In 1069 it
was decided that some military stations in Shensi should be abandoned. Cavalry
and infantry units were reduced from 327 to 270. The total reduction throughout
the country was from 545 to 355 units. It is impossible to say how much of this
policy of reduction was due to Wang An Shih, but we know it was one of the
major points of his policy.

resentment and disaffection from showing itself. Take warning
from the incident which occurred in the Liang Dynasty when
an attempted interference with the paid troops led to the
insurrection of Chang Yen (張 彥)."

Despite these warnings, the policy of disbandment was
persevered with, and although a reduction of about 50 per cent
was effected during the next six years,[1] bringing the figures for
the regular army down to 568,688 at the time of Wang An
Shih's retirement from the Grand Council, the Histories contain
no record of any mutiny or revolt such as the Emperor and
Ssu Ma Kuang had predicted.

Reduction of the regular forces was only one part of Wang An
Shih's policy. The training of the Militia to take the place of the
disbanded regulars, and to make them suitable for use in
co-operation with the Standing Army, was the main object now
before him. This could only be secured by gradual modification
of the original Militia Act, which we have already said was more
in the nature of a police than a military measure at the start.

The history of this modification will be gleaned from the
following extracts from the Court discussions and reports
as found in the Histories.[2]

The eventual object of this development was evidently to
get the Militia to consent to take service outside their own area
for the purpose of garrison duty in some military centre, or
even to proceed to the borders for defensive work. This, of
course, involved the people in some strict military training and
discipline, provision for which was now made under the
Militia Act.

Reports began to reach the court of the distress which these
developments were causing to the people. Fear of separation
in the family which border service might involve was a great
source of anxiety and grief in the homes and to the parents
of the enrolled men. Many were inflicting self-injury in order
to make themselves ineligible for this service.

---

[1] Quoted Liang Ch'i Ch'ao, p. 166.
[2] The material in this section is taken from the Dynastic Histories, vol. 192,
section 145, vi, iii.

To this Wang An Shih replied that the Militia were only to be called upon for border service or distant garrison duty after their written consent had been obtained. He admitted that cases of self-inflicted injuries might arise (although the one particular case which he had caused to be investigated proved to be that of a carpenter who had accidentally cut off his finger in the regular course of his work), because as the generality of the big officials were against the measure it was quite natural to expect that they might have incited the people to resort to such means in order that opposition to the Act might be increased.

He argued that such opposition as had arisen against the measure arose in the main from those whom the measure affected deleteriously, such as robbers and harbourers of fugitives from justice. He quoted an instance from Ch'ang She Hsien (長 社 縣), where recently thirty robbers who had been driven from the capital district by the working of the new Act had been captured. Such people as these naturally would do their utmost to stir up the people against an Act which had led to their undoing.

And as regards the injunctions about the Militia attending for drill at specified times, it was inevitable that a certain measure of compulsion should be brought to bear, and he agreed that it was quite feasible that coercion by legal means, though necessary in this case, might be followed by a certain amount of resentment. However, he thought that if the measure was carefully explained to the people such resentment might be minimized or even eliminated.

For there were undoubted advantages connected with the Act, not only to the general public, such as the elimination of robbers, but also to individuals. There was the fact, for instance, that this military training would make the local people less subject to intimidation and attack by bandits. The law provided for suitable rewards and promotion for those who reported the seizure of robbers and other criminals, and then there was to be exemption from taxation for those of the Militia who enrolled for regular service on police patrol or garrison duty.

The Militia Act was very gradually introduced, and the sphere and nature of its operations gradually extended.

During the year 1070, in the 11th month, a mandate was issued calling the Militia officers to enrol for military drill at a time convenient to them, and, of course, in the intervals of the agricultural seasons. According to the skill in arms which each displayed they would be divided into four classes. The first class would be reviewed by the Emperor in person and given official status.[1] The second class would be exempted from the usual spring tax of fodder (forty bundles), and relieved of part of the service tax (i.e. to the amount of 2,000 cash). Should the amount they were liable to pay under this head be less than that, they had the privilege of nominating someone else who should be relieved in their stead to that extent. Militia officers, who themselves failed in the archery tests, could still qualify for first-class status if their own levies came up to standard, or if their seizures of robbers in their area or absence of robbers in their own companies and regiment justified it.

Stringent injunctions were issued against leaders compelling their Militia men to train to the detriment of their ordinary avocations. Those who resorted to bribery or indulged in any other form of illegal practice were to be subject to imprisonment. Informers of such malpractice would be rewarded. If one of the official class should offend in any of these particulars his name was to be removed from the official roll.

The above applied only to the company officers and to the capital district first of all.

Wang Chung Cheng (王 中 正) and Ti Tzu (狄 諮) were appointed Superintendents of Instruction.

In twenty-two counties (縣) eleven drill grounds were selected. The officers called in numbered 2,825. Instruction and tests comprised the use of the bow and crossbow, also mounted archery. Military instructors were appointed from the regular army to the number of 270. Thirty supervisory instructors were also appointed, with ten special liaison officers

---

[1] Culled from the Dynastic Histories, vol. 192, section 145, vi, iii.

from the official circle. During the instruction period each man was to be provided with a food allowance and a cash bonus of three " strings " per month. Weapons and mail would be provided at Government expense if necessary, and prizes of silver dishes and wine were awarded for special proficiency. Promotion in official rank would be granted for outstanding merit.

When these company officers had become efficient a system of group instruction was drawn up for the men. The company officers were to act as instructors to these, and the Militia were to be drilled on waste ground near to the homes of the company officers. Each officer was to give five days at a time to this work, their duties being arranged in rotation by the local authorities. The Militia were to be divided into three sections, consisting of cavalry, bowmen, and cross-bowmen.

When these regulations were operating successfully in the capital district, they were later extended to the three Circuits of Hopei, Hotung, and Shensi. One civil and one military official were appointed to supervise the working of the measure in each circuit. Ti Tzu (狄 諮) and Liu Ting (劉 定) were commissioned for Hopei, Chang Shan Fu (張 山 甫) to Shensi, Huang Lien (黃 廉) and Wang Ts'ung Cheng (王 崇 拯) to Hotung.

The Military Treasury was ordered to provide the expenses for the scheme. As this marked the completion of the first year of operation of the new measure, the Emperor held a special review of the Militia of the capital district. Records were kept of the tests, and special prizes were conferred by the Emperor. This would be about the end of 1071.

Another important development was made in the 7th month of 1071, when Wang An Li (王 安 禮), younger brother of Wang An Shih, was commissioned to suggest plans for the reorganization of the Volunteers (義 勇) in the three circuits of Hopei, Hotung, and Shensi, with a view to bringing them more into line with the provisions and regulations of the Militia Act.

This reorganization scheme evidently was attended with special difficulty, and called for the exercise of some diplomacy. For the last year or so the Volunteers and the Militia had been operating side by side, out of five men three being of the Volunteer type and two of the Militia. This suggests that the Volunteers were of the three higher grades of residents and the Militia of the two lower grades. There would be this delicate distinction to obliterate if the two were to come together and function as a unit. Then under the Volunteer regulations only one out of three males was liable for enrolment, while under the Militia Act one out of every two was to be called upon.

The History notes that Wang An Shih suggested that the change should be introduced so gradually and in so diplomatic a manner that the Volunteers would be converted into Militia almost without their knowing it. He made much of the advantage that would accrue to the Volunteers in that under the old regulations they were liable for border service or distant garrison duty, whereas under the Militia Act they were liable only for local duty. But we have already seen that the ultimate object of the Militia Act was to make real soldiers out of the people, so that this may have been a part of the " hoodwinking " process to which the Historian refers.

The following extracts from the discussions [1] which took place at Court on this measure will show something of its nature and the difficulties which attended its promulgation and development.

Feng Ching (馮 京) asked " Under the old regulations governing the Volunteers (I Yung), the officers had all been drawn from the residential families of position and influence. Who would officer the men under the new Militia Act ? "

In reply Wang An Shih quoted ancient precedents under which the civil leaders of groups became the military officers of the levies. This system could still be observed.

Feng Ching rejoined : " It will be very difficult to persuade the Militia to take periodical service like the Volunteers had

---

[1] Culled from the Dynastic Histories, vol. 192, section 145, vi, iii.

given, and it is impossible to make them take the place of the regular forces."

Wang An Shih replied that they would be called upon for such duties only after training, but that once trained they would prove superior to the regulars. The latter consisted for the most part of the rag-tag and bobtail of the countryside, whereas the Militia would be drawn from the stolid farmer-class and the residential families. These would make far better soldiers.

Feng Ching raised the quibble that Sung T'ai Tsu (宋 太 祖) had gained and consolidated the empire without using farmer-soldiers.

Wang An Shih replied that that was a time of special difficulty following on the disorderly period of the Five Dynasties. In those days the influential people joined the army for their own advantage, when there were good posts and high rank to be secured as a reward for their services. But now, after a long period of peace, that type of person had become inured to the luxuries of civil life and had ceased to take up posts in the army. So that now the regular forces consisted of rabble chiefly. (In effect he needed the influence of the residential families in order to enhance the prestige and efficiency of the armed forces.)

Wen Yen Po (文 彦 博) urged that after all the way to help the ruler was by way of inculcating moral principles, and not to seek to strengthen the empire by taking such military measures.

To this lofty precept Wang An Shih replied : " Quite true, the use of military force to strengthen the State is not the ideal way of doing things But it is still consistent with principle to adopt mild measures at one time and strong measures at others. Force may sometimes be necessary to the preservation of the State. But force should never be the only consideration. The ancient kings held their armed forces in high esteem, but at the same time gave moral principles their proper place in their policy. The two ideas may consistently be combined."

The Emperor then raised the old " bogey " that reduction of

the Regulars would invalidate the security of the State, and asked how the cost of maintaining the Militia was to be met.

Wang An Shih replied : " It may not be necessary to carry out drastic reductions in the regular forces, as every quarter reductions naturally occurred by death, resignation, and expulsions." If recruiting were stopped the necessary reductions could be gradually and quietly effected. He would admit that the numbers of armed forces at the disposal of the crown was insufficient, but hoped that by getting to work speedily on the training of the Militia, and by the institution of a system of appropriate rewards and promotions, in a very few years their efficiency would not only exceed that of the old Volunteers but also that of the Regulars.

And as regards the expense of instituting the change, that might be secured by reductions which would take place in the paid forces. Equal numbers of the Militia could be supported at one-tenth or one-fifth of the cost of the regulars.

So the Militia Act was introduced and developed very gradually and with considerable difficulty. Although in 1071 the Militia began to devote special periods of the year to military training, it was not until the following year that they commenced to take up regular official duties, and those were only of a local police character. In 1072 Tseng Pu reported that large numbers of the Militia had expressed their willingness to take a regular part in police or military duty under the officials.

This idea roused great discussion amongst the various officials at the capital, but eventually the following mandate was issued upon the subject, viz. :—

" Peasant proprietors in the Militia who wish to serve as local police may do so. Ten days shall be regarded as one period of service. Should illness prevent service being given at the prescribed period, transfer to the next rote may be effected. Food and other out-of-pocket expenses would be granted.

" Each corps shall consist of fifty men, with three officers, two of company rank and one of regimental-officer rating.

" The latter will receive 7,000 cash and the former 3,000 cash a month.

" The police force thus organized must confine its activities to its own district.

" If a large force of bandits had to be dealt with the forces on duty at the time should be supplemented by others on the rote, and allowances would be paid to all. But when the particular task for which they were called had been completed those not on duty at the period should return to their homes and occupations. The service thus specially rendered would count towards their next period on the rote."

In addition the local officials were ordered to replace the old People's Corps by Militia who had at least reached third-class grading. All the latter were to be registered and enrolled for regular service on the rote. If famine occurred or crops failed to yield less than half the normal harvest, such men were to receive official relief, varying in amount from three to fifteen piculs of grain.

In the 11th month of 1071 an edict was issued ordering the Militia to take up regular patrol duty.

At the end of that year the Militia enrolled in the capital district and Hopei, Hotung, and Shensi numbered 691,945 men, enrolled in 3,266 sections.[1] As regards expenditure, there was a saving on the regular army budget for that year of 1,661,483 " strings ". Against this had to be put extra expenditure incurred by the operation of the Militia Act amounting to 313,166 " strings ", with a round figure estimated at 1,000,000 " strings " for rewards in connection with the same.

It is presumed that the saving on the regular army was effected by stopping recruiting in accordance with Wang An Shih's former suggestion.

Instances also of the effectiveness of the measure in suppressing banditry and robbers may be quoted. There had been an annual average of two hundred cases of robbery with violence in the capital district before the measure was promulgated. These were practically eliminated after the measure became operative.

[1] Dynastic Histories, vol. 192, section 145, vi, iii.

These facts are taken from the records of the capital district only. Unfortunately figures are not available from the other districts, so that it is impossible to make a nation-wide comparison. However, taking the above figures as a basis, it is justifiable to surmise that considerable economy on the National Budget had been effected on the military side, and that banditry was being suppressed by the operation of the measure.

By the year 1076 the total forces enrolled under this Militia Act for the whole country, including those corps not bearing the same designation, but which were to be regarded as of kindred type and which it was designed to bring eventually under the Act, numbered 7,182,028.[1]

Liang Ch'i Ch'ao [2] says that this Act which caused Wang An Shih most thought was also provocative of most resentment. Other measures which were devised by him were seen by the generality of the people to be of some benefit to them, opposition arising in the main from the wealthy and official classes. The Militia Act, however, aroused also the resentment of the generality of the people, in that it compelled them to submit to regular periods of military drill and discipline. This is always difficult to secure in any country from the civilian population, but it was peculiarly difficult in China of the mid-Sung times.

Apart from that general opposition, there were other classes whose peculiar circumstances naturally caused them to resent and resist the measure. There was, for instance, the bandit type, whose activities the Militia Act was particularly designed to curb or suppress. These would naturally resist this attempt to deprive them of their livelihood.

And, again, there was a large section of the people which the disbanded soldiery represented, either in person or indirectly through their families or friends. For a certain number were disbanded apart from those reductions which naturally occurred. These, too, would just as naturally resent a measure which deprived them of a comparatively easy means of livelihood.

---

[1] Dynastic Histories, vol. 192, section 145, vi, iii.
[2] Liang Ch'i Ch'ao, pp. 185-6.

However, the character and value of this particular Act may be partly appraised by an account of its succeeding history,[1] which we will now proceed to outline. During the period in which Wang An Shih was in power, i.e. from 1068 to 1077, the Militia Act was gradually extended in accordance with his original ideas. After his retirement in the latter year, and for the rest of Shen Tsung's reign, i.e. until 1085, there is no note in the Histories of any substantial alterations having been made in it. It is possible that it was not further developed, but we can assume that it was maintained for that period.

With the death of Shen Tsung and the advent of Ssu Ma Kuang to power during the regency of Shen Tsung's mother, the Militia Act was rescinded, together with all the rest of the Reform measures instituted by Wang An Shih and his colleagues.

Ssu Ma Kuang was the first to appeal for its abrogation. Immediately after the death of Shen Tsung, or to use Liang Ch'i Ch'ao's more expressive phrase, "before Shen Tsung's corpse had become cold," [2] he sent in a long memorial to the throne, the details of which are given below :—

"The idea of making soldiers of the people may be said to have originated in ancient times, and to have been the ancient practice. But under the old regulations only three men of mail and seventy-two troopers were called from eight hundred families.[3] Moreover, in those days idle folk were very numerous, and to call them in one season out of four for military training was in no way detrimental to the work of agriculture.

"Further, the officers from the Liang Ssu Ma (兩 司 馬) upwards were all from educated and official families. So that

---

[1] Taken from the Dynastic Histories, vol. 192, section 145, vi, iii.
[2] Liang Ch'i Ch'ao, p. 184.
[3] This would compare favourably with Wang An Shih's advocacy of the demand from 128 families, but the latter seems to have been the rule in later Chow times. Prior to that there are indications that these demands for war service were made of a still larger district than the "Ch'iu" (丘), namely from the "tien" (甸), which again was four times the size of the "Ch'iu" and comprised 512 families.

peculation or intimidation did not arise, the most friendly and cordial relations subsisting between them and their men. Therefore success attended the operation of those regulations.

" But now one out of every two villagers is enrolled, arms are distributed, and military instruction is given to them, so that practically half of the able-bodied male population is being made into soldiers.

" During the last three or four years on the drill grounds in Hopei, Hotung, and Shensi the Militia have been compelled to attend for training with utter disregard of the time of year.

" For every man who has to attend for review and practice, another man is required to attend to his needs while there. And although five days only is stipulated as the period of attendance, the officers make a variety of pretexts, such as building or grass cutting which must be done, to detain the Militia for much longer periods than that. As a matter of fact, it often happens that they can only purchase their release by bribes. As the direct outcome of these practices the work of agriculture in the three circuits has suffered tremendously.

" This impressing of the farmers into military service is generally resented, and they are losing their feeling of attachment and loyalty to the State.

" The number of officials required to administer the Act, the expense of reviews, travel, and awards have involved the National Exchequer in enormous outlay.

" If the Militia are required for police duty only, why enrol such large numbers ? If they are expected to fight along with the Regulars, then those living near to the borders will have to give most of their time to military duties, with no leisure at all to devote to the work of agriculture. It may be that farmers on the drill grounds can be drilled into some sort of soldierly shape, but it cannot be expected that they will make any show in presence of an actual enemy.

" The time already spent in the capital district on drill and other military training has already seriously interfered with farming (practically ruined it).

" Robbery has increased rather than diminished in the

Hotung, Shensi, and Chinghsi circuits. If that is true in a time of peace and general well-being, what may we expect in famine times, or when disorder arises, when all the people will have weapons in their possession. In effect this Act is an inducement to the people to resort to banditry for a livelihood."

Ssu Ma Kuang therefore appealed for the rescindment of the Militia Act, urging that it should be supplanted by the older regulations governing the Archers or "Kung Chien Shou" (弓 箭 手). He proposed that one archer should be provided from every fifty families : that the family from which he hailed should be granted two " ch'ing " of land, and that they should also be exempt from all taxation. The duties of the archers should be limited to police work, and suitable rewards should be offered for captures of robbers.

All the archers should be assembled on the voluntary principle as the first step. There were already great numbers of the old Militia available who had the courage and skill desired. If there should be more than two applicants for a vacancy the local official should be empowered to select the one most suitable, his basis of judgment being that of military efficiency. The rejected candidates would then have to be open to challenge by any other who might displace him in the race for future appointments. In this way competition would be stimulated, and official drills and reviews rendered to a large extent unnecessary. The strongest would be enrolled in the levies and the weaklings who had been rejected would not dare to create any trouble.

Should the voluntary principle not produce sufficient men, then impression would have to be resorted to, but whenever the volunteers were coming forward in sufficient numbers those who had been thus impressed should be allowed to resign.

All the older types of People's Corps must at the same time be revived on the lines of the old regulations.

As a result of his strenuous opposition it was decreed in the 7th month that dating from the first month of the following year the Militia in the four circuits of the Capital, Hopei, Hotung, and Shensi should all be abolished. But the drill of the archers and other local levies was still to be retained in the intervals of the agricultural seasons and in a place convenient to their homes. The detailed arrangements for this were left to the discretion of the officials of the Board of War.[1]

But in the interim between the decision to rescind the measure and the actual date of rescindment, Wang Yen Sou (王 巖 叟) entered the field, and submitted two lengthy memorials on the subject, which expedited the rescindment in certain aspects. The essential points of his appeals are given below :—

" The distress and turbulence of the people in regard to the Militia Act was not necessarily due to the character of the measure itself, but to the way in which it was being administered. He thought that by far the greater proportion of the trouble was due to the character and practices of the officials in charge of it, who had no real desire to benefit the nation."

As a result of his appeal a mandate was issued in the 10th month cashiering the chief officials in charge of the Militia Act. The local officials who had administered the regulations were also dismissed, their places being taken by local military officials, who would supervise the Militia as a part of their other work. It was also decided to limit the season for public drill to three winter months.

This did not satisfy Wang Yen Sou, for in the 11th month he appealed for the total abolition of the special Supervisory Bureau which had been established in connection with the Act.

He took the opportunity of once more outlining the suffering of the people from the working of this particular measure. Apart from the actual hardship of the constant drilling, there was the tyranny of the officers, their various pretexts for calling on the time and strength of the Militia, their actual beatings or other ways of intimidating the levies. He affirmed that it had become a common saying that " one should not enter the drill ground with an empty purse ". Bribery and corruption were such that the Militia had lost all desire to live. They had

---

[1] T'ung Chien.

resorted to self-inflicted injuries, separation of families, or actually absconding in order to avoid enrolment. If a Militia-man ran away the officials then pounced on his family (already impoverished by the loss of an able-bodied son) for a fine of 10,000 cash in lieu of a substitute. This very thing had given rise to hundreds of cases of litigation by the poor and aged of the different counties.

He then proceeded to attack the Militia Mounts measure, too, asserting that it was considered a disability among the people to own a horse. Their animals were impressed for the drill periods, ill-used, badly fed, and often died as the result of their treatment.

Summing up, he described all the officials in charge of the Militia regulations as a heartless crowd, and urged the Emperor to give the question his close attention.

He had one or two suggestions to make by way of improvement. Apart from abolishing the special Bureau and cashiering the special officials, he thought that it would be wise to confine the training period to two months in the year, viz. the 11th and 12th months, when the people would be quite free to engage in military pursuits. He urged, too, that it was quite unnecessary for officers from the capital to be sent out for inspection purposes. Local officials could do the work quite well. As a further step he appealed for the abolition of the local Militia Stores and Treasuries.

All these suggestions were adopted.

Then in the 1st month of the following year, 1086, the Board of War reported that the group instruction under the Militia Act regulations had been completely abolished in the four circuits, and that all the arms and equipment used on these occasions had been returned to the officials. They had also issued stringent instructions against the revival of this aspect of the measure.

In the 2nd month the superintendents of these circuits were ordered to take over concurrently all matters connected with the Militia Act, and to establish a new Bureau on the lines of the " T'i Hsing Ssu regulations " (提 刑 司 例),

presumably for control and development of other types of People's Corps.

In the 3rd month Wang Yen Sou impeached Ti Tzu (狄 諮) and Liu Ting (劉 定), special officers previously appointed to Hopei to supervise the Militia Act, and they were relieved of their posts.

In the 11th month in response to an appeal of Lu T'ao, an old enemy of Wang An Shih, it was decreed that even in cases where there were three or more males in a family they should not be compelled to attend for special drill. (This referred to residents of the fifth class who had less than 20 "mou" of land.)

All this suggests that the Militia were not altogether disbanded, but only that special drill, special officers, special Bureaux were all given up.

It was part of the national military system, even under Ssu Ma Kuang, that there should be People's Corps more or less organized. So that from the above mandates and the progress of events during the short period in which he was in supreme power, we may infer that the name at least and some semblance of the form of the Militia Act were maintained. But, as far as effective organization and training are concerned, it would seem that the Act was abrogated, at any rate in the letter, and as regards its spirit the various modifications that were made were such as to deprive it of all resemblance to the original.

After the regency of Che Tsung's grandmother ceased, when Che Tsung became independent, the Emperor in 1094–5, assisted by ministers like Chang Ch'un, Tseng Pu, and Ts'ai Ching, sought to revive the Militia Act as part of his general policy of restoring the regime of Shen Tsung and Wang An Shih.

In the 7th month of this year, 1095, answering an inquiry of the Emperor as to the numbers of Militia enlisted, Chang Ch'un, the Grand Councillor, reported that in the times of Shen Tsung there were over 700,000 men enrolled in the Capital, Hotung, Hopei, and Shensi circuits. . . . These men after training were superior to the regulars. . . . Expenses

were met by the Military Treasury, or by means of reductions
which were made in the regular forces. . . . No money had been
taken from civil taxes for this measure. It was extremely
unfortunate that it had been abrogated in the reign of Yuan
Yu (元 祐).

In the 9th month of the same year An Ch'un appealed
for the restoration of the Militia Act complete with the
monthly review and drill features, and for the appointment of
special officers to supervise the same.

Tseng Pu counselled delay, as in the Shensi and Hotung
circuits for several years in succession the people had been
impressed for public work, and the task set had not yet been
completed. In Hopei serious floods and famine had been
experienced which had led to the scattering of the people, and
it was inadvisable to reinstate the measure just now.

The Emperor, however, was keen to make a start and
suggested that at least a beginning might be made in the capital
circuit. Ts'ai Pien (蔡 卞) thought that if certain modifications
were made in the regulations of Shen Tsung's day it could be
carried out.

Eventually Tseng Pu was won over, and the attempt was
made. He reported that in the capital district there were
260,000 Militia, of whom over 70,000 had received training in
Shen Tsung's day. He thought, however, that as fifteen years
had elapsed since those regulations had ceased to be operative,
it would be advisable to reintroduce the measure gradually.

Later on in 1105 (reign of Hui Tsung (徽 宗)) the Board of
War reported that no less than 871 petitions had been received
from the capital district alone asking that the drill regulations
of the Militia Act should be repealed. It was, however, decided
that the Militia in the four circuits should be called up for drill
in the intervals of agricultural work, and that special officers
should be appointed to supervise the measure.

In 1113 the Board of War reported that under the regime of
Shen Tsung the regulations had called for fifty days in each
year as the prescribed period for each man on military drill
within the four circuits. But in the case of those who attained

to special skill with their weapons this period was reduced, so that at the most twenty-seven days and at least eighteen days were demanded in the year. In cases of famine or other calamity arising they might be completely exempted from this service.

As in the Chingtung and Ching Hsi circuits no real instruction had been given, although the name of " Militia " was used, they appealed that the Act might be extended in full force to those circuits.

This appeal was granted.

In the 8th month of the same year the Board of War reported that 610,000 men were enrolled in the Militia in all circuits, and that the people generally were willing to enrol.

In 1119 stringent orders were issued for the inspection of the Militia, and called for a report from the various districts as to the way in which the regulations were being carried out. One month's interval was allowed to all circuits to put the measure into effect.

The next year an edict was issued, outlining the advantages of the Militia Act as promulgated and administered in the reign of Shen Tsung, but admitting that after many years of experiment the local officials had practically made the measure ineffective as far as the original intention of it was concerned. By their calling upon the people out of the stipulated times and giving them work which they were never meant to do, and by other wicked, deceitful and tyrannical practices they had prevented the levies functioning as a proper police force, and made a dead letter of the Act.

The Shang Shu Sheng (尚 書 省) was thereupon instructed to depute certain officials to get accurate records of numbers and other important facts connected with the Militia in each district. They were also ordered to see that Militia leaders were appointed who were to take regular service. The Militia were to take up police duty once again, and in general to function as was originally intended.

In the 3rd month of 1126, just before the capital was moved to the south, and during the onslaught of the Chin Tartars, Ch'ien Kai was deputed to organize the Militia of the Capital district, and drill them into shape to assist with the defence of the area.

In the 6th month Hu Shun Chih (胡 舜 陟) appealed that Ch'in Yuan (秦 元), a military strategist of thirty years' experience, should be appointed to drill and lead the Militia of the Capital district. This appointment was made with the approbation of everyone.

But when in the 11th month Ch'in Yuan had assembled 30,000 of them and offered to lead them against the advancing foe, the Emperor withheld his consent.

When the Chin armies had actually appeared in the vicinity of the capital itself, Ch'in Yuan renewed his offer, but Liu Ho (劉 韐), Defence Commissioner, opposed the idea, as he wished to incorporate the Militia into his own regular forces.

Liang Ch'i Ch'ao is of the opinion that Wang An Shih devised the Militia Act with the idea of resisting the northern invasion, and that the disaster of 1126–7 was due in the main to its first being rescinded in Ssu Ma Kuang's time and then only partially revived later on.

We will close this section with a quotation from Ch'en Ju Ch'i (陳 汝 琦), of the Ming Dynasty,[1] viz. :—

" The Dynasty of Sung was weak and decadent from the military standpoint. The power and authority of the old military leaders was dissolved in their winecups. The Border forces got weaker and weaker. The Imperial bodyguard was then used to strengthen the Border garrisons, but that left the Capital weakly defended. To make up for this deficiency a crowd of riff-raff was enrolled. This excited the opposition of the local gentry in every place, and the people were burdened by the extra imposts and taxes that their maintenance rendered necessary. The Border and Garrison forces were in addition very poorly equipped.

" Then like a peal of thunder the Tartar hordes rolled on. Capturing Shuo Chow, Tai Chow, and T'aiyuan (朔 州, 代 州, 太 原), they marched via Peking (北 京) and Chi-Chow (薊 州), and appeared before Kaifengfu

---

[1] Quoted Liang Ch'i Ch'ao, p. 188.

" After the removal of the capital to the south, the southern Sungs began to complain that the calamity was due to lack of men, and that even if they had had the men they lacked the spirit that was required to deal effectively with the emergency.

" But if the Militia Act (of Wang An Shih) had not been rescinded : if the people had been trained at the proper seasons, they would have become accustomed to obeying military orders, they would have had weapons in their homes, and the fighting spirit in their blood. In which case even if the Tartars had advanced within the borders they could not possibly have marched so many thousands of li without opposition. But as it was, they rushed on like a river that had burst its banks with nothing to stem the flood."

CHAPTER XV

PROMULGATION OF THE PUBLIC SERVICES ACT

(TWELFTH MONTH, 1070)

COINCIDENT with Wang An Shih's promotion to the office of
Grand Councillor, another important reform measure was
promulgated, which we have called the " Public Services Act "
or " Mu I Fa " (募 役 法), the main idea of which was that
certain services which had hitherto been rendered by the people
to the officials as part of their obligation to the State, should now
be paid for by the Government out of taxation receipts.

This measure was the outcome of one year's deliberation
by Wang An Shih and his colleagues in the Financial
Reorganization Bureau, and the details were finally presented
and passed in the 12th month of 1070. The History [1] notes
that Lü Hui Ch'ing and Tseng Pu had been successively engaged
on the work of drawing up the various regulations comprised
in the Act.

A system of conscription for public services had been
operative prior to this. It was called the " Ch'ai I Fa "
(差 役 法), or " Commissioned Services Act ". The system
as such dates back to very ancient times in Chinese history.
The normal practice, if we are to take the regulations at face
value, would not seem to have been in any way oppressive,
as in the first instance only three days in the year were demanded
of the individual who was conscripted for public work.[2] But
this regulation must have been more often kept in the breach
than in the observance, evidence of which is found in the words
of Mencius : " The people are hauled away for Government
service when they should have been at work on their fields,

---

[1] " T'ung Chien " (通 鑑).
[2] Liang Ch'i Ch'ao, p. 137.

213

such service resulting in separation, hunger, and death." [1]
It is easy to see that once a system of using the people for public
work is permitted abuses must inevitably arise.

According to the Dynastic Histories the procedure in this
matter during the times of the Sung Dynasty—prior, of course,
to the institution of this new measure by Wang An Shih—
followed on the lines of preceding dynasties. [2]

The services demanded of the people under the older measure
were varied in character, but in the county districts, "hsien"
(縣), practically all the work connected with the "yamen"
or local office of the Government, was provided in this way.
The cooks, servants, messengers, coolies, scavengers, gate-
keepers, watchmen, the yamen guard, local police, clerks,
workmen for building and road work, escort and transport
services, collection of taxes, supervision of the local markets,
and even the finances and banking business all came under the
regulations.

In the sub-prefectural districts, " Chow " (州), very similar
regulations obtained.

Responsibility for the execution of these services, and the
provision of the necessary finance, men, animals, etc., was laid
upon the local residents according to their classification, which
in its turn was based upon property qualifications. The most
important office of all was that carried by the Official Agent,
termed " Ya Ch'ien ", [3] who was responsible for the obtaining
of transport, labour and general supplies, supervision of markets,
and banking. The next in order of importance was that
connected with the collection of taxes, responsibility for which
was placed upon the " elders " or " Li Cheng " (里 正).
Police services were devolved upon the " Leaders ", or " Ch'i

---

[1] Legge's edition of the Chinese Classics, Works of Mencius, book 1, pt. 1,
ch. v, par. 1.
[2] Dynastic Histories, Sung Dynasty. "Shih Huo Chih," sec. 130
(食 貨 志), book 5, ch. i, from which most of the historical material in
this chapter is taken.
[3] (衙 前).

Chang ",[1] who commanded the local bowmen. The duties of escorting, messenger work, and sundry services were imposed upon the " Gangers ", or " Ch'eng Fu " (承 符), and their subordinates.

The manner in which the older system was administered during the Sung Dynasty prior to the promulgation of Wang An Shih's " Public Services Act " will appear from the following account of its operation, as found in the Dynastic Histories.[2]

" During the reign of T'ai Tsu (太 祖), A.D. 960–975, the people were divided into nine classes, only the first four of which were liable for the public services. But as this classificatior. was based on property qualifications, which were constantly varying, it was found necessary to limit the more important services to the first two classes only, the rest of the services being carried by the 2nd grade Regular Army forces which were quartered in the district. The latter procedure was in vogue in the reign of T'ai Tsung (太 宗), A.D. 976–997."

It is quite evident, however, that although prime responsibility for these services was limited to the wealthier classes, the lower orders were by no means exempted in actual fact, for no matter who took responsibility for the work the actual labour had to be found amongst the farming classes generally, and this exposed the system to serious abuse.

For instance, in 1012, during the reign of Chen Tsung (眞 宗), 200 labourers were transferred from Chung Mu Hsien (中 牟 縣) to the capital to carry out repairs to the fodder store of the Imperial stables. But the officials of the Imperial Stud impressed these men to act as stable-boys. As a result of this particular incident, which doubtless was typical of many, a mandate was issued prohibiting the transfer of labourers from one place to another unless very extensive and important public work demanded it.

" But," continues the History, " unjust, oppressive, and deceptive practices arose in connection with this system, due to the prolonged period of peace."

---

[1] (耆 長).
[2] " Shih Huo Chih," as above.

It was necessary, for example, in the last year of Chen Tsung (1022) to issue an edict limiting the area of land which could be owned by any individual. The necessity for this had arisen in connection with the operation of the "Commissioned Services Act" [1] of the time. The landowners, in their desire to avoid classification as "Elders", i.e. "Li Cheng" (里 正) and "Hu Chang" (戶 長), had begun to make false deeds of sale of land to the official classes (who by law were exempt from the public services), the real owners assuming the role of leaseholders. By this edict any person lodging reliable information about such transfers would be rewarded by the gift of a third of the land in question.

This shows that this practice must have been fairly common, and also suggests the burdensome nature of the services which these "Elders" were called upon to render.

Instances of arbitrary and unfair classification of the people must have been numerous, too, for an order was issued early in Jen Tsung's reign (1023–1063) that when new classifications were made they were to be published and the people given sufficient time in which to lodge their objections and appeal for reassessment. The History also notes that very extensive demands were being made upon the people to provide the more laborious forms of public service at this time.

During Jen Tsung's reign several attempts were made to improve the regulations. In the period 1034–8 an edict was published ordering business men of experience to transact the duties of Official Agent, as there had occurred many cases of bankruptcy amongst those who had been impressed for this very onerous work. It will be remembered that transport and banking were part of the Official Agent's responsibilities, and it was quite possible under the regulations which obtained at the time that some wealthy farmer with no business acumen or experience would be called upon for this service.

Buddhist priests were exempted from the public services. So the people resorted to the device of classifying themselves

---

[1] (差 役 法) or Labour Conscription Laws.

as priests in order to avoid these public responsibilities. This led to another edict ordering that all who reported themselves under this category should shave their heads after the manner of the Buddhist priests. Only then would they be granted exemption. Doubtless this led to a reduction of the number of this type of malingerer. It had been reported that in a single sub-prefecture (" Chao Chow " 趙 州) over 1,000 such cases had occurred. This, again, is evidence of the burdensome character of the regulations.

Jen Tsung made another attempt to lighten the burden, which in the main had fallen hitherto upon the farmers and country residents, by making the city residents and merchants carry an equal share. But this was not maintained for any length of time, as later memorials submitted on the subject show.

Han Ch'i (韓 琦) pointed out the grievous nature of the system in connection particularly with the offices of " Official Agent " and " Elder ". He quoted cases of families deliberately splitting up in order to avoid classification which would make them liable for these services. Also of families selling their land or even giving it away with the same object in view. Some, he averred, had even committed suicide in order that the family might not be liable for these positions. " In a variety of ways," he continued, " they seek to avoid the ruinous fate which attends occupancy of these posts."

He then proceded to quote instances of the inequitable working of the law. " In one district there are two villages. In the first there are fifteen first-class families whose total possessions are valued at 3,000,000 ' strings '.[1] In the second there are five such families, whose total property is valued at 500,000 ' strings '. But the law is administered in such a way that the families in the first village get their call for these public

---

[1] The expression " strings " is used to denote a unit of currency. The coins, which had a hole in the middle, were strung together in units of a thousand. In more modern times a thousand of these coins would be worth about 1s. 8d. of British money. But in the times of the Sung dynasty these coins were worth much more than that. The salary of a district magistrate was less than ten of these " strings ". These are rapidly dying out.

services only once in fifteen years, while those in the second village get their call once in every five. In this way the wealthier people are serving less frequently than the poorer ones. Such practices are hardly consistent with the theory that the officials should act as the parents of the people." [1]

An experiment made by Wang K'uai (王 達) in the Chinghu Circuit of allowing the people to pay money in lieu of service proved very profitable, as he was able to transmit to the National Exchequer a sum of 300,000 " strings " derived from this source. As this received the special commendation of the Emperor, other districts began to emulate the practice. But evidently this system left much to be desired, for in the period 1049–1054 another edict was issued, stating that as the positions of " Official Agent " and " Elder " had been otherwise provided for (being paid for by the original nominee), it was illegal to call upon the people generally for contributions towards these posts.

Evidently the officials were trying to get these posts provided for twice over as far as the finances were concerned.

This same edict prohibited the officials from calling upon representatives of the farming classes, called " Hsiang Hu " (鄉 戶), for the position of " Official Agent " or the various " Elder " posts.

Undoubtedly this was designed to prevent these men from incurring serious financial losses such as frequently attended the occupancy of these positions by men lacking the requisite business knowledge and experience.

Later a new division of the people into five classes was made, the first and wealthiest of which was to be called upon for the Official Agent's work and the other classes given responsibilities in proportion to their classification. But it was specially ordered that the " Li Cheng " should be superseded by the " Hu Chang " or " Village Elder " in the work of tax collection. A term of two years was set for each of these.

In the period 1054–6 a new system was tried of selecting one hundred men from each county for the more onerous

---

[1] The classical definition of the ruling caste.

positions under the " Commissioned Services Act ". These were to be divided into groups of ten, the group to act together for one year. This meant that one family was called upon once in ten years, and to shoulder one-tenth of the responsibility. For the second grade of public service groups of fifty were to be selected, who would act seriatim in groups of five, so that these also served once in ten years.

This measure, which the History notes was really equivalent to eliminating the practice of impressing the people (as individuals) for the two most difficult and onerous positions under the Act, brought considerable relief.

But all these attempts at relief were either only temporary in character or applied only to certain sections of the country. Evidence for this is fully supplied by the following memorials presented during the period 1064–8, or the time immediately preceding the reform work of Wang An Shih and his colleagues in the Financial Reorganization Bureau.

The first is by Ssu Ma Kuang, and reads as follows :—

" Since the system of impressing the country residents for the work of the ' Official Agent ' was instituted, the distress of the people has been greatly accentuated, so much so that they are afraid of improving their financial status. For under this system it is better to be poor than wealthy. In a tour which I took through the villages recently I inquired how it was that their implements and appurtenances were so meagre. They all replied that they were afraid of adding to their possessions. For if they planted an extra mulberry, purchased a new cow, stored up sufficient food for two years, or had about ten rolls of cloth in the house, their neighbours would regard them as a rich family, and this would render them liable for the post of ' Official Agent '. If that was so, it was still less reasonable to expect these people to add to their land holdings or extend their living accommodation.

" I was greatly grieved at this state of things, and said to myself, ' With a good ruler on the throne, and peace prevailing in the country, how comes it about that the laws are such as make the people afraid of getting on ? ' "

The second memorial is by Wu Ts'ung (吳 充), written
shortly after Shen Tsung ascended the throne (1067–8). It
reads :—

"As the time for selection of the ' Official Agent ' comes
round, the clerks from the yamen make their trips of inspection,
entering each home. They take the most careful note of every
cup, rolling-pin, spoon, and chopstick in the place, making
a record of the value.

" There are cases of men who after having been called upon
for this service have lost everything. They have become
bankrupt and, possessing no descendants, have had to look to
their neighbours to guarantee their credit. This accounts for
the people adopting every kind of device to escape the burden
of this service. They dare not cultivate much land lest their
classification should be raised. Kinsfolk dare not live together
lest they should be appointed to ' Headship ' positions. There
are none who are seeking to improve their financial status.
I implore your Majesty to make early investigation into the
working of the ' Commissioned Services Act ',[1] and to make
such modifications as the times demand."

The third memorial is from the pen of Han Chiang (韓 絳),
also written in the year 1068, when he was Minister of Finance.
It reads as follows :—

" There is nothing more injurious to agricultural interests
than the current system of impressing the people for the public
services. The biggest burden is carried by the ' Official Agents ',
who are often ruined financially by having to serve in this
position. The next in order of disability are those who serve
in the sub-prefectures (州) as ' Elders ', for these are always
involved in heavy financial outlay.

" I have heard of a case in the Ching-tung Circuit of a family
comprising only father and one son, but who were likely to be
called upon for the post of ' Official Agent '. The father said
to his son, ' It is preferable that I should kill myself rather

---

[1] (差 役 法) or Labour Conscription Laws.

than you should have this position thrust upon you.' So he committed suicide.

"Another case has come under my notice in the Chiang-nan Circuit of a man who married off his widowed grand-mother, and still another of a son who deserted his mother in order that they might avoid being selected for these positions. This, of course, is contrary to all the dictates of humanity.

"There are many others who are selling their land to official families (who are not liable for these services) in order that their classification may be lowered. This, of course, leads to still heavier burdens being imposed upon those who are of the class originally liable for these services.

"Other matters connected with this system which are inimical to the livelihood of the farming class are too numerous to mention here. I hope you will call for reports on the working of the system from all your officials, and call a Conference of your high officials at Court, and that you will ensure, by instituting more of the ancient practices in this matter, that the burden for these public services is more equitably shared by all classes. Only in that way will the farmer be encouraged to industry and prosperity."

It is evident from this that the main burden for these services fell upon the farming classes. We know that the officials as a class were exempt, and that priests shared in this privilege. It would seem that families with only one male member were also exempt. The merchant and artisan class were either wholly exempt or had relatively lighter dues imposed. But, despite that, from an extra clause in Wu Ts'ung's memorial we gather that farmers of the first class were giving up their farms and becoming merchants and artisans, and in the last resort even turning to banditry, rather than submit to the regulations.

From all that has been recorded above it will be evident that conditions at the time Wang An Shih began his reform work were such as called for radical changes in this matter of the public services. Men like Fan Wen Cheng (范 文 正) had suggested that a number of districts might be amalgamated but be liable only for the services hitherto required of one.

Han Ch'i proposed that a fresh land survey be made and the districts reassessed on an area basis. Ssu Ma Kuang sent in an appeal that the post of " Official Agent " should be made a paid appointment under the Government, and that the rest of the public services might be carried by the farming class. These were all measures of relief, but dealt with the problem only partially. It was left to Wang An Shih to make a proposal sufficiently radical and comprehensive as to be worthy of the name of really constructive and just reform.

It will be remembered that during the year 1069 the Financial Reorganization Bureau had sent out a Commission of eight to make inquiry into the working of the Commissioned Services Acts and Taxation Measures, and to make a report. This having been received, the Emperor ordered the Bureau to present their detailed proposals for reform.[1] This was done as follows :—

" After a full and detailed examination into all the proposals which have been made, we have reached the conclusion that the best plan is to order the people to pay money to provide for the public services. That we assume is what is meant by the ancient practice of using the monetary contributions of the people for the support of those who were employed on official work.[2]

" Our present suggestion is that we first draw up a detailed scheme looking to reform on these lines, that this scheme be published broadcast throughout the country, and that opinions be solicited as to the advisability or otherwise of proceeding with this matter, before any actual new law be framed."

This suggestion gained the Emperor's approval, and the following circular was issued, viz. :—

" Great difficulty has arisen in connection with the practice of using ' Official Agents ' especially on the financial side, it having been found impossible to secure an equitable allocation of funds for this onerous position.

[1] " Shih Huo Chih," as above. Also Liang Ch'i Ch'ao, p. 141, quoted from " Wen Hsien T'ung K'ao " (文 獻 通 考), vol. xii.

[2] " Shu Jen Tsai Kuan " (庶 人 在 官), quoted from Chow Li (周 禮).

"As a measure of relief and reform it is now proposed to put the city market taxes and the sale of wines, which were formerly managed by the 'Official Agent', under the direct supervision of the Government, but that the proceeds from these sources shall, as heretofore, be set aside for the expenses of the 'Official Agent'. In addition monies which shall hereafter be collected in lieu of public services, formerly rendered by the people as part of their State taxes, shall also be devoted to this particular purpose. Further, the proceeds from country and suburban markets which had also formerly been a special perquisite of the 'Official Agent' and under his sole control, shall be made a definite figure and offered as a reward to any who volunteer for the post of Official Agent in the future.

"It is further proposed that in future the 'Official Agent' should be relieved of all responsibility for official land and water transport, of official granary and treasury supervision, of the Government Courier services, and of market and Government banking business.

"In this way it is hoped that those features which under the old regulations often involved these men in double or manifold the stipulated expenditure, will be eliminated, and free them from all financial outlay of their own.

"Further, the grievous burdens which were formerly carried by the 'Gangers' and others responsible for the sundry services of the yamen, we propose to lighten by a revision of the existing regulations, so that in future there will be no cause for complaint.

"Finally, it is proposed that those classes who own property and whose financial resources are equal to it, but who hitherto have been exempt from all contribution to the public services, shall now be required to take a financial share towards the expense involved in the same."

This circular having been issued for some time, the matter was advanced a step by the presentation of the following proposal from the Land Revenue Bureau (司 農 寺):—

"We would call your attention to the fact that once these new regulations become Law, those who benefit from them will be the inarticulate and simple rustics of the countryside, while those who are going to suffer from them are the official, rich, and influential folk who can stir up a good deal of popular agitation.

"We would also ask you to note that once these regulations are promulgated, the local Government officials will be deprived of their most powerful instrument of intimidation and graft.

"We fear, therefore, that if we continue to give such men opportunity to express themselves on this new measure by further delay, it will be more difficult to carry out than was at first expected. So we suggest that we once more take steps to make the regulations more clearly understood, and then, without further parley, that an actual experiment be made first in one or two sub-prefectural districts. Then if found satisfactory and successful in a limited sphere they may be applied to the whole country.

"In places where the measure should be operated with real benefit to the people generally, we suggest that suitable rewards be given to the responsible authorities."

The Emperor concurred in this suggestion.

This memorial gives some idea of the nature of the difficulties confronting the protagonists of this new measure. It was an open attack upon the privileges of the wealthy and influential classes, and at the same time would deprive the local officials of their most powerful weapon of intimidation and their most profitable medium of graft. Hence the need for determined action with a preliminary experiment, and a gradual extension of the sphere of operation.

This experiment was evidently made in the capital district first, for the History records that Chao Tzu Chi (趙 子 幾), the Superintendent of the Capital Circuit, presented a report on the working of the proposed regulations in his area, which were handed to the officials of the Land Revenue Bureau, Teng Chien (鄧 綰) and Tseng Pu (曾 布), for consideration and report.

Then after more than a year of consideration and practical experiment in a limited area, the details of this new scheme were presented to and approved by the Emperor, and in the 12th month of 1070 were issued to the country as the proposed law of the land.[1] But before actually becoming law the people were given an interval of one month in which to voice their criticisms.

The actual measure, which we have styled the " Public Services Act ", was as follows :—

1. The people are to be divided into classes according to their property and financial qualifications.

2. City residents of the first five classes shall be assessed for the public services tax, others being exempt.

3. Country residents of the first three classes shall be likewise assessed, others being exempt.

4. The tax shall be paid twice a year, once in summer and once in the autumn.

5. In the case of a family holding property in two counties the tax shall be paid in both if the resident is of the higher classification, but only in one if of the middle class.

6. Members of one family living in separate districts shall only be called upon to pay the tax according to the classification as modified by such separation.

7. Members of official families, families with no male member, monks, priests, and minors (under twenty years old) will be assessed for the tax, but at half-rate.

8. The money received from these various sources is to be devoted to the employment of members of the first three classes on the various public services, salaries being paid proportionately to the nature of the task. (The services demanded of these three classes would, of course, be of the more important type.)

It was estimated that in the county district of K'ai Feng Fu, i.e. the capital, there would be over 22,600 families who would be liable to this assessment. From these a sum of 12,900 " strings " would be realizable. It was proposed to use 10,200 " strings " for the payment of salaries, leaving a balance of 2,700 " strings " which were to be held in reserve as a con-

---

[1] " T'ung Chien " (通 鑑).

tingency fund against famine years (when it might be impossible for the people to pay the tax).

Other counties (縣) were ordered to make their assessments and allocation of the money received on this basis.

It was further ordered that a new classification of all residents should be made once every three years in cities, and once every five years in the country, this to be based on a careful investigation into the real financial status of the people, and to be undertaken at a time when agriculture would not be interfered with. Deceit on the part of the people or unjust classification on the part of the officials would be subject to severe penalties.

The following regulations were also part of the final scheme :—

9. All who offered themselves for the work of the public services should be guaranteed by three persons.

10. Those who offered for the position of " Official Agent " should possess property of a certain amount as " bond ".

11. All archers engaged should submit to tests in bowmanship, and all clerks and accountants were to be examined in penmanship and book-keeping before being appointed.

12. Contracts for two or three years duration were to be drawn up, on the expiration of which the appointment would be subject to reconsideration.

The prescribed interval of one month having elapsed without any opinions to the contrary having been voiced, the above regulations were duly promulgated as the law of the land to be universally applied.

A certain amount of liberty was allowed to local officials [1] in applying them, and they were permitted to make such

---

[1] As an instance of this liberty, one might quote the Circuit of Liang Che (兩 浙), where the city residents whose possessions were valued at less than 200 " strings " and country residents whose possessions were valued at less than fifty " strings " were exempted from the tax. Later, however, this was changed, and all became liable. At least the History notes that those whose possessions were valued at less than fifty " strings " should also pay.

adaptations in them as would make them uniformly just in the various districts.   It was recognized that customs varied, and that the type of service and general financial status differed in different sections of the country.

The tax which was paid by the classes hitherto liable for the public services was termed " Mien I Ch'ien " (免 役 錢) or " Exemption money ".   That which was now to be paid by classes formerly exempt [1] from public services was termed " Chu I Ch'ien " (助 役 錢) or " Aid money ".

The total amount to be assessed in each county and sub-prefecture was to be based on the actual public service needs of each district.   This was to be raised by assessing the residents proportionately to their various grades.

But in addition a sum equal to one-fifth of the total assessment for the actual needs of each district was to be collected, to be held in reserve as a contingency fund against famine years. This extra money was termed " Mien I K'uan Sheng Ch'ien " (免 役 寬 剩 錢), or " Exemption Surplus money ".

Several concrete instances of the result of putting this measure into operation are given by the Histories.   In the prefecture of K'ai Feng Fu 830 men who had acted as " Official Agents " under the old regulations were now freed from their former obligations, and the number of those who had been responsible for other public services in the capital district amounted to several thousands.   These likewise were relieved of their old duties.   The old " Official Agents " were in the majority of districts abolished altogether and military officials appointed in their place, with a monthly salary of three " strings ".   " This plan," says the historian, " was considered most convenient by all."

But criticism and opposition was not lacking.

Hsieh Hsiang (薛 向) complained that in the Liang Che (兩 浙) Circuit a sum of no less than 700,000 " strings " had been collected under the head of " Aid money ".   This evidently surprised the Emperor, who referred the matter to Wang An

[1] The classes so exempted were city residents, families with no male or a single male representative, priests and monks, and officials.

Shih. The latter remarked : "The supervisors of this Act
take only what the regulations allow. But if you wish to be
generous, you may reduce the specified exaction."

Yang Hui (楊 繪) and others complained that in the Suan
Tsao Hsien (酸 棗 縣) the regrading of the people had been
done without proper inquiry, and that certain injustices had
resulted. People from the lower grades had been deliberately
promoted to the higher grades with a view to extracting more
money for the public services fund. On this being brought to
Wang An Shih's attention, he said if that was the case it must
be that the exemption clause with reference to the fourth class
of country resident was not being observed.[1]

Liu Chih sent in two memorials approving the new measure
in one respect, but pointing out its defective and injurious
character in several others. He approved the method of basing
the assessment on actual property qualifications, as under the
old regulations, though a man should have thirty times as much
land as another, he might still be of the same class and called
upon for the same type and amount of public service. Now
under the new law this was impossible.

His criticisms included the following points :—

1. On the new basis of property qualification grading
the rich were better off than before, and the poor were worse
off than formerly.

2. Under the new regulations the sums contributed by
the people would be the same year by year, irrespective
of harvest conditions, whereas under the old system the
numbers of men and amount of service demanded varied
according to economic circumstances.

3. Taxes were reduced or even totally remitted in famine
times under the old regulations, but the new regulations
made no such provision for this.

4. As the public services under the old regime were
provided by respectable peasant proprietors, they maintained

---

[1] Referring to country residents only, the top three classes of which only
were liable.

the services with care and conscientiousness. But under the new system all these services would be supplied by hired labour, under which defalcations, deception, neglect, and losses were to be expected.

5. Especially in the cases of hired police or those on military duty, also in connection with clerical work and other matters, connivance at or actual association with treacherous schemes was to be feared.

6. It was unfair to expect city residents to pay the same amount of " Aid Money " as the country folk, as while the services in the country depended on this for their maintenance, the city residents had only been taxed for these in cases of emergency.

7. He thought a trial might be made of using only the market receipts and proceeds from the sale of wines for the support of the " Official Agent ", and that it might be found unnecessary to use the " Aid Money " for this purpose.

8. The farming people grew wheat and other grains. It was unreasonable to expect them to pay actual " cash " for their taxes.

9. To " hire " men for service in towns on the borders would but induce to treachery.

10. The method of assessing the land taxes varied in different places, and to aim at uniformity in this matter meant that injustice must be done to some.

11. To " hire " men for the police services would not conduce to the suppression of banditry.

12. The policy of hiring men for the work of the Official Agent's post would inevitably lead to serious losses of Government property, etc., etc.

In answer to the above and similar criticisms, Tseng Pu (曾 布) submitted the following :—

" 1. The upper classes in the capital district have been relieved of the duties of " Official Agent ", and they are paying 40 to 50 per cent less under the new regulations than they were under the old.

2. The middle classes are freed from their former liability for the services of bowmen, artisans, clerks, and elders, all these being now provided for by money from the upper classes. In addition city residents, priests, officials, families with only one male, all help these expenses with their contributions, so the amount now paid by the middle classes has been reduced 60 to 70 per cent as compared with their old assessment.

3. The lower classes are now compelled to take service with the Militia only, whereas they had to provide all manner of services under the old regulations. They are not asked to pay a single " cash " in actual money. Their expenses in connection with the public services have been reduced 80 to 90 per cent as compared with former years.

It was quite clear from the above that compared with the demands made under the Commissioned Services Act all classes of the people were contributing less. Further, it was obvious that the upper classes received a proportionately smaller reduction and the lower classes a proportionately higher one. So he failed to understand what the critics meant by their assertion that the new measure favoured the upper classes and was hard on the lower.

4. Revision in the grading of the people was a necessity. Even under the old regulations this was done once every three years. Moreover, the people had been notified that if in any respect they considered that injustice had been done in this matter, they were permitted to report and due consideration would be given to their case.

5. It is said that in regrading the people the only aim we have in view is to get more and more money for the Public Services' Fund. It is said that we have even deliberately increased the numbers in the higher grades with that sole object in view. But, as a matter of fact, in certain districts, Hsiang Fu (祥 符 縣), for instance, we have actually reduced the numbers of residents in the higher classes. This our critics are careful not to mention.

6. It is quite reasonable that all kinds of labour for the public services should be hired. In more than half the empire the system of allowing men to volunteer for the position of " Official Agent " has been put into effect. These men have proved themselves satisfactory in such important services as supervision of the granaries and other stores for the transport and market services.

Other departments like clerical and coolie work have been quite successfully maintained on the paid system for some time.

The police and military duties required under the new regulations are comparatively light in character,[1] and there is no necessity to hire men for these. They can be satisfactorily maintained by the rotary system of family service.[2]

7. Such fears as have been expressed about the Official Agents misappropriating or losing public property if paid for their work, or of police services proving ineffective for the suppression of banditry if maintained on the hired system : that border districts will suffer from treachery or incendiarism if guards and police are hired, I consider ungrounded. (Three guarantors had to be secured under the new regulations for any of these posts, which would help to minimize these dangers.)

8. The new regulations permit the people to pay either in grain or in cash. It is the contention of our critics that if cash is demanded the price of silk, cloth, rice, and millet will fall. They also assert that if commodities are demanded in lieu of cash, that there will be endless trouble in fixing the cash value of the same, to say nothing of the evils that will arise in connection with the acceptance or rejection of goods offered. I fail to see how this can affect the livelihood of the people in any injurious way. They have been allowed to choose whether they will pay in cash or goods, so what else can be done ?

[1] That is, under the Militia Act (保 甲 法).
[2] The Militia Act.

9. With regard to provision for famine years, this is more satisfactorily guarded against under the new than under the old regulations. For the surplus of 2 per cent over actual needs is to be devoted to this very purpose, enabling the tax to be suspended either in whole or in part according to circumstances.

The balance, if any, is to be devoted to land reclamation projects or the increase of official salaries.

10. As regards the further contention of our critics that the " Aid Money " is not on the same footing as ordinary taxation, and that the people will refuse to pay on the slightest pretext, or pay it only in part, I would ask whether there were not such features attendant upon the working of the old regulations ?

11. It is said also that the new measure was devised solely with a view to the enrichment of the official exchequer, and that officials who could report big balances on the working of the fund counted that a matter for congratulation.

Against that I would quote the instances of the Liang Che Circuit, where from 1,400,000 families the revenue amounts to 700,000 " strings ". The proceeds from the Capital Circuit containing 160,000 families comes to 160,000 " strings ". So we see the people in the Liang Che Circuit pay only half the amount subscribed by the people in the capital precincts. But that is because the public services in the capital are naturally much heavier in proportion than those in the provinces. Yet in the Capital Circuit this fund reports no balance (how can you expect balances from the provinces where only 50 per cent of the amount proportionately is collected ?)."

Further opportunity was afforded to Yang Hui and Liu Chih to answer these arguments. The Histories do not give any details of these, but quote the latter's assertion that it was only possible to carry out this new measure because all the big officials at the capital were sponsoring it, and their protégés in the country were in charge of its administration. But it was certainly not in accordance with the wishes of the people as such.

As a result of this controversy Yang Hui was transferred to Cheng Chow and Liu Chih to the Salt Administration at Heng Chow (衡 州).

But with a view to doing justice to the scruples of the opposition, the special inspectors who were sent out into all districts to press for the furtherance of the new regulations, and to supervise the initiation of the necessary changes, were ordered to prevent any compulsion being brought to bear on any who were unwilling to take up the " paid " duties.

The following incident throws some light on the way in which the assessment was carried out in the districts.

Li Yü (李 瑜), the transport officer of the Li Circuit (利 路), wished to fix the " Aid Money " from his district at 400,000 " strings ", but his assistant Hsien Yü Hsien (鮮 于 侁) said that 200,000 " strings " was sufficient, especially as the people generally were poor.   Both men sent in memorials giving their individual points of view.   The Emperor decided in favour of Hsien Yü Hsien and the smaller amount.

However, Teng Chien (鄧 綰) later reported that the actual needs of the area would have been met by an assessment of something over 90,000 " strings ", whereas Li Yü had actually called for 333,000.   Teng Chien also asserted that the superintendent of the Circuit Chow Yueh (周 約) had collaborated with Li Yü in this exorbitant assessment.

In consequence of this report both Li Yü and Chow Yueh were punished and Hsien Yü Hsien, who had advocated leniency to the people, was promoted.

It was only after full opportunity had been given for discussion as above, and after the widest and closest inspection in the districts, that eventually the report of the Financial Reorganization Bureau as handed in to the throne was accepted and the measure applied to the whole country.

The sums received under the head of " Exemption Money " were used to pay the salaries of the officials connected with the administration of the Act and those employed on the public services.

In this connection the following comparison will be suggestive. In the first year of Shen Tsung's reign, i.e. 1068, the amount paid on account of salaries for taxation officials was only 4,000 " strings " per annum for the capital. Eight years later, i.e. 1075–6, over 380,000 " strings " were allocated for the same item.

The Emperor's approval was also obtained to devote any surplus balances from the " Exemption Money " to the purpose of pensioning retired officials, and for the provision of food allowances to subordinates.

In 1076 the total amount from all districts received under the head of " Exemption Money " was 10,414,553 " strings ".

In 1077 Lü T'ao (呂 陶), official at P'eng Chow (彭 州), complained that the officials in different districts were adding all sorts of improvised taxes under the heading of " Surplus Money ". The door for this kind of practice had possibly been opened by an earlier regulation that for every 1,000 cash collected under this head an additional 5 cash should be received for the repairs to yamens, yamen furniture and utensils, and the transport of grain, and that if this sum should prove insufficient it could be supplemented by fines imposed on those convicted of light offences against the law.

Lü T'ao added that in the period 1073–7 the surplus fund received from the four districts which formed his area amounted to 48,700 " strings ". This year he had been ordered to collect another 10,000. If the whole of the Ssu Ch'uan Circuit was to subscribe in the same proportion it would realize a sum of 500,000 or 600,000 " strings ", and if applied to the whole empire it would mean that a sum of six to seven million " strings " would be in the hands of the Government on the " Surplus Money " account.

This he considered would soon lead to a serious shortage of ready money, that trade would be interfered with, and that merchants and farmers would suffer greatly.

He suggested that possibly the Court was ignorant that this " Surplus Money " was being collected in such huge sums.

He therefore appealed that this part of the measure might

be suspended for some years, or that only one-tenth of the 2 per cent might be accepted temporarily.

Certain modifications which were made in the original measure should be noted here.

In 1075 the official class were granted a rebate of one-half their contribution to the " Aid Money " fund, on condition that the amount of the rebate was not to exceed 20 " strings ".

In 1079 (after Wang An Shih had resigned) city residents were commanded to pay the " Exemption Money " on the same basis as country residents.

The same year, on the appeal of Liu I (劉 誼), official salaries which came under the Act were reduced by 2 " strings " a month per capita. In the Kuang Hsi Circuit, which Liu I represented, this reduced the total paid for salaries under this head by 1,200 " strings ". This reduction was made on receiving his report that from the Kuang Hsi Circuit 190,000 " strings " had been contributed by 200,000 people under the heading of " Exemption Money ", which he thought excessive.

In 1084 the total proceeds from this tax for the whole empire amounted to 18,729,300 " strings ", or more by one-third than had been received in 1076.

The type of criticism prevalent about this time was that although receipts connected with this measure had greatly increased, the number of people employed under the Act had not increased in proportion. It was also frequently averred that the officials could not be prevented from making demands in excess of the legitimate needs of the public services in their particular district.

After the death of Shen Tsung in 1085 and the return of Ssu Ma Kuang to power, he at once pressed for the abrogation of the Act in favour of the revival of the old " Commissioned Services Act " with certain modifications.

His memorial is given in full below :—

" Under the ' Commissioned Services Act ' the only people who suffered serious financial loss were the ' Official Agents ' who had been drawn from the farming classes. It was quite possible that this was due to their lack of the requisite business ability, and not to the necessities of the case. Some of the loss, again, might be put down to fire or flood, or possibly through deceptive practices on the part of officials and their subordinates. In this way it was conceivable that the Agent might have been called upon to make good deficiencies which in no way represented real expenditure.

"I propose, therefore, that in future the office of ' Official Agent ' be confined to those who have the necessary business acumen and skill, namely, the ' Chang Ming ' (長 名) class. These men have a way out of every difficulty, and numbers of them have become very wealthy from the proceeds derived from the collection of the market taxes. If this is done, all this talk about bankruptcy in connection with this business will cease.

" Under the ' Commissioned Services Act ' the upper classes alone were called upon for the public work, the lower classes and certain specially privileged classes being exempt. But now all without distinction are ordered to pay money in lieu of service, which I consider an instance of excessive taxation. Since the promulgation of the new Act, the upper classes have been carrying lighter responsibilities than before, while the lower classes are worse off.

" The actual administration of the measure permits of the possibility of inhumane practices on the part of the local officials. The feature which causes most distress is the taking of the ' Surplus Money ' in addition to the Exemption Money. Tens of thousands of ' strings ' are collected from the districts under this head simply with the hope of securing the Imperial favour.

" Further, ready money is demanded for the most part, but the country residents do not mint money. They must barter goods in order to get it, and in so doing in good years they lose half the real value. In bad years they have no grain to sell, so they offer their land. Should there be no purchaser they slaughter their animals and sell the meat. They cut down their mulberries and sell the wood for tinder. They have no means whatever of making any provision for future years. These are the reasons why they are so distressed.

" My own opinion, stupid though it may seem, is that the
' Exemption Money Measure ' should be abrogated, and that
all public services in the districts should once more be based
on the old impressment method. Further, that all those engaged
under the present hiring system should be dismissed

" The position and work of the ' Official Agent ', however,
calls for special consideration. My proposal is that the position
should be thrown open to those who volunteer for the work.
That only those who have had considerable business experience be appointed, and that they should be paid for their
services.

" Should volunteers not be forthcoming in sufficient numbers,
then let compulsion be exercised.

" Should the duties and expenses of the office become too
burdensome, some method could be devised to relieve them,
more or less in line with the former practice. They could be
rewarded by being given the relatively light but profitable
services in connection with the markets.

" As regards the amount now in hand in connection with
the Public Services Act, I suggest that it be distributed among
the different districts, to be utilized as a capital fund for the
operation of the old Granary Laws. A census should be taken of
the present population, and sufficient should be retained from
this fund to keep the people in food for three years. Any balance
which remains after this has been done should revert to the
Transport Officers.

" The Public Services Act relieved the wealthy classes, who
had formerly been responsible for all public services, but taxed
the poor, who formerly had carried no responsibilities in connection therewith. I reaffirm that this Act has worked out to
the advantage of the upper classes and to the disadvantage of
the lower.

" At the present time there is still opportunity to revert to
the old impressing system, but if we delay much longer the
rich will have become inured to their privileges, and the poor
so unaccustomed to labour that it will be found very difficult
to institute the change."

Su Shih (蘇 軾) ventured to "apply the brakes" at this juncture, saying that both the old and new methods had their own peculiar advantages. The great defect of the Public Services measure was that it tended to pile up money in the hands of the officials, and this tended to create a dearth of the same commodity amongst the people. The big defect of the "Commissioned Services Act" was that it prevented the people from getting on with their agricultural work at the proper season, and that it gave the local and subordinate officials too much opportunity for extortion and "squeeze". He thought that these considerations put the two measures about on a level footing.

He added : "In the times of the Three Dynasties the farmers were the soldiers and the soldiers were the farmers. In the times of Ch'in (秦) they began to distinguish between them, but only in the mid-T'ang times was the idea of a regular standing army instituted. Then the farmers gave of the fruit of their toil to maintain the army, and the soldiery gave their lives for the protection of the farmers.

"This was regarded as the most convenient and beneficial arrangement by the whole empire, and even though a sage should arise he would find it difficult to improve on the system.

"The Public Services Act is akin to the idea.

"Ssu Ma Kuang's idea of displacing this by the impressing method is practically equivalent to eliminating the regular army and making soldiers of the people. Is not that the same thing as Wang An Shih has advocated under another name ?"

To this Ssu Ma Kuang demurred.

Later, however, Su Shih continued to press his case in the Government Council Chamber, " Cheng Shih T'ang " (政 事 堂), and Ssu Ma Kuang lost his temper. On Su Shih's quoting a precedent in which Ssu Ma Kuang had conducted an argument with Han Wei Kung on the subject of the Shensi "I Yung " (Volunteers), when he had continued to argue the case in spite of Han Wei Kung's expressed displeasure, Ssu Ma Kuang apologized.

Fan Ch'un Jen (范 純 仁) then took up the cudgels on

Su Shih's behalf, urging Ssu Ma Kuang to take the most careful thought before reintroducing the " Commissioned Services Act ", and requesting him to seek opinions from other quarters and not to rely upon his own judgment alone. He was afraid that unless the measure were reintroduced very gradually, beginning with one circuit, that the distress of the people would be increased.

Ssu Ma Kuang ignored this and expressed his determination to put the change into effect. Whereupon Chang Ch'un (章 惇) replied : " But that is stopping people's mouths. If I must flatter you to ensure my own position and honours, I had far rather have adopted a similar policy long ago with Wang An Shih, and have been rich and influential all these years."

This brought forth an expression of thanks from Ssu Ma Kuang, but a note of rebuke from Lü Kung Chu, who said that Chang Ch'un merely wanted to win the argument regardless of facts.

As the discussion proceeded, the question of revival of the impressment method raised another, as to the numbers of men who should be called upon for the Public Services. It was first suggested that the figures of the year prior to Shen Tsung's accession might be taken as the basis. This was advocated because the numbers employed under Wang An Shih's Act were much fewer than those used under the " Commissioned Services Act ".

This brought forth an interesting memorial from Su Che (蘇 轍), quoted here not only for its intrinsic interest but also for the testimony it affords to his change of front in regard to Wang An Shih's particular measure. Before that had been instituted he had said that " the farming class are as indispensable to the Public Services as educated men are to the Government Services ".

The following are the points of his memorial :—

" The arrangements regarding the ' Official Agent ' were quite satisfactory under the Act of Wang An Shih, and need not be changed. . . . After ten years of experiment with the

' paid ' system the fears of those who said that serious losses would thereby be sustained have been proved groundless. . . . The market taxes for one year amounted to 4,200,000 ' strings '. Of this not more than two-thirds would be required for the general services of the Official Agent, and for the transport services a sum of 1,500,000 ' strings ' would be ample. This aspect of Wang An Shih's measure was thus shown to be commendable.

" He thought that the idea of placing the city residents upon the same footing as the country residents in the matter of the Public Service taxes was good. But he was of opinion that too much had been taken, and that half the amount should be sufficient.

" With regard to the numbers to be employed, he thought that the basis of the year before Shen Tsung's reign was excessive, and that the numbers of the men employed at the present time should be enough.

" He thought, too, that subordinate posts in the districts should all be ' paid '. But it was important that only a sum requisite for the actual needs of the district should be demanded."

However, the rescindment of the Public Services Act was proceeded with, the official mandate to that effect having been issued during the third month of 1086.[1]

But as the result of the above and kindred memorials the Emperor finally decided that the numbers to be called for under the revived " Commissioned Services Act " should be based on current figures. This must have been a hard knock for Ssu Ma Kuang and Ts'ai Ching, for the latter in his capacity as Governor of K'ai Feng Fu had added 1,000 names to the list of those to be " impressed " for the public services.

From another memorial of Ssu Ma Kuang submitted about this time, we note a certain measure of self-contradiction. For whereas he had formerly said that under Wang An Shih's measure the upper classes were better off than under the older Acts, he now said that they were called upon for greater

---

[1] " T'ung Chien."

monetary outlay than before, as although formerly they had their regular terms of compulsory service, they also had been allowed periods of rest, whereas now (under the Public Services Act) there was no such thing as a cessation of payment.

In this memorial he also suggests that it might be permitted that any who were impressed under the revived " Commissioned Services Act " should provide money for a substitute, and then they themselves might be free of obligation. Should the one hired fail in any respect, then the " hirer " should be held responsible.

Further, he advocated that should the method of reimbursing the " Official Agent " prove inadequate, possibly something on the lines of the " Aid Money " of Wang An Shih's Act might be reinstated to help out.

In the revived Impressment measure as finally promulgated, however, we note that in the case of the " Official Agent " (which was to be a paid appointment) the proceeds of markets and fords were to be devoted to their maintenance. Should that prove insufficient, then the extra work required should be " impressed ". The " Aid Money " feature was not to be maintained.

After the old measure had been promulgated once more, it needed but a short interval to prove that there was a lack of means for the post of " Official Agent ", so the term " hiring " (雇 募) was altered to that of " calling " (招 募), which was practically equivalent to " impressment " or " conscription ".

Evidently, too, it was just as necessary to prohibit certain malpractices on the part of the local officials as it had been under the regime of Wang An Shih.

Su Shih (蘇 軾) now entered the field under Wang An Shih's banner, and affords another interesting instance of " change of mind " with regard to this particular measure.[1]

Formerly he had said : " The country people are as necessary to the Public Services as the grains are for food, as silk and hemp are for clothing, as oars and boats to the crossing of

---

[1] Liang Ch'i Ch'ao, p. 146.

rivers, as oxen and horses are to travel. Possibly there may be some other way of meeting the need, but it would have to be something of a heterodox character.

" Officials leave their families and their ancestral graves in order to perform their duties to the State. It is only right that in their leisure hours they should have the opportunity of entertaining themselves. But if they had to go without cooks and messengers that would be very mean treatment indeed, endangering both the peace and the prosperity of the State."

But now he asserted most strongly that the " hiring " system ought to be adopted, and that any system which involved the " impressing " of the people for the Public Services should not be revived.

All that was requisite to the beneficial operation of the Public Services Act of Wang An Shih was to ensure that only the actual amount needed for the Public Services of any district should be demanded.

Ssu Ma Kuang objected to this, saying that the " Impressing " method was the law and that it was already in operation. If the regulations were altered now, the law would cease to get the respect of the people.

He did, however, admit that in some districts the " hiring " system was still in operation, while others were adopting the " calling " system.

He said, too, that it would be better to keep this variety than aim at uniformity by recalling the mandate.

Su Shih, however, was not satisfied. In 1087 he again opposed the idea of Labour Conscription. He said : " The whole empire is against it. The money spent is now much greater than under the Public Services Act. The hardships of the people have been increased tenfold. Men called to undertake a certain piece of work found they could not do it themselves, so had to hire men to help them. So their expenses were greatly increased. Even a sage could not improve upon the ' hiring ' system."

In 1089 Li Ch'ang (李 常), who also had formerly been an opponent of Wang An Shih's measure, was accused by Liu An Shih (劉 安 世) of being a traitor, because he had said that

under the " Impressing " system the higher classes were relieved
of some of their obligations, and that the lower classes had had
their burdens greatly increased. Where the rich had been paying
100 to 300 " strings " under the Public Services Act, they were
now paying only 30 to 40. But the lower classes, who under the
Public Services Act had paid only two or three " strings " were
now compelled to pay the equivalent of about 30. He, therefore, suggested something in the nature of a compromise
between the two methods. That he thought would be in the
interests of the people.

In 1094, when Che Tsung became independent, the tables
turned again in favour of Wang An Shih's policy. Under the
advocacy of Ts'ai Ching (蔡 京), whom Liang Ch'i Ch'ao
dubs a vacillating puppet (反 復 小 人), the Public Services
Act of his regime was reinstated together with others. It will
be remembered that Ts'ai Ching had assisted Ssu Ma Kuang
to rescind Wang An Shih's measures eight years previously,
but now he had become the chief protagonist of their restoration.

It has to be said, however, that considerable modifications
were introduced, and that the method of administering them was
not the same as had obtained in Wang An Shih's day.

In some form or other the idea of " hiring " men for the Public
Services persisted through the Sung Dynasty and has, in fact,
persisted to the present day. There has also been a good
deal of the " impressing " system maintained as well, and is
much in evidence nowadays in a land distracted by civil war.

CHAPTER XVI

STATE TRADE AND BARTER MEASURE

市 易 法

THIS measure had much in common with the Equitable Transport Measure which was first promulgated in 1069. In fact, as has already been suggested above,[1] it would seem that this new measure incorporated the older one. The Economical Transport Measure was concerned primarily with the Land Revenue Services, but this new measure was much wider in scope, being more in the nature of a State Trade Monopoly, affecting all kinds of goods.

The main object of the measure as it eventually developed through experiment seems to have been to relieve the small farmer, artisan, and trader of surplus stocks, which were to be purchased by the Government at fixed prices. Exchanges of goods could be effected through the agency of the Government Bureau established for this purpose, and loans could be contracted either of goods or money at fixed rates of interest.

In this, as in other economical measures promulgated under the regime of Wang An Shih, there was also included the idea of controlling the wealthy " combines " and money-lenders, who took advantage of the small merchant's or farmer's lack of a market to buy up their surplus stocks at very low prices, or to offer loans at exorbitant rates of interest, when they were in financial need. This enabled the " Combine " to store the goods thus purchased until there was a dearth of any particular commodity, which could then be sold out at high prices.

So one idea of this measure was to secure Government control of this business. This would ensure that the prices of things either for purchase or sale were fixed more equitably with a view to relieving the people's economic distress.

[1] See Chapter XII.

Credit for originating the measure seems to belong, not to Wang An Shih but to Wang Shao (王 韶), who, in the 10th month of 1070, proposed something of this character in connection with his scheme for colonizing the north-west.[1] His great purpose was to cultivate friendly relations with the border tribes in the area of the T'ao River (洮 河), hoping thereby that they would be brought into allegiance to China. If this could be done the Hsi Hsia would be deprived of one of their most powerful allies ; China would be able to recapture the Ho Huang (河 湟) territory, and thus close one of the most accessible routes of the threatened invasion.

Wang Shao, having been appointed Pacification Commissioner for the Ch'in-Feng (秦 鳳 路) Circuit, i.e. modern Shensi and Kansu, outlined his scheme as follows :—

"The territory from Wei Yuan (渭 源) to Ch'in Chow (秦 州) was, he affirmed, suitable for cultivation. This area, which comprised some 10,000 ch'ing (頃), needed colonists. But before farmers could be induced to settle there, it was necessary to encourage trade. If that could be done under Government auspices, the land could soon be settled and brought under cultivation, and the territory would naturally come to be regarded as part of the Chinese empire.

" His suggestion was that the Government should initiate the project by granting a capital sum, which would enable purchases of goods to be made, and permit of the organization of a Trade and Barter Bureau. Branches of this would be set up at various points along the frontier, which would offer the natives both within and outside the border facilities for the exchange of goods ; the opportunity to cultivate friendly relations would be afforded thereby ; and an alliance of mutual advantage to China and the border tribes would result."

This scheme having received the approval of the Emperor and Wang An Shih, a sum of money was allocated from the Ch'in Feng Bureau of Finance, and the project duly launched.

[1] Dynastic Histories, " Sung Shih Huo Chih," vol. 139, ch. 8, second half, p. 3 (宋 史 食 貨 志).

Considerable discussion arose as to the site of the proposed central Bureau. It was Wang Shao's idea to locate this at Ku Wei (古 渭). In this he was opposed by Li Jo Yü (李 若 愚), the Intendant of the Ch'in Feng Circuit, on the ground that the accumulation of large stocks in any one place in the area would but serve as an incitement to plunder, and that it would seriously affect private enterprise in horses and other livestock in the Ch'in Chow district. He denied that the land was good and affirmed that it was really only suitable for leasing to bowmen in return for their services.

He was supported in his opposition by such notables as Wen Yen Po, Tseng Kung Liang, Feng Ching, and Ch'en Sheng Chih.

This roused Wang An Shih to make a detailed statement of the policy which had led to the proposal.[1]

He was not convinced that it was essential to the scheme that the central Bureau should be established at Ku Wei, but he had no doubts such as had been raised by Li Jo Yü about the accumulation of stocks there being an incentive to banditry. He continued, " The wealthy families along the border often retain stocks amounting to 200,000 or even 300,000 ' strings ' in value. If *they* have no fears of banditry, why should the Government ? To act in such a way would be to demonstrate weakness."

" Our purpose is to make of the border tribes in the neighbourhood a people subject to China. It is therefore essential that we should establish intimate relationships with them in order that our influence should be enhanced.

" Ku Wei is well suited for the purpose. It can serve as a garrison town, and is quite conveniently situated for trade. As the population increases, we shall be able to establish a military post with resident commander. This will add considerably to our prestige in the eyes of the natives, and give the various border tribes full opportunity to conduct trade with our representatives.

[1] Dynastic Histories, " Sung Shih Huo Chih," vol. 139, ch. 8, second half, p. 3 (宋 史 食 貨 志).

" Hitherto our people have been allowing trade debts to accumulate, and this has excited bad feeling on the part of the frontier tribes. The scheme as at present proposed will give the Government a measure of control, and this habit of delaying payment of debts will cease. This ought to have a favourable effect upon our relations with the tribes, and bring them more readily to our allegiance.

" From the revenue which should accrue from this business, fresh tracts of land can be brought under cultivation, and this will help to provide the necessary military expenses. It ought to be quite feasible eventually to station an army there (to be in readiness for the Hsi Hsia)." [1]

The History contains no details as to the progress of this particular scheme in the Ch'in Feng area. But in the 3rd month of 1072,[1] at the suggestion of Wei Chi Tsung (魏 繼 宗) and with the full approval of Wang An Shih, a central Trade and Barter Bureau was organized at the capital (K'aifengfu).

Wei Chi Tsung's memorial which led to this being done reads as follows :—

" The prices of goods in the capital are under no regular control. The Government ought to be able to adopt some measure of control in this matter which will be beneficial to the poor. For the wealthy houses take advantage of the people's difficulties to make excessive profits. In this way money which might be used to relieve the financial stringency of the National Treasury gets into the hands of one section of the people.

" Therefore I appeal that funds be granted from the proceeds of Government Trade Monopolies to establish what shall be called ' The Ch'ang P'ing Trade and Barter Bureau '. Further, that one financial expert and another thoroughly versed in commerce be appointed to supervise this. They should be given every opportunity to procure information about prices of goods. When these are cheap they will buy available stocks at a price slightly higher than current rates, and later on

[1] Dynastic Histories, " Sung Shih Huo Chih," vol. 139, ch. 8, second half, p. 3 (宋 史 食 貨 志).

when goods are dear sell out again at slightly lower than pre-vailing prices. Any balance remaining from the proceeds of these trade transactions would of course revert to the National Exchequer."

This proposal was then incorporated in a memorial from the Chung Shu Sheng (中 書 省) requesting that the suggested appointments be made, and that goods which were likely to remain on the hands of the people should be purchased on a fixed price basis.

It was also suggested that, if desired, exchanges of goods might be effected, and that if any wished to purchase from the officials on credit it should be permitted. This transaction would be regarded as a loan, either five guarantors or adequate property assets to be regarded as essential in such case. Interest would be charged on such transactions at the rate of 24 per cent per annum. From the proceeds would be taken the salaries of the officials employed, and fines would be imposed if repayment was delayed.

Lü Chia Wen (呂 嘉 問) was then appointed to supervise the Bureau, and a grant of 1,870,000 " strings " was made from the Capital and Ching-Tung Treasuries to initiate the scheme.

Criticism, of course, soon became rife. Some of it was levelled at Lü Chia Wen, who was accused of taking more interest than the regulations permitted. Some accused the Government of rewarding Lü Chia Wen for his illegal gains. Other criticism was directed against the measure as being beneath the dignity of the Government, as it involved the officials in dealing in fruits, ice, coal, silk, salt, etc.

Tseng Pu and Lü Hui Ch'ing got at loggerheads over the discussion of this matter, the merchants raised a storm at Court, and the Emperor wished to rescind the measure.

This, however, was not done, the name of the central Bureau was changed to " Central Trade and Barter Bureau " and six branches were set up in the Ch'in-Feng and Liang Che circuits, and at Chien Chow (黔 州), Ch'eng Tu (成 都), Kuang Chow (廣 州), and Yün Chow (鄆 州).

Later again each prefectural city had a local Bureau of this type.[1] In this way that which had been initiated as a local measure of expediency in the north-west was extended to the whole country.

Very few details are given in the records of the subsequent history of this measure. Men like Wen Yen Po emphasized the indignity which was attached to the sale of small commodities by the Government, and stressed the fact that nothing but resentment on the part of the people had resulted from it.

This brought forth from Wang An Shih the following reply :—

" The Trade and Barter Measure has been drawn up with the utmost care, with a view to removing difficulties which for long have confronted the generality of the populace, and also with the idea of eliminating the baneful influences of the wealthy and monopolizing classes. No financial advantage accrues to the Government from it."

Whatever may be our opinion about the character of this measure and Liang Ch'i Ch'ao [2] criticizes it as the least practicable of those introduced by Wang An Shih's regime, this last statement of his that " no financial advantage accrued to the Government " would seem to be justified, for that was the main reason urged for its rescindment in the 12th month of 1085.[3]

The memorial which led to this rescindment reads as follows [3] :—

" The capital devoted to the initiation of this scheme amounted to 12,000,000 ' strings '. This was supposed to produce interest at 2 per cent per month. After fifteen years of operation the capital ought to have been many times increased. But as a matter of fact an amount equal to the original capital is all that is in hand.

" And as regards the goods dealt with, the quality has

---

[1] Dynastic Histories, " Sung Shih Huo Chih," vol. 139, ch. 8, second half, p. 4 (宋 史 食 貨 志).

[2] Liang Ch'i Ch'ao, p. 135.

[3] T'ung Chien (通 鑑).

decreased, and stocks are gradually diminishing. In effect the measure has become a dead letter."

Han Ch'uan (韓 川) also said that the measure was not paying its way, the income not equalling the expenditure. So the measure was abrogated the same month.

Criticism of this measure is reserved for the chapter on Wang's economic policy in general.[1] It should, however, be noted here that Wang An Shih's main idea in promoting it was not to gain anything for the Government, but to ensure that expenses of operation should be met from the proceeds ; that the poor should be relieved of the exorbitant demands of the wealthy monopolists ; and that trade should be stimulated by relieving the farmer and artisan of surplus stocks.

[1] See Vol. II of this work, in which is contained a full critical discussion of Wang An Shih's economic policy.

CHAPTER XVII

SUNDRY MILITARY MEASURES

IT will be convenient at this point to give some account of three other matters connected with the military policy of Wang An Shih. These concerned the distribution of the regular forces, the provision of mounts for the Militia, and the establishment of an Arsenal Board for the whole country.

These three measures were all promulgated during the period of Wang An Shih's first term as Grand Councillor, viz. 1070—12th month to 1072—5th month, when he first attempted to resign.

I. DISTRIBUTION OF THE REGULAR FORCES

In the military System of the Sung Dynasty, prior to Shen Tsung's reign, there seems to have been a five-fold division. There was first the Imperial Army, consisting of two sections, one termed the Bodyguard, or "Wei Chün" (衛 軍), which was always stationed at the capital, the other called the "Chin Chün" (禁 軍), whose headquarters were also at the capital or within the immediate precincts, but who were transferred in relays at regular intervals to important garrison posts. These two units formed the Standing Army or First-class Regulars.

Next came a class of troops known as the Country Force, or "Hsiang Chün" (廂 軍). These were also Regulars, but of a second-class type. They were stationed usually in the main provincial towns, or "Chow" (州), and were mostly engaged in police, patrol, road repairs, or other work of a public character. These apparently were paid at half the rates of the First-class Regulars.[1]

Then came a class of Local Levies or People's Corps, styled "Hsiang Chün" (鄉 軍). These functioned under a great

[1] See under Chapter XIV, p. 193, note 2.

variety of names [1] in the smaller towns and villages as local police or guards, and seem to have been called up for periods of service on a rotary system as part of their contribution to the Public Services. Men either served themselves in this capacity or if sufficiently wealthy hired a substitute. The Volunteers, or " I Yung " (義 勇), referred to in the chapter on the Militia Act, came under this heading, although their services were more of a voluntary character than the ordinary Local Levies undertook, and they had their special regulations and privileges.

Finally there were troops of an Irregular character known as the Border Guards, or " Fan Chün " (藩 軍). These consisted of friendly border tribes not natives of China Proper, who were in alliance with the Empire and acted as " buffer " forces between enemy tribes and the Imperial armies.[2]

Wang An Shih's Redistribution Measure was concerned solely with the Imperial Army and particularly with the " Chin Chün " (禁 軍).

It had been the practice of the Sung Emperors hitherto to concentrate these Regular Forces in the Capital precincts, whence they were despatched under Imperial orders for garrison duty at specified intervals. This probably took place once every three years.[3] This policy of concentration under direct control of the Emperor had arisen from the fear that military commanders, if left for prolonged periods in charge of their own troops at some remote centre, might revolt and declare independence. This fear, too, had led to the device of constantly changing the officers of those forces stationed in garrison posts, lest by prolonged stay in one place, causing too great an intimacy arising between the chiefs and their subordinates, attempts should be made to plot against the throne.

The policy of concentration gave rise to many evils. For one thing the soldiers at the Capital were not called upon for

---

[1] Dynastic Histories, " Sung," vols. 190–2, where the various types of People's Corps are outlined in detail.

[2] " T'ung Chien," under date of 1070—12th month, and compare with Dynastic History, " Sung," vol. 187, section 140, i.

[3] See Memorial of Su Shih (蘇 軾), translated in Chapter XIV, p. 190.

any public work, and because drill was very irregularly conducted they tended to become lazy and arrogant. For another the country was involved in enormous expense by having to transport grain and supplies for the army from the distant portions of the Empire. These were obvious evils. There were others not quite so obvious but still no less real, such as the drawing of hundreds of thousands of men from their homes in the country to live a life of idleness in the Capital, instead of using them to develop the agricultural resources of the State.

The frequent transfers of these troops to the distant garrison posts also was a constant drain on the National Exchequer, and involved the country people in heavy toil on the transport services.

Then again the constant changes which were made in the personnel of the commanding officers, while it tended to minimize the possibility of disloyalty and limited their power and influence, had corresponding drawbacks. For these aims were secured at the expense of cohesion and *esprit de corps*, as the officers were not given sufficient time with any particular force to gain the confidence and loyalty of the men.[1]

It seemed necessary, therefore, that some change should be introduced from the standpoint of both economy and efficiency, not to mention that the morale of the army and people generally was in grievous need of the stimulus of new policy.

So we find under the date of the 12th month of 1070 that the History [2] records the introduction of a measure for distributing the regular forces at different centres throughout the Empire. The control of all these forces was still to be invested in the Emperor ; commanding officers were to be given sufficient time with their troops to gain their confidence and respect ; strict discipline was to be enforced and regular drill instruction given. It was hoped by this means to avoid the evils which had

---

[1] See Memorials of Ou Yang Hsiu (歐 陽 修), Fan Chen (范 鎮), and Su Shih (蘇 軾), translated in Chapter XIV, pp. 186–192.

[2] " T'ung Chien."

been attendant upon the old system, and in particular to free the forces and the people from the burdensome toil of frequent transfers.

This redistribution could be effected only gradually, but the following statistics from the Histories [1] show the results of this new policy after a few years of operation :—

In 1074 there were thirty-seven divisions in the Capital and precincts, comprising the Capital itself and the Circuits of Hopei (west) (河 北), Chingtung (京 東), and Chinghsi (京 西).

In 1075 there were forty-two divisions stationed in the north-west comprising the Circuits of Lu Yen (鄜 延), Tzu Yuan (涇 原), Huan Ch'ing (環 慶), Ch'in Feng (秦 鳳), and Hsi Ho (熙 河).

In 1081 there were thirteen divisions stationed at various centres in the South and South-Eastern areas, comprising the Circuits of Huai-Nan (淮 南), Liang Che (兩 浙), Chiang Nan (江 南), Ching Hu (荆 湖), Fu Chien (福 建), and Kuang Nan (廣 南).

As the History [2] records that the Capital and North-West divisions were reorganized shortly after the idea was first mooted, we may conclude that the above distribution as far as these two areas were concerned was made almost immediately.

A division varied in strength from 3,000 to 6,000 men, but in addition to the ninety-two divisions mentioned above there were twenty-five auxiliary divisions affiliated with them. We know that at the time of Wang An Shih's final retirement from the Grand Council in 1076 the numbers enrolled in the Regular army were 568,688,[3] which would give an average of about 5,000 to a division. The latter figure also indicates that the policy of disbandment or reduction of the Regular forces must have formed part of this policy of redistribution.

The distribution of the forces in the relative strength outlined

---

[1] " T'ung Chien," under 12th month, 1070, also Dynastic History, vol. 187, section 140, i.

[2] " T'ung Chien," as above.

[3] Dynastic History, vol. 187, section 140, i.

above serves to show the nature of the military situation of the times. The thirty-seven divisions in the Capital and Northern areas were held in readiness for the threatened invasion of the Ch'itans. The forty-two divisions in the north-west were so stationed to cope with the menace of the Hsi Hsia, while the divisions in the south and west were to deal with internal revolt or border risings in the remoter south and west.

The History [1] then proceeds to outline the evils which resulted from this new policy, without however giving any dates, or suggesting any other possible reason for their rise. The account reads :—

" But as the Imperial Forces had now come under the personal control of their officers, they began to spend their time in drinking and feasting and idle sports. They became proud and insolent. The military officials began to wrangle with the local civil officials in matters of authority. As each division had its own group of officials and as in each prefecture the old official system still functioned, there was a great deal of unnecessary duplication and expense.

" Although," continues the record, " those versed in military matters knew the system was pernicious, they were unable to prevent its being carried through."

Liang Ch'i Ch'ao [2] traces these evils, which, the History suggests, arose from the institution of some sort of dual control, to the changes which took place in the regulations after the death of Shen Tsung in 1086. Certain modifications then introduced tended to loosen the control of the central authority, which was an essential element in the scheme as originally propounded, and the old fear of military commanders getting possession of their own forces seems to have been realized to some extent. He agrees that this was one of the chief causes of the progressive military decadence which characterizes the Dynasty after this date.

But the guilt for such decadence is not necessarily to be ascribed to the original promoters of the change. Central

---

[1] " T'ung Chien," as above.
[2] Liang Ch'i Ch'ao, p. 170.

control was safeguarded by them. It is the later modifications of their scheme which account for the trouble.

II. Mounts for the Militia

Horses were very scarce in the times of the Sung Dynasty, and of course this considerably affected military policy. The Government had established a special Bureau for the securing and care of animals for the army, which was styled the " Ch'un Mu Chien " (羣 牧 監). This was under the control of the Board of War through the appointment of one of its chief officials to the supervision of the Bureau.[1]

It was Wang An Shih's purpose to increase the number of the mounts that would be available, not only for the Regular army, but also and in particular for the Militia, who were to be enrolled under his new Militia Act (保 甲 法).

Though a good deal of money was being expended on the Government services in this connection, the regulations were not very effectively administered, and in particular the breeding processes had failed to produce any substantial results. By getting families and individuals to keep and care for animals which in time of need might be placed at the disposal of the Militia, he hoped to remedy existing defects and save a good deal of waste.

At the same time he hoped to create a mounted auxiliary to the Militia which would have its own particular value, both for local patrol duty and the necessities of escort and scouting.

The measure, which we will call " The Militia Mounts Measure " (保 馬 法), first appears in the History under the date of the 5th month, 1072,[2] when after Wen Yen Po (文 彥 博) and Wu Ts'ung (吳 充) had raised certain objections, Wang An Shih instructed Tseng Pu (曾 布) to draw up a set of regulations which might be presented to the throne. The details of the proposal follow :—

1. Any of the Militia resident in the Capital district, or in the five adjacent circuits, who were willing to keep a horse,

[1] Liang Ch'i Ch'ao, p. 189.
[2] " T'ung Chien."

should be provided with one at the expense of the Government. If an individual could afford to keep two animals it should be permitted, or if any particular unit offered to keep two that should also be allowed. As an alternative to the Government providing the mount, the people could purchase their own with money provided by the officials. No one was to be compelled to keep the mounts against his will.

2. Not more than 3,000 horses were to be allocated in the Capital district, and in the five adjacent circuits the maximum was set at 5,000 animals.

3. In case the mounted Militia were called upon to drive out bandits they were not to proceed more than 300 li (100 miles) from their base.

4. Every year the animals were to be subject to inspection, and unsatisfactory animals were to be replaced.[1]

5. Those who kept mounts in the Capital district were to be exempted from an annual contribution of 250 bundles of straw, and in addition they would be granted gifts of money and cloth. Those who were resident in the five circuits [2] and kept a mount would be exempted from the annual horse maintenance tax.

6. Should the mount die it was to be replaced at the expense of the individual owner or unit if they were of the first, second, or third grade of resident, but only half the cost of replacement would be demanded from those who were of the fourth or lower grade. It was suggested that the people might form clubs of ten so that the burden of making these replacements might be shared.

The proposal was accepted by the Emperor and promulgated by Imperial decree. But the provisions of the measure were first to be applied to the Capital district, and later to the whole country.

[1] Probably by the people, however, as animals which died had to be replaced by the people.
[2] Probably the five circuits to the north and north-west, mainly in Shensi Shansi, and Hopei.

Liang Ch'i Ch'ao's one criticism [1] of this measure is that it was hard upon the people to have to replace mounts that died. Epidemics might kill off large numbers no matter how careful the people were.

Against that it must be said that the people had the use of the mount for their own purposes throughout the year, and that it was necessary to have some system of penalties attached to the scheme. Otherwise the people might not care sufficiently for the animals and the measure fail of its objective, namely, to have mounted Militia available for the north and north-west frontiers in case emergency should arise.

III. THE ARSENAL BOARD

This was set up in 1072 as the result of a memorial presented by Wang An Shih's son Fang (雱). The latter had been appointed Expositor to the " Ts'ung Cheng Tien " (崇 政 殿) in the 8th month of 1071.[2] He must therefore be given credit for the promotion of the scheme, but we include it here as it formed part of the military reform policy of the time, and must at least have had his father's approval.

The following is a synopsis of the memorial [3] which he presented :—

" Han Hsuan Ti (漢 宣 帝), 73–48 B.C., is styled the best ruler of Mid-Han times, and we read in the times of his two successors Yuan Ti (元 帝) and Ch'eng Ti (成 帝), 48–6 B.C., that the artisans were particularly skilful.

" It may be argued that in the matter of armaments the smaller officials should bear responsibility. But it is also an important aspect of government, and at a time like the present, when we are faced with the menace of powerful neighbours on the border and with the need for dealing with robbers and bandits within the empire, it is a question that the Government should seriously consider.

---

[1] Liang Ch'i Ch'ao, p. 190.
[2] " T'ung Chien."
[3] Quoted Liang Ch'i Ch'ao, pp. 190–1. Cf. Dyn. Hist., Sung, vol. 197, sec. 150, i.

" While it is true that enormous quantities of bows, crossbows, and suits of mail, which have been collected as one form of taxation, are stored in the various arsenals,[1] they are practically useless.

" Further, I have noticed that in the workshops skilled men are very scarce and that idlers are often impressed from the market places to make up the numbers. The weapons which such men turn out have merely the shape and appearance of weapons.

" Also that when officials of these arsenals make their reports they say nothing about the condition of the weapons in stock, as they are concerned merely to report quantities.

" Is it therefore reasonable to expect that we shall be able to intimidate or overcome our foes unless something is done to reform the present thinking and practices in this matter of armaments ?

" If it is thought to be good policy to try to hoodwink the people by pretending that there is no need to prepare for war, why collect all this metal, timber, skin, etc., the products of the people's time and strength, and then waste the materials thus collected by using inefficient workmen to turn out a lot of useless weapons ?

" My suggestion is that we plan for the centralization of arms manufacture much as is done in the case of the coinage. An official skilled in the work should be selected to supervise it. Hire skilled artisans as instructors of the workmen in the various centres. Appoint one of the Court Ministers to inspect the work turned out, who also shall be empowered to offer rewards for good work done. In that way keen competition will be stimulated and better weapons result."

This proposal gained the approval of the Emperor, and in the following year a National Armaments Board was established, which was to control the manufacture of arms throughout the country. Two officials were appointed to superintend the work.

---

[1] See below, reference to materials collected for the making of arms.

The manufacture of arms had previously been under the supervision of the Board of Finance, but this was now transferred to the new Board. Recommendations as to possible new weapons or improvements in the old were sought from officials and people alike.

Wang Fang shares in the vilification of his father at the hands of the Historians.[1] They class this memorial of his as an attempt to curry favour with the Emperor. But no doubt there was plenty of room for reform in this as in other aspects of the Government system of the Sung Dynasty.

Even according to the Dynastic Histories this new measure was quite effective, for we read that after it had been in vogue but a short time there was a sufficiency of all kinds of armaments.

However, along with the other measures associated with Wang An Shih's name and regime, it was repealed in the year 1086 or thereabouts, and responsibility once more laid on the local officials for the production and supervision of weapons.

---

[1] Dynastic History, vol. 197, section 150, i.

CHAPTER XVIII

WANG AN SHIH AS GRAND-COUNCILLOR

FIRST PERIOD (from the 12th month of 1070 to the 5th month of 1072)

WANG AN SHIH had been increasingly influential in affairs at Court during his period of office as Vice-Grand Councillor, so that his appointment as Grand Councillor in the 12th month of 1070 occasioned no great surprise.[1] For three months Han Chiang acted with him as co-Grand Councillor. But in the third month of 1071 he was degraded and transferred to Teng Chow (鄧 州) following on a defeat of the Chinese forces at the hands of the Hsi Hsia, and the loss of Fu Ning (撫 寧), Lo Wu (囉 兀), and other cities, for which, in his capacity as Commissioner for military affairs in Shensi, he was considered to have been responsible.[2] This transfer of Han Chiang left Wang An Shih the sole Grand Councillor, a condition of affairs which persisted for the next three years. Feng Ching (馮 京), Wang Kuei (王 珪), and Wu Ts'ung (吳 充), the latter in his capacity as Vice-President of the Board of War, co-operated with him in conducting the affairs of the Government as Vice-Grand Councillors.

The first act of Wang An Shih recorded in the History after his assumption of sole authority in the Grand Council was the promulgation of an order that a strict watch should be kept on all officials who were not faithfully carrying out the various new measures.[2]

The next incident of note was the resignation of Ssu Ma Kuang, in the 4th month of 1071, from his appointment at Yung Hsing (永 興) and his transfer to Lo Yang (洛 陽) to take charge of the "Hsi Ching Liu T'ai" (西 京 留 臺).[3] This

---

[1] See Chapters X and XI, etc.
[2] "T'ung Chien" Hsi Ning (熙 寧), 4th year, 3rd month.
[3] "T'ung Chien" Hsi Ning (熙 寧), 4th year, 4th month.

was in the nature of a sinecure, affording him full facilities for prosecuting his literary and historical research work. His memorial of resignation is of interest, reading as follows :—

" I am inferior in forethought to Lü Hui, and in public-spirit and uprightness I fall far short of Fan Ch'un Jen and Ch'eng Hao. I cannot be compared with Su Shih and K'ung Wen Chung for outspokenness, and lack the determination of Fan Chen (all these officials had either resigned or been degraded for their opposition to Wang An Shih).

" You (the emperor) now rely solely upon the counsel of Wang An Shih. Those who are of one mind with him are regarded as good and loyal servants of the throne, but those who oppose him are despised as vilifiers and slanderers. That which I now write will doubtless be regarded as akin to vilification and slander. If I am considered to be equally guilty with Fan Chen then I trust I may be allowed to resign, but should I be regarded as still more blameworthy than he, then shall I meekly await your sentence of banishment or death."

However, as has been noted above, neither banishment nor death awaited him, but transfer to a post which afforded him an opportunity for indulging his literary tastes.

Teng Chien (鄧 綰) was promoted in this month from the prefecture of Ning Chow (寧 州) to the Censorate, and also to the Land Revenue Bureau in association with Tseng Pu. The Historian states that he gained this promotion by adroit flattery of the Emperor and Wang An Shih, and that those who knew him best " jeered at the appointment ".[1]

Lü Hui (呂 誨), who had made such a determined attack upon Wang An Shih's character soon after the promotion of the latter to high office, died in the 5th month of 1071. Prior to this he had resigned all his Government responsibilities on account of illness. The disease had first affected his feet, being in the nature of paralysis. In his letter of resignation he had compared his sickness to the current policy of the Government and had expressed his great fear that eventually it would affect his heart !

---

[1] " T'ung Chien " Hsi Ning (熙 寧), 4th year, 4th month.

Ssu Ma Kuang paid him a visit before he died, arriving just in time to hear his farewell message, " Don't lose hope, your opportunity to take part again in public life will come." [1]

Han Wei (韓 維), the younger brother of Han Chiang, resigned the governorship of K'aifengfu the same month, as a gesture of disapproval of the Agricultural Loans Measure. Tho Historian notes that this action was contrary to the Emperor's own wishes, as he wanted to retain Han Wei at the Capital, and the incident is quoted as an illustration of Wang An Shih's arrogance, as the latter suggested that his resignation be accepted.[1]

Ou Yang Hsiu retired into private life in the 6th month of 1071. The Historian notes that he had once before requested that he might be allowed to retire, having reached the age of sixty. But on that occasion he had been given the military governorship of Ts'ingchowfu. While there he appealed for permission to stop the distribution of the Agricultural loans in the area, but this was not granted. The Emperor had then expressed a desire that Ou Yang Hsiu might be recalled to the Grand Council, but owing to Wang An Shih's opposition he had been transferred to Ts'ai Chow instead. This only increased his determination to retire altogether. However, Feng Ching appealed that he might be retained in Government service, whereupon Wang An Shih is reported to have said :—

" Ou Yang Hsiu is a partisan of Han Ch'i, whom he regards as a pillar of State. To appoint such a man as he to a prefecture will have a ruinous effect, and if you find him a position at Court the result will be equally disastrous. What is the use of retaining him ? "

" So," says the Historian, " he was given the honorary title of Junior Tutor to the heir-apparent, and allowed to retire." [2]

In the same month Fu Pi (富 弼), who had been Grand Councillor for many years under Jen Tsung (仁 宗) and who had also held similar office during Shen Tsung's reign, was transferred to Ju Chow (汝 州). The Historian notes that

[1] " T'ung Chien " Hsi Ning (熙 寧), 4th year, 5th month.
[2] " T'ung Chien " Hsi Ning (熙 寧), 4th year, 6th month.

Fu Pi had a personal liking for Wang An Shih, but had raised serious opposition to the Agricultural Loans Measure, which had led to his being degraded in rank and position.[1]

Yang Hui (楊 繪) was the next to go. He had criticized the character of the Public Services Act, and had incurred the enmity of Wang An Shih by a remark to the effect that all these famous and loyal representatives of the old guard had been compelled to leave the Court on account of his unreasonable attitude.[2]

Liu Chih (劉 摯), who had associated himself with Yang Hui in this outburst, was also degraded and transferred to Heng Chow. He made a severe attack upon Wang An Shih and Tseng Pu, asserting that all the ills of empire could be laid at their door.[2]

In the 8th month of 1071, Wang Fang (王 雱), son of Wang An Shih, was appointed Tutor to the heir-apparent, and concurrently as Expositor in the Hall of Classics (崇 政 殿 說 書).[3]

The expedition for the recovery of the Ho Huang (河 湟)[4] region was set on foot at this time, Wang Shao (王 韶) being appointed special Military Commissioner for the area.[3]

In the 10th month of 1071[5] the National University was divided into three departments, for the details of which the reader is referred to the chapter on Wang An Shih's Educational Policy, in Vol. III of this work.

During the 1st month of the next year (1072) a detective agency, styled the "Lo Tsu" (邏 卒), was established at the Capital, the object of which was to intimidate all officials who were inclined to hinder the reform policy.[6]

Ts'ai T'ing (蔡 挺) was appointed Vice-President of the

[1] "T'ung Chien" Hsi Ning (熙 寧), 4th year, 6th month.
[2] "T'ung Chien" Hsi Ning (熙 寧), 4th year, 7th month.
[3] "T'ung Chien" Hsi Ning (熙 寧), 4th year, 8th month.
[4] See Chapter XVI and also XXI.
[5] "T'ung Chien" Hsi Ning (熙 寧), 4th year, 10th month.
[6] "T'ung Chien" Hsi Ning (熙 寧), 5th year, 1st month.

Board of War in the 2nd month. The Historian credits him with having shown great zeal in equipping and training the Militia in his district, and with being a man of great resource. But having said that in his favour, the writer then proceeds to dub him a crafty fellow, who wrung the heart strings of the Emperor and Court officials by the composition of a song which contained the line " I am a man who has grown old in the wilds of Yü Kuan " (玉 關 老 人). His long period of service there had so far gone unrecognized, but by this song he so played upon the sympathies of those at Court that they gave him this important appointment ! [1]

The death of Li Jih Tsun (李 日 尊), king of Nan P'ing (南 平), i.e. Annam, was reported in the 3rd month, and a mandate was issued by the Emperor confirming the appointment of his son, Ch'ien Te (乾 德), as his successor.[2]

Fu Pi finally retired from official life at this juncture. He had been at Ju Chow only two months when he submitted a memorial to the effect that he was unable to administer the New Measures in his district. He appealed that he might be allowed to retire to Lo Yang for medical treatment, and his request was granted. He was given the honorary rank of Minister of Works, with other titles and emoluments. The Historian notes that he continued to manifest an interest in affairs at Court, and frequently expressed himself on the more important questions of public interest.[2]

The Trade and Barter Measure was promulgated in the 3rd month [3] and the Militia Mounts Measure in the 5th month of 1072.[4]

Wang An Shih sent in his resignation at this point,[5] being considerably perturbed, so the Historian relates, with the Emperor's partiality for a certain Li P'ing, an official of the

---

[1] " T'ung Chien " Hsi Ning (熙 寧), 5th year, 2nd month.
[2] " T'ung Chien " Hsi Ning (熙 寧), 5th year, 3rd month.
[3] See Chapter XVI.
[4] See Chapter XVII.
[5] " T'ung Chien " Hsi Ning (熙 寧), 5th year, 5th month.

Board of War, who was said to have excited the enmity of Wang An Shih by his opposition to the Public Services Act. He was charged with securing the dismissal of a Court functionary on false evidence, and Wang An Shih demanded his punishment. The Emperor admitted that Li P'ing (李 評) was guilty, but took no steps to publicly incriminate him. On the following day Wang An Shih asked the Emperor for a transfer to a post in the south-east. The Emperor replied, " Such intimacy as has subsisted between us is almost unknown in the annals of history. Prior to your admission to the Literary Council I remained uninformed on matters of the greatest import, but since you have been associated with me I have gained great enlightenment. Why should you wish to desert me now that Government matters are just beginning to assume good shape ? "

As Wang An Shih persisted in his intention to resign, the Emperor said, " I suppose my attitude to Li P'ing has rendered you dubious about my confidence in you. But remember that we have been intimate since the time you were appointed to the Edicts Board. Later on, after you had been appointed Vice-Grand Councillor, when Lü Hui, in his attainder, likened you to such infamous fellows as Shao Cheng Mao (少 正 卯) and Lü Ch'i (盧 杞), I in no wise wavered in my regard for you. Can you imagine, after that, that anyone could shake my confidence in you ? "

Still Wang An Shih persisted, and handed in his resignation to the Emperor in person. The latter, however, refused even to look at it, and eventually, after much palaver and persuasion, he was induced to return to his post.

The above incidents are taken from the Histories, and have been recorded with little or no comment as to their feasibility or otherwise. As a special section has been devoted to this subject,[1] we are not burdening the narrative at this stage with criticism of the traditional records. However, as this chapter contains so many references to the resignation of famous men on account of their attitude to Wang An Shih's policy, and as there are suggestions here and there that Wang An Shih was conniving

[1] See Vol. II of this work.

at the employment of inferior men in the Government services, it is only just that something should be said on the other side straightaway.

With that in view we will now introduce a memorial which was submitted to the throne by Wang An Shih about this time. It is entitled " Five Matters of Government " (五 事 劄 子), and reads as follows [1] :—

" During the five years that your Majesty has been on the throne numerous reforms have been instituted. Each of these has been carefully devised, with proper regulations for administration, and now they have been incorporated as part of the recognized law of the land. Great benefit is already discernible from the institution of these reforms. But amongst these are five measures of relatively greater importance which have excited a very great deal of discussion and criticism. I would, however, point out that these measures are of such a character that their effectiveness or otherwise can only be gauged after a comparatively lengthy period of trial.

" The five measures to which I refer are : (1) The north-western military policy, aiming at the placation of the area ; (2) The Agricultural Loans Measure ; (3) The Public Services Act ; (4) The Militia Act ; (5) The Trade and Barter Measure.

" With regard to the first, it should be noted that in the Ch'ing T'ang (青 唐) and T'ao Ho (洮 河) region, comprising some three thousand li of territory, the hitherto unsubdued Jung tribes (戎 羌), numbering over 200,000 people, have surrendered and become willing subjects of the empire. So that our policy there has already been proved to be effective.

" As regards the second, I would draw your attention to the fact that formerly the people paid interest on loans contracted from the money-lenders, and that now they take loans from the Government, which exacts lighter rates of interest. The people are thereby much better off than before in this respect, which was the main purpose of the Agricultural Loans Measure.

" But it should be observed that this measure, together with the Public Services Act and the Trade and Barter Measure,

[1] Prose Works, vol. 10, p. 2.

are of such a character that everything depends upon the way in which they are administered as to whether they turn out to be beneficial or injurious to the livelihood of the people. If the right type of man is secured for the administration of them, great benefit is bound to accrue, but if unsuitable men are employed for their operation considerable injury will result.

" In the Classic of History we read : ' Policy that diverges from ancient precedents cannot be permanently successful.' The three measures under notice may all be said to be modelled on ancient precedents. But it is only as one understands the principles underlying these ancient precedents that revival of them can be successfully accomplished. This is what I had in mind when I warned you that these particular measures might be executed in such a way that either good or ill might result.

" The precedent for the Public Services Act is found in the Chow Kuan (周 官) in its reference to the ' Fu, Shih, Hsü, and T'u ' (府 史 胥 徒).[1] A somewhat similar idea is found in the Classic of Rites (禮 記), where in the section ' Wang Chih ' (王 制) we find the expression ' Shu Jen Tsai Kuan ' (庶 人 在 官) or ' The employment of the people on Government service.'

" In this connection it should be observed that in former times the poor and wealthy have not been equitably classified. Further that a considerable variety of practice has obtained in different parts of the country. The result is that the responsibility for the Public Services has in no sense been fairly apportioned. We now propose, under this new measure, to re-assess all classes of the people exactly in proportion to their financial condition, so that each household should bear its just share of the Public Services. We have also proposed that payment should be made for public work of every kind. This will enable the farmers to get on with their agricultural work at the proper season.

" If, however, we fail to secure the right type of man for the administration of this measure, the classification which we

---

[1] " Chow Kuan Hsin I " (周 官 新 義), vol. 6, p. 3.

suggest should be made under the provisions of the Act will not be fairly adjusted, and defects are sure to emerge in the operation of the ' hiring ' regulations.

"The precedent for the Militia Act is found in the ' Ch'iu Chia Fa ' (丘 甲 法) of the Three Dynasties, which was successfully adopted by Kuan Chung of Ch'i (齊 管 仲), Tzu Ch'an of Cheng (鄭 子 產), Shang Chun of Ch'in (秦 商 君), and Chung Chang T'ung of the Han dynasty (漢 仲 長 統).

"We are not therefore in this connection proposing something which is entirely new. It has, however, to be observed that for thousands of years our people have been free to remove from place to place at will, without any supervision on the part of the Government. But now we are proposing a radical change in this respect, by organizing the people into groups of fives and tens, and bringing the populations of different villages together to form troops of definite numbers and status.

"The object of this Militia Act is two-fold, namely to sift out the lawless elements of the countryside and also to instil into the minds of the people the idea that they are to be prepared to act as soldiers in a time of emergency.

"If, however, we fail to secure the right type of man to administer the regulations of the Militia Act, disaffection will be caused by their harassing of the people, and by threatening to send them off to distant outposts or to engage in actual warfare.

"The precedent for the Trade and Barter Measure is found in the ' Ssu Shih ' (司 市) or Supervision of Trade Regulations of the Chow dynasty. It is also akin to the ' P'ing Chün Fa ' (平 均 法), or ' Equalizing Measure ' of the Han times.

"Our object in proposing this measure is also two-fold, namely to regulate the prices of all commodities, and to encourage trade by unified control. This will involve the Government in the provision of large capital outlay of millions of ' strings ', and will require of the people the payment of tens of thousands of ' strings ' to the Government by way of interest.

"One realizes only too well that as the trade of the country is still far from being properly organized, there is a danger that the officials in their desire for fame and rewards, or in their eagerness to get results too speedily, might nullify the beneficent object of this particular measure.

" Therefore I repeat that if these measures are to function beneficially to the people it is essential, first, that the right men be secured to administer them, and secondly, that the measures should be introduced gradually. If we fail to secure the right men, or if we aim only at getting speedy results, disaster will follow.

" But if the Public Services Act can be properly administered, the people will gain in two respects : They will not be called off from their agricultural labours at seasons inconvenient to them and their financial responsibilities to the State will be more equitably adjusted. If the Militia Act can be properly administered, banditry and internal disorder will be eliminated and our military prestige greatly enhanced. If the Trade and Barter Measure can be properly administered, the circulation and distribution of all kinds of goods will be greatly promoted and the national Treasury will be provided with adequate resources."

It is quite clear from the above that Wang An Shih had none but just and beneficent ideals in promoting these important reform measures, and that he was fully aware of the danger of employing unsuitable men for their administration. It would also appear that the Emperor Shen Tsung was in a greater hurry to see results from the operation of these measures than was wise, and that Wang An Shih would have developed them much more gradually if he had had his way.

The great difficulty facing Wang An Shih, and in fact, any reformer of that age, was the lack of able and conscientious men to supervise the administration of such measures as were then proposed. It is to this more than any other factor that we are to look for the eventual failure of the reform policy.

CHAPTER XIX

WANG AN SHIH AS GRAND COUNCILLOR

SECOND PERIOD (1072, 5th month, to 1074, 4th month)

HAVING been reassured of the Emperor's confidence and favour, Wang An Shih was now ready to persevere with his reform policy, despite the continuance of strong opposition.

'In the 7th intercalary month Chang Ch'un was appointed as Special Inspector of the Ching-Hu Circuit (north) to deal with an appeal from certain Man (蠻) tribes in the area that the Chinese Government should come to their help against the oppression of their chieftains.[1]

This, says the History, arose out of the Emperor's desire to overawe the border tribes by strong military action.

In the 8th month reports of a victory over the Thibetans and the fortifying of Wu Sheng (武 勝) by Wang Shao, reached the Capital.[2] Some discussion occurred at Court between the Emperor, Wang An Shih, and Wen Yen Po about the expense of this expedition. Wang Shao had hoped to get the expenses of this expedition out of the proceeds of the Trade and Barter Measure, but evidently it had been found necessary to call upon the National Exchequer. Wen Yen Po was overruled in the argument, so ceased to discuss the matter.

Ou Yang Hsiu died this month.[2] He had just completed the History of the Five Dynasties which the Emperor had commissioned him to undertake. " He was a man of high principle and great moral courage," says the record, " a great scholar and protégé of Han Yü. All the men he recommended to the throne became famous." (We remember that Wang An Shih was one of these.)

The same month one T'ang Chung raised a great storm at court. He had been promoted to various educational posts on

[1] " T'ung Chien " Hsi Ning (熙 寧), 5th year, 7th month (intercalary).
[2] " T'ung Chien " Hsi Ning (熙 寧), 5th year, 8th month.

Wang An Shih's recommendation, " because," says the History, " he had attributed the difficulty of administering the Agricultural Loans Measure to the opposition of big officials like Han Ch'i (who ought to have been beheaded)."[1] However, just as Wang An Shih was contemplating giving him still further promotion to the Censorate, he became suspicious of the loyalty of his protégé, and gave him only a subsidiary appointment instead.

This roused T'ang Chung's wrath, and he submitted no less than twenty memorials on current affairs, all of a critical character, which were allowed to lie unnoticed.

T'ang awaited his opportunity for revenge. This was afforded him at the conclusion of a general congratulatory audience, when he requested private conversation with the Emperor. The latter suggested that he might wait until another day, whereupon T'ang prostrated himself upon the ground and resolutely refused to rise. Seeing there was no alternative, the Emperor called him to ascend the stairs. He said as he approached, " All that I have to say affects the important officials, and as I am about to accuse them of illegal practices I hope you will permit me to go into the matter in considerable detail." So putting his ivory tablet into his girdle he took out his manuscript. Then fixing his gaze upon Wang An Shih he said, " Come a little nearer, Wang An Shih ! "

Seeing that Wang An Shih was very slow in responding, he yelled, " You see how this fellow behaves in the Imperial presence ; that is nothing to what he is like outside."

Wang An Shih then advanced in slow and dignified fashion and listened while T'ang read from his manuscript, which contained about sixty different points. The chief were that Wang An Shih had acted in an autocratic and arbitrary fashion, and that Tseng Pu had usurped authority unlawfully. He affirmed that the whole empire feared Wang An Shih, who had overawed the Emperor.

He asserted that men like Wen Yen Po and Fang Ching knew

---

[1] " T'ung Chien " Hsi Ning (熙 寧), 5th year, 8th month.

how matters stood but were afraid to speak, and that Wang
Kuei was nothing more than Wang An Shih's menial. As he
read this passage T'ang looked steadfastly at Wang Kuei, who
was trembling with bowed head. He went on to describe
Hsüch Hsiang and Ch'en I as Wang An Shih's puppets, Li Ting
and Chang Tsao as his teeth and claws, and Chang Shang Yin
as his sleuth hound or falcon. . . . And as regards Wang An
Shih himself, he could only compare him to the two notorious
villains of the T'ang Dynasty, Li Lin Fu (李 林 甫) and Lu
Ch'i (盧 杞).

"The Emperor had tried several times to stop his reading of
this manuscript, but he continued without a qualm right to the
end, when with a double obeisance he retired from the Imperial
presence.

"After he had left, the greatest concern was manifest on the
faces of all present. The Usher accused him of contempt of
court, so T'ang was degraded and transferred to Ch'ao Chow
(潮 州)."

The "Equitable Land-tax Measure" (方 田 均 稅 法)
was promulgated in this, the 8th month.[1]

In the 9th month the small Hua Shan (少 華 山), or
Hua mountain, collapsed during an earthquake, burying several
hundreds of homes. One historian [2] says that this was a warning
to the Emperor for using a wicked fellow like Wang An Shih.

Progress with the military campaign in the north-west was
reported by Wang Shao, and so at this juncture, in the 10th
month, the territory of the Hsi Ho (熙 河) was proclaimed
a Circuit of the empire. The Historian notes, however, that the
cities of Ho (河), T'ao (洮), and Min (岷) had not yet been
reduced.[3]

Chang Ch'un also reported progress with the Man (蠻)
tribes, the Su tribe of the Mei Shan T'ung Man (梅 山 峒 蠻)
having submitted, and An Hua Hsien (安 化 縣) been fortified.[4]

[1] See Chapter 20.
[2] " T'ung Chien " Hsi Ning (熙 寧), 5th year, 9th month.
[3] " T'ung Chien " Hsi Ning (熙 寧), 5th year, 10th month.
[4] " T'ung Chien " Hsi Ning (熙 寧), 5th year, 11th month.

In the 12th month, Ch'en Sheng Chih was appointed President of the Board of War.[1] He had resigned from the Grand Council in the 10th month of 1070 on account of his mother's death. In the 1st month of the following year he had been offered his old appointment, but had refused.

In the 2nd month of 1073,[2] Wang Shao captured Ho Chow (河 州), taking as prisoners the wife and family of the chief, Mu Cheng (木 征).

This same month one Shen Ch'i (沈 起) was appointed to Kuei Chow (桂 州) with the express object, says the History,[2] of inciting the Annamese to revolt, and thus give China an excuse for openly attacking them. " This was in line with the plans of the Emperor and Wang An Shih, the latter outlining detailed plans which Shen Ch'i was to follow to the letter." The History also records that Shen Ch'i had been given this appointment in place of the original nominee, Hsiao Chu (蕭 注), because he had publicly said that the Annamese could be subjugated with little trouble, whereas Hsiao Chu had emphasized the difficult nature of the task.

A Bureau for reinterpreting the Classics in line with Wang An Shih's ideas was set up in the 3rd month of 1073.[3] Responsibility for this work was primarily undertaken by Wang An Shih himself, but he was assisted by Lü Hui Ch'ing and his own son, Wang Fang. The Emperor had wished to appoint Ch'eng Hao (程 顥) as well, but Wang An Shih had disapproved, so he was left out.

An eclipse of the sun had been foretold to occur on the 1st of the 4th month of this year.[4] So from the 3rd month the Emperor had refrained from attending public assemblies, and had observed fasting regulations. He had also lightened the sentences of all criminals by one degree with a view to placating Heaven. However, on the day of the eclipse it was so cloudy

[1] " T'ung Chien " Hsi Ning (熙 寧), 5th year, 12th month.
[2] " T'ung Chien " Hsi Ning (熙 寧), 6th year, 2nd month.
[3] " T'ung Chien " Hsi Ning (熙 寧), 6th year, 3rd month.
[4] " T'ung Chien " Hsi Ning (熙 寧), 6th year, 4th month.

that it was not observable. Here, according to the Historian, Wang An Shih and his clique took a leaf out of their opponents' note-book, and proceeded to congratulate the Emperor on the fact that the eclipse had been thus screened because of his virtuous character and righteous rule.

(Had it not been screened the Historian would certainly have discovered someone who had said that it was a warning to the Emperor that Wang An Shih was overshadowing his Majesty.)

Wen Yen Po at this juncture once more entered the lists, protesting strongly to the Emperor against his relying solely upon the advice of Wang An Shih in everything that pertained to the Government. He said that the Court should make it their first business to secure the unity and loyalty of the people. With that in view it was essential that the opinions of the majority should be sought and given due consideration. The people were greatly disturbed by the recent policy of change and innovation. Surely the laws and regulations of former rulers and officials were not so useless that they must all be discarded. He would admit that perhaps they left room for improvement. But it was very important that they should not be altered without just reason.

Wang An Shih perceived that this alluded to him, so he proceeded to deliver his soul against the policy of conservatism and *laissez-faire* which he understood Wen Yen Po and others like him to be advocating. He insisted that in attempting to relieve the sufferings of the people anything that could be done should be done, regardless of the old regulations.

Wen Yen Po thereupon pressed his appeal for resignation, so he was transferred first to Ho-Yang (河 陽) and later to Ta Ming Fu (大 名 府). The Historian notes that though he was absent from the Court the Emperor continued to show him many favours.[1]

In this same month, i.e. the 4th of 1073, a Law Course was instituted in the National University as part of the scheme for

---

[1] " T'ung Chien " Hsi Ning (熙 寧), 6th year, 4th month.

educational reorganization, and Fan Tzu Yuan (范 子 淵) was appointed superintendent of the River Conservancy Bureau.[1]

In the 5th month Hsiung Pen (熊 本) was appointed to the Tzu K'uai region (Ssuch'uan) to inspect border conditions and take such steps as he considered necessary to deal with problems as they arose.[2]

The National Arsenal Board was instituted in the 6th month on the suggestion of Wang Fang, Lü Hui Ch'ing being made superintendent.[3]

Chow Lien Hsi, the famous philosopher, died this month at the age of 57. He was of the same school as Shao Yung (邵 雍), Chang Tsai (張 載), Ch'eng I (程 頤), Ch'eng Hao (程 顥), and (later of course) Chu Hsi (朱 熹). The reader will remember the controversy about Wang An Shih's meeting with Chow Lien Hsi, which is said to have seriously disturbed the former's peace of mind. The fact that a man with so fine an intellect had been allowed to spend his life in positions of comparative obscurity gives the Historian another opportunity to inveigh against Shen Tsung and Wang An Shih. It is, however, quite conceivable, as even the commentator on the text remarks, that he suffered in no way from this lack of recognition. He was probably best employed in the quieter spheres of the provinces, where he had leisure for the elucidation, development, and expression of his philosophical ideas.[3]

This month also an extensive plague of locusts is noted, and like earthquakes, eclipses, floods, drought and the like, is attributed by the recorders to the wicked policy of the Emperor and Wang An Shih.

In the 9th month, at the instigation of Wang An Shih, certain changes were introduced into the system of examining candidates for military posts. Formerly it had been possible for a candidate to pass the examination by writing out from memory sections of the books prescribed for study. This was now

[1] " T'ung Chien " Hsi Ning (熙 寧), 6th year, 4th month.
[2] " T'ung Chien " Hsi Ning (熙 寧, 6th year, 5th month.
[3] " T'ung Chien " Hsi Ning (熙 寧), 6th year, 6th month, and also pp. 258-260 of this work.

supplanted by questions of a type designed to test the candidate's practical knowledge of military matters.   Tests in riding and archery also formed part of the examination.[1]

During the same month the news of Wang Shao's great victory over the Thibetans was received at Court, and in the felicitations which followed, Wang An Shih received the gift of the Emperor's gem-studed belt for the share he had taken in planning the expedition.   The victory included the capture of Min (岷), Yen (宕), T'ao (洮), and Tieh (曡) cities.

The commentator on the History [1] says this was the outcome of Wang An Shih's restless war-making policy, which was entirely uncalled for.   Former rulers had managed to keep the Thibetans under control without the bloodshed and expenditure which had been involved in this campaign.

The " Trade Tax Measure " was instituted at this time.   It was styled "Mien Hang Ch'ien" (免 行 錢), and seems to have applied only to the capital.   The details are given in the chapter on Sundry Economical Measures, to which the reader is referred.

In the 10th month, the scheme for straightening a bend in the Yellow River was mooted, and Chang Ch'un reported a victory over the Southern Man tribes and the fortification of Yuan Chow.

In the 1st month of 1074, Hsiung Pen was rewarded for a victory gained over the Lu tribes (瀘 夷) in Ssuch'uan.

The Iron or " Liao " (遼) Tartars sent an embassy in the 2nd month to consult about the border line between China and their territory.   Their complaint was that China had erected many forts along the northern boundary of the Hotung Circuit and that Chinese forces had presumed to invade the districts of Wei (蔚), Ying (應), and Shuo (朔).   So they had sent an ambassador, Lin Ya Hsiao Hsi (林 牙 蕭 禧), to demand the destruction of these forts and the drawing of a definite boundary line.

It was decided to send Liu Ch'en (劉 忱) to recommend to

---

[1] " T'ung Chien " Hsi Ning (熙 寧), 6th year, 9th month.

the Liao ruler that a Commission should be appointed to go into the boundary question on the spot. It was suggested that this Commission should meet at Tai Chow (代 州). Meanwhile the whole matter was referred to the Board of War, and the order given that the opinions of old officials such as Han Ch'i, Fu Pi, Wen Yen Po, and Tseng Kung Liang, who were all in provincial appointments, were to be solicited.[1]

Han Ch'i submitted seven reasons for the suspicion of the Iron Tartars. The first was that China had accepted tribute from the Coreans. The second was the despatch of the expedition to the Hsi Ho (熙 河) region and the fortification of several towns there. The third was that China had planted elms and willows in the western hills which was interpreted as a move to interfere with the free movement of enemy cavalry. The institution of the Militia Act was the fourth. The fifth was the fortification of the northern towns. The establishment of the Arsenals Board and the distribution of bows and arrows of new style was the sixth, and the seventh was the distribution of thirty-seven military divisions in the northern sectors.

" It was to be remembered," he said, " that the Ch'itans, i.e. the Liao, were old enemies, and it was quite natural that their suspicions should have been aroused by all these preparations."

He then went on to criticize the reform policy of Wang An Shih and his associates, saying : " I myself have always been ready to advise your Majesty. But those who have been formulating your policy recently, have said it is necessary to deal first of all with matters which are fundamental, which they have interpreted to mean the assembling of great funds of money and stocks of grain, and the recruiting of troops from the farming class to meet the enemy on the four borders. To this end the Agricultural Loans Measure and the Public Services Act have been promulgated, and the Trade and Barter Bureau has been established. In a great variety of ways money has been collected, new regulations are issued almost every day, and there is no certainty about anything.

[1] " T'ung Chien " Hsi Ning (熙 寧), 7th year, 1st month.

" The executive officers think that the more money they can extract from the pockets of the people the cleverer they will be thought. The farming class is broody and resentful. The merchants and officials are all dissatisfied. There are many things of which your Majesty is ignorant. In your desire to punish the tribal enemies on the borders, and in your hope of establishing a notable and permanent peace, you have first thrown the empire into this state of confusion and distress, and have incited the people everywhere to resentment and induced their disloyalty. These things are due to those who are advising your Majesty.

" As regards this embassy from the Liao, I suggest that you explain that in all the preparations we have recently made we have no aggressive designs upon them, and that you refuse to admit that we have transgressed in the matter of the border line. That you urge them not to make these things a pretext for war, and thus disturb the friendly relationships which have subsisted between us for so long.

" But at the same time I would urge that the policy of stationing all these divisions in the north, which is one of the main causes of their suspicion and unfriendliness, should be abandoned. I would suggest further, in order to arouse the patriotic spirit of the people, that you select men of real worth and ability to fill high official position. If you can but bring the hearts of the people into a state of willing co-operation, the necessary preparations on the borders will have been already accomplished. After that, should the Liao still be determined to break the treaty, then by one terrific onslaught in demonstration of our military might, let us recover the ancient boundary, and wipe out the long standing disgrace." [1]

Fu Pi, Wen Yen Po, and Tseng Kung Liang also sent in their proposals, confining their remarks to criticism of current policy.

In the 4th month the History records that for seven months there had been no rain. The Emperor was deeply grieved, and suggested that anything connected with the administration of the

---

[1] " T'ung Chien " Hsi Ning (熙 寧), 7th year, 3rd month.

laws which might be unjust should be eliminated (with a view to placating Heaven and bringing the rain).

Wang An Shih replied, "Floods and drought occur in the ordinary course of Nature. Even sage rulers like Yao (堯) and T'ang (唐) could not avoid such calamities. All that is necessary is that the Government should do all in its power to relieve the people. That is the right and adequate way of responding to the situation."

The Emperor rejoined, "That is just what I fear has not been done. I fear that too much money has been exacted under the new Trade Tax regulations, and that this naturally has excited the resentment of the people. All at Court, including the great officers and members of the Imperial Household, have talked of the injurious character of this Measure."

Feng Ching having interposed to the effect that he had also heard of such criticism, Wang An Shih retorted, "Yes, of course. All the officials who fail to get their own way flock to you, and so you hear these things. But I have heard no such criticisms."

Han Wei said, "I fear that fasting and the cutting of certain Court expenses is not an adequate response to this warning of Nature. In addition to examining your own heart in all sincerity, you ought to seek for frank criticism from the people."

This suggestion received the approval of the Emperor, who then and there instructed Han Wei to draw up and issue such a mandate.

Then occurred the incident which led to the resignation of Wang An Shih and his transfer to Chiang Ning Fu for a time. As this is an event of considerable importance, we will give a detailed account of the matter.[1]

One Cheng Hsieh (鄭 俠), who was in office at Kuang Chow in connection with the Military services and who had been recommended by Wang An Shih, returned to the Capital to report on one period of service. "He came," says the Historian, "out of gratitude to his patron to offer him his loyal help and advice."

---

[1] "T'ung Chien" Hsi Ning (熙 寧), 7th year, 3rd month, possibly 4th.

Meeting with Wang An Shih on arrival, and being asked what news he brought, Cheng Hsieh replied, " I cannot help feeling anxious about certain recent actions of the Government." He then proceeded to enumerate the difficulties connected with the Agricultural Loans and Public Services Acts, the Militia Act and the Trade and Barter Measure, the various military expeditions which had been organized, etc.

Wang An Shih had no reply to make to this.

Later Cheng Hsieh was appointed to take charge of the An Shang Gate (安 上 門). Drought and famine prevailed at this time, but taxation was very heavy, for the State was collecting money to meet the urgent needs of the Exchequer. Cheng Hsieh observed the poor refugees from the north-east, travelling along the roads in the driving wind, with the heavens darkened by storms of dust, supporting their aged parents, and leading their young children. The roads were blocked with their numbers. He noted their sicknesses, their weakness, their evident sorrow and pain. Some he saw were practically naked, some had only leaves, or seeds, or the bark of trees for their food. Some were even toiling along in chains and handcuffs (probably those who were unable to pay their taxes). Others had taken away the tiles from their roofs or the timbers from their doors and windows in order to pay their taxes.

Cheng Hsieh then made a sketch of all that he had seen, and submitted it with a memorial to the Emperor. But no one would receive it by any of the ordinary channels. So he adopted the subterfuge of labelling it a secret message of great urgency, and got it delivered by mounted messenger to the Yin T'ai Ssu (銀 臺 司).

Appended to his memorial were the words, " The drought is caused by Wang An Shih. If you dismiss him, and if rain does not fall within ten days afterwards, you may cut off my head outside the Hsuan Te Gate. I shall regard that as just punishment for my deception of you."

The Emperor could not take his eyes off the memorial, but sighing deeply, eventually put it up his sleeve and returned to his own apartments. That night he could not sleep, and arising very early he issued orders that eighteen different matters connected with the Government were to be attended to immediately. Amongst these were the following :—

The Trade Tax Measure was to be temporarily suspended. The Bureau of Finance was ordered to reconsider the provisions of the Trade and Barter Measure. The Land Revenue Bureau was commanded to distribute grain from the Ch'ang P'ing Granary to the famine victims. The Board of War was ordered to report on the progress and objects of the Hsi Ho expedition. Each Circuit was commanded to report on the reasons for the prevalence of refugees in the country. No pressure was to be brought to bear upon the people to take the Agricultural Loans. The Public Services Act was to be administered with less stringency. The Equitable Land Tax Measure and the Militia Act were to be rescinded.

As the result of the publication of this proclamation (which was probably confined to the Capital), the Historian reports that the people went wild with joy, and ran about on missions of mutual congratulation. "And on that very day heavy rain fell, and everyone was greatly relieved."

The record continues, "When the high officials entered the palace to congratulate the Emperor on the rainfall, he produced the sketch drawn by Cheng Hsieh, and reprimanded the officials for not telling him the truth about conditions in the country.

After they had retired Wang An Shih submitted his resignation, and then for the first time the officials of his faction realized the trend of events leading up to it. This made them wild with rage. They handed over Cheng Hsieh to the criminal authorities, accusing him of getting his memorial through to the Emperor by false pretences. Lü Hui Ch'ing and Teng Chien interviewed the Emperor, and said, "Your Majesty has neglected food and sleep these last few years in the interests of these New Measures, and now, just at the time when the country is about to reap the benefit of all this thought and labour, you have nullified by one stroke of the pen almost everything that has been done, and that at the instigation of a madman. This is too pitiable for anything."

The officials then congregated in the Imperial presence, weeping and wailing over the Emperor's action. So, with the exception of the Equitable Land Tax Measure, which was temporarily suspended, the whole of the New Measures were once more restored.

The matter of Wang An Shih's resignation had not yet been acted upon, so the History dilates upon the subject as follows [1]:—

"Wang An Shih had been a member of the Grand Council for over six years. He had changed all the old laws, extended the frontiers, and degraded or transferred the whole of the old guard of loyal and experienced officials of the Court. In their places he had promoted a band of clever but arrogant young men, who had gained very responsible positions in quite an irregular manner. The whole nation groaned with resentment, and yet the Emperor continued to enhance Wang An Shih's prestige and authority.

"The Empress Dowager had frequently urged that the laws of their ancestors ought not to have been lightly changed. She now said that she had often received reports of the injurious character of the Agricultural Loans Measure and the Public Services Act, and she expressed her conviction that these should be repealed.

"To this the Emperor replied that these measures had been devised with the express object of relieving the people, and with no idea of inflicting still greater hardship upon them.

"The Dowager rejoined, 'I know that Wang An Shih is a man of great learning and considerable ability. But the number of influential people who harbour resentment against him is very great. If you desire to save him from still greater trouble, I suggest, as a measure of expediency, that you transfer him temporarily to a provincial appointment.'

"The Emperor replied that all the officials regarded Wang An Shih as the only one capable of dealing with current affairs of State.

"Ch'i Wang (岐 王), also known as Hao (顥), the Emperor's

---

[1] "T'ung Chien " Hsi Ning (熙　寧), 7th year, 4th month.

brother, proffered the suggestion that the Dowager's advice was most opportune, and that the Emperor ought to think very seriously about it.

" This brought from the Emperor the angry retort, ' By this you imply that it is I who have mismanaged the empire, and that I have ruined it. You had better take over from me.'

" ' Whatever makes you make a statement like that ? ' said Ch'i Wang, weeping.

" Gloom descended upon the royal group, and nothing was said for some time. Then the Dowager broke the silence with the remark, ' It is Wang An Shih who is responsible for all this confusion. What are you going to do about it ? '

" So the Emperor began to waver in his allegiance to Wang An Shih. With Cheng Hsieh's memorial and sketch in mind, and noting that Wang An Shih was obviously ill at ease, eventually, after several attempts to detain him, he permitted him to resign. He was transferred to the Governorship of Chiang Ning Fu, in the 4th month of 1074, with the rank of Grand Councillor of the Kuan Wen Tien (觀 文 殿 大 學 士)."

Lü Hui Ch'ing made desperate efforts to prevent Wang An Shih's departure, even resorting to the device of sending in memorials for his retention in office under forged signatures (of opponents of his policy). For this the Historian records that Wang An Shih was extremely grateful.[1]

Such is the account of Wang An Shih's resignation as found in the Histories. But in order that a more balanced view of the incident may be gained, we will translate two of his six appeals for resignation at this time. These show in themselves that it was only after frequent and urgent appeals on his part that Wang An Shih was permitted to leave his post at this juncture. The following represents his first appeal [2] :—

" I was but a lonely wanderer when I received your gracious

---

[1] Certain changes were introduced during Lü Hin Ch'ing's regime, e.g. the promulgation of the " Shou Shih Fa " (手 實 法) or Personal Testimony Measure; also the banishment of Cheng Hsieh must also be regarded as a deviation from Wang An Shih's policy. But see next chapter.

[2] Prose Works, vol. 10, p. 15.

call to office. For the last four years I have exposed myself
to the penalties of high office in the Chung Shu Sheng. From
the moment you consented to the initiation of the reform policy,
great opposition arose from every quarter of the official world,
for which I must take the blame. If it had not been for your keen
intelligence and insight, I should have had to leave my post
long ago.

"I am fully conscious of my obligations to you, and in
taking the present step am actuated by no motives of disloyalty
to you personally. I have suffered from ill-health for the whole
of the past year, and this has rendered me incapable of fulfilling
the duties of my onerous position.

"You know I have been desirous of resigning before, but
so far you have refused to allow me to do so. So I have striven
to carry on. But recently my difficulties have greatly increased,
for I have found myself so enfeebled in body and mind, just at
the period when your Majesty is keenest on putting everything
into good shape, that I have been like a 'corpse in office'
for some time. I realize your kindness in overlooking my guilt
for so long, but I have come to see that opposition has become
so serious that it is impossible for me to hold on any longer. If
I were to remain on, I feel that not only should I be doing
violence to my own conscience, but that I should also involve
your Majesty. For you would be accused of lacking the requisite
knowledge of men. Hence I am bold enough to appeal to you
in this manner.

"I appreciate your request that I should still continue in
my present position, and have been greatly exercised in mind
about it. But I have finally come to the conclusion that I
would rather expose myself to the charge of disobeying your
orders than incur the greater guilt of failing to fulfil my duty.

"It is, moreover, a well-established principle of our Dynasty
to give to each minister of State his fair proportion of labour and
recuperation. Such office as I have held naturally carries heavy
responsibilities. Criticism for faulty administration naturally
reverts to the chief minister. Those who in the past have been
over presumptuous in this matter of holding on to office have

usually suffered indictment and degradation in the end. One can quite see that the above principle is well grounded.

" So far, I am happy to say, I have come through a fairly long period of high office without any mishap of that kind. But I hope most earnestly that you will give due regard to the practice followed by your forerunners in their treatment of their high ministers of State, and that you will grant me my due period of rest and recuperation.

" If, on some future occasion, you should choose to recall me to a responsible position, I promise not to refuse."

With a view to retiring at this juncture, Wang An Shih had submitted the names of Lü Hui Ch'ing and Han Chiang as suitable men to carry on his work, the latter to be Grand Councillor and the former Vice-Grand Councillor.

His sixth request for resignation reads as follows [1] :—

" Your Majesty's favour in promoting me to such intimacy with you in the public cause is humbly acknowledged. For despite my lowly origin and lack of prospects, you extended your favour to me when others despised me. Further you have, in opposition to the opinion of the many, entrusted me with the responsibility for State affairs through a period of eight years.

" I have appealed on several occasions that I may be permitted to resign, but so far you have not seen fit to accede to my request.

" When you initiated the reform policy, which has been so successfully promoted, your ministers were ignorant of your great purpose. Although at that time it was my real object to co-operate with them, I must say I was ignorant of the strength and influence of their opposition. But your own wisdom and forethought exceeded my powers of execution. I have made many mistakes, and my puny toil day and night cannot suffice to repay one ten-thousandth part of your grace and favour.

" I have, however, presumed on this grace too long. The doubts and suspicions of your great officers have been revealed. The resentment of all merges in my person, and I fear it will be

[1] Prose Works, vol. 10, pp. 16 and 17.

impossible to avoid the penalty of my guilt (i.e. I must leave the Court).

"In addition there has come upon me this serious sickness, sent, as I believe, by the will of Heaven, which has affected mc not only physically but mentally as well, so that although I might wish to rouse myself to fresh efforts and continue in office for another spell, it seemingly cannot be.

"Therefore, I have reached the conclusion that I must risk your wrath and ask again to be relieved of my appointment. I regard you as I would regard Heaven and Earth. I think of you as the parent of the people, and appeal to you to exercise your prerogative of mercy. Although I realize that my failures deserve punishment, I am hoping that because of my real desire to succeed, you will extend to me your gracious pardon, and enable me to finish my official course without misfortune, that is, if you really wish to free me from still greater difficulties in the future.

"I would remind you that I have not yet received your gracious permission to retire. I understand that you wish me to pull myself together and continue in my post. If I felt that I could really be of any help in furthering your noble purposes I would undertake the task even if I and my ancestors should perish by my so doing. But as I contemplate my failure and perceive how at the present time it is involving you with other officials, I simply dare not continue.

"Your Majesty's intelligence is like that of sun and moon combined, enlightening every place. If it be possible for me still to be the recipient of your illustrious favour, be it ever so small, then I aver in all sincerity that I shall not dare to resist your will.

"I await your gracious commands and venture to express the hope that your favour will speedily be made known."

After this letter had been submitted, the Emperor gave Wang An Shih a private note permitting him to resign from his position as Grand Councillor, but urging him to remain in residence at the Capital, where he might be consulted on important matters.

This note Wang An Shih acknowledged as follows [1] :—

" I beg to acknowledge your Majesty's note of hand, expressing your desire that I should remain in the Capital as an adviser on State affairs, and urging upon me that I ought to sympathize with your Majesty's purpose and give you my speedy consent. . . .

" Physically I am getting weaker and weaker, my guilt daily accumulates, and I consider myself most fortunate in having secured your gracious permission to resign my responsible position. I regard your present request, delivered by Lü Ch'ing, as a further mark of your favour.

" As I contemplate the magnitude of your favour, the intimacy which has characterized our relationships, and the opportunity which this affords, I really cannot bear the idea of leaving your service. But after the most careful thought I have reached the conclusion that I ought not to take up this position (as advisor in the Capital) and that I should prefer to be given an outside appointment, something in the nature of a sinecure if possible.

" You have already appointed suitable men to take up my work who are quite capable of carrying out your Majesty's plans. Should I elect to remain in the Capital it seems to me it would only further the slanderous purposes of my fellow-officials. But if you will give me an appointment in a provincial district I must of course nerve myself to the task. At some other time, if your gracious commands should come to me, I shall not presume to disobey, as indeed I have made clear to you in my former petitions."

The above documents give us more insight into the facts of Wang An Shih's resignation at this period. He had been carrying the sole responsibility for public affairs for some three years, and had pushed his own ideas against the rigid opposition of all the old officials. Their slanders and innuendoes had added to his mental burdens, and a breakdown in health was evidently imminent. On these grounds alone his desire to resign is understandable.

---

[1] Prose Works, vol. 10, p. 17.

To have resigned before would have been premature. But now he was convinced of Shen Tsung's purpose to push the reform policy ; Han Chiang and Lü Hui Ch'ing he considered quite loyal and capable of maintaining his policy, so there seemed to be no difficulty in the way of his resignation and retirement for rest and recuperation.

It is evident from the succeeding history and correspondence that he in no way considered this retirement as final. He would come again to the Capital when the time seemed opportune, and his health permitted.

But of course the Histories must seek to give the impression that the Emperor was wavering in his allegiance to Wang An Shih, and doubtful of the wisdom of his policy, That I think is adequately controverted by the evident desire of the Emperor to retain him, first in his old office, and failing that to keep him in residence at the Capital in an advisory capacity. Further evidence of lack of suspicion on the part of the Emperor is afforded by his acceptance of Wang An Shih's own nominees to succeed him in ministerial appointments.

Chapter XX

SUNDRY ECONOMIC MEASURES

In addition to the measures which have been discussed above, there were several other projects of an economical character, initiated and fostered by Wang An Shih, which should be mentioned. These dealt with the problems of land reclamation, river conservancy and control; the question of land survey, division and assessment; matters connected with transport; the coinage; Government monopolies in tea and salt, trade taxes, etc.

We shall give some account of each of these in the order outlined above.

I. Land Reclamation and River Conservancy Work

In the 4th month of 1069 a Commission of eight men was appointed [1] to travel through the country for the purpose of exploring (amongst other things) the possibilities of land reclamation and river control. They were instructed to look out for men versed in agriculture and those who had tackled the problem of land reclamation or river control with any success. Such men were to be requested to offer their suggestions to the Government, and rewards were to be given for those who presented schemes which proved to be of a practicable character.

Under the 11th month of the same year the History [2] records the reception of many plans and suggestions of this character, and notes that in the period from 1070 to 1076 reclamation work had been carried out in 10,793 different places, representing the reclaiming of 361,178 " ch'ing " of land.

---

[1] " T'ung Chien " (通 鑑), from which most of the historical material in this section on Land Reclamation is taken.
[2] " T'ung Chien."

Extensive projects for deepening and directing river channels were undertaken in connection with the Chang River (漳 河), the Yellow River (黃 河), and the Pien River (汴 河), details of which are given below.

In the 4th month of 1071 work was opened on the Chang River to the north of K'aifengfu, with the object of deepening the channel for a distance of 160 li (over 50 miles).[1]

This aroused considerable discussion at Court. The Emperor thought that the number of men engaged on the work, amounting to over 10,000, made the project too expensive, considering the straitened condition of the National Exchequer. Some of these men would doubtless be from the provincial troops (廂 軍), while others would be from the farming class, paid at official rates under the Public Services Act.

Wen Yen Po said that financial considerations were of secondary importance. What was much more important was that the people should be placated, and the only way to do that was to free them from burdensome public work of this character. Moreover, he said that no work had been done on this river for years. If it did not overflow to the east it would overflow to the west, so that it was immaterial whether anything was done or not.

Wang An Shih replied, " If we do not keep the Chang River in its proper channel it will overflow. No matter whether it should overflow to the east or to the west the damage would be equally serious. But by ensuring that it keeps to its proper channel no damage at all would result, so this project may be described as beneficial and constructive."

Then occurred a great typhoon in the north, which considerably alarmed the people. The Emperor prepared an edict on the subject to the effect that in view of the typhoon it would be better to stop the work on the river, as it was interfering with agriculture, and that it would not be too late to take up the work again next year. The History relates that Wang An Shih· retained the edict in his office, so we infer that the work was proceeded with.

[1] " T'ung Chien."

Anyone acquainted with China knows that one of her most important problems awaiting solution is that of river conservancy. The Yellow River, which has been termed "China's Sorrow", frequently changes its course, or breaks its banks. The floods which ensue cause inestimable damage and loss of life. The main cause is the silting up of the river channel by sediment brought down from the loess regions through which the river mainly flows. Constant dredging seems to be the only solution.

Wang An Shih also gave his attention to this important problem.

In the 4th month of 1073 a discussion took place at Court [1] concerning a project for deepening the Yellow River channel. The river had overflowed its banks in the Hopei Circuit, between Ta Ming Fu (大 名 府) and Hsia Ching Hsien (夏 津 縣), the former being in modern Hopei and the latter in Shantung.

The Emperor commented on the fact that large numbers of men had been transferred from the Chingtung Circuit for the restoration work, and that many of them had suffered serious financial losses thereby. He said he had also been informed that the breaking of the banks was a negligible factor after all, as no matter where the river flowed it still only occupied the space of a river, so it really made no difference whether it flowed east or west. (This looks strangely like Wen Yen Po's argument above.) "Would it not be better to leave matters as they were and cease these efforts at control?"

Wang An Shih replied, "If we let the river flow northwards and make no efforts at control, the flooding of enormous tracts of public and private land will result. As the river silts up it spreads out over the plain. Is this to go on indefinitely? We have already cut two channels at very little expense, and much land that was formerly alkaline has already been reclaimed and made suitable for agriculture. May we not claim that this is success?

"Moreover, the number employed on the project is con-

---

[1] "T'ung Chien."

siderably less than last year, and as the work on the embankments progresses less labour will be required."

Eventually the Emperor approved a plan for regular work on the river, and the Yellow River Conservancy Bureau was set up.

One or two interesting schemes were suggested for dredging the river.

Liu Kung I (李 公 義) proposed the use of a big iron rake which might be dragged along the bed of the river to keep the silt in motion. He thought that if some plan was devised for keeping rakes of this character in constant use the channel might eventually be deepened by a few feet. Huang Huai Hsin (黃 懷 信) thought the idea good, but considered that the rake proposed would not be heavy enough for the work. So Wang An Shih suggested that they should devise a fresh scheme between them.

In the end they proposed the adoption of a " river deepening plough ".[1] This consisted of a heavy wooden beam 8 feet long, fitted with iron spikes 1 foot in length. This was to be weighted with stones and suspended from two boats equipped with windlasses, by means of which the plough could be lowered into the river and the raking process begun.

The History [2] records that although everybody else was convinced that the idea was hopeless, Wang An Shih thought it excellent, and sent the plan and arrangements for the use of this " plough " to Ta Ming Fu, ordering the Director of the River Conservancy Board, Fan Tzu Yuan (范 子 淵), to conduct an experiment in co-operation with the local officials. These all came to the conclusion that the scheme was impracticable. Later, when Fan Tzu Yuan met Wang An Shih at the Capital, the latter asked him why the project had been rejected. Fan Tzu Yuan, not daring to tell the truth, said that while he himself thought the idea quite good, the rest of the officials could not agree on the matter.

" This remark," says the History, " gave Wang An Shih great

---

[1] 浚 川 耙 " Chun Ch'uan Pa ".
[2] " T'ung Chien."

pleasure, and after he had made plans for deepening the river from Wei Chow to the river mouth, Liu Kung I, the original inventor of the ' plough ', was appointed Assistant to Fan Tzu Yuan." It would seem, though the History is a bit confused at this point, that an order for several thousands of these " ploughs " was issued, and an experiment made.

Wang An Shih also proposed a scheme for straightening a bend in the Yellow River by the cutting of a channel. This proposition was made in the 10th month of 1073.[1]

Ou Yang Hsiu opposed the idea,[2] saying that the cutting of a river channel was like deliberate incendiarism, whereas not to do so might be likened to an accidental fire. There was no difference in effect. But in cutting a river channel it was necessary to burden the people with long and grievous toil, so that in his opinion it was better not to do anything at all.

This brought the customary sort of reply from Wang An Shih, in which he likened the work on such schemes of public benefit to " trouble which the people are willing to endure ". He said there were only two alternatives in matters of this kind, either to adopt an attitude of lazy indifference, or set about the work with a feeling of conscientious responsibility. " It should not be difficult," he said, " to see which course we ought to adopt."

The deepening of the Pien River was also one of Wang An Shih's ideas, but the actual work was not begun until 1078, after he had retired from high office. The scheme was carried through and the work completed in forty-five days.

Ssu Ma Kuang opposed these river schemes, as also did Su Shih.[2] The latter wrote : " The empire has enjoyed a long period of peace, and economic conditions have greatly improved. Whatever is of benefit to the country has already been done. If these river projects are now started, there will be endless trouble and disaffection amongst the people."

It is not possible to estimate aright the value of these river

[1] " T'ung Chien."
[2] Liang Ch'i Ch'ao, p. 152.

schemes promoted and encouraged by Wang An Shih. The Histories are silent on the matter. But one thing stands out clearly, and that is Wang An Shih's earnest desire to grapple with this great economic problem of his time. Such efforts as he made are undoubtedly more commendable than the attitude of many of his famous contemporaries, whose policy was " do nothing and see what happens ".

II. LAND SURVEY AND CLASSIFICATION [1]

'The following account of this scheme is given in the History [2] under the date of the 8th month, 1072, viz. :—

"The Emperor was dissatisfied with existing methods of assessing the land tax, on the ground that it was not equitably administered, so he ordered the Board of Revenue to draw up new regulations and publish them throughout the empire."

The regulations as finally issued included provisions for land survey, and also a more equitable assessment of the land tax.

It was decreed that the land should be divided into plots of 1,000 paces square, i.e. about one square mile. In Chinese measurements the area was 41 ch'ing 66 mu 160 paces. In the 9th month the local official and his assistants were ordered to conduct the survey, measuring off the land into plots of the stipulated size, and at the same time to classify the land. The classification was to be based first on the general type of the land, whether it was hilly, elevated, level, or marshy. That having been done, the type of soil was next to be noted, whether it was red or black, more or less fertile, etc. Each plot was then to be classified in one of five divisions, and on that the land tax would be determined.

In the 3rd month of 1073 the survey was reported to have been completed, and an announcement of the classification published. An interval of three months was allowed, during

---

[1] Fang T'ien Chun Shui (方 田 均 稅).
[2] " T'ung Chien."

which any question which arose might be settled. After that period had elapsed without incident, notices were served on the landowners, and a full statement and plan of the village district delivered as well. This was to serve as the land tax agreement.

Certain other regulations were connected with this scheme which directly affected taxation, as follows :—

Each county was to take its old land-tax figure as the maximum. But under the old regulations fractions were ignored, e.g. if the tax was to be collected in grain nothing less than a pint was accepted, while in the case of silk or cloth being contributed no fraction less than an inch was taken into account. Under the revised regulations as now issued the exaction of more than the actual amount prescribed was prohibited regardless of the extra trouble that fractions might cause.

It was also enacted that waste land, salty land from which the people could derive no food, hill and forest land, marshy land, roads, ditches, cemeteries, etc., were not to be taxed.

Mounds were ordered to be erected at the corners of the plots, and trees planted to define the boundaries. Each plot was to have a separate deed, also each village, and each owner or group was to have separate documents provided. In case of dissolution of partnership, mortgage, sale or transfer, a new deed was to be drawn up and delivered to the owner by the officials. Local yamens were ordered to keep the records accurately and up-to-date. But all the plots as now surveyed and defined were to be maintained intact, i.e. no alteration was to be made in the boundary stones.[1]

Wang Wan (王 曼) was appointed as the Superintendent of this survey and classification work. A beginning was to be made in the Ching-tung Circuit, and then extended to the whole country.

---

[1] Obviously to save the trouble of making fresh surveys and remeasurement of the plots.

III. Improved Transport System [1]

The main bulk of Government supplies came from the south and east, so the question of transport was one of the important matters of finance in the days of the Northern Sung.

Prior to the initiation of Wang An Shih's reforms, all sorts of malpractice occurred in connection with the public transport services. Officials and their subordinates alike were engaged in the nefarious traffic of stealing, smuggling, and selling. On occasions the whole cargo of a boat would be reported as missing, and sometimes a boat would be deliberately scuttled so as to conceal the theft from the higher authorities. In this and other ways the Government suffered serious losses, as much as a million bushels of grain being unaccounted for in a single year.

In 1069 Wang An Shih recommended Hsieh Hsiang (薛 向) as Transport Officer for the Chiang-Huai and adjoining circuits, and a new scheme was inaugurated. This consisted of enabling hired private boats to compete with the public service boats in connection with the transport work. The main idea of this was that each of these competitors would keep a close watch on the other. The old defects were in this way largely eliminated. There were practically no losses reported in connection with the official returns, and in addition to the amount formerly reported as the regular annual yield, 250,000 extra bushels (annually) were delivered in the Capital by the private boats.

IV. The Coinage

Two matters affecting the coinage are sometimes associated with the name and regime of Wang An Shih, which have called forth considerable criticism. One was what is regarded as a depreciation of the currency measure, styled " Che erh ch'ien " (折 二 錢), and the other his lifting of the embargo on the export of copper. As this subject is of a complicated character, and the records vague, we have dealt with it in Vol. II, to which the reader is referred.

---

[1] Shih Huo Chih, vol. 128, ch. 3, p. 10.

V. Government Rents and Monopolies

In the Biography of Wang An Shih, as found in the Dynastic History of Sung,[1] following on the account of the more important reform measures associated with his name, which have been outlined in the preceding chapters, there occurs the following paragraph :—

" A mandate was issued ordering the people to bid, by sealed tender, for market stands and sites, and this led to an increase in prices. The quantities of official tea and salt, which each district was compelled to take, were increased. In Hopei a Government Purchasing Bureau was established in order to ensure that large stocks of grain were always ready at set points along the waterways for transport."

The Histories seem silent on the sealed tender business, and there is very little of importance recorded about the salt regulations during Wang An Shih's tenure of office. There is, however, one reference to the matter. This notes that the salt tickets (issued to the merchant classes) ceased to have their face value. There are two documents on the " Tea " question included in his Works, which give us some idea of his attitude to it.

Tea was one of the Government monopolies, which seems to have been operated on the following lines in Wang An Shih's day. It was grown by private enterprise, the planters being regarded as leaseholders of the land. The planters delivered the tea to their landlord, who in turn sent it on to the Government officials. The latter then turned it over to the big merchants, to whom the Government looked for a definite sum by way of revenue. The salt monopoly would seem to have been operated on somewhat similar lines to this. In both cases the big merchants were entitled to assess the people, according to their financial rating, and compel them to take certain specified quantities of both commodities.

It is evident that Wang An Shih was really opposed to this system, and was an advocate of " free-trade " by the people,

[1] Pen Chuan (本 傳).

at any rate as regards tea. He outlines twelve reasons why he considered the extant system detrimental to the interests of Government and people alike :—

1. As the tea merchants were so few, it was easy for them to combine, and in times when tea was plentiful to cut down the prices offered to the planters.

2. Again, because the merchants were so few, a good deal of damage resulted from the large stocks which were kept. This meant reduced revenue from the commodity, and proportionately large assessments had to be made in the way of general taxation to make up for this.

3. This in its turn led to the planters producing less tea.

4. The extant system was virtually a point monopoly of the Government and the merchants, which encouraged illicit dealing in the better grades of tea. Much expense was involved in the attempt to control this traffic.

5. The receiving depots being so few, they were of necessity widely scattered, which led to great losses during transport.

6. Stocks gradually deteriorated, and much loss ensued.

7. The Government demanded very high capital qualifications, so the registered merchants were perforce very few.

8. The system offered no encouragement to private enterprise.

9. Litigation expenses were greatly increased, as it was practically impossible to prevent smuggling.

10. The merchants compelled the people to take inferior tea from their large stocks at unfair prices.

11. Middle-men and retailers were also compelled to take set quantities from the merchants, and this involved them in the accumulation of stocks which they could not sell, and much damage and loss resulted.

12. In places where the tea was sold directly by the officials, they had to resort to various subterfuges to get the tea out to the people. Although ostensibly they sold at reduced prices, the difference was always made up in some form or other.[1]

---

[1] Prose Works, vol. 17, p. 22.

There is no date to this document, but it follows on another document dealing with the question of the tea monopoly. In this Wang An Shih advocated the surrender of monopoly rights, and urges the importance of permitting the people to trade freely in the commodity.

The following are the essential points from the document in question, which is styled " Discussion on the Tea Regulations " (論 茶 法)[1]:—

" The Government's surrender of the tea monopoly and permission to the people to trade freely in the commodity is truly beneficial, and quite in accordance with the ancient ideas of what is right. Those who oppose the surrender are solely concerned with minutest fractions of profit, and seem to be oblivious of the fact that ' by giving it will be possible to receive ' (不 知 與 之 爲 取).

" Tea is as essential to the life of the people as grain and salt. They cannot do without it for a single day. The tea which comes from the officials' hands is of poor quality and practically unsaleable. So it comes about that the tea drunk by the people is in the main the product of illicit dealing. The attempt to deprive the people of a commodity of which they are so fond can only result in a continuous policy of repression and prohibition. Though banishment be the order of the day, though beating be resorted to continually, the illicit trade will go on. If the monopoly is surrendered these things will cease.

" Should Government proceeds from tea be altogether lost, I would still suggest that it was right to surrender the monopoly. But my contention is that under this free-trade system the revenue from the sales will equal the old figures under the monopoly.

" When Sang Hung Yang (桑 宏 羊) made the proposal to make wine a Government monopoly, everyone thought that this was the method they had long been waiting for to ensure a sufficiency of Government revenue, and thought it

[1] Prose Works, vol. 17, p. 21.

a measure that would never be altered. But when Ho Kuang (霍 光), that unlearned and ignorant fellow, came on the scene, he opposed Sang Hung Yang and secured the abolition of the measure. So right prevailed over the desire for gain for a long period.

" In these days the Court is desirous of eliminating the defects and evils of a hundred generations, and is seeking to restore the ancient glories of the Age of Yao and Shun. And yet some are anxious that our modern laws and regulations should follow on the lines of a scheme of which even Ho Kuang was ashamed. Is that reasonable ?

" I feel that although the Government might not be expected to surrender a monopoly in other commodities, it can make a start right away by surrendering the monopoly in tea. This will give the people a demonstration of the Government's sympathy with them in their difficulties, and give them the hope that the surrender of other monopolies might follow. . . .

" I consider this surrender of the tea monopoly an attempt to deal radically with the economic situation as it exists at present and that the financial situation will be greatly improved if such policy is maintained."

It is obvious from the general trend of this argument that Wang An Shih was opposed to Government trade monopolies in general. In this he seems inconsistent, when we remember his Trade and Barter Measure, which partook of the nature of a Government monopoly in everything, at least according to his critics. But the first idea of this measure was to enable the people to dispose of surplus stocks of their own produce, and not to traffic in everything in the name of the Government to the detriment of private enterprise.

No details are given in the Histories about the Hopei Purchasing Bureau in connection with the granary system.[1] This may have been simply a measure of convenience, under which stocks of grain would be purchased and collected at various points, possibly by the agents of the Trade and Barter Bureau, for convenience of transport.

[1] See p. 298.

VI. TRADE TAX

This is referred to in the Sung Histories as "Mien Hang Ch'ien" (免 行 錢). Under the date of the 9th month of 1073, the History (T'ung Chien) has the following :—

"Formerly there existed in the Capital a 'hang' (行), or trade-centre, for every kind of goods, from which the officials drew their necessary supplies (and through which the Government trade tax had been collected). But this system resulted in the small trader of the poorer classes suffering considerable loss. So Lü Chia Wen (呂 嘉 問) requested that an agreement should be made on the basis of the profits made by these various 'hangs' whereby all traders should pay a money-tax on all transactions (direct to the Government), to meet the expenses of the officials required (for the operation of the new system) and also to make up for the deficit caused by the loss of the goods formerly handed to the officials by the different 'hangs'."

So the main idea of this measure was to eliminate the practice whereby small traders had passed their goods through "hangs", paid their taxes, and then either received permission to sell, or left them at discretion in the "hang". The new system meant that these small traders would deliver their goods for inspection, fixing of prices, taxation purposes, etc., directly to Government officials. It was expected that in this way they would receive considerate and fairer treatment.

From a further narrative in the History (T'ung Chien), under date of the 5th month of 1074, we find that Lü Chia Wen came under fire for his administration of this particular measure, and also for his connection with the Trade and Barter Measure. On this occasion the Emperor is reported to have said that "the 'Mien Hang Ch'ien' involved the officials in very troublesome small transactions". To this Wang An Shih replied that "permission to the people to hand in money direct to the officials instead of doing so via the 'hangs' was because they were thus more likely to rest content and get on quietly with their avocations, instead of being subject to the former troublesome annoyances attendant upon the old method. If the law was rescinded, on the one hand there would be no means of getting the required goods supplied to the Court, and on the other, as the pay of the officials concerned was low, it was inevitable that they would seek for some ' squeeze ' from the people. The repression of such customs would involve the State in the drawing up and execution of very strict measures which to his mind would be unfair as long as salaries remained at their low level. Under the ' Mien Hang Ch'ien ' regulations, very little was taken from the people by way of taxation, but the officials concerned were able to maintain their self-respect. That was his main reason for devising the measure. . . ." He said further, " the underlings in the ' hangs ' intimidated the people excessively, so that if a trader should incur their resentment, they would be punished in spite of their willingness to pay money. Although the salaries of the officials (under the new measure) might be said to be fairly large, yet they did not equal (in the total) half the figure which the ' hangs ' had formerly taken from the people."

The object of this measure is thus seen to be in line with Wang An Shih's general idea of relieving the small trader of troublesome and excessive exactions on the part of the semi-official tax gatherers, represented by the " hangs ". From the standpoint of the conventional official it seemed a " loss of dignity " for the Government to be dealing in such commodities as fruits, ice, coal, etc., and to be receiving revenue in such small sums as taxation on smaller commodities implied. But " trouble " and " loss of dignity " of that type did not bother Wang An Shih in his desire to control the wealthy in the interests of the poor.

CHAPTER XXI

MILITARY CAMPAIGNS

WE have seen that in the times of Wang An Shih the greatest menace, from the military standpoint, which threatened China arose from the north and north-west. In the former region the danger first arose from the Liao (遼) Tartars, and later from the Golden (金) Tartars, who eventually defeated the Sungs and occupied the whole of North China for over a hundred years. In the north-west, China was threatened by the Hsi Hsia (西 夏) or Tanguts, who became the allies of the Golden Tartars and helped to reduce the Sungs to impotence.

Wang An Shih foresaw the peril of all this, and his military policy was designed to forestall the alliance which in the end brought about his country's downfall.

There were also a number of tribes in Hunan and Ssu Ch'uan which as yet had not become wholly submissive to the Chinese Government, and these Wang An Shih purposed to bring into complete dependence or allegiance.

In the south-west the kingdom of Chiao-Chih (交 趾), or Annam, which had hitherto acknowledged the suzerainty of China, rebelled during Wang An Shih's regime, and called forth a punitive expedition.

In all there were four military campaigns or expeditions undertaken by Wang An Shih, of which we will proceed to give some account.

First, then, we must refer to the Ho Huang campaign, in the north-west.

This was undertaken with a view to crippling the Tanguts and preventing their joining forces with the Liao or Iron Tartars. They were considered the relatively easier foe to subdue, so Wang An Shih turned his attention to them first.

The preliminary step was designed to recover a strip of territory known as Ho Huang (河 湟), or Hsi Ho (熙 河),

which had been in the possession of the Chinese empire in the time of the T'ang dynasty, but was now in the hands of Thibetan tribes, who were considered possible allies of the Tanguts. As this strip of territory formed the gateway from the northwest into China, it was considered necessary that the Chinese Government should gain control over it.

The territory in question lay along the T'ao (洮) River, flowing through the west of modern Kansu, comprising the cities of Min Chow (岷 州), T'ao Chow (洮 州), and land west of Kung Ch'ang Fu (鞏 昌 府), a tract now represented by the line of the T'ao River from the Min Mountains in the south to Lan Chow Fu in the north, near to the Great Wall.

It was felt by the Chinese that if this territory remained in the possession of actual or potential enemies that the whole tract of Ho Hsi (河 西), i.e. the country west of the Yellow River, would be endangered. From the middle of the T'ang dynasty and throughout the period of the Five Dynasties, it had remained in the hands of Thibetan tribes. But hitherto no one had thought of attempting to regain it.

The first suggestion for its recovery came from Wang Shao (王 韶), Secretarial Adviser of the Chien Ch'ang forces (建 昌 軍), who in the year 1068, the first of Shen Tsung's reign, made the following proposal[1] :—

" If the Court wishes to subjugate the Tanguts we must first recover the territory of Ho Huang. If that can be done, the Tanguts will have to guard against frontal and rear attacks. Each year they attack Ch'ing T'ang (青 唐), but so far have not succeeded in their efforts to conquer the area. Should they succeed, the way will be open for them to unite their forces and make a southern drive. They will be able to ravage the country between Ch'in and Wei (秦 渭), pasture their horses in Lan Hui (蘭 會), and cut off the Ku Wei territory (古 渭). They could then reduce the Ch'iang (羌) tribes in the Ho Huang region, fortify Wu Sheng (武 勝) on the west, sending expeditions occasionally to ravage the T'ao Ho area, and

---

[1] " T'ung Chien," Hsi Ning (熙 寧), 3rd year, 10th month.

by threatening Western Kansu and Ssu Ch'uan will disturb the whole region. In which case the brothers Hsia and Cheng (瞎 征) will be unable to make any effective resistance against the Tanguts.

" Of the descendants of the Chueh (唃) clan, only Tung Chan (董 氈) can take independent action at present, and that with difficulty. Hsia, Cheng, and Ch'i Pa Wen (欺 巴 温) exercise very limited authority, their Government orders extending only one or two hundred li. So that in any case they would be unable of themselves to oppose an advance of the Tanguts.

" The territory south of Wu Wei (武 威) to the T'ao River and Lan Shan (蘭 鄯) was at one time all part of the domain of Han (漢). The soil is fertile, all kinds of grain may be cultivated there, and the inhabitants may be called upon for the public services of the empire.

" Fortunately for us the various Thibetan tribes are all disunited, so the time is opportune to bring them into subjection.

" I suggest that you appoint someone who is thoroughly conversant with the district and the people, and order him to visit the various tribes in turn. In this way he will be able to discover those who are inclined to be friendly with us. He should of course seek to get their alliance by diplomatic methods, for if we can get six or seven of the more important chiefs on our side, the rest will be forced to submit. When all the rest have been won over, the Chueh clan will be compelled to yield. After that the Li (李) clan of Ho Hsi (the Tanguts) will be in our hands. If you wish to accomplish their speedy subjugation you may take steps to attack them in their lairs and strongholds, but it might also be possible to win them over gradually by enlisting their co-operation. The immediate aim will be to gain the Thibetan's alliance, but the ultimate and greater success will be achieved in our new relations with the Tanguts."

This plan appealed to the Emperor and also to Wang An Shih, who forthwith requested that Wang Shao might be placed in charge of the military side of the Shensi and Kansu administration.

Wang Shao then proposed that the upper and lower cities

of Wei Ching (渭 涇) should be fortified and a corps stationed there with the object of securing the submission of the Thibetan tribes in the T'ao River region. This proposition was referred to Li Shih Chung, the Commissioner for Shensi and Kansu, who, however, disapproved of it, and was forthwith deprived of his command.

Wang Shao then made a further proposal with regard to the cultivation of the area under discussion. He said : " From the source of the Wei River (渭 河) to Ch'in Chow (秦 州), a distance of over 600 li along the river, the land is still uncultivated. The total area represented by this tract amounted to 10,000 ' ch'ing '. If only one-tenth of that could be brought under cultivation, it would produce a yield annually of 1,500,000 bushels."

So he further suggested that a Trade Exchange should be set up, from which profits would accrue, which might be devoted to agricultural development.

Wang Shao was granted a capital sum to initiate the scheme and he himself appointed to supervise it.

From Wang An Shih's speech on this particular aspect of the project we infer that it was regarded as a part of a definite plan for bringing the Thibetans in the Hsi Ho region into submission by peaceful means.

In the 8th month of 1071 Wang Shao was duly appointed Pacification Commissioner for the T'ao Ho region,[1] and the following year the Ku Wei garrison force was reorganized as the Army for the Pacification of the Furthest Regions under his command.

He first gave his attention to the most powerful leader in the Ch'ing T'ang (青 唐) sector, whose name was Lung O (龍 珂), who soon surrendered with 20,000 followers, and was given the title of " Submissive " (包 順).[1]

In the 8th month of 1072 Wang Shao attacked some of the Thibetan tribes, capturing Wu Sheng (武 勝), which he fortified and made into the headquarters of the T'ao River Army.

---

[1] " T'ung Chien," Hsi Ning (熙 寧), 4th year, 8th month.

A little later he reduced another influential chieftain called
Mu Cheng (木 征) at Kung Ling Ch'eng (鞏 令 城).[1]

Wang An Shih wrote Wang Shao a letter at this time,
probably in acknowledgment of his report of the capture of
Wu Sheng. The letter reads as follows [2] :—

" The east and west banks of the T'ao River were formerly
in joint possession of the Thibetans and the Dynasty of Han,
and so it was considered essential that Wu Sheng should be
made the military headquarters for that region. If nowadays
we contemplate the building of a city there, I fear it will have to
be very big and a difficult piece of work with all you have in
hand already. Again, if we build a large city there a big force
will be needed to defend it. So in view of all the circumstances,
and looking to the future, I think it will be best not to relinquish
the old city. In the meantime you might make observations
of the general lie of the land, and possibly undertake the enlarge-
ment of the city later.

" When your work of reconstruction is complete, we ought to
establish a branch of the Trade Exchange Bureau there. We
should also make it the headquarters of the Thibetan Border
Corps. Then we should enlist the help of wealthy Chinese
and lend them Government funds for the opening up of markets
and stores. These would serve the interests of both Chinese
and Thibetans and be of public and private benefit. An
adoption of a plan of this type will make it much easier for us
to hold the place, and the submission of the tribes will be the
more speedily accomplished."

In the 10th month of 1072 the Hsi Ho area was made into a
separate Circuit, the force under Wang Shao was promoted
from the status of the Chen T'ao Army (鎮 洮 軍) to that
of Hsi Chow Defence Force, with headquarters at Hsi Chow (熙
州). Wang Shao was made Commissioner for the Circuit and
appointed to the concurrent post of Governor of Hsi Chow.[3]

---

[1] " T'ung Chien," Hsi Ning (熙 寧), 5th year, 8th month.
[2] Prose Works, vol. 18, p. 9 (與 王 子 醇 書).
[3] " T'ung Chien," Hsi Ning (熙 寧), 5th year, 10th month.

In the 11th month the chieftains of the Ho Chow (河 州) tribes, Hsia Yo (瞎 藥), surrendered. In the 12th month suburbs were added to Hsi Chow city and many fortifications erected.

Wang An Shih then sent Wang Shao another letter,[1] as follows :

" I hear that you have fortified Wu Sheng, and that you have subdued some of the Thibetan tribes. That is excellent. I also hear that Ch'eng Ch'eng Ko (郢 成 珂) and other chieftains have assembled their united forces to ward off the Hsi Hsia (西 夏). These things demonstrate the success of your gracious yet awe-inspiring policy.

" I fear, however, that if we demand of these tribes prolonged service in the field, involving them in considerable distress and financial outlay, it will be difficult to retain their good-will, for they may thus fail to see any advantage in their being our allies. I think we might instruct Ch'eng Ch'eng Ko and his associates to disperse the main body of their following, retaining only their better equipped levies as a defence force against the Hsi Hsia. These should be generously treated, so that they may feel under obligation to us. When the fortifications are completed, you should offer them still greater inducements to loyalty. The advantage of limiting the numbers engaged will be twofold, the amount required for their upkeep will be reduced, and we shall be able to offer more generous treatment to those who are retained. I am not sure of your own opinion on this matter, but you might give my proposal your careful attention.

" If you plan to deal radically with the non-submissive elements, you will need victuals for the Regulars and land for the bowmen. My only fear is that new recruits will be unsatisfactory, and if you could somehow arrange for an exchange of these with the older soldiers from the Shansi Circuit they should be better able to keep control of the recently subjugated tribes. It is impossible for me to estimate the situation properly at this distance, but I am telling you all that is in my mind."

[1] Prose Works, vol. 18, pp. 9 and 10.

In the 2nd month of 1073 [1] Wang Shao captured Ho Chow
(河 州) and took as prisoners the wife of the Thibetan chieftain,
Mu Cheng, and other members of his family.

A third letter written by Wang An Shih to Wang Shao
reads as follows [2] :—

" The most important task before you at present in the
Hsi Ho Circuit is to make adequate preparations for defence
and you should issue stringent warnings to all your generals
against their taking any hasty action. . . . You have acted
with good faith and in a generous manner to the Thibetan
tribes. You might make use of those who show good ability.
Our available resources for the expenditure in that region,
which is heavy, are only sufficient for defensive purposes. . . .
If we can really get the co-operation of the tribes, that will
free us not only from the danger of internal trouble, but be
of great assistance in our campaign against the external foe.
Our forces should be used in a compassionate and just manner.
We have no desire for wholesale slaughter, which can only
induce resentment. The exercise of justice and mercy will be
infinitely the better policy in the long run. . . .

" I hear too that amongst the subdued tribes there are many
destitute. Unless we provide them with the means of livelihood
they will turn to banditry. I hope you will be able to find them
employment on public works. In any case I trust that you will
act in a compassionate manner. I am too far away from the
field to be acquainted with all the details, but I am confident
you have some definite policy. . . ."

In the 9th month of 1073 a revolt occurred. Mu Cheng,
taking advantage of Wang Shao's absence, recaptured Ho Chow.
Later, however, Wang Shao defeated him. After this Mu Ling
Cheng (木 令 征), another chieftain, surrendered with the city
of Min Chow (岷 州), and when Wang Shao had actually
entered that city the chieftains of Tang (宕), T'ao (洮), and
Tieh (疊) all capitulated.

---

[1] " T'ung Chien," Hsi Ning (熙 寧), 6th year, 2nd month.
[2] Prose Works, vol. 18, pp. 10 and 11.

During this campaign Wang Shao's army was in the field for fifty-four days. They had marched 1,800 li, captured five cities, killed several thousand of the enemy, and had taken 10,000 animals. These cities are all located in the Tung Ch'ang Fu (東 昌 府) prefecture of modern Kansu.

When the news of this victory reached the capital, the Emperor held a congratulatory audience in the Tzu Ch'en Tien (紫 宸 殿), during which he took off his gem-studded belt and presented it to Wang An Shih as a reward for his wise counsel which had proved so successful in connection with the Ho Huang campaign.

Wang An Shih then read a speech which he had prepared for the occasion. In this he refers to the capture of the five cities, the expansion of the national territory by over 2,000 li, the killing or capture of 19,000 rebellious Thibetans, and the submission of over 300,000 former aliens.[1]

He also sent a letter of thanks to the Emperor for his gift of the royal girdle.[2]

In the 4th month of 1074 Wang An Shih sent Wang Shao a fourth letter as follows [3]:—

" Now that Mu Cheng has surrendered, there is nothing more to fear in the Hsi Ho territory. But we must avoid extraordinary expenditure, and draw up suitable taxation regulations, so that a permanent and progressive policy may be ensured.

" The Emperor is highly gratified by your fidelity and success. Our opponents at Court can no longer obstruct our border policy. You ought now to give full scope to your ideas and respond adequately to the Emperor's favour. You need have no anxiety about other matters."

One gathers from the various speeches and documents referring to this campaign that it was the original intention of its promoters, certainly of Wang An Shih at least, that the tribes might be won over by diplomacy and peaceful measures

---

[1] " T'ung Chien," Hsi Ning (熙 寧), 6th year, 9th month.
[2] Prose Works, vol. 15, p. 1 (賜 玉 帶 謝 表).
[3] Prose Works, vol. 18, p. 10, letter No. 4.

and the offering of generous treatment. In the end most of the territory was reduced by actual fighting. This gave a handle to Wang An Shih's political opponents, who contended that there was no need to use force at all.[1]

It is difficult to form any opinion on this controversy with such information as is at our disposal, but as a piece of military strategy the expedition seems to have been justified. There is further every indication that Wang An Shih intended to treat the subjugated tribes with the utmost clemency and even generosity. Note how repeatedly he urges this upon the attention of Wang Shao.

The following sketch will give the reader an idea of the subsequent history of the relationships of the Sungs with this area and people.

In 1086, when Ssu Ma Kuang assumed the office of Grand Councillor-in-Chief, he wished to relinquish all responsibility for the Hsi Ho region. He would actually have done so if Sun Lu (孫 路) had not produced a map of the area and demonstrated how the Shensi Circuit as a whole would be endangered by so doing.[2]

However, in the 4th month of 1086 the special Hsi Ho Finance Bureau was abolished.[3]

In a memorial notice on the death of the Empress-Regent, Hsuan Jen,[4] it is recorded that during her regime she presented the Hsi Hsia with territory. From this we conclude that some at least of the land recovered by Wang Shao was lost in that period.

In 1097 it is recorded that Lü Hui Ch'ing (呂 惠 鄉) recovered Yu Chow (宥 州),[5] and in the 3rd month of 1099 that the Hsi Hsia suffered a defeat at the hands of the Chinese

---

[1] See Vol. II of this work.
[2] Liang Ch'i Ch'ao, p. 213.
[3] " T'ung Chien," Yuan Yu (元 祐), 1st year, 4th month.
[4] " T'ung Chien," Yuan Yu (元 祐), 8th year, 9th month (畢 邊 砦 之 地 以 賜 西 夏).
[5] " T'ung Chien," Shao Sheng (紹 聖), 4th year, 8th month.

which led them to make a treaty of alliance with the Liao or
" Iron " Tartars.

However, in the 7th month of 1099 [1] the Chinese retook
Ch'ing T'ang from the Thibetans and in the next month they
walled Hui Chow (會 州).[2]

In 1105 the " Iron " Tartars requested China to hand back
the territory which they had taken from the Hsi Hsia and
withdraw all their forces from the region.[3]

An overwhelming defeat was inflicted upon the Chinese
forces by the Hsi Hsia in the 8th month of 1115,[4] and from then
onwards their prestige and power greatly increased. They
did their utmost to assist the " Iron " Tartars in their campaign
against the Sungs, but in 1122 suffered defeat at their hands.

In the 1st month of 1124 the Histories [5] relate a treaty of
alliance between the Hsi Hsia and the " Golden " Tartars, who
by this time had conquered the " Iron " Tartars and had become
the most formidable enemy of the Sungs.

In 1126 it is recorded that the Hsi Hsia captured Hsi An Fu
(西 安 府), so they must have been a powerful factor in the final
debacle which resulted in the capture of K'ai Feng Fu by the
" Golden " Tartars, and the transfer of the Sung capital to the
south.

It would therefore seem that the peril which Wang An Shih
foresaw, and did his utmost to prevent, actually did arise and
led eventually to the downfall of the Dynasty.

The Second Campaign of note which was undertaken under
the regime of Wang An Shih was the Hunan Expedition.

The so-called aboriginal tribes of China, viz. the Man (蠻)
and the Miao (苗), were gradually driven from the central parts
of the country to the south and west. The process of subjugation
was described by Chinese historians as " civilizing " them. The

---

[1] " T'ung Chien," Yuan Fu (元 符), 2nd year, 7th month.
[2] " T'ung Chien," Yuan Fu (元 符), 2nd year, 8th month.
[3] " T'ung Chien," Ts'ung Ning (崇 寧), 4th year, 4th month.
[4] " T'ung Chien," Cheng Ho (政 和), 5th year, 8th month.
[5] " T'ung Chien," Hsuan Ho (宣 和), 6th year, 1st month.

tribes which took refuge in Ssu Ch'uan were "civilized" by the Emperor Wu Ti (武 帝) of the Han dynasty (B.C. 140-86), but there were frequent outbreaks of rebellion which had to be suppressed by force of arms.

Hunan was occupied by large numbers of aborigines even in the times of the Sung dynasty.

A short sketch of their relationship to China from the earliest times will be of use here.[1]

The Man tribes of Hunan were first brought under Chinese rule by the Ch'u State (楚) in the period known as Spring and Autumn (春 秋 時). Later on, in the period known as "Warring States" (戰 國 時), a general of Ch'in (秦), Pai Ch'i (白 起) by name, incorporated more of their territory, and established the military post of Ch'ien Chung (黔 中). During the Han dynasty this military post was termed Wu Ling Chun (武 陵 郡).

During the Later Han (後 漢) the tribes of this area frequently made incursions into Chinese territory, so the general, Ma Yuan (馬 援), led an expedition against them and inflicted a severe defeat. From this time on to the period of the Sui dynasty (隋 朝), A.D. 589-618, rebellion and submission alternated. But during the Sui dynasty Ch'en Chow (辰 州), in the heart of the area, became Chinese.

During the T'ang dynasty military posts were established at Chin Chow (錦 州), Hsi Chow (溪 州), Wu Chow (巫 州), and Hsü Chow (敘 州). The natives, however, were by no means exterminated, the land reverting to China on a policy of arrangement between the Government and the chieftains of the various tribes. During the later stages of the Dynasty, when much confusion existed, the Man tribes occupied territory at will, their chieftains assuming official rank and titles. Quite a formidable rising of the Man tribes occurred when Ma Hsi Fan (馬 希 範) was Imperial Commissioner for Hunan. In this they were assisted by the Yao (猺) tribes. Later again, during the administration of Chow Hsing Feng (周 行 逢),

---

[1] Liang Ch'i Ch'ao, pp. 214, 215.

there were frequent uprisings, the natives harassing Ch'en Chow (辰 州) and Yung Chow (永 州), slaughtering and carrying off large numbers. Scarcely a year passed without fighting.

In the times of the Sung dynasty, when the military prestige of the Empire was low, the tribal chieftains still held on to their territory. It was considered good policy by the Chinese Government to recognize the *status quo*, and to confer mandates upon them for the control of their areas. This, however, only increased their pride and incited them to reckless acts.

The strongest tribe was known as " P'eng " (彭) of the Pei Chiang (北 江) district, who held the triple city of Hsi Chow (溪 州) and seventeen other " chow " (州) or counties. Other tribes were located in the Nan Chiang (南 江) district, comprising territory from Ch'en Chow (辰 州) to Ch'ang Sha (常 沙). These tribes were called respectively Shu (舒), T'ien (田), and Hsiang (向), each of which occupied four or five " chow " (州).

These tribes were at constant strife with one another, cruel and oppressive. They frequently indulged in reckless slaughter, often raised the flag of rebellion, and represented a fearful menace to law-abiding and peace-loving people.

Shortly after Shen Tsung ascended the throne, Chao Ting (趙 鼎), chief Administrator of Hupei (湖 北), reported that the chieftain of Chia Chow (峽 州) had been raiding the neighbourhood, that he had been seriously maltreating the people, and that the latter were appealing for the protection of the empire. A resident of Ch'en Chow (辰 州), Chang Ch'iao by name (張 翹), submitted a memorial asserting that terrible atrocities were being perpetrated in the Pei Chiang and Nan Chiang territories.

This happened at the time when Wang An Shih and Shen Tsung were contemplating the sending out of expeditions to bring the border tribes under proper control, so in the 7th month of 1072 Chang Ch'un (章 惇) was commissioned to make investigation into conditions obtaining in Hunan and Hupei with a view to the reduction of the Man tribes.

In the 11th month of that year Chang Ch'un reduced the Su

(蘇) tribe of the Mei Shan (梅 山) region, which for a very long time had had no relationship with China. This district bordered on T'an (潭) on the east, Shao (邵) on the south, Ch'en (辰) on the west, and Ting Li (鼎 澧) on the north. This added 14,800 families to the national population register and 260,000 " mu " of land to the territory of the empire. Regulations were issued calling upon these people to pay taxation as regular subjects of the empire. The cities of Wu Yang (武 陽) and K'ai Chia (開 峽) were built. An Hua Hsien (安 化 縣)[1] was also fortified, also Hsin Hua Hsien[2] (新 化 縣).

In the 10th month of 1073 two chieftains of the Nan Chiang area, called Hsiang Yung Wu (向 永 晤) and Shu Kuang Yin (舒 光 銀), surrendered to Chang Ch'un. The T'ien tribe were also defeated and their city of I Chow (懿 州) taken. The city of Yuan Chow (沅 州)[3] was then fortified, and the new city of I Chow was made the headquarters of the Government for the whole region. Later the head of the Ch'eng and Hui tribes (誠 徽), called Yang Kuang Fu (楊 光 富), surrendered with the population of twenty-three districts. Then the city of Ch'eng Chow (誠 州)[4] was established.

In the 1st month of 1076 Chang Ch'un brought the lower Hsi tribe (下 溪) and their chieftain, P'eng Shih Yen (彭 師 晏), into subjection. This tribe had gradually extended its influence over twenty counties. They had conducted their affairs entirely independently of the Imperial Government for many generations. Aided by Li P'ing (李 平), the Commissioner for Hupei, Chang Ch'un, defeated their armed forces and brought the whole tribe with their territory under Chinese rule. These districts are represented by the modern Ch'en Chow Fu (辰 州 府). The lower Hsi city was rebuilt, named Hui Hsi (會 溪), and made into a garrison town. Taxation similar to

---

[1] The modern An Hua Hsien (安 化 縣), in Ch'ang Sha prefecture.
[2] The modern Hsin Hua Hsien (新 化 縣), in Pao Ch'ing prefecture.
[3] The modern Yuan Chow Fu (沅 州 府).
[4] The modern Ching Chow (靖 州).

that imposed on regular subjects of the empire was imposed upon them.

So we see that in a little more than three years Chang Ch'un reduced three great chieftains and brought over forty counties within the Imperial domain. From Yung Chow (融 州) in Kuangsi he fortified villages and established a line of communication with Ch'eng Chow (誠 州).

In the early years of Che Tsung's rule, Fu Yao Yü (傅 堯 俞) and Weng Yen Sou (王 巖 叟) submitted a memorial to the throne proposing that all these districts brought under the Imperial sway during the reign of Shen Tsung should revert to the control of the various tribes, on the ground that the Man (蠻) peoples had become inured to living in peaceful relationship with the empire. If the Emperor thought it inadvisable that the whole of the territory should be surrendered, it was suggested that Ch'eng Chow should be given up and Yuan Chow retained. The road which Chang Ch'un had built and all the fortifications and barricades which he had erected were destroyed, and from this time the tribes were once more cut off from connection with the Government and lived their independent life.

Wang Ch'uan Shu (王 船 山), of Manchu times, who usually is unfavourably disposed to Wang An Shih's policy, thinks that Chang Ch'un's work in Hunan was worthy of special recognition. He admits that he had succeeded in " civilizing " the Man tribes in Hupei and Hunan, and the bringing of these hitherto lawless elements into orderly and settled relationship with the empire he considers commendable. He considers it unfortunate that he did not finish his work, for the unsubjugated tribes like the Miao are still far from being " civilized ".[1]

The third campaign of note we will call the Ssu Ch'uan expedition.[2]

Since the times of the Han dynasty the numerous tribes of the Ssu Ch'uan borderland had given the empire considerable

---

[1] Liang Ch'i Ch'ao, p. 217, synopsized.
[2] Liang Ch'i Ch'ao, pp. 219–221, synopsized, in translation.

trouble. In the early days of Shen Tsung's reign there were two chieftains of the Lu Chow (瀘 州) district (connected with the Wu Man tribes), called respectively Yen Tzu (晏 子) and Fu Wang Kuo Shu (斧 望 箇 恕). These chieftains were very powerful, who had already made a savage onslaught on the Nei Hsi (納 溪) " barbarians " and were then planning to invade the Imperial domain from Yü Ching (淯 井).

In 1073 Hsiung Pen (熊 本) was commissioned to investigate the situation in the Tzu (梓) and K'uei (夔) areas, and take such measures as he thought advisable to bring the border tribes into a more reasonable frame of mind. Hsiung Pen reported that the success which had attended the raids of these tribes in the past was due to their having secured the assistance of local dare-devils as guides. So the first step he took was to execute one hundred of these at Lu Ch'uan (瀘 川). This example of severity brought their associates to their senses, and they offered their services to the Imperial Government as a measure of atonement for their past crimes.

Hsiung Pen then appealed that substantial rewards might be conferred upon the local people, a move which brought all the tribes in the area with one exception into willing submission.

That solitary exception was the tribe headed by Ko Yin (柯 陰). Hsiung Pen then collected the fighting forces of nineteen tribes in the Yen Chow (晏 州) area, and aided by some irregulars from Kueichow (貴 州) inflicted a severe defeat upon Ko Yin. As a result of this lesson, the tribes of Yü Ching (淯 井), Chang Ning (長 寧), Wu Man (烏 蠻), Lo Shih (羅 氏), and Kuei Wang (鬼 王) all tendered their submission and expressed their willingness to remain under Chinese rule for ever. The District Commissioner, Fan Pai Lu (范 百 祿), published a proclamation warning them to continue in loyal relationship with the empire or suffer the consequences. This was set up in the form of a stone tablet at Wu Ning (武 寧).

When Hsiung Pen returned to the capital to report, the Emperor said : " You have neither wasted public funds nor injured the people. In one day as it were you have eliminated a source of anxiety and trouble which has been our bane for over a century."

The Emperor then duly thanked and suitably rewarded Hsiung Pen.

From that time onwards the border tribes continued sub missive, with the exception of one Liao Mu Tou (獠 木 斗), who revolted at Yü Chow (渝 州) in 1075. Hsiung Pen defeated him at T'ung Fo Pa, which brought the leader of the revolt into submission, surrendering all the territory which had been under his control, including Ch'in Chow (泰 州). The total area was about 500 li. Four forts and nine military outposts were erected by Hsiung Pen. He also fortified T'ung Fo Pa, naming it Nan P'ing Chün (南 平 軍). Yu Chow and Ch'in Chow are represented by the modern Ch'ung Ch'ing Fu (重 慶 府).

The fourth campaign of importance undertaken under Wang An Shih's regime was the Chiao-Chih (交 趾) or Annamese expedition.[1]

During the winter of 1075 the king of Annam, named Li Ch'ien Te (李 乾 德), made an incursion into Chinese territory, capturing the cities of Ch'in (欽) and Lien (廉) in Kuangtung. The following spring he captured Yun Chow (邕 州) in Kuangsi. Kuo K'uei (郭 逵) was mandated as Pacification Commissioner for Annam, with Chao Hsieh (趙 高) as his second in command. As the troops set out on their punitive expedition Wang An Shih published the following proclamation written by his own hand, viz. :—

" To the peoples of Chiao Chow (交 州) and the Thibetans of the Imperial Border Territory. Our country has hitherto treated the people of Annam with the utmost generosity, allowing their ruler to retain the rank and title of king. China has refrained from any punitive action up to the present time. But now they have captured our cities, slaughtered our officials and subjects, and offended the majesty of our empire. These are crimes which we cannot overlook, and which we feel must

---

[1] Liang Ch'i Ch'ao, pp. 221–6, synopsized, in translation.

be punished in the name of Heaven. This has demanded that a military expedition be sent, so our forces are now advancing against them both by sea and land. Heaven has given indications favourable to our cause, and there are already many signs of a new state of things to come.

"Everyone knows that they have taken the initiative against us, and we are determined to avenge the insult.

"But you need not flee from the presence of the Imperial troops, no matter where they shall penetrate, for you have our full sympathy in your sufferings from the enemy's oppressive tactics. If you manifest your willing submission to the Imperial sway, and take steps actively to submit with all your people, you will be rewarded with unusual favours of rank and presents, and you are offered a free pardon for all past offences.

"Li Ch'ien Te is after all but a youth, the policy of his Court is not in his hands, and if he will present himself at our Court he will be treated with the same respect as before. The Imperial commands will not be changed, let all obey without wavering. We are aware that your families have been suffering extreme hardship from the oppressors and exorbitant demands of the enemy. I have already given orders to our officials that they are to make known our gracious will, but at the same time they are commanded to exterminate all who resist with armed force, in the hope that the whole area may enjoy perpetual peace." [1]

In the spring of 1076 Kuo K'uei reached Ch'ang Sha (長 沙), whence he sent off two expeditions, one to recover the Yun and Lien cities, the other, led by himself, to proceed westwards as far as the Fu Liang River (富 良 江). The Man tribes came up in boats to join issue. The Imperial forces could not cross the river, so Chao Hsieh sent off his men to fell trees, and made implements of attack which could hurl stones like rain. The enemy craft were all smashed up. The attack was made from ambush, and several thousands of the enemy were killed. The false prince Kung Chen (洪 真) was killed. Li

[1] Prose Works, vol. 12, p. 1 (勅 牓 交 趾).

Ch'ien Te then became alarmed, and sent an ambassador with the message that he was willing to surrender at the entrance to the camp.

The district of the Fu Liang River is very remote, but only 80,000 men were sent. Of these more than half perished from the heat and swampy fever. They returned after reducing Kuang Yuan Chow (廣 源 州), Men Chow (門 州), Ssu Lang Chow (思 浪 州), Su Mao Chow (蘇 茂 州), and Kuang Lang Hsien (桄 榔 縣). Kuang Yuan was renamed Shun Chow (順 州). Li Ch'ien Te was pardoned and restored to his original status, and right up to the end of the Sung dynasty there was no further instance of revolt on the Annamese border.

The History narrates that they presented tribute as usual to the Chinese Court in the Autumn of 1078.[1]

---

[1] " T'ung Chien," Yuan Feng (元 豐), 1st year, autumn.

CHAPTER XXII

EDUCATIONAL POLICY

It is well known that education in China, up to comparatively recent times, has been almost entirely confined to the preparation of men for the Government services. This general statement holds true of the times of the Northern Sung Dynasty and of the period during which Wang An Shih was wielding his political influence.

There was, however, very little, if anything, in the way of a Government system of education, even of this limited type, operative in those days. There were, it is true, a great many schools organized by private enterprise, into which candidates for literary fame, and the official recognition and Government appointment which they hoped would follow on that, enrolled in considerable numbers.

While there was no regular school system under the auspices of the Government, there was in vogue a properly organized examination system. By means of this the candidate for official position could advance by definite stages until he became eligible for admission into the official hierarchy, which entitled him to hope for the highest positions in the Government service. This has given China the not inappropriate designation of " The Scholars' Empire ".[1]

This system in the times of Sung seems to have operated on the following lines. The candidate studied privately for the first examination, styled " K'o Chü " (科 舉), which was taken at some provincial centre, and success at which entitled him to the appellation of " Scholar " or " Hsueh Shih " (學 士). This made him eligible for entrance to the examination for the doctor's degree or " Chin Shih " (進 士). This latter examination was always held at the capital of the Empire. If the candidate was successful at this examination he was usually

---

[1] Holcombe, " The Chinese Revolution."

appointed to some subordinate post in the provinces for a period of probation, usually three years in duration, after which he was entitled to submit a thesis to the Government examiners. If this was accepted the candidate was enrolled as a member of the " Kuan Chih " (館 職) or Official Hierarchy. The successful candidate at this examination was expected to serve again on probation at one of the Literary Bureaus in the Capital before receiving definite appointment in one or other of the Government offices. He might as an alternative be appointed to the provinces as magistrate of a county, " Hsien " (縣), for a period of another three years, then rise to a sub-prefectural appointment, or " Chow " (州). Students who had qualified for the " Doctor's degree " (進 士) were also eligible for these county and sub-prefectural appointments, even though they did not submit the special thesis for the " Kuan Chih ". Wang An Shih himself provides a case in point. The usual term of office in these county or sub-prefectural posts was three years, at the conclusion of which the appointee's record was reviewed by the Government authorities, and he received either a renewal of his old appointment or a fresh one according to circumstances. Officials of prefectural status " Fu " or " Chün " (府 郡), and those in positions of any importance at the Capital, were, in the normal course, all of the Kuan Chih qualification. In special circumstances, and on the Emperor's initiative, certain exceptions might be made to this procedure, which, however, in the main was that generally followed.

It should, however, be noted that at the Capital there was established what was known as the " Kuo Tzu Chien " (國 子 監),[1] a kind of Government University, in which the sons of the official hierarchy received an education, graduation from which entitled them to the same privileges as those who had taken the regular examinations in the provinces. Both the provincial scholars and the graduates from this University had, however, to take the doctor's degree or " Chin Shih ".

[1] Dynastic Histories, Sung Dynasty, book 157, " Hsuan Chü Chih " (選 舉 志), vol. 110, sect. 111.

This National University was divided into two departments, the students of which were styled respectively the "Kuo Tzu Sheng" (國 子 生) and the "T'ai Hsueh Sheng" (太 學 生). Admittance to the former was confined to the sons of officials of the seventh grade and above, the numbers being limited to two hundred. Students of the latter were primarily the sons of officials of the eighth and ninth grades, but opportunity to take an entrance examination to this was afforded to students from non-official families who showed exceptional ability.

We may take the above sketch as typical of the educational system in vogue during the earlier days of the Sung Dynasty.

During the reign of Jen Tsung (仁 宗), who was on the throne from 1023–1063, attempts were made to establish something like a Government system of education throughout the country. Shortly after his accession he donated a piece of land in the district of Yen Chow (兗 州) to be used for school purposes, and issued an edict that in the more important Government centres of the Empire schools should be set up.[2]

In the year 1044 he issued another edict,[2] ordering each sub-prefectural district (州) and county (縣) to establish a school. Under this mandate the Chief Civil Administrator of the area was to appoint teachers from the members of his own staff. In case there should not be enough of these available, then he was to select suitable men from the village scholars to fill the posts.

How ineffective this edict proved to be may be seen from Wang An Shih's famous Memorial of a myriad characters, where he writes : " It is true that each sub-prefectural district and county is supposed to have its school, but in reality nothing but the shell exists, i.e. they are just so much bricks and mortar. There are no regular teachers, nor is any real instruction being given in them." [3] From this we may infer that the scheme

---

[1] Dynastic Histories, Sung Dynasty, book 157, " Hsuan Chü Chih" (選 舉 志), vol. 110, sect. 111.

[2] " T'ung Chien," Ch'ing Li (慶 曆), 4th year, 3rd month.

[3] See page 60, " Myriad Character Memorial " (萬 言 書).

for a national system of education in Jen Tsung's day remained very largely on paper. The request that the teaching staff should be provided out of the entourage of the local officials meant that little or nothing would be done.

Conditions in the Government University evidently were equally bad in those days, for we read in the History [1] that out of a possible total attendance of a thousand students, only ten or twenty were to be found in their classes. So Jen Tsung made an effort to improve matters by appointing some efficient person to take charge. In 1053 one, Hu Yuan (胡 瑗), known popularly as An Ting Hsien Sheng (安 定 先 生), who had been running very successfully a large private school in Che Chiang for over twenty years, was appointed a professor in the University. Some few years later he was given the post of Imperial Tutor and concurrently appointed as Deputy-Director of Education.

The Historian [1] notes that while in those days scholars held the rhyming essay in highest esteem, Hu Yuan in his school laid special emphasis on classical interpretation, and instruction in practical matters of administration.

After his promotion to the capital, Hu Yuan tried assiduously to introduce certain reforms, and pressed them against considerable opposition. In the intervals of official examinations he would assemble the students in a great hall and give them instruction in music and poetry. So keen was the interest aroused by this experiment that students would stay on all night in some instances, or travel great distances to put themselves under his instruction. Eventually his method gained general approval, and he was requested to apply his ideas to the reform of the National University.

Just how much was done in this way the Histories do not relate, but Wang An Shih in his Memorial [2] says : " It is true there are instructors in the National University, but they are not selected with any care. The conduct of Court ceremonies, music, and practical matters of administration have no place

---

[1] " Hsuan Chü Chih," vol. 110, sect. 111 (選 舉 志).
[2] " Myriad Character Memorial " (萬 言 書). See page 61.

326 WANG AN SHIH

in the curriculum . . . Instruction chiefly consists of explanations of the text of the Classics, split up into chapters and sentences."

It should be said both in fairness to Wang An Shih and to Hu Yuan that the latter was not in office at the time this was written. But it is evident that education generally, from the Government standpoint at any rate, was at a very low ebb when Shen Tsung came to the throne and when Wang An Shih began his reform movement.[1]

In his memorials to the throne the latter made many references to the subject of education, and after his promotion to high office gave a good deal of thought and attention to the educational system. He made definite attempts at reform, particularly in the National University, also in regard to Classical Interpretation, and in reference to the method of selecting officials on the examination basis.

With regard to the first, the History[2] narrates that in the year 1068 the numbers of students in the University were increased, the total in the " Kuo Tzu Sheng " department being advanced from 200 to 300. In the year 1071 we read[3] : " Since schools have been established in the sub-prefectural and county districts, the accommodation in the ' T'ai Hsueh ' department of the University is much too limited. It was then decreed that the whole of the Hsi Ch'ing Palace (錫 慶 院) and a portion of the Ch'ao Chi Park (朝 集 院) should be taken over for this purpose. Ten professors were added to the staff."

The " T'ai Hsueh Department " was now divided into three sections,[3] styled respectively the " Wai She " (外 舍) or External Section, with 700 students, which were later increased to 2,000, the " Nei She " (內 舍) or Internal Section with

[1] There was another attempt made in Jen Tsung's day to extend educational facilities by setting up the four gate colleges, " Ssu Men Hsueh " (四 門 學). These colleges seem at one time to have been located in the provinces, but were now moved into the Capital for convenience. Into these colleges sons of the lower grades of officials were admitted, and also sons of non-official families. This attempt was, however, abandoned after a short period.

[2] " Hsuan Chü Chih," vol. 110, sect. 111.

[3] " T'ung Chien," Hsi Ning (熙 寧), 4th year, 12th month.

300 students, and the "Shang She" (上 舍), or Advanced Section, with 100 students. The External Section was the lowest of the three. Candidates for admission to this section were required to produce a certificate of identification from their local official and to pass an entrance examination. After admission to the school the student's progress was recorded month by month by his own teacher, conduct as well as intellectual attainments being taken into account. Each term he was examined by five different persons, and at the end of the year, after another examination, his average standing was determined. Each student was required to specialize in the meaning of one classic. At the examinations he was given papers on the interpretation of the Classics, essays, and questions in practical subjects. If he was successful at this examination he was admitted to the Internal Section, where he studied for two years, being examined much in the same way as the students in the External Section, and then promoted to the Advanced Section by examination at the end of the course. Those who passed in the highest grade at the graduation examination from this Section were styled First Class Graduates, were excused the usual examination for the doctor's degree or "Chin Shih" (進 士), and entitled to direct appointment to Government service by the Emperor. Those who were classed in the Second Grade were excused the first part of the examination for the doctor's degree, taking only that part which was personally supervised by the Emperor, and if successful in that were considered eligible for official appointment. Those who only reached Third Class standing had to take the whole of the doctor's degree examination, in the same way as the students from the provinces who had passed the "Sheng Shih" (省 試), i.e. provincial tests.

Special appointments of an educational character were thrown open to First Class Graduates, they being either given posts as teachers or recorders in the University, those of specially fine abilities being given professorships, and at the same time recommended for appointment to the Chung Shu Sheng (中 書 省).

In 1073 Wang An Shih introduced four professors of Law

into the University, and suggested that the officials resident in the Capital might take special courses in this subject. The candidates for the doctor's degree and the sons of officials (probably those in the " Kuo Tzu Chien ") were all ordered to take examinations in Law and Administration.[1]

He also set up a Department of Medicine in the University, teachers being appointed by the Medical Officer of the Han Lin Academy, physicians of repute being also invited from the provinces. After a preliminary examination three hundred students were admitted to this Medical School. Pharmacy, medicine, the use of the needle, and elementary surgery were the subjects of instruction. A proper system of examinations was instituted in connection with the department, the best students being appointed to the Imperial Household medical staff, with official rank, others were given appointments in the school as teachers, or allocated to Government departments at the capital or in the provinces.

A Military Academy was established by Wang An Shih in 1072. This was set up in the Wu Ch'eng Wang Temple (武 成 王 府), the professors being men skilled in both literary and military subjects. There were a hundred students in residence, who were taught military tactics, studied the causes of success or failure in the great wars of history, and made a special study of the lives of soldiers of repute.

The above material is taken from the " Wen Hsien T'ung K'ao ",[2] very little of it being found in the Canonical Histories. It seems as though Wang An Shih made a beginning with a scheme which promised to develop along the lines of the modern university system.

He did not, however, confine his attention to the University in his educational projects. In 1071 he ordered the setting up of additional schools in the five circuits adjacent to the capital, i.e. Ching Tung, Ching Hsi, Ho Tung, Ho Pei, and Shensi.

Lu Tien (陸 佃) and others were appointed Education Officers. Later on every prefecture (府) and sub-prefecture

---

[1] " T'ung Chien " and " Hsuan Chü Chih ", vol. 110, sect. 111.
[2] Quoted Liang Ch'i Ch'ao, p. 199.

(州) established a school, and fifty-three educational officers were appointed for their supervision.

Ma Tuan Lin (馬 端 臨), author of the Wen Hsien T'ung K'ao (文 獻 通 考), says: "Education was greatly advanced at this period. The reason why Educational Officers were few was because they were very carefully selected."[1]

It has already been noted that the Government system of examinations aimed at the securing of men for the Government services. Wang An Shih paid great attention to this, and was a very severe critic of the current method. This subject occupies a big section of his famous memorial to Jen Tsung.[2]

His main criticism was levelled at the amount of memorizing work required and at the type of essay called for under the existing regulations. The tests involved the memorizing of practically the whole of the Classics. This it will be readily seen absorbed an enormous amount of time, and in the end did not necessarily give the student any real knowledge of the general ideas or great principles underlying the text. The essay tests called for rhyming-parallel phrasing and poesy. As a test of a man's literary skill this might be very effective, and might be regarded as a great accomplishment. It was, however, of no help to a man faced with practical problems of an administrative character when he received his appointment to govern a district, which might include several hundreds of thousands of people.

Wang An Shih contended that such a method of selecting officials was not only useless, in that the students could find nothing in it of practical help in actual administration. It was also positively injurious in that the time and energy devoted to such subjects and accomplishments prevented them from learning those things that would be of practical value later on. The fact that some who had been selected by this system had shown themselves capable administrators was no credit to the system as such. They were skilled in government because of their native genius for such work rather than because of the help the system and its prescribed studies gave them.

[1] Liang Ch'i Ch'ao, p. 195.

[2] i.e. the Myriad Character Memorial (萬 言 書). See pp. 69–73.

It will be well at this point to introduce the reader to one of Wang An Shih's essays on this subject. It is entitled " The Selection of Men of Ability " (取 材), and reads as follows[1] :—

" An Artisan in making his preparations for a piece of work first hardens and sharpens his tools, selects his materials, and estimates the amount required. In these ways he economizes his strength when actually at work, and produces better results. In like manner the sage in the sphere of statecraft will take steps to procure men of character and talents. With a view to ensuring that such are obtained, he will look carefully into their previous record, noting not only their reputation, but also their actual achievements. In that way he will be saved much anxiety in regard to their actual service, and their contribution to the public cause will be of real value.

" It is therefore of the utmost importance that a proper method of securing men for the public services should be adopted.

" Those rulers in the past who adopted the literary test system of securing officials, all had the idea that they might obtain men of character and ability thereby. It is true that sometimes such men were secured by this method, but in many cases it failed of its object, . . . and sometimes mistakes were made in certain appointments. . . .

" My proposal is that something after the method of Tso Hsiung (左 雄) of the Eastern Han Dynasty (東 漢) should be adopted, viz. ' Candidates for official position should be tested in their knowledge of the various schools of thought. Candidates for the civil service should in particular be tested in their knowledge of documents and memorials. This would lead to all civil officials having not merely gifts of literary composition, but also to their being conversant with ancient and modern laws and regulations, the principles of astronomy, and their bearing on the affairs of the State. They would have some idea of political economy, and know how to initiate necessary reforms. In a word they would be able to apply their know-

---

[1] Prose Works, vol. 17, p. 16 (取 材), " Ch'ü Ts'ai."

ledge to the duties of their office. When discussion of important matters of government arose, they would be able to make their own contribution thereto out of their knowledge of ancient and modern ideas.

" ' Those who are termed " Scholars " would be acquainted not only with the fine art of phrase-making, but would receive instruction in law, ceremonies, public administration, and in the right relationships that should subsist between ruler and officers. They would know how to adapt the method of government to the needs of the times, and to apply their knowledge to whatever sphere of public service they were called. No longer would they make a " mockery " of government, but would be able to solve all problems of the State by a true classical method, being guided always by ancient precedents.'

" The modern ' Chin Shih ' (進 土), or Doctor of Literature, is the equivalent of the old civil official, and the modern exponent of the Classics is the equivalent of the old ' Scholar '. But in the tests for the doctor's degree, too much emphasis is laid upon one's ability in phrase making and the linking of rhyming couplets, which ability after all is of a very minor type. In the realm of Classical knowledge, precedence is given to memorizing ability, the real and practical meaning of the text being ignored. This calls for but inferior gifts of intellect.

" The upshot of all this is that a man of real administrative gifts remains unemployed, and a man of really exceptional ability for such work is boycotted by his conventional contemporaries. The educated class say one to another, ' We can hunt or fish as much as we please, for all that is required in the examinations is a mere veneer of learning. What, after all, can we contribute to the work of Government ? ' The student of the Classics says : ' We only need to copy out the ancient texts and hand them on to others. We need only devote ourselves to memorizing, why bother about the meaning of underlying principles of the text ? ' Fathers are thus influenced to encourage their sons to be content with mere surface accomplishments, as sufficing for current requirements. What hope is there of their making any real contribution to the government in their day and generation?

"What kind of criticism can such men make of any important question of government? What contribution can they make in the Great Hall, when the question is raised of making some important change in the constitution or laws and regulations of the land? What share can they take in solving some fine point of law? What can they do towards enhancing the prestige of the Government by making useful comparisons between the past and the present? In a word, all they will be able to do will be to acquiesce in the opinion of the majority.

"The statement of Wen Chung Tzu (文 中 子) is apropos, viz. : ' Letters, letters ! Does the art of Letters consist merely of writing essays? Such writing should relate itself to fundamental principles. Learning, learning! is that only a matter of memorizing texts? Learning should make a positive contribution to the advancement of the cause of Justice.'

"We may see from this that in ancient times very great importance was attached to the selection of officials. In my opinion, if we are desirous of securing capable men for the government services to-day we should proceed along the lines laid down by Tso Hsiung. In the examination for candidates for the doctor's degree, questions should be asked about the most important factors to be taken into consideration when formulating any principle of government, and their views should be ascertained as to the relative urgency of any matter that is suggested. They should be required to show their knowledge of how the people may be educated in regard to their duties to the State, and to give some idea as to where to begin with the settling of border problems. In each case the candidate should be asked to discuss the matter from the standpoint of current needs. It is futile to muddle their minds with the details of textual exposition and rhyming puzzles.

"In testing the classical knowledge of the students they should be questioned on the relationship of rites and ceremonies to practical government, and on the import of changes in the natural order, and on what should determine the order of precedence in the regulations for ceremonies. Each candidate should be told to give prime attention to the meaning of passages, and not be compelled to give his whole attention to repetition and memory work.

" If some such method as this is adopted a proper classification of the candidates will be feasible and a sound basis will be secured whereon they can be either promoted or degraded. With this as their guiding principle, students will know what is acceptable to the examiners, and they will no longer despise the knowledge which is practical and cease devoting their time and strength to useless studies. The latter after all is the more laborious course of the two, so they should learn to give themselves to the type of study which is relatively easier and much more valuable.

" For if only the students will cease working so hard at what is of no practical value, they may specialize in some form of knowledge which will bring them success in administrative affairs. They will begin to concentrate on the principles of Government and learn to make valuable contributions to administrative problems. No matter whether this type of man be employed at Court or in the provinces, his work will be of real benefit to the people and that, rather than the present method of promoting men merely according to their length of service, should be the criterion of a man's worth." [1]

It will be of interest, while on this question of the examination system, to quote a selection of the questions which were set by Wang An Shih himself. From these it will readily be perceived that mere memorizers of the Classics would look in vain to their memories to supply the answers. The questions are appended,[2] as follows :—

" 1. The appointment of Kun (鯀) by Yao (堯) is related in detail in the Book of History. Did Yao know that Kun was incapable, and at the same time wish to try him out, or was he ignorant of his inability for the post ? If he was ignorant of his incapacity it would seem wrong to term Yao a sage ; if he

[1] Essay ends here.
[2] Prose Works, vol. 17, p. 23.

knew he was incapable, but still wished to give him a trial, then it was surely wrong to distress the people with nine years of inefficient administration. Later on the Court ministers recommended Shun (舜) and Yü (禹), but if perchance they had recommended another ' Kun ', would he (Yao) have given him a further trial of nine years?

" Seeing that Yao was really an illustrious sage, we may assume that he would know Kun to be a worthless fellow. But his knowledge should have led him to trust his own judgment unhesitatingly. Why then did he follow the advice of his ministers? You might reply that he ought to accept the advice of his ministers and not trust to his own opinion. However, the mind of a real sage is most concerned about the relief of the people from any distress, and his selection of men for the public service should have regard to this very matter. Would you, then, think that a ruler should always act as Yao did (i.e. follow the advice of his ministers in spite of his own opinion), so as to set a standard for future generations, and by making it a precedent prevent some unintelligent ruler from bringing ruin upon his country?

" Perhaps it will be urged that Yao knew that the period of the flood was ' decreed ', and so first made use of Kun (the length of time which the floods lasted being ' decreed ' it was a matter of no consequence as to who was employed to cope with them). Others again might say: ' He deliberately prolonged the distress of the people in order to enhance the glory of Yü (禹).'

" In my (Wang An Shih's) opinion, both these suggestions are wrong. For we cannot conceive of Yao extending the period of the people's distress merely to add greater glory to Yü, nor can we imagine that Yü would consent to the enhancing of his reputation at the expense of the people's distress. If they had so acted they would both have forfeited the right to be termed such as we know Yao and Yü to be. The suggestion that Yao might be slavishly addicted to the fatalistic notion of ' time ' in this connection is quite unworthy of the character of the sage. If, indeed, the time of the flood was ' decreed ', why then should Yao have set Kun a task which in the end would inevitably result in his death?

" I find it impossible to explain why Yao took this action, but anticipate that you (the candidate) will be able to do so."

Such was poser Number 1. It will be of interest to note here that although Wang An Shih in this question professed ignorance of Yao's reason for employing Kun, he attempted to solve the riddle himself in his essay on Kun.[1] In this he candidly admits that Yao used Kun because he thought he was the only man at Court who had the kind of knowledge that was required for flood control. This reduces Yao to the level of an ordinary mortal (very healthily, too), who acted to the best of his intelligence and made use of a man whom he thought might do for the job, but who failed. The conventional notion of Yao as a perfect sage, possessed of all knowledge, and foreknowledge as well, would land the candidate in a very deep morass as he attempted to answer this question.

" 2. Discuss Kao Yao's (皋 陶) remark, that ' All depends upon one's capacity for recognizing men, and on one's ability to placate the people.' [2]

" The ancient custom of mutual admonition which obtained between a ruler and his ministers was very fine. If a ruler lacked one of these two qualifications, though he should possess the other, he would still be unfit to govern the people. But having due regard to the majesty of the Emperor, the economic well-being of the empire, and the number of civil and military officials required, there must be one sure method whereby the right men may be recognized. Of this you (the candidate) will doubtless be able to inform me."

Wang An Shih's own ideas on this subject are clear from his essay on the " Securing of Capable Men " (材 論),[3] Ts'ai Lun.

In this he first stresses the importance of securing men of ability for the Government services, and points out the crime of those in authority who are not doing their best to get them,

[1] Prose Works, vol. 16, p. 7.
[2] Prose Works, vol. 17, p. 24.
[3] Prose Works, vol. 16, p. 24 (abbreviated), " Ts'ai Lun " (材 論).

either because the presumption of the Emperor is such that he thinks his own dignity will suffice to keep the empire in peace and order, or through his thinking that rank and emoluments will suffice to entice such to the service of the State.

He then goes on to say that the great reason for the current scarcity of such men in the Government service is that no efforts are being made to find them, probably because it is idly assumed that they do not exist. The essay continues :—

" The conventional argument is that genius will show itself sooner or later, as an awl in a sack is sure to work its way through. But that is only one side of the matter. The other may be represented by a common saying about horses. ' As long as they remain in the stall it is difficult to distinguish between them. The only way to discover their differences is to lead them out and try them on the road.' There is a way of discovering men of ability. First of course it is necessary that the attempt be made to find them and then devise some method of testing them. They should be given a trial in a position for which they are thought suitable.

" Education will find its appropriate place after a number of able men have been placed in office and proper regulations have been devised, and will then be of assistance in discovering those who have the qualifications for the more important Government positions."

From this we gather that it was one of Wang An Shih's ideas to revive, as a temporary expedient, one of the more ancient methods of selecting officials, that is, to secure that a number of men should be recommended by local groups, on the grounds of their high character and known ability, regardless of whether they had observed the customary official procedure or not. Such men would then be placed in a position on probation and, if found satisfactory in that, they could then be given greater responsibilities.

But this was only to be a temporary measure. For undoubtedly Wang An Shih's great idea was to establish a Government school system, by means of which the right men could be discovered and employed. The following extracts from one of his memorials on the subject [1] will serve to make this clear :—

"The ancient method of selecting officials was essentially dependent upon the establishment of schools. For this tended to produce uniform thinking amongst the officials on ethical matters and practical methods ; it also contributed to the cultivation of correct practices among the people generally. This, too, enabled the Government to have a constant supply of men available for the various services.

"Of recent times, however, the method adopted for producing this supply of men has shown no particular regard for these fundamental principles. So that, although it is true that the country possesses a number of scholars, they have become such solely because of their natural ability. For there have been no schools, no tutors, nor any corporate educational life, in which their natural capacities might be developed and perfected.

"This is a matter of the greatest concern to critics of the current system. It is of course necessary, if we wish to revive the ancient ideas in this matter that reform should be introduced gradually, and we admit that that has its peculiar difficulties. But at least steps can be taken to eliminate the rhyming-couplets and parallel-phrasing style of essay and to require the students to make the ' meaning ' of the Classics the main object of their studies.

"Let this be adopted as a temporary measure until the Government shall have instituted a school system throughout the country. Then it should be feasible to revive the system of education and method of selecting officials which obtained in the period of the Three Dynasties. When education is made universal we shall have approached very nearly to the ancient pattern."

Su Shih (蘇 軾) was an advocate for the retention of the current system, arguing as follows [2] :—

"The essential thing in the securing of suitable men for the

[1] Works, vol. 10, p. 8 (乞 改 科 條 制 劄 子).
[2] Liang Ch'i Ch'ao, p. 201.

Government services is that those who select them shall have a capacity for knowing men, and that the candidate for office shall be actually tried out in some way after full investigation has been made of his character, ability, and actual attainments. Provided that this is ensured, the type of examination which they must pass is of no great consequence. A man's literary ability is no criterion of his administrative gifts or capacity. The existing system has produced some very famous officials, so why go to the trouble of changing it and of introducing at great expense something which would be no better ? "

It would seem from this that Su Shih was largely at one with Wang An Shih in the method to be adopted. They were agreed that selection should depend upon ability and personal character, and that there should follow a period of trial. They differ, however, in the fact that Wang An Shih wanted the existing system essentially altered in some respects, whereas Su Shih was content to retain it. He had at the same time no great opinion of its value in itself, saying in effect " We have got to have a system of some kind, and this will do as well as any other."

After having been consulted by the Emperor on this subject, Wang An Shih produced the following reply [1] :—

" It is admitted that the present examination system has produced a number of good men, but that is because it is the sole avenue to official preferment. But I deny that the system is a good one. For any system which compels a man in the robust strength of his youth, when he ought to be studying the fundamental principles of philosophy and government, to shut himself up in his room and devote all his time and energies to the making of poetry and the composition of rhyming couplets is of necessity utterly injurious. For such a man entering upon the duties of official life will have been denied all chance of gaining that knowledge which would be of practical value to him in that work. The fact that present-day officials fall far behind those of ancient times is adequate proof of the ineffectiveness of the system."

[1] " T'ung Chien," Hsi Ning (熙 寧), 4th year, 2nd month.

As a result of this discussion it was decided in the 4th month of 1071 that the existing system should be supplanted by the following, viz. [1] :—

" Each candidate for the official examinations (presumably for the doctor's degree (進 士)), should be required to make a special study of one of the five Classics, i.e. History, Poetry, Changes, Chou Li, and Li Chi, and should be tested further in his knowledge of Mencius and the Analects. The examination should be divided into four sections. The first would be on the particular Classics in which the student had specialized. The second would be on the other Classics, on which ten questions would be set, all on the meaning of the text. The third paper would consist of an essay, and the fourth of three questions on practical administration.

" In addition the Board of Rites would set two questions for candidates taking the special part of the examination which was under their auspices.

" The ' Chung Shu Sheng ' (中 書 省) would publish specimens of the questions to be set on the meaning of the Classics for the guidance of the candidates.

" The ' Tien Shih ' (殿 試), or part of the examination which was held under the personal supervision of the Emperor, would consist entirely of practical questions, the answers to be limited to 1,000 characters. The successful candidates would be divided into five grades, the first four of which would be entitled ' Chin Shih ' (進 士), or Doctor of Literature, and the last would be styled ' Hsueh Chiu ' (學 究), or ' Probationer '.

" The former practice which required the successful candidate to subscribe a hundred taels when he entered the Court to offer thanks for his selection, was to be abolished, a registration fee of 2,000 cash only being demanded."

It is quite refreshing to note that the Historical Commentator,[2] who usually has nothing good to say of Wang An Shih's

---

[1] " T'ung Chien," Hsi Ning (熙 寧), 4th year, 2nd month.
[2] " T'ung Chien," Hsi Ning (熙 寧), 4th year, 2nd month, " Kuang I " (廣 義).

proposals, has a word of praise for this attempt to reform the examination system. He does, however, qualify this by criticizing the fact that the " Annals " (春 秋) were not included amongst the books to be studied. This he considered made Wang An Shih guilty of doing grievous despite to the ancient literature.[1]

We may conclude that the method which Wang An Shih himself would have adopted for the securing of capable and worthy men for the Government service was to devise a Government system of education which would include the establishment of schools in every important centre. In these the subjects to be taught would be such as would tend to prepare men practically for their life work. Their presence in the schools would give their tutors the opportunity to find out their real character and ability. These would make their recommendations to the higher authorities, and guard as far as possible against the appointment of the wrong man.

But the introduction of such a system would take time, and it was necessary to take certain preliminary steps at once. These to his mind consisted of reforms in the existing examination system, the elimination of useless and positively injurious features, and requiring that the questions should be of a more practical character. This would lead to a more intelligent study of the Classics, and prepare the candidates to some extent for the facing of the practical problems of public administration.

It will be as well while we are on this subject to note another contribution made by Wang An Shih to the reform of this examination system. This consisted of a new edition of the Classics, in which the meaning was interpreted afresh, inducing the student to regard the ancient texts as adaptable in their significance to modern times and current needs.

In the 3rd month of 1073 a special bureau for the preparation of these new interpretations was set up,[2] under the supervision of Wang An Shih, with his son Fang and Lü Hui Ch'ing as

---

[1] (于 古 叛 經 之 罪 人).
[2] " T'ung Chien," Hsi Ning, 6th year, 3rd month.

editorial assistants. This work was completed and presented in the 6th month of 1075.[1] It comprised three books only, viz. the Chow Li, styled the " Chow Kuan Hsin I " (周 官 新 義), which was from the pen of Wang An Shih himself, and which is still extant, and new interpretations of the Books of History and Poetry which were the work of Fang and Lü Hui Ch'ing more particularly, but over which Wang An Shih exercised some supervision.

The Emperor accepted these new interpretations and issued an edict ordering all the educational authorities to adopt them.

There is a note in the Histories [1] to the effect that " this was done with a view to unifying the method of interpretation of the Classics, and also with the idea of unifying men's thinking on moral and philosophical subjects. The students of the time were compelled to study these new books, as the superintendents of the official examinations required candidates to use in their answers the interpretations they contained. In this way the old commentators on the Classics were ignored, being supplanted by this New Interpretation ".[2]

Liang Ch'i Ch'ao [3] agrees that if Wang An Shih intended by this step to ban all interpretations of the Classics except those which he himself favoured, the move would be open to serious criticism. He is of the opinion, however, that this was not Wang's idea. Rather was he out to get students to think of the Classics as having practical value for the affairs of Government. It was therefore justifiable to demand of them an acquaintance with these particular interpretations, which had been prepared specifically with the idea of showing the practical value of the classical teachings. Other interpretations were not " banned " in the sense that no one was allowed to study them.

Unfortunately, only one of the three Classics published by this bureau is extant, the " Chow Kuan Hsin I " (周 官 新 義). Liang Ch'i Ch'ao [4] thinks that this is the best interpretation

---

[1] " T'ung Chien," Hsi Ning, 8th year, 6th month.
[2] (先 儒 傳 註 一 切 廢 而 不 用)·
[3] Liang Ch'i Ch'ao, p. 195.
[4] Liang Ch'i Ch'ao, p. 197.

of the Classic since the times of the Han dynasty. "But," he says, "scholars never read it or in their ignorance vilify the work."

It will be of interest here to give a short summary of the succeeding history of this special literature.[1]

In 1086 Huang Yin (黃 隱), of the National University, burned the type blocks of the new interpretations, and prohibited the students from reading any of these works. In the following year the works were "banned" from the official examinations, together with the use of Wang An Shih's Dictionary (字 說).

It is evident, however, from a study of the course of events that students continued to study these works, for in the year 1126 we find Yang Shih (楊 時) appealing that Wang An Shih's writings should be pronounced "heretical", as they were blinding the minds of scholars. In this memorial he demanded that Wang An Shih should be deprived of all his posthumous honours and rank, as that would discourage men from the study of such heretical works, which only confused and deceived their minds.

Yang Shih was a famous disciple of the Ch'eng (程) school of philosophical interpretation.

New light is thrown on the subject by a study of another memorial submitted about this time by Wang Kuo T'ing (王 過 庭), the Censor, which reads :—

"It is very difficult to ascertain the real meaning of the Classics, and it is inevitable that different schools of interpretation should arise. It is a common failing to regard one's own interpretation as correct and all others as wrong. Some time ago the interpretations of Su Shih were banned as heretical, but recently the ban has been lifted. The correct attitude to adopt on these questions, to my mind, is to accept the good points of each interpretation.

"Yang Shih has quite overstepped the mark in adopting this militant attitude to Wang An Shih's writings. It is well known that the students, who had become quite accustomed to the use

---

[1] Liang Ch'i Ch'ao, p. 197.

of Wang An Shih's interpretations, made a hostile demonstration at the residence of Yang Shih, compelling him to keep to his room. They only dispersed after considerable time had elapsed. This shows that Yang Shih's views were not those of the majority."

It is evident from this that Wang An Shih's works were still popular towards the end of the Northern Sung Dynasty.

However, in the year 1136, in the reign of Kao Tsung (高 宗), his works were again prohibited by Imperial decree, and up to comparatively recent times have been greatly neglected by the generality of Chinese students.[1]

We will close this section with the selection of a few questions set by Wang An Shih at the official examinations, viz. [2] :—

" The sages in their policy of government were careful to differentiate between fundamental and secondary things, and in carrying out any item of that policy they observed a certain order of precedence according to the relative importance or urgency of the matter.

" The empire to-day is suffering from the lack of a reform policy, the present defects having been allowed to go unreformed for too long. The method of government, the educational system, the manner of administration, and the various laws and regulations fail to conform to the ideas of the sages. That which is fundamental has been lost in the search for what is secondary, and priority has been given to matters which are of subsidiary importance. Gradually the empire is verging on disaster. That is the result of not following out·the ideas of the sages. An official who is ignorant of the reasons why the sages were successful in their government is not worthy of the name. Discuss in full the thesis at the head of this question."

Take another question [3] characteristic of Wang An Shih's own policy, viz. :—

" The laws of Hsia (夏) were changed by Shang (商), and the laws of Shang by Chow (周). These changes were made

---

[1] Liang Ch'i Ch'ao, p. 197.
[2] Prose Works, vol. 17, p. 24.
[3] Prose Works, vol. 17, p. 25.

because of the changing times, and with a view to the well-being of the people. But as regards the ideas behind the laws, as originally devised and as later reformed, were they not akin ? "

A further question [1] emphasizes Wang An Shih's own ideas about current astrological notions, viz. :—

" The principles which guided the sages in their practical administration of government consisted of a humane or sympathetic consideration for their fellows. If, after consideration, any proposed course of action was found to be either non-utilitarian or unrighteous, it was at once rejected. In the Book of History, in the chapter on the Great Plan (洪 範), the Five Businesses (五 事) which are discussed there are all of utilitarian value, and in accord with righteousness.

" But I am in some doubt as to the so-called verifications, favourable and unfavourable, which are attached to these.

" The ruler is supposed to take his cue from Heaven in arranging for the conduct of government. When Heaven displays phenomena of an unusual character it is considered right that the ruler should regard such as a warning, and take steps to bring his administration more into line with the revealed will of Heaven.

" It would seem to follow logically from that, that if the ruler acts in accordance with what is right, Heaven should display a correspondingly favourable aspect. But is that really so ?

" The text reads : ' Wildness is emblemed by constant rain, and Assumption is emblemed by constant sunshine.' But history seems to afford no real ground for such theories, for if we are to posit wildness or assumption in the conduct of the ruler when floods or drought are prevailing, what are we to say of the floods of Yao's time, or the drought which lasted for three years in the times of T'ang. What crimes had these rulers committed which induced such calamities ? I suppose these words need very deep thought and cannot be explained in any superficial way. Will you give me your ideas on the subject ? "

[1] Prose Works, vol. 17, p. 24.

One sees here Wang An Shih's critical and logical mind at work, and affords a hint as to his reason for attempting a reform of the current and merely conventional methods of interpreting the Classics. Obviously questions like this were intended to arouse the critical and reasoning faculties of students, forming a glaring contrast to the more conventional type of question which could be answered by making copious quotations from the Classics.

We will quote one more question [1] for the light it throws on Wang An Shih's own opinions on current affairs and the extant method of government, viz. :—

"Discuss the following statement, viz. : 'The conducting of military expeditions against the border tribes is inimical to the welfare of the people. Hunting expeditions, musical entertainments, elaborate expenditure upon palaces, parks, and official residences, cause impoverishment of the State.'

"None of these things are being done to-day, and yet the conferences of the responsible officials are always concerned with ways and means of securing income for the State. Still there is financial stringency.

"'Undue reliance upon relatives, or the families of the feudal princes, undue honouring of the great official families, and allowing really worthy commoners to lie in seclusion, and preventing them from rising to high office, are among the reasons why official duties get neglected.'

"Although none of these things exist to-day, and the official positions are all open to competitive examination, there is still a serious scarcity of capable officials.

"At previous times in our history great armies were maintained without great expenditure. Nowadays the able-bodied are called to the colours in great numbers, and the land taxes are all earmarked for their maintenance, and still we have not sufficient troops for our needs.

"In olden times large herds of horses were available for the military, but no land was wasted on that account. Nowadays

---

[1] Prose Works, vol. 17, p. 25.

thousands of ' ch'ing ' of arable land are being used for pasture only, and large sums are expended on the purchase of mounts from the border tribes.   Still there is a serious scarcity of horses.
" What are the reasons for these things ? "
There remains one minor item to note under the head of Wang An Shih's contribution to education.   Evidently members of the imperial clan, near and remote alike, had hitherto been regarded as eligible for official appointments without taking any examination.

In the 5th month of 1072 an edict [1] was issued that those members of the imperial clan of a kinship remoter than descent from the cousins of the great-grandmother of the Emperor should be compelled to take examinations before being considered eligible for official appointment.   Those who failed to pass one test, and who showed no literary promise, would be ineligible for further tests.   Those who showed some promise, though failing at the first attempt, should be given another chance.   Should they fail at the second attempt, some subordinate post might be found for them, but nothing of a responsible character would be given them.

We gather from the above that Wang An Shih's contribution to the educational system was by no means negligible. He did not succeed in carrying his scheme to full fruition, but took several steps in a comparatively short period along the road.   If his idea had been further promoted by his successors, or if he himself had been given a longer time in which to carry out his policy, the value of his contribution would doubtless have been considerably enhanced.

[1] " T'ung Chien," Hsi Ning, 5th year, 5th month.

Chapter XXIII

WANG AN SHIH AS GOVERNOR
OF CHIANG-NING-FU

(1074, 4TH MONTH, TO 1075, 2ND MONTH)

BEFORE the departure of Wang An Shih from the capital, his nominees for office, viz. Han Chiang as Grand Councillor, and Lü Hui Ch'ing as Vice-Grand Councillor, had been duly installed by the Emperor.[1]

There is no record in the Histories of Wang An Shih's doings at Chiang Ning Fu during his temporary retirement from the capital. His correspondence, however, reveals the fact that he actually assumed his new duties on the 15th of the 6th month,[2] also that his brother, Wang An Kuo, died during this period.[3] It is evident, also, from a letter of thanks written to the Emperor, that his son, Wang Fang, must have been with his father at this time, and the fact that he had been attended by the Court physician[4] is sufficient evidence of the Emperor's continued solicitude for Wang An Shih during his absence from the capital.

The Histories lay great emphasis on the fact that Han Chiang and Lü Hui Ch'ing maintained without change the whole of Wang An Shih's policy during his absence from the Court, and state that on account of this servile adherence to their patron's ideas Han Chiang was given the nickname of " The Propagating Abbot " (傳 法 沙 門), while Lü Hui Ch'ing

---

[1] " T'ung Chien," Hsi Ning, 7th year, 4th month.
[2] Works, vol. 15, p. 8.
[3] Works, vol. 23, pp. 4 and 5. The expression used in this letter is 七 年 八 月 十 七 日 不 起, which I interpret as meaning that Wang An Kuo died on that date. Otherwise another date for death would surely have been indicated.
[4] Works, vol. 15, p. 22.

was dubbed " The Divine Protector of the New Laws " (護 法 善 神).

They also relate that Lü Hui Ch'ing, in his desire to maintain the New Laws unimpaired, resorted to subtle strategy immediately Wang An Shih had gone. On the one hand, he issued a circular to all responsible officials that they should report on the working of the new measures, and on the other induced the Emperor to issue a mandate to the effect that the officials must not expect to secure the repeal of any of the measures by refusing to carry them out in accordance with the regulations. In this way he hoped to earn the reputation of ostensibly seeking for criticism, while in reality he was suppressing it under cover of the Emperor's seal. " In this way," continues the record, " Wang An Shih's measures were maintained without change." [1]

But, as a matter of fact, considerable changes were made in this interval, both in policy and in the personnel of the higher Government Councils. It would seem, further, that these changes were largely responsible for necessitating the return of Wang An Shih to the capital after a very brief interlude of ten months.

We must now proceed to note these changes, keeping as far as is reasonably possible in line with the traditional Histories.

The first thing to be noted after his resignation was the institution of a Government monopoly in tea in Ssu Ch'uan. Prior to this the tea plantations in that province had been operated by private enterprise, the Government receiving from the planters a sum of 300,000 " strings " annually, on what was known as the " two-tax system ", i.e. the total sum was divided into two halves, and paid twice a year. But now Li Ch'i (李 杞) and P'u Tsung Min (蒲 宗 閔), the agents of Wang Shao, set up Government Trade Bureaus in every district, and imposed severe restrictions on private trade in tea. This was part of Wang Shao's policy in the Ho Huang area. For he commissioned his agents to proceed to Ssu Ch'uan, take over the

---

[1] " T'ung Chien," Hsi Ning, 7th year, 4th month.

control of tea sales there, and secure horses for his expedition from Shensi with the proceeds. In one year it is stated that they secured 767,000 " strings " by this monopoly, which was more than double the sum previously raised.

The commentator on the History states that the Government monopoly in tea dates from this time. Monopolies in salt, wine, and iron had existed before.[1] It has been noted that Wang An Shih was opposed to such monopolies.[2]

During the 5th month further progress was made in connection with the Civil Service examinations, the " Chih K'o " (制 科), or special examination conducted by the Emperor, being abandoned.[3]

Dissension occurred between Lü Hui Ch'ing and Tseng Pu shortly after Wang An Shih's departure, and also between Tseng Pu and Lü Chia Wen. Tseng Pu was head of the Bureau of Finance, and Lü Chia Wen had been supervising the Trade and Barter Bureaus, and also the working of the Trade Tax Measure. The upshot of this controversy was that both Tseng Pu and Lü Chia Wen were transferred to provincial appointments.[4]

In the 7th month Lü Hui Ch'ing adopted the proposal of his brother Lü Ho Ch'ing to introduce certain changes in the method of determining the classification of the people for the purposes of the Public Services Act. The changes were incorporated in what was called " The Self-Assessment Act " (" Shou Shih Fa " 手 實 法). The procedure observed was as follows :—

Printed forms were issued to the people, on which were outlined lists of property items with fixed prices attached to each. Individuals were then ordered to assess all their property ` on the basis of this list and a new division of the people into five classes was made. The Historian notes that although it was the intention of Lü Hui Ch'ing to make provision for the

---

[1] " T'ung Chien," Hsi Ning, 7th year, 4th month.
[2] See Chapter XX, p. 301.
[3] " T'ung Chien," Hsi Ning, 7th year, 5th month.
[4] " T'ung Chien," Hsi Ning, 7th year, 5th month.

suspension of the tax altogether in case of serious famine or other loss, he yielded to the suggestion of P'u Tsung Meng that, as the people were to assess themselves, the measure might be allowed to function without regard to harvest conditions. " In this way the property of the people was minutely assessed to every foot of land and every inch of timber. Even chickens and pigs were included. The operation of this measure left the people destitute." [1]

One should note, however, that in the original draft of this measure those items of property which were regarded as nonproductive of income were to be assessed at only one-fifth the value of productive property, and that utensils and foodstuffs required for the family were not to be subject to assessment at all.

In the 9th month a great fire broke out in the Bureau of Finance, over one thousand " chien " (間) being gutted. This is interpreted by a commentator as a display of Heaven's wrath against the promoters of the " Self Assessment Act ".[2]

A special department for investigation into the national finances was created in the 10th month of 1074 with Han Chiang in control. This evidently was the result of criticism of the great increases in official salaries which had taken place under Wang An Shih's regime. The Ministry of Finance reported that the increase in recent years had amounted to 1,110,000 " strings " per annum. The Historian takes the opportunity to relate that the idea of the promoters of the New Measures was that the bigger the salary paid to an official the less likely would he be to descend to " graft " and other base practices, and that they hoped in this way to save the expense of much litigation. " But," continues the Historian suggestively, " honest officials were extremely scarce, and took their ' pickings ' as before." The main idea in establishing this special department was to bring the finances of the country under the

---

[1] " T'ung Chien," Hsi Ning, 7th year, 7th month.
[2] " T'ung Chien," Hsi Ning, 7th year, 9th month.

purview of one department.   It was styled the "K'uai Chi Ssu " (會 計 司).[1]

Wang Shao (王 韶), the hero of the Ho Hsi expedition, was appointed Vice-President of the Board of War in the 12th month of 1074.[2]

The year 1075 opened eventfully, for in the 1st month Ts'ai T'ing was dismissed from the Board of War, Cheng Hsieh, of famine sketch fame, was banished to Ying Chow, in South Fuchien, and Feng Ching was dismissed from the Grand Council to Po Chow for his supposed connivance at Cheng Hsieh's doings.   It is also stated that Wang An Kuo, brother of Wang An Shih, was dismissed from all offices.[3]

The last item would seem to be a glaring instance of deliberate falsification of the facts, for included in Wang An Shih's works is the memorial notice for Wang An Kuo's grave, which states clearly that he died on the 17th of the 8th month, 1074.[4]

The narrators of this period seem determined to add to Wang An Shih's guilt by making his own brothers appear to be critical of his policy, and in particular by representing them as bitterly opposed to Lü Hui Ch'ing.

The banishment of Cheng Hsieh by the latter was a definite departure from Wang An Shih's customary policy.   For, although he had transferred opponents to provincial appointments, he had not actually banished any of them.   The Historian relates that Lü Hui Ch'ing demanded that Cheng Hsieh should be executed, but that the Emperor had opposed that drastic suggestion.

From the above incidents it is evident that the removal from Court of Wang An Shih's powerful personality had led to the break-up of his adherents, largely it would seem through the personal ambition of Lü Hui Ch'ing and the inability of the others to co-operate with him.

Han Chiang, who was in control of the Chung Shu Sheng,

[1] "T'ung Chien," Hsi Ning, 7th year, 10th month.
[2] "T'ung Chien," Hsi Ning, 7th year, 12th month.
[3] "T'ung Chien," Hsi Ning, 8th year, 1st month.
[4] Works, vol. 23, pp. 4 and 5.

found that Lü Hui Ch'ing was obstructing business. Finding, too, that he had no means of preventing this, he privately appealed to the Emperor for Wang An Shih's return.[1]

On the face of it, it would seem that the Government was in a parlous state at this time, so the Emperor issued a mandate recalling him to the capital in the 2nd month of 1075, and after some hesitancy Wang An Shih consented to return.

[1] "T'ung Chien," Hsi Ning, 8th year, 2nd month.

CHAPTER XXIV

WANG AN SHIH'S RESTORATION TO POWER

(2ND MONTH, 1075, TO 10TH MONTH, 1076)

THE Histories dilate upon the alacrity with which Wang An Shih responded to the Emperor's summons to return,[1] and quote this as evidence of his insincerity in resigning and lack of principle in resuming office at this time.[2] But the conditions obtaining at Court as outlined in the previous chapter, suggest that the situation was sufficiently serious to demand Wang An Shih's return, and that in returning he was actuated by no other motive than the endeavour to restore harmony at Court and stability to the Government. He had done his best to convince the Emperor that others were capable of doing this, but after his two refusals to resume office had been ignored he felt it incumbent upon him to make the attempt himself.[3]

He was not destined to remain in office long, however. His own party, if such it may be called, showed signs of dissolution. The Emperor's mother was unfavourably disposed towards him, Lü Hui Ch'ing seemed in no mood to welcome his return, and Wang An Shih's own health had been seriously impaired. These difficulties must have been present to his mind as he once more resumed his old post, and it therefore redounds greatly to his credit that he eventually responded to the call of the Emperor to meet the urgent need of the Government at this juncture.

The first matter of importance awaiting attention after his

---

[1] "T'ung Chien," Hsi Ning (熙 寧), 8th year, 2nd month (安 石 承 命 倍 道 而 進 七 日 至 汴 京).

[2] "T'ung Chien," 8th year, 2nd month, of "Hsi Ning" (熙 寧), "Kuang I" commentary (廣 義) (欺 天 罔 人 而 絕 無 忌 憚 之 心).

[3] Prose Works, vol. 15, pp. 9 and 10.

return was the old question of the northern boundary which the " Liao " Tartars (遼) had raised.[1] Several conferences had been held on this subject, but so far no satisfactory decision had been reached. The Chinese wanted the boundary line to be drawn along the course of the southern or inner wall, which was in accordance with the most recent treaties made with the Tartars. The latter, however, demanded that it should be drawn on a line 30 li to the south of this.

After the representatives of the two nations had met six times without result, Wang An Shih advised the Emperor to submit to the demands of the Tartars as a temporary expedient, hoping that eventually they would not only recover what was surrendered on this occasion, but more besides.

So Han Chen was forthwith commissioned to proceed to the border, and hand over the territory demanded. This stretched from east to west, a distance of 700 li (230 miles).

According to the Historian [2] this led to war later on.

By this the Historian probably implies that the surrender was a sign of weakness, of which the Liao were only too ready to take advantage.

Certainly this action aroused a good deal of criticism. But it would seem that Wang An Shih was merely recognizing un fait accompli. For the " Liao " were in possession of the disputed territory, and to contest their claim at this time would probably have led to open warfare, for which the Sungs were by no means prepared. During the reign of Jen Tsung the Chinese had adopted the device of sending tribute to these foes in the hope that they would desist from their aggressive tactics. However, they continued to advance into Chinese territory. Several conferences which had been held prior to Wang An Shih's return had settled nothing, and it was left to him to deal decisively with the question. Had he taken strong action war would have resulted and the verdict of history would have been

---

[1] " T'ung Chien," Hsi Ning, 8th year, 2nd month, possibly 3rd month.
[2] " T'ung Chien," Hsi Ning, 8th year, 7th month (遂 爲 異 日 與 兵 之 端).

just as strongly against him. He had to make a definite decision where others had either procrastinated or failed. The only course that seemed open to him was to submit to the claim of their too powerful foe.

This decision was reached in the 7th month of 1075.

Two events prior to this must be briefly noted. The first was the appointment of Wu Ts'ung to be president of the Board of War, and the transfer of Ch'eng Sheng Chih from that post to Yang Chow. This occurred in the 4th month. Ch'en Sheng Chih was nicknamed " the fish-trap Minister ",[1] which implied that he was solely concerned to further his own selfish ambition.

The second event was the presentation of the New Interpretation of the Classics, i.e. the Odes, the History, and the Chow Li. These it will be remembered had been prepared under the supervision of Wang An Shih, assisted by his son and Lü Hui Ch'ing. A mandate was issued ordering the publication of these, and their use by the Educational Authorities. By way of celebrating this notable event, Wang An Shih was appointed " Tso P'u She " (左 僕 射), or " Left Imperial Bodyguard ", and honoured with other rank and emoluments as marks of the Emperor's appreciation. This occurred in the 6th month.[2]

The same month Han Ch'i (韓 琦) died. He had been a very famous official, who had rendered great help to Wang An Shih in his younger days. He was honoured as one of the " pillars of State " and the Emperor wrote a panegyric with his own hand commemorating his great services to the country. He was given the posthumous title of " Loyal and Worthy " (忠 獻), and later had the title of Duke of Wei (魏 公) conferred upon him, by which he is generally known.[2]

In the 8th month Han Chiang resigned. The Historian [3] relates that for some time he had been at variance with Wang An Shih. The final divergence of opinion arose over the question of the employment of one Liu Tso (劉 佐). Wang wished to

---

[1] " T'ung Chien," Hsi Ning, 8th year, 4th month (號 爲 筌 相).

[2] " T'ung Chien," Hsi Ning, 8th year, 6th month.

[3] " T'ung Chien," Hsi Ning, 8th year, 8th month.

employ him, but Han Chiang objected. The matter was referred to the Emperor, but Han Chiang offered to resign. " But," said the Emperor, " why resign on this very trivial matter ? " Han replied : " If one cannot get justice in a small matter like this, how can one expect to get it in still more important affairs ? "

The Emperor then proposed that Liu Tso should not be employed, and this was actually agreed upon. But Han, on the pretext of illness, still persisted in his determination to resign, so he was transferred to Hsü Chow (許 州) as governor.

At the same time the Treasury Department, of which Han Chiang had been head, was closed by Imperial decree.

In the 10th month Lü Hui Ch'ing received his *coup de grâce*, being transferred to Ch'en Chow (陳 州). The events leading up to this open breach between Wang An Shih and his old colleague are narrated in the Histories [1] as follows :—

" Wang An Shih's son Fang had been offered a post as librarian in the Lung T'u Ko (龍 圖 閣) soon after his father's return to power. As Fang himself had asked to be allowed to refuse this post, Lü Hui Ch'ing suggested that he might be excused from accepting it. This led to open suspicion between Wang An Shih and Lü Hui Ch'ing.

" The censor Ts'ai Cheng Hsi then accused Lü Hui Ch'ing of some illegality, which caused him to leave his post and return home to await the issue. Teng Chien and Fang then conspired together, the former indicting Lü Hui Ch'ing and his brother of compelling the wealthy people of Hua T'ing Hsien to loan the officials 5,000,000 ' strings ' (Chang Jo Chi (張 若 濟) being the official) and asserting that with this they had bought land, and derived substantial proceeds from the transaction.

" This resulted in Lü Hui Ch'ing being transferred as above. Chang Ch'un was also implicated in this matter of land purchase, so he was transferred to Hu Chow."

" The same month a comet appeared in the constellation " Chen " (軫). This represented the culmination of a series of

---

[1] " T'ung Chien," Hsi Ning, 8th year, 10th month.

extraordinary astronomical phenomena which had occurred since Wang An Shih returned to Court, and naturally caused great commotion. In the 6th month a big meteor (殞 石) had fallen. In the 7th month the planet Venus (T'ai Pai) (太 白) was visible in the daytime. On the 1st of the 8th month there had been an eclipse of the sun. The appearance of the comet, which in the minds of astrologers denoted the sweeping away of the old, caused the Emperor a great deal of anxiety. He avoided making any public appearances, and instituted a fast. He also called for general criticism of the Government, issued pardons for criminals, etc.[1]

Wang An Shih and his associates then presented the following memorial :—

"In the 5th year of the Emperor Wu Ti of Chin (晉 武 帝) (A.D. 265–290), a comet appeared in Chen, and another, " Po " (孛), in his 10th year. The Emperor reigned for twenty-eight years, and this did not agree with the predictions of the diviners. The ways of Heaven are difficult to understand. Although in ancient times the rulers employed diviners in an official capacity, they only paid attention to actual happenings and facts that were observable by everyone.

" Astronomical phenomena are extremely numerous, and it is inevitable by forcibly interpreting them so as to bear upon matters of government that some fortunate coincidences should occur.

" We all have the greatest respect for the memory of such worthies as Chow Kung and Shao Kung (周 公 ; 召 公). It is unthinkable that they should attempt to deceive their ruler, Ch'eng T'ang (成 湯). But note their remark to him when he called their attention to the long reign of T'ai Wu Ti (太 武 帝) of the Shang Dynasty (1637–1562 B.C.). They said : ' Be dignified, cautious, reverent and obedient, and then you yourself can determine the length of your reign. Let there be no false peace in the government of the empire.' From this it may be seen that Chow Kung and Shao Kung considered

---

[1] " T'ung Chien," Hsi Ning, 8th year, 10th month.

that only the moral character of the ruler affected the length of his reign.

"Take another incident. P'i Tsao (裨 竈) had foretold that a fire should occur and his prophecy came true. When he predicted a second time that there would be a fire in Cheng, the people wished to offer sacrifices to avoid the catastrophe, and to show their respect for his foreknowledge and perspicacity. Kuo Ch'iao, however, refused to comply with this request. Whereupon P'i Tsao reiterated his warning, but in the end no fire occurred.

"If such famous astrologers as P'i Tsao could make faulty predictions, what can we expect of our present day exponents of that art? We know, too, that the ancient and traditional books on divination have been banned for many generations. It is also impossible to know how many errors have crept in from the process of copying.

"You are superior to T'ai Wu Ti in your personal character, you have carried out the dictates of the two Dukes Chow and Shao, of what use is it to seek the advice of these stupid and ignorant astrologers?

"We hear that the Empress Dowager and the Queen are distressed about the appearance of this comet. We hope you will comfort them with the advice which we your ministers give you."

The Emperor on receipt of this said: "But the people are seriously distressed by the operation of 'the new laws.'"

To this Wang An Shih replied: "But the people resent all manner of natural phenomena, like cold, heat, drought or rain, so why be particularly concerned about this?"

The Emperor retorted: "How I wish they had no cause for resentment, even on those grounds."

This remark displeased Wang An Shih, who went home and kept to his bed on the pretext of being ill.

The Emperor sought to comfort him, and implored him to return to his post.

Then Wang An Shih's faction said to him: "Unless you return as the Emperor wishes, those of whom we disapprove will seize the opportunity to introduce their ideas, and we shall lose our influence. It will also give our opponents a chance to discover our mistakes."

This led Wang An Shih to return, which so delighted the Emperor that he complied with every suggestion which he made.

Teng Chien then prepared a memorial pointing out the injurious nature of the "Self-Assessment Measure", in which the chief points were as follows :—

"Under this Measure everything of importance to the people's livelihood has to be reported, accurately and completely. Each family goes in dread of being accused of practising deception. But it often happens that the merchants carry stocks in spring which are scattered to the four winds before the autumn. Their autumn stocks again are exhausted by the winter. How is it possible in such cases to render accurate reports, and how can the people avoid incrimination ?

"It is just another opportunity for the 'leeches' (informers) to get big rewards, and so the more timid elements of the people accept without murmuring whatever conditions are imposed upon them, feeling that ruin is inevitable in any case."

In the 12th month Yuan Chiang (天 絳) was promoted from the Literary Council to be vice-Grand Councillor. The Historian remarks that he was a fawning flatterer of Wang An Shih.[1]

At the same time Tseng Hsiao K'uan (曾 孝 寬), son of Tseng Kung Liang, was promoted to be secretary of the Board of War. The Historian says that this was out of gratitude for the services his father had rendered to Wang An Shih.

Ch'en Hsiang, who had been promoted by Fu Pi to the Censorate, submitted a memorial requesting the Emperor to dismiss Wang An Shih, Lü Hui Ch'ing, and Han Chiang. As the memorialist was somewhat of a favourite with the Emperor, he suffered in no wise from this effort, though Wang An Shih tried several times to get him cashiered.

---

[1] "T'ung Chien," Hsi Ning, 8th year, 12th month.

Later he was appointed as an official of the Literary College (學 士 院), and the Emperor asked him to mention suitable men who might be recommended for office. Ch'en Hsiang thereupon produced a list of thirty-three names, including Ssu Ma Kuang, Han Wei, Lü Kung Chu, Su Sung, Fan Ch'un Jen, Su Shih, etc. These were all old opponents of Wang An Shih. The latter then indicated some minor faults in Ch'en's memorials and correspondence, and got him transferred to Ch'en Chow.

In the 2nd month of 1076 Kuo K'uei [1] was appointed Pacification Commissioner for Annam, with Chao Hsieh (趙 卨) as second-in-command of the punitive expedition. With his own hand Wang An Shih issued the proclamation of war against the Annamite king and ordered the troops of Chan Ch'eng (占 城) and Chan La (占 臘) to attack the Annamese from the south. [2]

In the 7th month Teng Chien was convicted of illegality in the matter of the Hua T'ing Hsien land purchase (see above), and was punished by degradation and transfer to Hao Chow (號 州). The details of this incident are important in the light of its effect on Wang An Shih's career, at least according to the Historian's narrative, which is given below [3] :—

" After Lü Hui Ch'ing had been transferred to Ch'en Chow, the land case at Hua T'ing Hsien still remained undecided. Wang An Shih's son Fang then incited two friends Lü Chia Wen and Lien Heng Fu, to support Teng Chien's indictment of Lü Hui Ch'ing in connection with this case, and by producing other documentary evidence managed at the same time to bring Chang Jo Chi (張 若 濟) under the ban of the law.

" This was done without reference to Wang An Shih and without his knowledge.

" Lü Hui Ch'ing got wind of this charge, and forthwith

---

[1] " T'ung Chien," Hsi Ning, 9th year, 2nd month.
[2] Two separate States to the south of Annam, and independent of it, but acknowledging suzerainty of the Sungs.
[3] " T'ung Chien," Hsi Ning, 9th year, 7th month.

impeached Wang An Shih, affirming that he had rejected all he had ever been taught (i.e. thrown all principles to the winds), that he had pursued a policy of faction and feud, that he had disobeyed the orders of the Emperor, and had issued mandates in his own name. He had done despite to the throne, and had forced the Emperor to act against his own will and desire."

The Emperor showed this indictment to Wang An Shih, who protested his innocence. Not understanding the reason for this attack of Lü Hui Ch'ing, he made inquiry of his son, who then told him the whole story. Wang An Shih seriously reprimanded Fang, who worked himself up into such a fury that a carbuncle broke out upon his back, from which later he died.

" The Emperor was disgusted with Wang An Shih's conduct."

Then Teng Chien, being afraid that possibly Wang An Shih would resign, and that he himself would lose all influence, made an appeal that Fang and Ts'ai Pien (son-in-law of Wang An Shih) should both be given good positions at the capital, and that Wang An Shih should not only be retained in office, but should be granted an official residence at the capital.

When this came to the ears of Wang An Shih, he said to the Emperor : " Teng Chien is a minor official. For such as he to beseech favours for a Grand Councillor is too undignified for words. He ought to be cashiered."

The Emperor, on the ground that Teng Chien was of a depraved character generally, and that he had overstepped his authority in these matters, duly punished him by degradation and transfer to Kuai Chow (虢 州).

The crowded record of Wang An Shih's official career now draws to a close. During this last period in office as Grand Councillor he had frequently asked to be allowed to resign on the grounds of ill-health. Now that his son Fang was dead, his grief was greatly intensified, and he submitted an urgent request that he should be permitted to resign all official responsibilities.

After several fruitless attempts to resign by sending in letters

direct to the Emperor,[1] Wang An Shih had perforce to appeal
to his friend Wang Kuei (王 珪), to whom he wrote the
following [2]:—
"The Emperor has once more forbidden me to resign. . . .
But I feel that I have occupied my ministerial post too long,
and I have been worried for some time about my inability to
discharge my public obligations. I have just lost my son, and
my health gets steadily worse. Not that I am in the least concerned about myself personally, but if in my present condition
I were still to carry on, it would certainly lead to many things of
importance being left undone. This would scarcely be a worthy
response to the Emperor's favour in appointing me. . . .
"Now I must depend upon the friendly offices of my
colleagues to secure my resignation. In my opinion it would be
wrong to incline the Emperor to keep me in office, as in the
end I should be compelled to resign despite his expressed wishes
to the contrary. . . ."
Evidently this letter came into the Emperor's possession, for
he once again appealed to Wang An Shih through his friend
that he would not give up. Hence the following letter from the
former to Wang Kuei [3]:—
"Since you visited me with the Emperor's request I have
been much perplexed as to the course I ought to take. As I recall
my lowly and hopeless condition before I received his favoured
appointment, and how intimate we have been since ; as further
I remember how he disregarded the slanders of court officials
and appointed me to the office of Grand Councillor, how could
I refuse to sacrifice even life itself for the Public Cause, if thereby
I might be of use to the State ?
"But as I view all the circumstances, and note that to the
majority my actions have been displeasing ; that anger and bitter
resentment have been directed against my dearest and most
intimate associates : that I have not exercised sufficient discrimination in choosing men, for dangerous men have emerged

[1] Prose Works, vol. 10, p. 18.
[2] Prose Works, vol. 18, p. 11.
[3] Prose Works, vol. 18, pp. 11 and 12.

amongst those whom I have selected as my colleagues : when again I take note of the length of time I have been in office, and that my authority has been so great, I fear I may be getting proud.

" I realize that my mental and physical energy is decreasing and fear I shall be quite unable to continue to discharge the duties of so onerous a post. As I look back over the pages of history for guidance in my present emergency, I find that those who through ignorance did not retire when they should, involved the country in great trouble in the end.

" For these reasons I cannot avoid the guilt of disobedience to the Emperor's command. But I wish before affairs reach their climax to retire to a country life, thus acting as ' one who knew when to retire without injury to the State '. In this way posterity will have no reason for mocking Shen Tsung for his employment and promotion of me.

" I avail myself of your proximity to the throne, of your authority in high matters of State, and of your acquaintance with the inner counsels of your associates, to do me the great favour of pleading my cause with the Emperor. I am prohibited myself from making any further direct appeal, so I am relying on you to say the one word which will secure my retirement. It is impossible to put into writing all that I feel, but trust you will understand."

Upon this the Emperor, seeing that further parley was useless, allowed Wang An Shih to resign, in the 10th month of 1076.

He loaded him with honours and titles. He retained the rank and title of Imperial Tutor (檢 校 太 傅), Left Imperial Bodyguard (左 僕 射), and Grand Councillor for Civil Affairs (同 平 章 事), Inspector in Chief of the Southern Area (鎮 南 節 度 管 內 觀 察 處 置 使), etc., etc. He was given actual administrative appointment as Governor of Chiang Ning Fu (判 江 寧 府), which he was to administer with the title of Imperial Commissioner for both civil and military affairs (使 相), a special and rare honour conferred on only the most famous ministers of the Sung Dynasty. He was further granted a special personal allowance of the revenue of a thousand (nominal), or four hundred (actual), families, and many other honorific titles were conferred upon him.[1]

When we compare all this with the account as found in the canonical histories, we get some idea of the prejudiced and mischievous character of such records. The account reads as follows [2]:—

" Wang An Shih and Lü Hui Ch'ing were at loggerheads. The Emperor was greatly displeased with Wang An Shih's conduct. After his son Fang died, his grief was unbearable, and he earnestly requested to be allowed to resign. This increased the Emperor's displeasure, so he dismissed him from office, and appointed him as governor of Chiang Ning Fu. The Emperor did not call him to Court again."

But we have seen that Shen Tsung repeatedly refused to consider his requests for resignation, so much so that at last Wang An Shih had to secure the interposition of his friends at Court. He was, moreover, given one of the most responsible, if not the most responsible, post in the provinces, viz., the governorship of Chiang Ning Fu. He was loaded with honours, and the Emperor throughout the rest of his life manifested the utmost solicitude for his welfare. Such facts as these are obviously in flat contradiction with the statement of the historian that Shen Tsung was displeased with his conduct, and therefore dismissed him.[3] Unless perchance we are to interpret the Emperor's displeasure as having reference to Wang An Shih's resignation. Then the statement sounds a little more reasonable.

[1] Prose Works, vol. 10, p. 20 (推 誠 保 德 崇 仁 翊 戴 功 臣). Also vol. 15, p. 10.

[2] Dynastic History, " Pen Chuan " (本 傳). See Vol. II.

[3] " Pen Chuan " (本 傳) reads 罷, " T'ung Chien " reads 免.

Chapter XXV

WANG AN SHIH IN RETIREMENT

Maintenance of the Reform Policy by Shen Tsung
1076–1085

THE Governorship of Chiang Ning Fu, with its heavy administrative responsibilities, soon proved to be too much for Wang An Shih's failing health. Several times he asked for permission to retire from official life altogether and that he might be granted a sinecure. He complained of dizziness, backache, and shortness of breath, and that he felt totally incapable of coping with the duties of such an onerous post. He objected also to receiving the heavy emoluments attached to this position, as it was obvious that he could not do the work. He assured the emperor that it would be easy to find someone else to fill the post satisfactorily.

Eventually, after five appeals,[1] he was permitted to resign his Governorship, but evidently he was still expected to act in an advisory capacity for civil and military affairs, as he retained the title of Imperial Commissioner for the area (" Shih Hsiang " 使 相).

This, too, he requested permission to resign, but had to write another four letters [2] before obtaining his desire. He wrote, " The emoluments attached to this title of Imperial Commissioner are quite undeserved. But such considerations aside, it is unprecedented for anyone to carry the emoluments of this type of office with him into retired life."

So eventually he was permitted to resign all administrative work, and to retire to a monastery with a pension.[3] This monastery was situated on Chung Shan (鍾 山) only fourteen li from the east gate of Chiang Ning. An anonymous writer

---

[1] Works, vol. 10, pp. 19 and 20.
[2] Works, vol. 10, p. 21.
[3] Works, vol. 15, p. 23.

in the Yin Chü Shih Hua (隱 居 詩 話) narrates the following incident : [1]

"In the third year of Shen Tsung's reign (1070) when Wang An Shih received the edict promoting him from vice-Grand Councillor to Grand Councillor, a crowd of his associates flocked to his door to offer their congratulations. But as he had not yet officially accepted the appointment he refused to see them." The writer continues, "He sat with me in an inner apartment. Suddenly as we were conversing quietly together, he seized his pen, and wrote the following lines on the window, viz.,

'I see the monastery on Chung Shan,
Its bamboos are bedecked with pure snow,
And bespangled with frost.
When in old age I retire
It is there I would live.'"

So evidently Wang An Shih was now to gratify a desire of his earlier days. Later he built himself a small house in the vicinity of Pan Shan (半 山), half-way between the city of Chiang Ning and Chung Shan. This he says was only ten feet square, but perhaps he is exercising the poet's licence. He says he had bought a large piece of vacant land round which he had planted trees, and in which he had excavated a pool. He had also dug a ditch around it, and planted some three hundred trees of a quick-growing variety. There he hoped to retire. Removed from the noise and bustle of the world, he could close his door and be dead to all around, or enjoy himself quietly feeding the birds or watching the fish in his pool.

Apparently the land had to be drained, for he speaks of opening a channel to convey the water which collected there to the moat surrounding Nanking city.[2]

In this neighbourhood Wang An Shih spent the rest of his days, following a simple and unpretentious life, reading voraciously, and labouring hard at literary pursuits. He revised

---

[1] Liang Ch'i Ch'ao, p. 236.
[2] Poetical Works, vol. 4, p. 1.

his New Classical Interpretation, completed his dictionary, wrote Commentaries on the Analects, Mencius, and Lao Tzu and essays on the Book of Changes and the Li Chi. He also continued his poetical writings, which became very extensive. He had always been a great reader, and in his retirement he continued to absorb everything in the literary way which came to his hand. This we gather from a letter written to his friend Tseng Tzu Ku (曾 子 固) in late life, viz.,[1]

"I have read the works of all the philosophers, the Nan Ching (難 經), the Su Wen (素 問), the Pen Ts'ao (本 草) (all medical works), and all the novels known to me. I have also delved into works on Agriculture, and those dealing with Women's pursuits.

"Students of the Classics differ in their interpretations. Unless I read widely I cannot expect to attain to a complete knowledge of the Sages' teaching. Men like Yang Hsün (楊 雄), having exhausted the resources of their own thought, proceeded to the study of other men's works in their search for truth. Thus they were able to discriminate between divergent theories, and were never misled by heretical teaching. I presume that was because of their firm grasp of principles.

"I hope that you friend will not fear that my reading of heretical works will lead me astray. The confusion of thought which characterizes modern scholarship arises not from the study of Buddhism, but because the minds of scholars and officials are besotted with passion and the lust for gain. They esteem one another in words only, and are utterly lacking in self-control. What do you think?"

This letter not only indicates the width of Wang An Shih's reading, but shows that he was giving considerable attention to religious writings, particularly Buddhistic literature. His numerous essays show that he must have gone very deeply into the study of the philosophy of all Schools, Taoist as well as Buddhist. He remained, however, a staunch disciple of Confucius, with certain Buddhistic trends. He was not, of

---

[1] Works, vol. 18, p. 12.

course, a conventional Confucianist. We have already seen that he was not satisfied with superficial interpretations of the Classical texts. His efforts were directed towards the discovery of their hidden meaning which would be applicable to every age and any situation.

Further light is thrown upon Wang's manner of life at this time by the following quotations :—

In the Hsü Chien K'ang Chih (續 建 康 志) occurs the following [1] :—

"After Ching Kung (荆 公), i.e. Wang An Shih, had retired from political life the second time, he held an honorary appointment at Chin Ling (金 陵) with the rank of Imperial Commissioner (使 相). Later he took up his residence at a place seven li outside the Pei Hsia Gate (白 下 門) of Nanking, and an equal distance from Chiang Shan (蔣 山). In his travels around the neighbourhood, visiting the monasteries and temples, he usually rode on a donkey, followed by a group of small boys. If he visited the city he would take a small boat. He never rode a horse, nor was he ever carried in a sedan chair. He lived on an open plot of land, in a very unpretentious house. It looked like a roadside inn."

Liu Yuan Ch'eng (劉 元 城) tells us that Wang was simple and economical in his manner of life. "He was a lover of learning all his days, and thought nothing of rank, wealth or fame." [1]

Tradition has it that he carried his economy a little too far, and that he rarely washed his clothes or bathed.[2] But as the histories are full of slanderous statements about his character and policy, we suggest that this reference to his unhygienic habits is equally unfounded, and may therefore be discounted.

Some of his leisure was evidently devoted to chess, though if we are to give credence to what the commentator on his poetry has to say upon the subject, he was both a poor player and a poor " sport ". Li Pi (李 壁) writes, " Wang An Shih displayed no great forethought at chess. When he perceived that

---

[1] Liang Ch'i Ch'ao, p. 320.
[2] Pen Chuan.

the game was going against him he would overturn the board or scatter the pieces, saying, ' I started this game with the object of forgetting my troubles, but I find it too toilsome. Let's give it up.' " [1]

After the retirement of his old favourite, the emperor continued to take a close interest in his doings, and bestowed upon him all the honours which he had at his command for loyal and famous ministers.

In 1077, on the occasion of the Great Imperial Sacrifice, he was honoured with the title of " K'ai Fu I T'ung San Ssu " (開 府 儀 同 三 司), which was the highest title of rank that could be conferred upon any retired official during the Sung Dynasty.[2] He was also invested with the Dukedom of Shu (舒 國 公) and later given the still more honourable title of Duke of Ching (荆 國 公), by which he is generally known to this day.[3]

In 1078 he was appointed honorary Warden of the Chi Hsi Kuan (集 禧 觀 使), a sinecure, which carried with it certain emoluments by way of pension. He was also allowed to retain his honorary title of Grand Scholar of the Kuan Wen Tien (觀 文 大 學 士).[4]

In 1082 his Dictionary entitled the " Tzu Shuo " (字 說), consisting of 24 volumes, was completed, and presented to the throne. As a reward for this work, the characters " Shang Chu Kuo " (上 柱 國) were prefixed to his title of Duke of Ching. He thus became the recipient of the highest title of merit which was within the power of the emperor to confer.[3]

These various honours were accepted by Wang An Shih after several refusals, as is evident from the many letters which are found in his Works regarding them.

Not only did the emperor shower these honours upon his

---

[1] Poetical Works, vol, 3, p. 4.
[2] i.e., An honour equivalent to holding the office of " San Kung " (三 公), the three highest honorary officials of the empire. " Tz'u Yuan " (辭 源).
[3] Chan Ta Ho, Biographical Table.
[4] Liang Ch'i Ch'ao, p. 233.

old minister, but gave him many other tokens of his personal regard and solicitude.

When in 1083 Wang An Shih became seriously ill, the emperor despatched his Court physician to attend him,[1] and sent him gifts of medicine,[2] favours which called forth his deep gratitude. He recovered in the following spring, and submitted a memorial to the emperor offering to place his residence at Pan Shan at the disposal of the government to be used as a monastery.[3] This offer was gratefully accepted by Shen Tsung, who thereupon named the place " Pao Ning " [4] (報 寧) or " Welcome News ". This shows how anxious the emperor was concerning the health of his minister, and how greatly he was relieved by the news of his recovery.

All this evidence of the respect, interest, and solicitude which the emperor showed for his old favourite is in glaring contrast with the impression which the historians seek to convey in such narratives as the following :—

" In the tenth month of 1076 Feng Ching (馮 京) was appointed to an important position in the Board of War. When Lü Hui Ch'ing impeached Wang An Shih he disclosed from his private correspondence such sentences as ' Keep this from the emperor ' and ' Don't let him who is of the same age as myself see this '. (The reference in this latter clause was to Feng Ching.) The emperor perceived from this that Wang An Shih had been deceiving both him and Feng Ching. So he inferred that the latter must have been specially faithful to him, and therefore gave him this appointment." [5]

But what has been reported above, absolutely contradicts the suggestion that there had grown up between Shen Tsung and the emperor any feeling of mistrust or lack of respect and friendliness. When we add to that the fact that throughout his reign, right up to the time of his death in the third month of

---

[1] Works, vol. 10, p. 16.
[2] Works, vol. 15, p. 21.
[3] Works, vol. 10, p. 15.
[4] Works, vol. 15, p. 27.
[5] T'ung Chien, Hsi Ning, 9th year, 10th month.

1085, the emperor maintained in its entirety the policy of Wang An Shih, one's conviction is strengthened that the emperor's confidence in his old minister never waned.

Just after Wang An Shih had retired, the history reports the appointment of Wu Ts'ung (吳 充) and Wang Kuei (王 珪) to the Grand Council, in the tenth month of 1076. The former was father-in-law to Wang An Shih's daughter. Despite the fact that he had this close personal relationship with the reformer, says the historian,[1] he was not favourably disposed towards his policy. In support of this the history relates that " soon after his appointment, Wu Ts'ung suggested to the emperor that Ssu Ma Kuang, Han Wei, Su Sung, Sun Chueh, Li Ch'ang, Ch'eng Hao, Lü Kung Chu, and several others who for various reasons had showed their disapproval of Wang An Shih's Measures, should be recalled to Court."

It should, however, be noted that the only one of these to receive actual appointment during the remainder of Shen Tsung's reign was Lü Kung Chu, who was connected with the Board of War from the sixth month of 1078 to the fourth month of 1082, and that there is no note of his having raised serious objection to the government policy during that time.

There is also extant a letter written by Ssu Ma Kuang to Wu Ts'ung about this time, which may or may not have been sent in response to this suggestion that he should return to Court. It may, of course, have been written to Wu Ts'ung on his assuming the office of Grand Councillor in succession to Wang An Shih, to represent the views of the Opposition leader to the new head of the Government. The essential points of this letter are as follows :—

" The New Laws are being administered in an oppressive manner and the people are suffering great distress. It is absolutely necessary for the Government to awake to the fact that the most urgent need of the country at present is that these laws should either be completely repealed or at least that they should be greatly modified. But there is no doubt that some of them should be repealed altogether, such as the Agricultural

[1] T'ung Chien, Hsi Ning, 9th year, 10th month.

Loans Measure, the Public Services Act, the Militia Act, the Trade and Barter Measure, and the aggressive military policy. Open criticism should be sought from the country, and fresh policy inaugurated on the basis of that. The condition of things generally is desperate but not quite hopeless. But unless something is done to remedy matters, disaster is certain." [1]

Now the implication of the suggestions made by Wu Ts'ung re new appointments is that Shen Tsung was desirous of introducing changes in the government policy after Wang An Shih had resigned, and from Ssu Ma Kuang's letter we are asked to infer that the country was in desperate straits and the people suffering great hardships from the operation of the New Measures.

But one looks in vain, even in the histories which are so biassed against Wang An Shih, for any signs of Shen Tsung's change of mind in regard to his policy, or for any signs of serious discontent amongst the people on account of its oppressive character.

With the exception of Lü Kung Chu and possibly Sun Ku (孫 固), both of whom had formerly had difficulties with Wang An Shih, the chief officials of the Yuan Feng regime were all men who had been loyal supporters of the reform policy, and who sought to maintain it after Wang An Shih's resignation. Such were Wang Kuei, Yuan Chiang (resigned 1079), Wu Ts'ung (resigned 1080), Ts'ai Ch'ueh, Chang Ch'un, Feng Ching (resigned 1081), Hsueh Hsiang (resigned 1081), Han Wei, Chang Tsao, P'u Tsung Meng, Tseng Kung, An T'ao, Han Chen, and Wang An Li, the younger brother of Wang An Shih, who was a member of the Grand Council from 1083 to 1085. [2]

These appointments indicate no change in Shen Tsung's attitude to Wang An Shih's policy in general.

There is further a lack of incident in the historical records of this period of Yuan Feng, a paucity of discussion on the government policy, and no instance of revolt amongst the people

---

[1] T'ung Chien, Hsi Ning, 9th year, 10th month.
[2] T'ung Chien.

against that policy, which is significant. Viewing these factors as a whole, and also bearing in mind the prejudiced character of the histories, one may be justified in assuming that the period was characterized by comparative quiet and stability. The war against the Hsi Hsia was prosecuted with energy by Li Hsieh, and with considerable success.[1]

This matter will be discussed in further detail in the chapter on Wang An Shih's policy,[2] but what has been written above should serve to show that Shen Tsung maintained that policy for nine years after the retirement of Wang An Shih to Chiang Ning, and that there is no evidence in the records in support of Ssu Ma Kuang's contention that the " New Laws were being administered in an oppressive manner, and that the people were suffering great distress ".

We must now return to Wang An Shih's personal affairs. In 1083, after his recovery from illness, he not only offered his residence to the government, but also donated his land to the Buddhist temple on Chiang Shan, called the " T'ai P'ing Hsing Kuo Ssu " (太 平 與 國 寺). The yield annually from this land he stipulated as 342 piculs of rice, 17,772 bamboo mats, 33 piculs of wheat, and 24 " strings " for rent. He made this gift through the emperor to the temple, with the request that the priests might pray for the souls of his mother and father, whom he confessed he had failed to serve as he ought, and also that prayer should be made for the soul of his son Fang.[3]

These gifts [4] are construed quite differently in the " Wen Chien Lu " of Shao Pai Wen. For there we read, " After the death of Fang, Wang An Shih dreamt that he saw the ghost of his son wearing the cangue and burdened with chains. Whereupon he donated his residence at Pan Shan to be used as a monastery to atone for his son's crimes." [5]

After surrendering his own residence Wang An Shih rented a house in the city of Nanking. Later Buddhists say that this

---

[1] T'ung Chien.
[2] See Vol. II.
[3] Works, vol. 10, p. 15.
[4] Works, vol. 15, p. 28.
[5] Liang Ch'i Ch'ao, p. 313.

was situated behind the old Chiang Ning Hsien yamen, and that it was afterwards converted into a dispensary for the poor, called "Hui Min Yueh Chü" (惠 民 藥 局).[1]

In the third month of 1085 Shen Tsung died. Thus ended that intimate relationship between sovereign and minister the like of which, to use Shen Tsung's own words, "had never been known in history." For throughout a period of twenty years, first at Court together, and later when living apart after Wang An Shih's resignation, their mutual esteem and affection had been maintained unimpaired. Wang An Shih had been most solicitous that the emperor should preserve high ideals of personal character, and of his duty to the people. He had repeatedly urged upon his attention the importance of securing able and worthy men for the government services, and that such men, once secured, should be favoured with the emperor's confidence and trust.

Evidence for this is found in the memorials which Wang An Shih presented to the emperor soon after his accession to the throne. From these we take the following extracts, as being pertinent to the subject. The first is taken from the "Chin Chieh Memorial" (進 戒 疏).[2] This was submitted after Shen Tsung had completed the prescribed period of mourning for his predecessor, and reads as follows :—

"Your Majesty has now completed the prescribed period of mourning. This time, according to the Classics, is one at which all your ministers should submit their exhortations and warnings. I am one of your more intimate officers, and my rank behoves me to be among the first to utter my mind. Confucius, in a discussion on government affairs said, 'Licentious customs should first be abandoned, and then and then only, can one begin to consider how specious talkers may be kept at a distance.'

"Chung Hui (仲 虺), lauding the virtuous character of T'ang (湯), said, 'First and foremost he suppressed his lustful desires for women, music, and material gain. Then he was

[1] Liang Ch'i Ch'ao, p. 320.
[2] Works, vol. 9, p. 11.

able conscientiously to say, " I am responsible for the employment of men "." This means that it is essential that one should
deny one's self in regard to the allurements of beauty and gain,
if one is to have a pure mind and will. If the latter is gained,
then moral principles will be clearly apprehended, and one's
knowledge of men will be trustworthy. That is the way to keep
specious talkers at a distance, and the way also to secure loyal,
virtuous, and high minded men for the times. These, if they
will do their utmost for the country's welfare, and devote
themselves to making the laws of the land function effectively,
will raise the level of public life on to the highest plane.

" On the other hand, if the ruler does not train himself in
early life to refrain from the following of his lustful desires,
no matter how able he may be, he will proceed to excesses,
his mind will get confused, and his will contaminated. He will
have but hazy ideas about moral principles, and he will afford
a splendid opportunity for the rise and promotion of heterodox
theories and lawless practices. That will readily bring the
country to a dangerous crisis.

" Since your Majesty came to the throne there have been
no complaints about your sensuality, or excessive love of
pleasure and sport. But we must remember that Confucius,
sage though he was, would not allow himself to be ruled by his
desires until he had reached the age of seventy. Your Majesty
is still in the heyday of youth, and you have been called upon
to carry the responsibility for the government of this great
empire. Naturally there will be much that will allure you.
It is only right therefore that your ministers at this juncture
should exercise forethought on your behalf, and urge you to be
extremely cautious.

" Heaven is sparing in its creation of sagely ability, and
rarely indeed do we get the opportunity of meeting with a
sage. Heaven has however endowed your Majesty with sage-
like qualities. It is therefore only natural that the people
should be expecting the initiation of a gracious rule in keeping
with such qualities.

" I beseech you therefore to have such a real love of your

self as will bring to fruition the virtuous possibilities of your character, and that you will devote yourself wholeheartedly to making a true success of your rule, so that later generations will continue to ascribe to you the title of sage, and the whole empire gain from your wise and benevolent reign. This is the sum of our hopes."

Take again the following from his memorial on the " Kuan Chih " [1] (館 職) or " the duty of high officials " :—

" Since the time when Yao and Shun formulated their principles of government, it has been regarded as the personal duty of the emperor to go exhaustively into the reasons and principles of things, and to select other men for the practical administration of affairs . . . The multitude of minor matters is no business of yours; they are not worthy of your own personal attention, and will be dealt with by your officers.

" But since I was given a place in the government circle, I have discovered that the chief subjects of discussion at Imperial audiences are not the great questions of government but just these trifling affairs. So that there is not sufficient time for a proper discussion of matters that are relatively more important.

" But viewing the state of the government as it exists at present, I fear there is no hope of reducing the country to order and giving it the type of government for which the times call, unless we go very thoroughly and in the greatest detail into a consideration of current conditions, and make it quite clear to your Majesty that there is need for fundamental, constructive, and orderly reform policy.

" Such officials as myself will not be able to express ourselves in any adequate way unless you extend to us special favours in this matter of time. The most successful rulers all began their work by giving a period of strenuous thought to the problems of the time, and so in the end were able to take their ease.

" Your Majesty has the making of a great ruler, benevolent

---

[1] Works, vol. 10, p. 4. The extracts translated are from Liang Ch'i Ch'ao, p. 103.

and wise. None since the times of Ch'in (秦) and Han (漢) can compare with you. I do not wish to convey the impression that we think you are not giving your mind to these matters, but I feel you are devoting your self to too many non-essential things. Some of your decisions show that you have not given full consideration to the best methods. I fear therefore that it will be difficult for you to take your ease in the end, and govern the empire without effort (as it is the function of the sage to do)."

Take again the following from his second memorial on " the official hierarchy " [1] :—

" Since your Majesty came to the throne, you have realized the dearth of really capable men in the government service, and this has led you to employ and promote a considerable number who are of inferior ability and of poor character. If this type of man is allowed to get his way, public life will become corrupt, and that will incline your more intimate officials to serve first and foremost for their own personal advantage. You will be kept ignorant of the real state of the country. This defect has already made itself manifest. It will be criminal not to have this matter thoroughly investigated. If you desire to remedy this state of things, all that is necessary is that you should commission your faithful and honest officials to deal with it."

Several things emerge from a consideration of the above memorials. First there is Wang's frankness and sincerity. He was not afraid of warning his emperor against possible perils. He had also the moral courage to tell the emperor wherein he thought he had failed, regardless of the odium in which that might place him. He was also determined to do his utmost to make Shen Tsung the ideal ruler, and to deal fundamentally with his country's ills. The fact that Shen Tsung used Wang An Shih for so long and in such important capacities shows his respect for his judgment, and also his sense of Wang's worthiness to receive his confidence and

[1] Works, vol. 10, p. 5. The extracts translated are from Liang Ch'i Ch'ao, p. 104.

trust. There existed between the two a remarkable intimacy, combined with the deepest respect and affection throughout.

The character of Shen Tsung is summarized by the Canonical Histories as follows :—

" The emperor was filial and amiable by disposition. During his younger days he gave the most thoughtful consideration and attention to his mother and grandmother. Nothing affected the fulfilment of his duties to them. He was constant in his solicitude.

" He studied diligently with his two younger brothers in the Eastern Court, and was a model of respect to his tutor Wang T'ao (王 陶), who gave him instruction in the Classics and History. Within and without the court, all alike spoke in highest terms of his character and demeanour.

" After he came to the throne he showed caution and humility, treating his ministers with the utmost respect and reverence. He sought for honest criticism : he investigated the problems and difficulties of the people : he was merciful to the poor and aged, and generous to the distressed.

" He refrained from indulging in expensive building programmes in connection with the Royal Household, devoted himself to no unlawful pastimes, nor did he indulge in any questionable pursuits.

" To the affairs of State he devoted himself wholeheartedly, and was obsessed of the idea of doing something great and notable for his country.

" But shortly after his accession, Wang An Shih became high minister of state. He was of a fiery and self-confident disposition. He realized that the ancestors of Shen Tsung's line had suffered many reverses in their efforts to recover territory in North Hopei and North-west Shensi and Kansu, and was aware that Shen Tsung was anxious to wipe out the long-standing disgrace of these defeats. He was also convinced that no satisfactory policy had yet been devised which would enable the country to achieve this end.

" Taking advantage of these factors in the situation, he proceeded with characteristic obstinacy and prejudice to propagate his heretical theories and promulgate his various measures of reform.

"When these had become the law of the land, the whole empire was thrown into the greatest confusion and turmoil, the distressed and weeping people treading on each other's heels, as they rushed to the Court with their grievances.

"Alas! the emperor did not realize the gravity of the situation, and drove out all the old and faithful ministers of the crown, ignored or dismissed all who were at variance with the reform policy, and persevered with marked confidence in his endeavour to make the new measures effective.

"In the end all the good laws of the previous reigns were either abrogated or changed. So from this time the depraved and unprincipled came into power, the people lost their spirit of loyalty and patriotism, and the country deteriorated continually." [1]

So that, according to the historians, the one great mistake which Shen Tsung made was to employ Wang An Shih. But all the evidence goes to show that he was a monarch of foresight and determination. His project for retrieving the disgrace incurred by his forerunners, coalesced with Wang An Shih's proposals for financial and military reform. Shen Tsung seems to have found in him the one man whose ideas and determination were of the type requisite for the carrying out of his great purpose. It is that which accounts for the intimacy and mutual confidence which characterized their period of fellowship and co-operation in the country's service.

---

[1] Dynastic History of Sung, vol. 16, p. 6. " Pen Chi " (本 紀).

Chapter XXVI

REPEAL OF THE NEW MEASURES: DEATH OF WANG AN SHIH

(1085, 4TH MONTH—1086, 4TH MONTH)

SHEN Tsung was succeeded by his son Che Tsung, then only ten years of age. For the first eight years of his reign, his grandmother the Empress Kao, later known as Hsuan Jen (宣 仁), acted as Regent, presiding at all Court ceremonies and over the various government assemblies.

Hsuan Jen, although she was the mother of Shen Tsung, had been entirely out of sympathy with his government policy. She had made no secret of her antipathy to Wang An Shih and had rigidly opposed his proposals. So that, immediately the reins of government were put into her hands, she drove rough-shod over all the scruples of kinship, and overthrew the whole of the policy which had been initiated and maintained during her son's regime.

Her first act was to abolish the special Inspectorate [1] which had been set up in the previous reign to keep watch over all who were opposed to the New Laws. She also abolished the River Conservancy Bureau, and rescinded the Trade Tax Measure (免 行 錢).

Then she recalled Ssu Ma Kuang from Lo Yang, where he had just completed his historical work, the " Tzu Chih T'ung Chien ". After some hesitancy he yielded to the importunity of Ch'eng Hao,[2] and in the fifth month of 1085 entered the capital. The history relates that he was received with tremendous enthusiasm. The guards at the palace gates all saluted him as the Prime Minister, while the common people crowded round him in such numbers on the street that he could only proceed with the greatest difficulty. They raised such cries as " You

---

[1] T'ung Chien, Yuan Feng, 8th year, 3rd month.
[2] T'ung Chien, Yuan Feng, 8th year, 4th month.

shall not return to Lo Yang ", " You must be minister of State," " Save the people," etc., etc. This welcome was very embarrassing to Ssu Ma Kuang, and he had thoughts of returning to seclusion. He was, however, detained by special envoy from the Regent, and escorted in state to the palace.

In an interview with the Empress he expressed the opinion that the first thing to be done was to ask for frank criticism from the people. A mandate was issued to this effect after some preliminary obstruction by certain influential officials, and as a result over a thousand memorials on current affairs were submitted.[1]

Ch'eng Hao was also recalled to Court at this time, but death intervened. The histories relate the following as being his statement, viz. :—

" The way in which members of my party opposed Wang An Shih, instigated him and his colleagues to promulgate the New Measures. I now regret that we failed to discharge our duty to the late emperor with full sincerity. The result is seen in the present sad state of affairs, for which we cannot attach sole blame to Wang An Shih." [2]

This statement shows, on the one hand, that Ch'eng Hao considered the New Measures defective and injurious, but also indicates one of the reasons for their being so, in that he and his party had been prejudiced and unreasonable in their opposition. We shall discuss this subject more fully in the chapter on the Reform Policy.[3]

Wang Kuei (王 珪), who had been a member of the Grand Council since Wang An Shih's retirement, died in the fifth month of 1085,[2] and after his death, Ts'ai Ch'ueh (蔡 確), Han Chen (韓 縝), and Ssu Ma Kuang (司 馬 光) were appointed Grand Councillors, and Chang Ch'un (章 惇) made President of the Board of War.[2]

Of these all but Ssu Ma Kuang had been connected with the previous regime, particularly Ts'ai Ch'ueh and Chang Ch'un.

[1] T'ung Chien, Yuan Feng, 8th year, 4th month.
[2] T'ung Chien, Yuan Feng, 8th year, 5th month.
[3] See Vol. II.

Despite that fact, however, Ssu Ma Kuang, whose views on the reform policy coincided with those of the Empress, made no secret of his purpose, which was to assist her to eliminate the last vestige of the Shen Tsung-Wang An Shih administration. He had publicly stated that " all that was good in Shen Tsung's government might remain unchanged for a century, but the laws which Wang An Shih and Lü Hui Ch'ing had drawn up were so injurious to the livelihood of the people, that it was as necessary to save the people from them, as it was to save them from drowning or fire." [1]

His later acts in rescinding every one of those measures suggest that he considered there was nothing good in Shen Tsung's government. When others rebuked him for taking such extreme action, on the ground that it was disloyal to the existing emperor to overthrow the regime of his father, he replied, " This is a case of a mother reforming her son, not of a son acting contrary to his father's policy." [1]

He soon found a kindred spirit in Lü Kung Chu, who in the seventh month of this year was appointed to the Grand Council.[2] Lü Kung Chu had held the important office of Chief Censor under Wang An Shih, but had raised his voice against the Agricultural Loans Measure, and had deliberately refused to appoint Lü Hui Ch'ing to his department. This has led to his being transferred to a provincial post. Later he had held posts in the Board of War, during Wang An Shih's retirement. Now on his being recalled to high office, he is reported to have said :—

" It was the first concern of Shen Tsung to save the people from their distresses, but those who were his advisers thought primarily of increasing the revenue. The consequence was that all who propounded different ideas were compelled to leave the Court. The result is seen in the ever-increasing distress which has been caused by the defective character of the Measures which were promulgated by those left in power. If, however, we can secure fair-minded and high-principled men to work

---

[1] T'ung Chien, Yuan Feng, 8th year, 5th month.
[2] T'ung Chien, Yuan Feng, 8th year, 7th month.

together with the sole object of improving matters, it should not be difficult to redeem the situation by introducing a number of changes."[1]

This "number of changes", as has already been indicated, involved the rescindment of every one of Wang An Shih's Measures. The Militia Act was repealed in the seventh month of 1085, the Equitable Land Tax Measure in the eleventh month, followed by the Militia Mounts Measure, and the Trade and Barter Measure in the twelfth month. The repeal of the latter was accompanied by the transfer of Lü Chia Wen (呂 嘉 問), who had been chiefly responsible for the administration of that and the Trade Tax Measure, to Huai Yang Chun (淮 陽 軍).[2]

The difficulties of conducting the affairs of the government with a "Coalition" cabinet soon proved insurmountable. The historian notes that at this juncture the Grand Council consisted of eight men, of whom half were "evil-minded". These were Ts'ai Ch'ueh, Chang Ch'un, Han Chen, and Chang Tsao (張 璪), all of whom had been connected with the regime of Shen Tsung. "In such circumstances it was impossible for one or two faithful ministers to carry out their ideas", says the writer.[3]

So the one or two faithful ministers proceeded to eliminate the opposition, much in the same way as Wang An Shih had done. For in the second month of 1086 Ts'ai Ch'ueh was transferred to Ch'en Chow (陳 州), and Chang Ch'un to Ju Chow (汝 州). The latter had strenuously objected to Ssu Ma Kuang's proposal to rescind the Public Services Measure.

Ssu Ma Kuang was growing very feeble at this time, and had to be supported by his son as he moved about. This in no way lessened his determination to push on with his policy of abrogation. The historian states that he was resolved not to die until he had rescinded the Agricultural Loans Measure, the Public Services Act, altered the revised Army Dispositions, and cancelled the policy in the north-west. He is also reported

---

[1] T'ung Chien, Yuan Feng, 8th year, 7th month.
[2] T'ung Chien, Yuan Feng, 8th year, 11th month.
[3] T'ung Chien, Yuan Yu, 1st year, 2nd month. Intercalary.

to have said to Lü Kung Chu, " I have committed my health
to the doctor, my personal affairs to my son, and government
matters I must leave to you." [1]

Lü Kung Chu was thereupon appointed head of the Men
Hsia Sheng; Li Ch'ing Ch'en and Lü Ta Fang to the chief
posts in the Shang Shu Sheng; Fan Ch'un Jen to the Board of
War; and Li Ch'ang (李 常) to the Board of Revenue.
Objections having been raised against the latter appointment,
on the ground that he lacked the requisite ability for financial
administration, Ssu Ma Kuang replied, " The election of Li
Ch'ang to this position will indicate to the people that we
have abandoned the ' profiteering ' policy of the preceding
regime, and that our chief aim is not to increase the public
revenues." [1]

The Agricultural Loans Measure was repealed in the second
month of 1086, and the old Granary Regulations revived.[1]
In the next month the Public Services Act was supplanted
by the old Labour Conscription Measure (差 役 法).[2]

Fan Tzu Yuan (范 子 淵), who had rendered such
conspicuous service in connection with Wang An Shih's
river conservancy schemes, was now impeached of extravagant
expenditure on useless projects, and of harsh treatment of the
labourers engaged on the work, and transferred to Chia Chow
(峽 州).[3]

The Special Finance Bureau which had been inseparably
connected with the military policy in the north-west was next
abolished.[4]

A Bureau of Appeal (訴 理 所) was now established,
The object of this was to enable all who had been degraded or
dismissed for their opposition to Wang An Shih's policy to
lodge appeals for a reconsideration of their case.[3]

Ch'eng I, now 50 years old, who had hitherto refused to
take up Court appointments, accepted the post of tutor to
the emperor.[4]

[1] T'ung Chien, Yuan Yu, 1st year, 2nd month. Intercalary.
[2] T'ung Chien, Yuan Yu, 1st year, 3rd month. Intercalary.
[3] T'ung Chien, Yuan Yu, 1st year, 3rd month.
[4] T'ung Chien, Yuan Yu, 1st year, 4th month.

Han Chen (韓 縝) was impeached, amongst other things, of having been responsible for the surrender of seven hundred li of territory to the Tartars in the preceding regime, and transferred to Pin Ch'ang (潁 昌).[1]

In the meantime Wang An Shih's health was gradually failing. The death of Shen Tsung must have been a great blow to him. The one " sop " that had been offered to him on the accession of Che Tsung, namely, the honorary appointment as Minister of Works (司 空), he had refused on the grounds of weakness.[2] In the short period of twelve months he had been compelled to witness the reversal of the whole of his beloved policy. The shock of all this proved too much for his already enfeebled physique, and he passed away in the fourth month of 1086 at the age of 65.[3]

It will be realized from the above account that Ssu Ma Kuang was adamant in his opposition to all that Wang An Shih had proposed in the way of government policy. Investigation into the subject has gradually led one to the conviction that his zeal for victory over his political opponents blinded him to the real character of many of Wang An Shih's measures, and that he was led to do Wang An Shih a serious injustice in pursuing this policy of " total abolition ". All the more grateful, then, are we that the following letter, written by Ssu Ma Kuang to his colleague Lü Kung Chu, also styled Lü Hui Shu (呂 晦 叔), has been preserved, viz. :—

" Wang An Shih in literary ability and purity of character possessed many points of excellence above his fellows, but he was not a practical man, and he was too fond of pursuing wrong ideas. This estranged the loyal and upright and led to fawning and specious fellows attaching themselves to his person. The result is seen in the present ruinous state of the government.

" But just as we have corrected the defective features of his policy, and eliminated all that was injurious in his measures, he has passed away. Fickle folk will doubtless find innumerable

[1] T'ung Chien, Yuan Yu, 1st year, 4th month.
[2] Works, vol. 15, p. 28.
[3] Chan Ta Ho, Biographical Table.

pretexts for reviling him, but in my opinion, the Court ought to honour him with special courtesy, and so tend to repress such baseless talk.

" If you think that my idea is worthy it might be presented to the throne. I do not know what your opinion will be, and you need not trouble to write a reply. But I am relying upon you to press the matter urgently at Court." [1]

The above was written after the receipt of the news of Wang An Shih's death, and was probably instrumental in getting the posthumous title of Grand Tutor (太 傅) conferred upon him. This was duly conveyed in the following mandate, which, it is interesting to note, was drawn up by Su Shih, another of Wang An Shih's old political enemies.

The document reads as follows [2] :—

" From my perusal of ancient lore I have reached the conclusion that it is the way of Heaven to produce exceptionally gifted men for extraordinary crises. Such men attain to great fame, and are conversant with the teachings of all time. They are given the wisdom to fulfil their ideals, and are endowed with such powers of reasoning and rhetoric that their proposals get carried out. Further they are equipped with great literary gifts so that all things are set forth in an attractive and æsthetic manner, and with such high-souled determination and perseverance that in a remarkably short space of time they are able to reform the ways of a whole nation.

" The late Grand Councillor Wang An Shih studied Confucius and Mencius in his youth, and pondered deeply on the teachings of Buddhism and Taoism in his later years. He was widely versed in all the literature pertaining to the Six Arts, and interpreted everything in his own peculiar fashion. He was not satisfied with the philosophy of the various teachers of ancient time, but determined to create a philosophy of his own. His great work was accomplished in association with Shen Tsung, under whom he surpassed all his contemporaries and

---

[1] Liang Ch'i Ch'ao, p. 238.
[2] Liang Ch'i Ch'ao, pp. 238-9.

became the first minister in the land. The trust which the emperor placed in him has never been surpassed.

" But just when his labours were on the point of culminating successfully, he retired to private life, despising worldly fame and honours as of no account. He mingled with fishermen and foresters, but maintained unsullied the purity and integrity of his character. His deliberation and conscientiousness in his assumption and relinquishing of office are most estimable.

" I have only just assumed my regal duties, and am oppressed with grief for my father's death. But I have the highest regard for you, the old and faithful servant of three emperors, as you lie away there to the south of the river. As I contemplate the greatness of your achievements, I perceive something ·of the man you were. It is incredible that you should have passed from the earthly scene just when I should be mourning the loss of my father.

" Why did you not live to be a hundred years old ? But sad to relate, one cannot resist Heaven in such matters as life and death or in the acquisition or loss of a valuable helper. It is however within my power to grant titles of honour to deceased ministers, so I hereby confer upon you, our teacher and minister, a title which to scholarly men is most illustrious, which I hope you still have the consciousness to appreciate and accept, namely the special designation of Grand Tutor."

One cannot refrain from expressing the wish that those in authority at this particular time had honoured Wang An Shih by giving his policy greater consideration, and a further trial. But at the same time, these tributes to his character and work, emanating as they do from former antagonists to his policy, are most welcome.

" Wang An Shih died." In these simple words, with no embellishment of rank or title, the History [1] records the passing of one of the highest-minded political reformers of China. The obituary notice with which the historiographer deigns to honour him, reads as follows :—

---

[1] T'ung Chien, Yuan Yu, 1st year, 4th month.

" Wang An Shih was a very self-willed man. He could not brook opposition. He was so convinced that his own ideas were right that he would hold them tenaciously against all opposition. He had remarkable ideas, and unusual powers of rhetoric, which helped him to further his political theories. He was convinced that he ought to reform the character and customs of his age.

" (Possessed as he was of such gifts and ideals) Shen Tsung ignored the opinions of the great majority, and gave him his complete confidence. When opposition was raised against his New Measures at Court on the ground of their impracticability, Wang An Shih so warped the meaning of the classics as to make them conform to his own notions. He was so voluble and forceful in discussion that the rest found it impossible to make him yield.

" His most extreme utterances were that ' Extraordinary phenomena in the natural world need not be feared ' : ' The example of our ancestors need not necessarily be followed ' : ' Opinions of others are not worth considering.' In this way resentment and criticism were aroused, and for the period of eight years which elapsed after his resignation to the death of Shen Tsung, he was not again called to the Court.

" He seemed entirely unconcerned whenever he was informed that others of his Measures had been rescinded, but when he heard that his Public Services Act had been supplanted by the Labour Conscription Measure, he nearly choked with rage, gasping, ' And have they rescinded this too ? ' When he had recovered his composure he remarked, ' This particular Measure ought never to have been rescinded.' He had formerly said, ' Tseng Pu was the one who held loyally by the New Measures right through, but Ssu Ma Kuang deemed them impracticable from beginning to end.' "

Criticism on these and other opinions of the character and work of Wang An Shih are reserved for the chapters which deal specially with these topics. (See Vol. II of this work.)

DATE DUE

2/7/74			